Lecture Notes in Computer Science 2995

Edited by G. Goos, J. Hartmanis, and J. van Leeuwen

T0218235

Springer
Berlin
Heidelberg
New York
Hong Kong
London
Milan
Paris
Tokyo

Christian Jensen   Stefan Poslad
Theo Dimitrakos (Eds.)

Trust Management

Second International Conference, iTrust 2004
Oxford, UK, March 29 - April 1, 2004
Proceedings

Springer

Series Editors

Gerhard Goos, Karlsruhe University, Germany
Juris Hartmanis, Cornell University, NY, USA
Jan van Leeuwen, Utrecht University, The Netherlands

Volume Editors

Christian Jensen
Technical University of Denmark
Informatics and Mathematical Modelling, 2800 Lyngby, Denmark
E-mail: Christian.Jensen@imm.dtu.dk

Stefan Poslad
Queen Mary, University of London
Department of Electronic Engineering, London, UK
E-mail: Stefan.Poslad@elec.qmul.ac.uk

Theo Dimitrakos
Central Laboratory of the Research Councils
Rutherford Appleton Lab. OX11 0QX, Chilton, Didcot, Oxfordshire, UK
E-mail: t.dimitrakos@rl.ac.uk

Library of Congress Control Number: 2004102311

CR Subject Classification (1998): H.4, H.3, H.5.3, C.2.4, I.2.11, K.4.3-4, K.5

ISSN 0302-9743
ISBN 3-540-21312-0 Springer-Verlag Berlin Heidelberg New York

Springer-Verlag is a part of Springer Science+Business Media

springeronline.com

© Springer-Verlag Berlin Heidelberg 2004
Printed in Germany

Typesetting: Camera-ready by author, data conversion by PTP-Berlin, Protago-TeX-Production GmbH
Printed on acid-free paper   SPIN: 10993781   06/3142   5 4 3 2 1 0

Preface

This volume constitutes the proceedings of the 2nd International Conference on Trust Management, held in Oxford, UK, during 29 March–1 April 2004. The conference followed a very successful 1st International Conference on Trust Management held in Crete in 2003. Both conferences were organized by iTrust, which is a working group funded as a thematic network by the Future and Emerging Technologies (FET) unit of the Information Society Technologies (IST) program of the European Union.

The purpose of the iTrust working group is to provide a forum for cross-disciplinary investigation of the applications of trust as a means of increasing security, building confidence and facilitating collaboration in dynamic open systems. The notion of trust has been studied independently by different academic disciplines, which has helped us to identify and understand different aspects of trust. The aim of this conference was to provide a common forum, bringing together researchers from different academic branches, such as the technology-oriented disciplines, law, social sciences and philosophy, in order to develop a deeper and more fundamental understanding of the issues and challenges in the area of trust management in dynamic open systems.

The response to this conference was excellent; from the 48 papers submitted to the conference, we selected 21 full papers and 6 short papers for presentation. The program also included three keynote addresses, given by Jeff Bradshaw from the Institute for Human and Machine Cognition at the University of West Florida (USA), Ian Walden who is Director of the Computer-Related Crime Research Centre at Queen Mary, University of London (UK), and Massimo Marchiori from the World Wide Web Consortium, as well as three panels and a full day of tutorials.

The running of an international conference requires an immense effort from all involved parties. We would like to thank the people who served on the program committee and the organizing committee for their hard work. In particular, we would like to thank the people at the Business and Information Technology Department of the Council for the Central Laboratory of the Research Councils (CCLRC) for providing the logistics for the conference, and especially Damian Mac Randal for his help in putting this volume together.

March 2004

Christian D. Jensen,
Stefan Poslad,
and Theo Dimitrakos

Organization

The 2nd International Conference on Trust Management was organized by iTrust, a Working Group on Trust Management in Dynamic Open Systems, and the Council for the Central Laboratory of the Research Councils in the UK. The conference was partially funded by the Future and Emerging Technologies (FET) unit of the European IST program.

Executive Committee

Conference Chair	Theo Dimitrakos, CCLRC, UK
Program Chairs	Christian D. Jensen, DTU, Denmark
	Stefan Poslad, Queen Mary College, London, UK
Tutorials	Peter Herrmann, U. of Dortmund, Germany
Demonstrations	Dimitris Tsigos, Virtual Trip Ltd., Greece
Panels	Simon Shiu, Hewlett-Packard, UK
Local Arrangements	Damian Mac Randal, CCLRC, UK

Local Organizing Committee

Dr. Theo Dimitrakos	CCLRC
Damian Mac Randal	CCLRC
Dr. Brian Matthews	CCLRC
Dr. Susan Hilton	CCLRC
Pat Athawes	CCLRC
Wendy Ferguson	CCLRC

Program Committee

Nikos Alivizatos	University of Athens, Greece
Elisa Bertino	University of Milan, Italy
Jon Bing	NRCCL, University of Oslo, Norway
Joan Borrell	Autonomous University of Barcelona, Spain
Jeremy Bryans	University of Newcastle, UK
Sandro Castaldo	Università Bocconi, Italy
Cristiano Castelfranchi	CNR, Italy
Manuel Castells	University of California, Berkeley, USA
Stefano Cerri	University of Montpellier II, and CNRS, France
David Chadwick	University of Salford, UK
Rosaria Conte	CNR and University of Siena, Italy
Mark Roger Dibben	University of St Andrews, UK
Theo Dimitrakos	CLRC, UK
George Doukidis	Athens University of Economics and Business, Greece
Rino Falcone	CNR, Italy
Andy Gordon	Microsoft Research, UK
Peter Herrmann	University of Dortmund, Germany
John Ioannidis	AT&T Labs Research, USA
Valerie Issarny	INRIA, France
Keith Jeffery	CLRC, UK
Christian D. Jensen	Technical University of Denmark, Denmark
Andrew Jones	King's College, London, UK
Audun Jøsang	DSTC, Australia
Paul Kearney	BTexact, UK
Angelos Keromytis	Columbia University, USA
Graham Klyne	Nine by Nine, UK
Heiko Krumm	University of Dortmund, Germany
Giuseppe Laria	CRMPA, Italy
Ninghui Li	Stanford University, USA
Peter Linington	University of Kent at Canterbury, UK
Ian Lloyd	University of Strathclyde, UK
Stephane Lo Presti	University of Southampton, UK
Manolis Marazakis	Plefsis, Greece
Fabio Martinelli	CNR, Italy
Fabio Massacci	Università di Trento, Italy
Zoran Milosevic	DSTC, Australia
Erich Neuhold	Darmstadt University of Technology, and Fraunhofer IPSI, Germany
Christos Nikolaou	University of Crete, Greece
Paddy Nixon	University of Strathclyde, UK
Stefan Poslad	Queen Mary College, London, UK
Dimitris Raptis	Intracom, Greece
Jeremy Riegelsberger	University of Newcastle, UK

Program Committee (contd.)

Elena Rocco	University of Venice, Italy, and University of Michigan, USA
Peter Ryan	University of Newcastle, UK
Babak Sadighi	SICS, Sweden
Jakka Sairamesh	IBM Research, USA
Giovanni Sartor	U. of Bologna, Italy
Simon Shiu	Hewlett-Packard, UK
Morris Sloman	Imperial College, UK
Bruce Spencer	National Research Council, Canada
Ketil Stølen	SINTEF, Norway
Yao-Hua Tan	Free University of Amsterdam, Netherlands
Sotirios Terzis	U. of Strathclyde, UK
Dimitris Tsigos	Virtual Trip Ltd., Greece
Stavroula Tsinorema	U. of Crete, Greece
Andrew Twigg	University of Cambridge, UK
Emily Weitzenboeck	NRCCL, U. of Oslo, Norway
Stefan Wesner	HLRS, Germany
Marianne Winslett	University of Illinois at Urbana-Champaign, USA

Table of Contents

Short Papers and Experience Reports

Addressing the Data Problem: The Legal Framework Governing Forensics in an Online Environment

Ian Walden

Head of the Institute of Computer and Communications Law, Centre for Commercial Law
Studies, Queen Mary, University of London and consultant to Baker & McKenzie
i.n.waldem@qmul.ac.uk

Abstract. This article considers some of the problems raised by data for law
enforcement agencies investigating network-based crime. It examines recent
legislative measures that have been adopted in the UK and other jurisdictions to
address some of these problems of criminal procedure and the extent to which
such measures achieve an appropriate balance between inevitably conflicting
interests.

1 Introduction

Digital information or data, zeros and ones, is the form in which our emerging
'Information Society' carries out it activities, whether through software applications,
emails, data feeds or the Web. Our economy has become increasingly dependent on
the processing and transmission of such data across networks to support its
infrastructure and carry out many of its functions. Inevitably, networks such as the
Internet also attract a criminal element, both to facilitate the commission of traditional
crimes as well as commit new types of crime.

Any criminal investigation interferes with the rights of others, whether the person
is the subject of an investigation or a related third party. In a democratic society any
such interference must be justifiable and proportionate to the needs of society to be
protected. However, the growth of network-based crime has raised difficult issues in
respect of the appropriate balance between the needs of those investigating and
prosecuting such crime, and the rights of data users. In addition, there are the interests
of the network provider, the intermediaries that build and, or, operate the networks
and services through which data is communicated.

This article considers some of the problems raised by data for law enforcement
agencies investigating network-based crime. It examines recent legislative measures
that have been adopted in the UK and other jurisdictions to address some of these
problems of criminal procedure and the extent to which such measures achieve an
appropriate balance between inevitably conflicting interests.

C.D. Jensen et al. (Eds.): iTrust 2004, LNCS 2995, pp. 1–15, 2004.

2 Forensics and Evidence

The investigation of computer crime and the gathering of appropriate evidence for a criminal prosecution, the science of forensics, can be an extremely difficult and complex issue, due primarily to the intangible and often transient nature of data, especially in a networked environment. The technology renders the process of investigation and recording of evidence extremely vulnerable to defence claims of errors, technical malfunction, prejudicial interference or fabrication. Such claims may lead to a ruling from the court against the admissibility of such evidence[1]. A lack of adequate training of law enforcement officers, prosecutors and, indeed, the judiciary, will often exasperate these difficulties.

In terms of obtaining evidence, relevant data may be resident or stored on the computer system of the victim, the suspect and, or, some third party, such as a communication service provider (CSP). Alternatively, evidence may be obtained from data in the process of it being transmitted across a network, generally referred to as intercepted data. Specific rules of criminal procedure address law enforcement access to both sources of evidence.

3 Stored Data

Communications involves at least two parties, the caller and the called. In data communications either party, or both, may be machines or more accurately software or files residing on machines, rather than people. Law enforcement agencies will generally access forensic data once it has been recorded or stored, whether on the systems controlled by the calling or called parties, or during the process of transmission.

The nature of computer and communications technologies bestows upon data the duality of being notoriously vulnerable to loss and modification, as well as being surprisingly 'sticky', at one and the same time. The 'stickiness' of data is attributable, in part, to the multiple copies generated by the communications process, as well as the manner in which data is stored on electronic media. However, access to stored data has raised a number of issues in relation to criminal procedure, in respect of the seizure of such data, access to data held remotely, secured data, communications data and the preservation or retention of data.

3.1 Seized Data

Data stored on the computer system of the suspect is generally obtained through the execution of a court order for search and seizure[2]. A search and seizure warrant can give rise to problems where the relevant material is held on a computer system being used at the time of the search, since any attempt to seize the material for further

---

[1] Police and Criminal Evidence Act, s.78.

[2] E.g. Computer Misuse Act, s. 14, or the Police and Criminal Evidence Act 1984, s. 8 and ss. 19-20.

examination may result in either the loss or alteration of the evidence[3]. Another problem for law enforcement is the volume of data that is generally subject to seizure, especially as the cost of data storage has fallen and capacity increased dramatically in recent years. The time and expense involved in shifting and scrutinising seized data is a serious impediment to the process of investigation.

One procedural issue raised by the volume of data stored on a computer subject to seizure is whether the scope of the warrant extends to all material contained on the disk. In *R v Chesterfield Justices and others, ex parte Bramley*[4], D.C., the potential vulnerability of the police was exposed when the court held that the Police and Criminal Evidence Act 1984 did not contain a defence to an action for trespass to goods in respect of items subject to legal privilege being seized during the execution of a search warrant[5]. The decision placed law enforcement in an invidious position: searching and shifting the data at the premises of the suspect was not feasible, but removal for subsequent examination could give rise to liability.

To address the potential liability established by *Bramley*, the Government added provisions to the Criminal Justice and Police Act 2001[6]. The Act grants law enforcement agencies the right to remove material, including material potentially outside the scope of a warrant, where it is "not reasonably practicable" to separate it (s. 50(1)(c)). An exhaustive list of relevant factors is provided for determining whether it is 'reasonably practicable', including "the apparatus or equipment that it would be necessary or appropriate to use for the carrying out of the determination or separation" (s. 50(3)(d)), which would presumably encompass the various software tools used in computer forensics.

The Act also details a number of safeguards for the handling of such data that are designed to protect the defendant's rights under the European Convention on Human Rights. First, written notice must be given to the occupier of the premises detailing, amongst other items, the names and address of a person to whom an application can be made to attend the initial examination of the material (s. 52(1)). The examination should not then be commenced without due regard to the desirability of enabling the relevant person an opportunity to be represented at the examination (s. 53(4)). Second, items subject to legal privilege must be returned as soon as reasonably practicable, except where it is not reasonably practicable to separate it from the rest of the property "without prejudicing the use of the rest of that property" (s. 54(2)(b)). Third, an application may be made to the appropriate judicial authority for the material to be returned, although the authority could order that the material be examined by an independent third party (s. 59). Fourth, where an application has been made, the person holding the data may be placed under a duty to secure the data

---

[3] See generally the 'Good Practice Guide for Computer Based Evidence' published by the Association of Chief Police Officers. See also US Department of Justice Report, *Searching and Seizing Computers and Obtaining Electronic Evidence in Criminal Investigations*, July 2002 (available at http://www.usdoj.gov/criminal/cybercrime).

[4] (2000) 2 WLR 409.

[5] Subsequently, it has been held that *Bramley* only extends to situations involving legal privilege material, not any situation where irrelevant material is seized in the course of taking a computer as evidence: See *H v Commissioners of Inland Revenue* [2002] EWHC 2164 (Admin).

[6] These provisions only came into force from 1 April 2003 under The Criminal Justice and Police Act 2001 (Commencement No. 9) Order 2003, SI No. 708.

pending the direction of the judicial authority, which includes preventing its examination, copying or use (s. 60-61).

Concern has been expressed that the safeguards do not go far enough to protect the interests of the accused. In particular, such is the absolute nature of the rule protecting legal privilege[7], it has been suggested that by default seized material be subject to independent examination, rather than relying on the discretion of a judicial authority[8]. However, such a procedure could potentially further compromise the ability of law enforcement to operate with the rapidity often required in situations involving network-based crime.

3.2 Remote Data

Another aspect of the use of search warrants in a networked environment concerns the geographical scope of such warrants. Under the Police and Criminal Evidence Act 1984, a constable may require 'any information which is contained in a computer and is accessible from the premises to be produced in a form in which it can be taken away...' (s. 19(4))[9]. This provision would appear to enable law enforcement officers to obtain information held on remote systems, since the reference to 'a computer' would seem to extend to a remote computer that can be accessed via another computer on the premises. Such a position has also been adopted in the Council of Europe Convention on Cybercrime (2001)[10], which states that the right to search and access should extend to any other computer system on its territory which "is lawfully accessible from or available to the initial system" (art. 19(2)).

However, where the remote computer is based in another jurisdiction, important issues of sovereignty and territoriality may arise. In *United States v Gorshkov* (2001)[11], for example, the FBI accessed computers in Russia, via the Internet using surreptitiously obtained passwords, to download data from computers operated by the accused already under arrest in the US[12].

In transborder circumstances, the Convention on Cybercrime provides that access to data stored in another jurisdiction may be obtained without authorisation of the state in which the data resides if:

a) access publicly available (open source) stored computer data, regardless of where the data is located geographically; or

b) access or receive, through a computer system in its territory, stored computer data located in another Party, if the Party obtains the lawful and voluntary consent of the person who has the lawful authority to disclose the data to the Party through that computer system. (art. 32)

---

[7] *Derby Magistrates' Court, ex parte B* [1996] AC 487.

[8] See Ormerod, D.C., [2000] Crim.L.R. 388, where he suggests off-site sifting be carried out by an independently appointed legal adviser.

[9] See also s. 20, which extends this provision to powers of seizure conferred under other enactments.

[10] European Treaty Series No. 185 and Explanatory Report. Available at www.coe.int.

[11] WL 1024026 (W.D.Wash.).

[12] The court held the Fourth Amendment of the US Constitution, prohibiting 'unreasonable searches and seizures', was not applicable to such actions and even if it was, the action was reasonable in the circumstances.

The former would presumably be applicable where information was contained on a public web-site. The latter would extend, for example, to a person's email stored in another country by a service provider. These two situations were the only examples upon which all parties to the Convention could agree, but does not preclude other situations being authorised under national law[13].

In the early 1990s, certain UK-based electronic bulletin boards, containing illegal material such as virus code, began placing messages at the point of access to the site stating that 'law enforcement officials are not permitted to enter the system'. Such a warning was considered to be an effective technique in restricting the police from monitoring the use made of such bulletin boards[14]. As a consequence, in 1994 the Computer Misuse Act was amended to prevent law enforcement agencies committing a section 1 offence of unauthorised access:

> nothing designed to indicate a withholding of consent to access to any program or data from persons as enforcement officers shall have effect to make access unauthorised for the purposes of the said section 1(1).

> In this section 'enforcement officer' means a constable or other person charged with the duty of investigating offences; and withholding consent from a person 'as' an enforcement officer of any description includes the operation, by the person entitled to control access, or rules whereby enforcement officers of that description are, as such, disqualified from membership of a class or persons who are authorised to have access[15].

The scope of this exception should perhaps have been more narrowly drafted so as not to legitimise the use of 'hacking' and related techniques by law enforcement agencies to circumvent data security measures utilised on remote systems. Such proactive techniques by investigators, as well as the deliberate alteration or modification of information held on a remote system, should perhaps be subject to specific procedural controls, akin to interception regimes.

3.3   Secured Data

Even when data has been lawfully obtained, a further problem that investigators increasingly face is that seized data may be protected by some form of security measure, such as a password or encryption, which renders it inaccessible or unintelligible. In the US, for example, when the notorious hacker Kevin Mitnick was finally arrested, many of the files found on his computers were encrypted and investigators were unable to access them[16].

The nature of data security technologies means that investigating authorities have essentially three options in respect of gaining access to such protected data:

☐ Require the person from whom the data has been obtained to convert the data into an intelligible plain-text format;

---

[13] See Explanatory Report, at para. 293-294.
[14] See Home Affairs Committee Report No.126: 'Computer Pornography', p. xii, para.31-32, HMSO, February 1994.
[15] The Criminal Justice and Public Order Act 1994, s.162, amending section 10 of the Computer Misuse Act 1990.
[16] See generally www.freekevin.com.

☐ Require the person to disclose the necessary information and, or, tools to enable the authorities to convert the data into a legible format themselves; or

☐ Utilise technologies and techniques that enable the data to be converted without the active involvement of the person from whom the data was obtained.

In respect of the first approach, the Regulation of Investigatory Powers Act 2000 provides that a notice may be served on a person requiring that they disclose the information in an 'intelligible form' (s. 49). Prior to this provision, the law only required that information be provided in a 'visible and legible form', under the Police and Criminal Evidence Act 1984, s. 19.

Addressing the second approach, the Regulation of Investigatory Powers states that, where necessary and proportionate, a person may be required by notice to disclose the 'key'[17] that would enable the investigators to render the information intelligible themselves (s. 51).

This second approach raises issues that may need further consideration in terms of balancing different interests. First, the data security technique being delivered up may either be specific to an individual or it may be a tool that protects the data of a community of users, such as a company's employee email over an Intranet. In the latter scenario, the obligation to disclose gives rise to potential vulnerabilities both in terms of the individual rights of others, i.e. other protected users, and the interests of legal entities, i.e. the corporation. Under European human rights jurisprudence, the potential for collateral infringements of third party privacy rights must be necessary and proportionate to the object of the interference. The potential exposure of the corporate entity to a breach of its security may have significant consequences for its commercial activities, particularly in relation to adverse publicity and perceptions of trust. Indeed, such concerns have historically meant substantial under-reporting of computer crimes, such as hacking and fraud[18].

Second, the person subject to the requirement may be the person under investigation or a related third party, such as a company or communications service provider. Again, where the requirement is imposed on a third party, adequate consideration needs to be given to the costs, in the widest sense, being imposed on that third party. For example, in terms of communication service providers, a requirement to disclose keys protecting the data of its customers could restrict the growth of the market for services such as 'key escrow', where a third party maintains copies of cryptographic keys as a safeguard against loss or destruction. The needs of law enforcement could, therefore, militate against the use of data security services that are seen as being important to the development of our 'Information Society'.

Where a legal obligation is imposed upon a person in relation to an investigation, a failure to comply will inevitably result in sanctions. Such sanctions may comprise either the commission of a separate offence[19]; an offence related to the exercise of the

---

[17] "key", in relation to any electronic data, means any key, code, password, algorithm or other data the use of which (with or without other keys)-

(a) allows access to the electronic data, or

(b) facilitates the putting of the data into an intelligible form' (s. 56(1)).

[18] See US survey by CSI/FBI, which reported that only 32% of respondents who had suffered an intrusion had reported it to law enforcement agencies: quoted in National Criminal Intelligence Service, 'Project Trawler: Crime on the Information Highways', 1999.

[19] E.g. UK Regulation of Investigatory Powers Act 2000, s. 53: Failure to comply with a notice.

enforcement powers[20], or some form of adverse or incriminating inference raised in the course of any subsequent related criminal proceedings, e.g. possession of obscene material. The latter approach may be statutorily based, as in the United Kingdom[21], or may comprise a factor in civil law jurisdictions where evidence is freely assessed with regard to all relevant circumstances, including the behaviour of the accused.

Where an offence is committed through non-compliance with a lawful requirement, any penalty will need to act as an appropriate deterrent against such a refusal to comply. However, it is obviously quite likely that a person may choose not to comply with the request to disclose, thereby accepting the penalty, rather than comply and potentially expose themselves to prosecution for a more serious offence with greater penalties. Whilst such a scenario may be unfortunate, it would seem be a necessary compromise where the rights of the individual are balanced against the need to protect society.

The raising of an adverse inference against a person in criminal proceedings for a failure to supply certain information could raise issues concerning the right to a fair trial, under Article 6 of the European Convention on Human Rights. In particular, it may be viewed as an infringement of the individual's right to silence, right not to self-incriminate and the principle that the prosecution has the burden of proving a case. Convention jurisprudence indicates that whilst a conviction may not be based solely or mainly on a refusal to supply such information[22], an adverse inference may in specified circumstances be drawn from such a refusal when assessing the evidence adduced by the prosecution[23].

The viability of the third approach to protected data, converting the data into an intelligible form through utilising available techniques, would seem to depend on a number of factors, including the strength of the security technology employed[24], and the period within which the data realistically needs to be converted. In the longer term, it will depend on developments in technology since techniques may be developed which are essentially incapable of being overcome. However, some governments have recognised the need to establish some such 'in-house' technical capability to assist law enforcement investigations. The UK Government, for example, has established a National Technical Assistance Centre, at an initial cost of £25 million, which is designed to provide the necessary technical expertise to law enforcement agencies to try and access protected data without the involvement of the suspect.

3.4 Communication Data

The most common third-party source of evidence is communication service providers,

---

[20] E.g. failure to assist in the execution of judicial warrant.

[21] Criminal Justice and Public Order Act 1994, ss.34-38.

[22] Except for a specific offence of non-disclosure.

[23] See *Murray v United Kingdom* (1996) 22 EHRR 29, at para. 41-58. See generally Jennings, A., Ashworth, A., and Emmerson, B., "Silence and Safety: The Impact of Human Rights Law", [2000] Crim.L.R, 879.

[24] I.e US-based hardware and software manufacturers, such as Intel, have been in discussions with law enforcement agencies about the possibilities of 'building-in' certain functionalities into their products to assist criminal investigations.

such as an ISP. Data stored on the systems of a communications service provider is currently accessed either under the Data Protection Act 1998, which provides a voluntary mechanism to enable the disclosure of stored personal data without the third party incurring liability[25], or the Police and Criminal Evidence Act 1984[26]. However, the Regulation of Investigatory Powers Act 2000 contains new powers that, when implemented, will establish a new regime to enable law enforcement agencies to require the disclosure of 'communications data' from communication service providers. 'Communications data' includes 'traffic data' (s. 21(6)), such as a telephone number; data concerning usage of the service and any other data held on the person by the service provider (s. 21(4)).

Under RIPA, the police force, certain crime and intelligence services, Inland Revenue and Customs and Excise can access communications data without a warrant or other judicial oversight for any of the public interest grounds set out in the Act, including national security, preventing or detecting crime or preventing disorder, the economic well-being of the United Kingdom, public health and safety, collecting or assessing tax, and preventing death or personal injury[27].

In June 2002 the Home Secretary proposed extending the list of authorities that can access communications data under RIPA to include numerous public bodies, ranging from local authorities, National Health Service authorities and even the Food Standards Agency and the Postal Services Commission. This proposal was met with a storm of controversy and the government quickly withdrew these plans, saying that it would consult with the public before allowing additional authorities to access communications data under RIPA.

On March 11 2003, the Home Office released a consultation paper, 'Accessing Communications Data: Respecting Privacy and Protection the Public from Crime', discussing such proposals[28]. The consultation document proposes that some twenty-one further authorities should have access to some kinds of communications data, subject where appropriate to certification and prior screening by an independent third party (such as the Interception Commissioner). RIPA already grants the Secretary of State the power to restrict the types of data that may be accessed by a public authority, as well as the purposes for which such data may be used[29]. Currently, the majority of requests for data are made in respect of subscriber data, rather than traffic or usage data; therefore it is envisaged that the right of access for the twenty-one authorities would be limited to subscriber data, except in specified circumstances.

The proposal also contains a number of safeguards against the misuse of communications data[30]. However, it notes that RIPA contains no explicit offence against the deliberate misuse of communications data by law enforcement agencies, although the Data Protection Act 1998 does contain a limited offence that may be applicable[31]. Although the consultation paper admits that the June 2002 proposal was too permissive, the list of authorities remains extensive. It remains to be seen whether

---

[25] Section 29(3).

[26] Section 9 concerning access to 'special procedure material'. See *NTL Group Ltd.v Ipswich Crown Court* [2002] EWHC 1585 (Admin).

[27] Section 22(2).

[28] Available from www.homeoffice.gov.uk

[29] Sections 25(3)(a) and (b).

[30] Chapter 3, para. 6 et seq.

[31] Section 55.

the government will convince the public that the legitimate investigatory functions of all the listed authorities justifies their access to communications data.

3.5   Preserved or Retained Data

As discussed in the previous section, access to communications data held by a communications service provider is to be governed by a new regime under the Regulation of Investigatory Powers Act 2000. However, such data will only be available to be accessed by investigators if the service provider has retained such information. Generally, such data is retained for relatively short periods of time, due both to the cost to the provider as well as compliance with data protection rules[32]. Criminal procedure in most jurisdictions enables law enforcement to request the preservation of real-time data by a communications service provider in specified circumstances. Indeed, the Council of Europe Convention on Cybercrime requires member states to harmonise such procedures to facilitate the investigative process[33].

However, with heightened concerns about the threat of terrorism, the issue of the potential unavailability of evidence has led to calls for the imposition of a general broad data retention obligation on communication service providers to enable access to historic stored data, as well as the preservation of real-time data[34]. Such data retention obligations have been adopted in the UK, France and Belgium; although other jurisdictions, such as the US and Germany, have rejected this approach.

As a consequence of the events of September 11th 2001, provisions were incorporated in the UK's Anti-Terrorism Crime and Security Act 2001, Part 11, establishing a regime for a voluntary code of practice on the retention of communications data. The scheme is to be agreed between the Secretary of State and communication service providers, with the alternative possibility of mandatory directions being imposed. However, such a scheme has yet to be adopted, amid concerns that the provisions would breach European data protection and human rights laws[35].

4   Intercepted Data

As well as stored data, evidence may be obtained during its transmission between computers across communication networks. Such evidence may comprise the content of a communication, such as a list of passwords, or the attributes of a communication session, such as the duration of a call or the location of the caller.

---

[32] E.g. under The Telecommunications (Data Protection and Privacy) Regulations 1999 (SI No. 2093), regulation 6, data shall be erased or rendered anonymous upon termination of a call, except in specified circumstances.

[33] Articles 16-17 in respect of national rules and articles 29-30 in respect of mutual legal assistance.

[34] E.g. see NCIS document, 'Looking to the Future, Clarity on Communications Data Retention Law: Submission to the Home Office for Legislation on Data Retention' (21 August 2000). The document was leaked to the Observer and is available at www.fipr.org.

[35] See the evidence submitted by the Home Office to the All-Party Parliamentary Internet Group inquiry on data retention at www.apig.org.uk.

Interception of the content of a communication is governed in the UK under the Regulation of Investigatory Powers Act 2000 (RIPA). The Act makes it an offence to intercept a communication being transmitted over a public telecommunications system without a warrant issued by the Secretary of State; or over a private telecommunication system without the consent of the system controller (s. 1). An interception is lawful, however, where both the sender and recipient have consented to the interception (s. 3(1)); or it is carried out by a communications service provider "for purposes connected with the provision or operation of that service or with the enforcement....of any enactment relating to the use of...telecommunications services" (s. 3(3)). This latter provision renders lawful an interception carried out by a telecommunications operator to prevent fraudulent use of a telecommunication service or its improper use, under the Telecommunications Act 1984 (s. 42, 43)[36].

The RIPA regime is not primarily designed to tackle the activities of those intercepting communications in the furtherance of their criminal activities; rather its purpose is to control the interception practices of law enforcement agents and the use of intercepted material as evidence. The European Court of Human Rights has at least twice found UK law to be in breach of the Convention in respect of protecting the right of privacy of those who have been subject to interception[37].

An interception warrant should only be issued by the Secretary of State on the grounds of national security, 'serious crime'[38] or the 'economic well-being of the United Kingdom' (s. 5); and must identity a particular subject or a set of premises (s. 8(1)). A procedure for scrutiny exists through the office of the Interception Commissioner, and a right of appeal to an Interception Tribunal.

One unique feature of the UK interception regime is that it does not generally permit information obtained through an interception being adduced as evidence in legal proceedings (s. 17)[39]. Such evidence is for the purpose of an investigation, not for any subsequent prosecution. The reasoning behind such a provision is to protect from disclosure information about the investigative activities of law enforcement agencies. Such activities would enter the public domain if intercept evidence was used in court and became subject to challenge by a defendant's counsel. Conversely, interception evidence is admissible where a service provider under the Telecommunications Act 1984 carries out the interception[40], or if the evidence comes from an interception carried out in another country[41], since neither would reveal anything about the activities of UK law enforcement.

---

[36] See *Morgans v D.P.P* [1999] 1 W.L.R 968, D.C. Similar provisions are provided for in the Communications Bill, currently before Parliament.

[37] I.e. *Malone v United Kingdom* [1984] 7 EHRR 14 and *Halford* v. *United Kingdom*, (1997) IRLR 471.

[38] I.e. "(a) ...an offence for which a person who has attained the age of twenty-one and has no previous convictions could reasonably be expected to be sentenced to imprisonment for a term of three years or more; (b) that the conduct involves the use of violence, results in substantial financial gain or is conduct by a large number of persons in pursuit of a common purpose." (s. 81(3)).

[39] S. 17. However, it may be retained for certain 'authorised purposes' (s. 15(4)), e.g. "it is necessary to ensure that a person conducting a criminal prosecution has the information he needs to determine what is required of him by his duty to secure the fairness of the prosecution", and may be subsequently disclosed to the prosecutor or trial judge (s. 18(7)).

[40] E.g. *Morgans*, op. cit. note 37.

[41] See *R v P & ors* : (2001) 2 All ER 58.

The interception rules would not cover the practice of 'electronic eavesdropping', where emissions from computer VDU screens are surreptitiously received and reconstituted for viewing on external equipment[42], since they are not in the course of transmission to a recipient. However, 'electronic eavesdropping' would probably constitute a form of 'surveillance', which is governed under a separate part of RIPA[43].

4.1   Content and Communications Data

Historically, national legal systems have distinguished between the interception of the content of a communications and the data related to the communication session itself, i.e. its attributes, such as telephone numbers and call duration. Such a distinction would seem be based on a commonly held perception that access to the content of a communication represents a greater threat to personal privacy than access to the related communications data. Such a sentiment can be found in the European Court of Human Rights:

"By its very nature, metering is therefore to be distinguished from interception of communications, which is undesirable and illegitimate in a democratic society unless justified."[44]

However, developments in telecommunications would seem to have led to a qualitative and quantitative shift in the nature of data being generated through the use of communications technology, such as mobile telephony data relating to the geographical position of the user. While the volume and value of communications data has expanded considerably; conversely, obtaining access to the content of a communication is increasingly hampered through the use of cryptographic techniques, either built into the technology or applied by the user. As a result, investigators are increasingly reliant on communications data as evidence.

It would seem to be arguable that the threats to individual privacy from obtaining communication attributes data as opposed to communications content is of similar importance in modern network environments and should therefore be subject to similar access regimes. However, although there would appear to be no current requirement in any jurisdiction's law to treat access to such categories of data under a similar legal regime, the new EU Directive addressing data protection issues in the communications sector would seem to implicitly recognise the idea of equality of treatment:

"Member States shall ensure the confidentiality of communications and the related traffic data by means of a public communications network and publicly available electronic communications services, through national legislation..."[45]

One issue raised by differential legal treatment is that in modern communications networks the distinction between communication attributes and content is becoming increasingly blurred. A web-based Uniform Resource Locator (URL), for example,

---

[42] See generally, O. Lewis, 'Information Security & Electronic Eavesdropping - a perspective', pp.165-168, *Computer Law and Security Report*, Vol.7, No.4, 1991.

[43] Part II, 'Surveillance and Covert Human Intelligence Sources'.

[44] *Malone v United Kingdom* (1985) 7 EHRR 14.

[45] Directive 02/58/EC of the European Parliament and of the Council concerning the the processing of personal data and the protection of privacy in the electronic communications sector, OJ L 201/37, 31.7.2002, at art. 5(1).

contains not only details of the IP address of the web site being accessed, akin to a traditional telephone number; but will also often contain further information in relation to the content of the requested communication, e.g. a particular item held on the site or a search string containing the embedded parameters of the search. The introduction of touch-tone technology has also enabled an individual to key in his credit card details when using a telephone banking service. Such so-called 'post-cut-through' data render any legal categorisation based on a technical distinction between signalling and content channels unworkable.

Under US law, a distinction is made between communications content and 'call-identifying information', which is defined as follows:

"...dialing or signaling information that identifies the origin, direction, destination, or termination of each communication generated or received by a subscriber by means of any equipment, facility, or service of a telecommunications carrier."[46]

From a law enforcement perspective, the communications attribute of primary interest in an investigation is such identifying information. Whilst this would seem a relatively clear statutory definition, a decision by the Federal Communications Commission to encompass 'post-cut-through dialed digit extraction' within this definition was overturned in the Appeals Court partly on the basis that "there is no way to distinguish between digits dialed to route calls and those dialed to communicate information"[47].

In the UK, the distinction is made between the content and 'traffic data':

"(a) any data identifying, or purporting to identify, any person, apparatus or location to or from which the communication is or may be transmitted,

(b) any data identifying or selecting, or purporting to identify or select, apparatus through which, or by means of which, the communication is or may be transmitted,

(c) any data comprising signals for the actuation of apparatus used for the purposes of a telecommunication system for effecting (in whole or in part) the transmission of any communication, and

(d) any data identifying the data or other data as data comprised in or attached to a particular communication,

but that expression includes data identifying a computer file or computer program access to which is obtained, or which is run, by means of the communication to the extent only that the file or program is identified by reference to the apparatus in which it is stored."[48]

Sub-section (c) is designed to cover situations of 'dial-through fraud', where calls are re-routed over circuit-switched networks to avoid service charges. However, it would seem to be so broadly defined that it potentially covers any signals sent using touch-tone technology, such as bank account details which should more appropriately be treated as content. The final phrase of the definition is designed to limit the concept of 'traffic data' in an Internet-context to the apparatus identified by the IP address and not any files or programs stored on the machine[49].

---

[46] 47 USCA § 1001(2).

[47] United States Court of Appeals for the District of Columbia, *United States Telecom Association, et., v Federal Communications Commission*, No. 99-1442, decided 15 August 2000.

[48] Regulation of Investigatory Powers Act 2000, s. 2(9).

[49] Ibid., at Explanatory Notes, para. 33.

Under UK law, 'traffic data' is a sub-set of a broader categorisation of data, 'communications data', which also includes data relating to usage of the communications service, e.g. call duration, and other information concerning the person to whom the CSP provides the service, e.g. subscriber address details[50]. Access to such data is subject to a different regime than that applicable to communications content, as discussed in section 3.4 above.

In the URL example given above, how would such 'call-identifying information' or 'traffic data' be technically separated from associated content, such as file details? Reliance on the agencies themselves to distinguish such data would seem unacceptable, which requires us to consider the role of the CSP over whose network the data is being sent during the interception process. To safeguard the rights and freedoms of the individual, the relevant CSP would need to be able to identify the relevant data and then automatically separate 'call-identifying' information for forwarding to the appropriate requesting authority. Under US law, such an obligation in enshrined in the law:

> Carriers are required to "facilitat[e] authorized communications interceptions and access to call-identifying information…in a manner that protects…the privacy and security of communications and call-identifying information not authorized to be intercepted;"[51]

However, the technical feasibility of such approach requires further examination, as well as the costs and how they are distributed.

The potential consequences of the blurring between communication data and content in a modern communications environment are significant. An individual's rights in the content of their communications may be significantly eroded. Communication service providers will face legal, procedural and operational uncertainties with regard to the obligations to obtain and deliver-up data that has been requested by an investigating agency. Finally, law enforcement agencies will be faced with greater legal uncertainties in respect of the appropriate procedures to be complied with when carrying out an investigation.

4.2   Communication Service Providers

One dominant feature of the current communications environment is the proliferation of communications service providers and networks utilising alternative access technologies, both wireline and wireless. As a consequence, it can be assumed that most data will be transmitted across a number of different networks owned and, or, operated by different legal entities. As such, relevant evidence may be obtained from various entities within the network.

In a traditional voice telephony environment, the general principle was that an interception would be carried out as physically close to the suspect as possible, which usually meant at a local loop or exchange level. In the current environment, the principle is no longer necessarily applicable as the proliferation of intermediary service providers within the network hierarchy structure presents a range of alternative points of interception, particularly in respect of certain types of communications (e.g. a web-based email service and cached web pages).

---

[50] Ibid., at s. 21(4).
[51] 47 USCA § 1002(a)(4)(a).

Historically, in order to enable law enforcement agencies to intercept communications, communication service providers have had legal obligations to maintain the technical capability to intercept communications. An issue presented by the current communications environment is whether such obligations should be extended to the new types of communication service providers that have entered the marketplace and the scope of any such obligation. A number of jurisdictions have already addressed this issue, but significant national differences exist across a number of issues[52]: e.g.

☐ Whether an 'intercept capability' should be imposed upon all providers of communication services and networks or only providers of 'public' services and networks;
☐ whether an 'intercept capability' should be imposed upon providers of communication networks, rather than providers of communication services;
☐ whether the 'intercept capability' should enable LEAs direct access to the point of intercept, without the involvement of CSP personnel; and
☐ who should bear the cost of implementing an 'intercept capability'?

Law enforcement agencies are inevitably keen to have access to the widest range of possible sources of relevant evidential data.

Communication service providers have a number of concerns arising from an obligation to ensure an 'intercept capability'. First, considerable reservations have been expressed about the feasibility of achieving a stable 'intercept capability' solution in a rapidly evolving communications environment. 'Intermediary service providers' in particular are concerned that their freedom to design, build and operate innovative data communications networks and services, in accordance with the dictates of newly available technologies and commercial imperatives, would be significantly restrained by the need to meet an on-going obligation to ensure an 'intercept capability'. In addition, at the level of the traditional circuit-switched local access network, significant change will be experienced as a result of the regulatory drive within Europe to unbundle the local loop, to encourage the roll-out of broadband communication facilities[53]. It is generally accepted that a single technological solution to the requirement for 'intercept capability' is not going to be available, which will have associated cost implications for CSPs and potentially procedural implications for law enforcement agencies.

Second, the costs arising from compliance with an obligation to provide 'intercept capability' is an important factor. Such costs can be distinguished into fixed costs, in relation to building the 'capability' into the network (e.g. switches with intercept functionality), and variable costs, arising from the operational aspects of carrying out an interception (e.g. personnel). It is beyond the remit of this article to suggest the most appropriate division of costs between governments, as holders of public funds, and the providers of communication networks and services. In many jurisdictions, fixed costs are borne by the CSP, whilst variable costs are covered by the relevant

---

[52] E.g. Germany: Telecommunications Law, para. 88; UK: Regulation of Investigatory Powers Act 2000, s. 12; Netherlands: Telecommunications Act 1998, s. 13.
[53] E.g. Regulation (EC)No. 2887/2000 of The European Parliament and of the Council on unbundled access to the local loop; OJ L 336/4, 30.12.2000.

public authority[54]. It is generally accepted that shifting some of the financial cost arising from an investigation to the investigating agency acts as an effective restraint on the use of such techniques.

Significant concerns have been expressed, however, particularly by those representatives of newly emerged 'intermediary service providers', that the costs involved in implementing 'intercept capability' in modern communication networks are likely to be substantial. Such concerns have been reflected in some jurisdictions through express statutory reference to the parties required to bear the costs. In the UK, the Regulation of Investigatory Powers Act 2000 provides that a CSP "receives such contribution as is…a fair contribution towards the costs incurred"[55]. In the Netherlands, the Telecommunications Act 1998 enables CSPs to "claim compensation from the national treasury for the administrative and personnel costs incurred by them directly"[56]

Were the costs associated with the provision of 'intercept capability' to lie exclusively with the communication service providers, this may impact on the commercial viability of certain SMEs entering the market for the provision of communication services and networks. The imposition of onerous 'intercept' obligations upon CSPs within Europe, in comparison with other jurisdictions, may also have an adverse effect on where CSPs choose to establish their business in the medium to long term.

5   Concluding Remarks

The nature of digital information raises serious policy and legal issues in respect of the handling of such data. Digitisation enables widely diverse sorts of information to be represented in a common format: one and zeros. One consequence of such a common format, however, is to render traditional legal categorisations invalid or effectively unenforceable. The merger that is being seen between historically distinct industries, in particular telecommunications broadcasting and IT, generally referred to as 'convergence' has challenged existing regulatory frameworks across a range of issues.

In the context of criminal investigations, the issue of handling data has given rise to a range of challenges in terms of reflecting and balancing the needs of the various interested parties. The nature of digital information makes it extremely difficult to ensure that the different types of information continue to be subject to distinct legal treatment. Our inability to practicably distinguish potentially erodes the protections granted to individuals by law. To address this data problem is likely to require a variety of approaches, both legal and procedural.

---

[54] In Belgium and Finland, the costs involved in a criminal investigation may ultimately be recovered from the perpetrator, if found guilty.

[55] S. 14(1).

[56] Art. 13.6.2.

KAoS: A Policy and Domain Services Framework for Grid Computing and Semantic Web Services

Andrzej Uszok, Jeffrey M. Bradshaw, and Renia Jeffers

Institute for Human and Machine Cognition (IHMC)
40 S. Alcaniz, Pensacola, FL 32502
{auszok, jbradshaw, rjeffers}@ihmc.us
http://www.ihmc.us

Abstract. In this article we introduce KAoS, a policy and domain services framework based on W3C's OWL ontology language. KAoS was developed in response to the challenges presented by emerging semantic application requirements for infrastructure, especially in the area of security and trust management. The KAoS architecture, ontologies, policy representation, management and disclosure mechanisms are described. KAoS enables the specification and enforcement of both authorization and obligation policies. The use of ontologies as a source of policy vocabulary enables its extensibility. KAoS has been adapted for use in several applications and deployment platforms. We briefly describe its integration with the Globus Grid Computing environment.

1 Introduction

Policy is an essential component of automatic trust systems [7]. Advances in Web Services (*http://www.w3.org/2002/ws*), Grid Computing (*http://www.gridforum.org*), P2P networks (*http://www.afternapster.com/*), Semantic Web Services (*http://www.swsi.org/*) and the convergence of all these environments creates a need for a highly adaptable, semantically rich policy mechanisms supporting the establishment of trust in all its aspects. OWL (*http://www.w3.org/2001/sw/WebOnt*), based on Description Logic [1], is an emerging standard for semantically rich services infrastructure that can be used effectively not only by people but also by software agents that represent them. Trust systems of the future will need to be able to recognize and reason about semantics used by services and agents; thus OWL is a natural choice for the development of next-generation policy service components of trust systems that will be up to the challenge of the Semantic Web. The KAoS policy and domain services framework [2, 3, 8] uses OWL both to represent policies, domains and other managed entities, and to describe their elements. The use of OWL enables flexible extension of the framework architecture, consistent with the advanced requirements of semantic applications.

C.D. Jensen et al. (Eds.): iTrust 2004, LNCS 2995, pp. 16–26, 2004.

2 KAoS Services Framework Architecture

KAoS is a collection of componentized services compatible with several popular agent platforms, including the DARPA CoABS Grid [9], the DARPA ALP/Ultra*Log Cougaar agent framework (*http://www.cougaar.net*), CORBA (*http://www.omg.org*) and Brahms [6]. The adaptability of KAoS is due in large part to its pluggable infrastructure based on Sun's Java Agent Services (JAS) (*http://www.java-agent.org*). While initially oriented to the dynamic and complex requirements of software agent applications, KAoS services have also been adapted to general-purpose grid computing [10] and Web Services [9] environments.

Under DARPA and NASA sponsorship, we have been developing the KAoS policy and domain services to increase the assurance and trust with which agents can be deployed in a wide variety of operational settings. *KAoS Domain Services* provide the capability for groups of software components, people, resources, and other entities to be semantically described and structured into organizations of domains and subdomains to facilitate collaboration and external policy administration. *KAoS Policy Services* allow for the specification, management, conflict resolution, and enforcement of policies within domains.

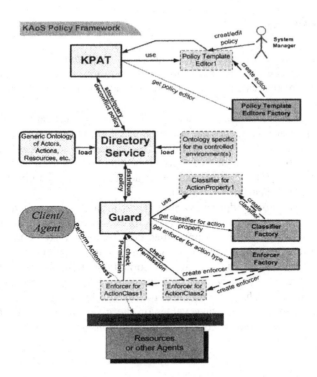

Fig. 1. Selected elements of the KAoS policy and domain services framework.

Figure 1 presents basic elements of the KAoS framework. Framework[1] functionality can be divided into two categories: generic and application/platform-specific. The generic functionality includes reusable capabilities for:

- Creating and managing the set of core ontologies;
- Storing, deconflicting and querying;
- Distributing and enforcing policies;
- Disclosing policies.

For specific applications and platforms, the KAoS framework can be extended and specialized by:

- Defining new ontologies describing application-specific and platform-specific entities and relevant action types;
- Creating extension plug-ins specific for a given application environment such as:
  - Policy Template and Custom Action Property editors;
  - Enforcers controlling, monitoring, or facilitating subclasses of actions;
  - Classifiers to determine if a given instance of an entity is in the scope of a given class-defining range.

3 KAoS Ontologies

The current version of the core KAoS Ontologies (*http://ontology.ihmc.us/*) defines basic concepts for actions, actors, groups, places, various entities related to actions (e.g., computing resources), and policies. It includes more than 100 classes and 60 properties.

The core *actor ontology* contains classes of people and software components that can be the subject of policy. Groups of actors or other entities may be distinguished according to whether the set of members is defined extensionally (i.e., through explicit enumeration in some kind of registry) or intentionally (i.e., by virtue of some common property such as types of credentials actors possess, or a given place where various entities may be currently located).

The core *action ontology* defines various types of basic actions such as accessing, communication, monitoring, moving, and so forth. An ontological definition of an action associates with it a list of properties describing context of this action or a current state of the system relevant to this action. Example properties of action classes are, for instance: destination of the communication, type of encryption used, resources accessed, time, previous history, and so forth. Each property is associated with the definition of a range of values it could have for each of the action classes. A particular instance of the action class can take values on the given property only from within this range. Actions are also divided into *ordinary actions* and *policy actions,* the latter

---

[1] Figure 1 emphasizes infrastructure supporting the specification and use of authorization policies. There are additional components to support obligation policies and other aspects of the system but they were omitted from the picture for simplicity and paper size restriction.

comprising those actions that have to do with the operations of the KAoS services themselves[2].

For a given application, the core KAoS ontologies are usually further extended with additional classes, individuals, and rules, which use the concepts defined in the core ontologies as superconcepts. This allows the framework to discover specialized concepts by querying an ontology repository for subclasses or subproperties of the given concept or property from the core ontologies. For example additional application-related context could be added to actions such as specific credentials used in a given environment.

During the initialization process, the core policy ontologies are loaded into the *KAoS Directory Service* using the namespace management capabilities of the *KAoS Policy Administration Tool (KPAT)* graphical user interface. Additional application-specific or platform-specific ontologies can then be loaded dynamically using KPAT or programmatically using the appropriate Java method. A distributed version of the KAoS Directory Service is currently being implemented. We are also studying possibilities for interaction among multiple instances of Policy Services [9].

The Directory Service is also informed about the structure of policies, domains, actors, and other application entities. This information is added to the ontology repository as instances of concepts defined in pre-loaded ontologies or values of these instance properties. As the end-user application executes, instances relating to application entities are added and deleted as appropriate.

KAoS employs the Jena Semantic Web Toolkit by HP Labs in Bristol (*http://www.hpl.hp.com/semweb*) to incrementally build OWL definitions and to assert them into the ontology repository managed by the Directory Service. In order to provide description logic reasoning on the OWL defined ontologies, the Java Theorem Prover (*http://www.ksl.stanford.edu/software/JTP*) inference engine has been integrated with KAoS. Performance is always an issue in logic reasoning; however, the steady improvement of JTP has led to a dramatic increase in its performance—an order of magnitude or more in some cases—in the last two years. The most time consuming operation in JTP is asserting new information, which happens mostly during system bootstrap. Currently, loading of the KAoS core ontologies takes less than 16 seconds on Pentium III 1.20 GHz with 640 MB RAM. Adding a policy takes usually less than 340ms. Querying JTP about ontology concepts and policies is much faster and takes only a few milliseconds.

4 Policy Representation

In KAoS, policies can express authorization (i.e., constraints that permit or forbid some action) or obligation (i.e., constraints that require some action to be performed, or else serve to waive such a requirement) for some type of action performed by one or more actors in some situation [2]. Whether or not a policy is currently applicable may be conditional upon some aspect of the situation. Auxiliary information may be associated with a policy, such as a rationale for its existence or a specification of some penalty for policy violation. In contrast to many existing policy systems [4;

---

[2] This distinction allows reasoning about actions on policies and the policy framework without resorting to the use of special "metapolicy" mechanisms.

http://www.policy-workshop.org], KAoS aims at supporting both an extensible vocabulary describing concepts of the controlled environment and also an evolution of its policy syntax. Such features are one beneficial consequence of defining policies within ontologies and using an extensible framework architecture [11].

In KAoS, a policy is represented as an ontology instance[3] of one of the four types of policy classes: positive or negative authorization, and positive or negative obligation. The instance possesses values for various management-related properties (e.g., priority, time stamp, site of enforcement) that determine how the given policy is handled within the system. The most important property value is the name of a controlled action class, which is used to determine the actual meaning of the policy. Authorization policies use it to specify the action being authorized or forbidden. Obligation policies use it to specify the action being obliged or waived. Additionally the controlled action class contains a trigger value that creates the obligation, which is also a name of the appropriate class of actions. Policy penalty properties contain a value that corresponds to a class of actions to be taken following a policy violation.

As seen from this description, the concept of action is central to the definition of KAoS Policy. Typically any action classes required to support a new policy are generated automatically by KAoS when a user defines new policy (usually using KPAT). Through various property restrictions, a given subject of the action can be variously scoped, for example, either to individual agents, to agents of a given class or to agents belonging to a particular group, and so forth. The specific contexts in which the policy constraint applies can be precisely described by restricting values of the action's properties, for instance requiring that a given action be signed using an algorithm from the specified group.

5 Policy Management

The real strength of KAoS is in its extensive support for policy life-cycle management. KAoS hides many elements of complexity of this process from the user. KAoS also provides a sophisticated policy disclosure interface enabling querying about policy impact on planned or executed actions.

5.1 Graphical Interface to Ontology Concepts

The KPAT graphical interface to policy management hides the complexity of the OWL representation from users. The reasoning and representation capabilities of OWL are used to full advantage to make the process as simple as possible. Whenever a user has to provide an input is always presented with a complete set of values he can choose from, which are valid in the given context.

As in the case of the generic policy editor shown on figure 2, a user, after selecting an actor for a new policy, is first presented with the list of actions the given type of actors is capable to perform based on the definition in the ontology relating actions to actors by the *performedBy* property. When the user selects a particular action type

---

[3] See *http://ontology.ihmc.us/SemanticServices/S-F/Example/* for an example of KAoS policy syntax.

information about all the properties, which can be associated with the given actions, are presented. For each of the properties, the range of possible values is obtained; instances and classes falling into this range are gathered if the user wants to build a restriction on the given property, thus narrowing the action class used in the build policy to its context.

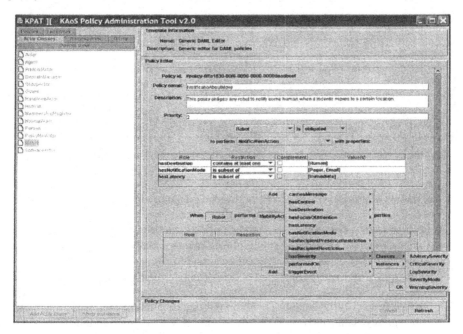

Fig. 2. KPAT generic policy builder – an example of ontology-guided interface.

5.2 Policy Administration

Each time a new policy is added or an existing one is deleted or modified, the potential impact goes beyond the single policy change. Policy administrators need to be able to understand such interactions and make sure that any unwanted side effects are eliminated. KAoS assists administrators by identifying instances of given types of policy interactions, visualizing them, and, if desired, facilitating any necessary modifications.

One important type of interaction is a policy conflict [2, 8]. For example, one policy might authorize actor A to communicate with any actor in group B while a new policy might forbid actor A from communicating with actor B1, a member of B. In general, if a new policy overlaps in key properties of a subset of controlled actions with an existing policy of a potentially conflicting modality (i.e., positive vs. negative authorization (as in our example); positive vs. negative obligation; positive obligation vs. negative authorization), some means must be used to identify the conflict and to determine, in the area of overlap, which policy takes precedence[4]. If precedence cannot be determined otherwise, KAoS will ask the administrator to determine the appropriate action (figure 3).

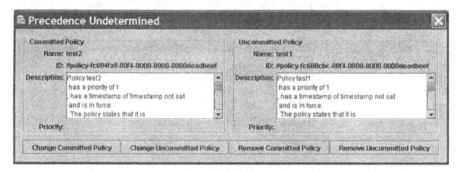

Fig. 3. Notification about policy conflict and options available to the administrator.

The following policy actions can be performed on a pair of overlapping policies:

- *Remove Policy*: one of the overlapping policies can be completely removed;
- *Change Priority*: priorities of the policies can be modify so they either do not conflict or they alter the precedence relation[5];
- *Harmonize Policy*: the controlled action of the selected overlapping policy can be modified using an automatic harmonization algorithm to eliminate their overlap; see [8] for details. This required modification of the restrictions in of the policy controlled actions by building either intersection (by using *owl:intersectionOf*) or differences (by using *owl:complementOf*) of the previous ranges in the two conflicting policies.
- *Split Policy*: the controlled action of the selected overlapping policy can be automatically split into two parts: one part that overlaps with the other policy and the other which does not. Then the priorities of these parts can be modified independently. The splitting algorithm is similar to the harmonization and is currently in development.

In the future, a more sophisticated user interface will allow for modification of entire sets of policies at once.

Whereas the goal of policy conflict resolution is to ensure consistency among the policies in force, other forms of analysis are needed to ensure policy enforceability. In

---

[4] If desired, precedence relations can be predefined in the ontology, permitting partially or totally automated conflict resolution.

[5] We currently rely exclusively on the combination of numeric policy priorities and update times to determine precedence—the larger the integer and the more recent the update the greater the priority. In the future we intend to allow people additional flexibility in designing the nature and scope of precedence conditions. For example, it would be possible to define default precedence over some policy scope based on the relative authorities of the individual who defined or imposed the policies in conflict, which policy was defined first, and so forth.

some cases, the implementation of policy may be impossible due to prior obligations of the actor or oversubscription of resources. In the future, KAoS will be able to suggest ways of relaxing such non satisfy constraints in certain situations.

In some cases, two complementary policies of the same modality can create unanticipated problems. For example, one policy may prevent communication among actors within domain A while another policy might prevent communication to actors outside of the domain. Though the two policies would not conflict, their combination would result in the inability of actors in domain A to communicate at all. It should be possible in the future to flag these and other situations of potential interest to administrators.

5.3 Policy Exploration and Disclosure

A human user or software component uses KAoS to investigate how policies affect actions in the environment. In general, the answers to these queries are decided by inferring whether some concrete action falls into a category of action controlled by one or more policies, and then determining what conclusions about the described action can be drawn. As part of KAoS policy exploration and disclosure interfaces we provide the following kinds of functionality:

- *Test Permission:* determine whether the described action is permitted.
- *Get Obligations:* determine which actions, if any that would be obligated as a follow on to some potential action or event. For instance, there might be an obligation policy which specified that if an actor were to receive information about a particular topic then the system would be obligated to log or forward this information to some other party.
- *Learn Options:* determine which policy-relevant actions are available or not available in a given context. For example, the actor may specify a partial action description and KAoS would return any missing (required) elements of the action with ranges of possible values—for instance, information about missing credentials.
- *Make Compliant:* transform the action an actor tries to perform from a policy non-compliant to a policy-compliant one by informing it about the required changes that would need to be made to the action based on existing policies. For instance, if the system attempted to send a message about particular subject to a few actors, the list of actors might need to be trimmed to some subset of those actors or else extended to include some required recipients. Or else maybe the content of a message would need to be transformed by stripping off sensitive information, and so forth.
- *Get Consequences:* determines the consequences of some action by observing and investigating possible actions in the situation created by a completion of the considered action(s) to the specified depth (consequences of consequences). This option has many variants currently under investigation.

5.4 Adapting Policy to Legacy Systems

When policy leaves the Directory Service, for performance reasons it typically has to map OWL into a format that is compatible with the legacy system with which it is being integrated. KAoS communicates information from OWL to the outside world by mapping ontology properties to the name of the class defining its range as well to a list with cached instances of that class that were in existence when the policy left the Directory Service. A particular system can use the cached instance for its computation; also in any moment it can refresh the list by contacting the Directory Service and providing the name of the range. Alternatively, the Directory Service can push changes to the system as they occur.

6 KAoS Policy Applications

KAoS is used in several applications ranging from the human-robotic teamwork for NASA and the Office of Naval Research [12], through massive societies of agents in the DARPA Ultralog project building next generation army logistic system, to Semantic Web Services interaction in the DARPA CoSAR-TS project [9][6]. Here, we briefly present a summary of how KAoS has been integrated with Grid Computing services on the Globus platform (*http://www.globus.org/*) [10].

   Globus provides effective resource management, authentication and local resource control for the grid-computing environment, but has a need for domain and policy services. KAoS seemed to be a perfect complement to the Globus system, providing a wide range of policy management capabilities that rely on platform-specific enforcement mechanisms. By providing an interface between the Globus Grid and KAoS, we enable the use of KAoS mechanisms to manage GSI (Grid Security Infrastructure) enabled Grid services. GSI was the only component of the GT3 (Globus Toolkit) we used in the integration. The interface itself is a Grid service, which we called a KAoS Grid service. It provides Grid clients and services the ability to register with KAoS services, and to check weather a given action is authorized or not based on current policies. The clients or resources use their credential to request to be registered into one or more KAoS managed domains. The credential is a standard X.509 certificate that Globus uses for authentication. The credential is verified using the GT GSI. If the certificate is valid the registration request is sent to KAoS for registration into the desired domains. If the resource uses an application specific ontology to describe its capabilities, it will have to be loaded into the KAoS ontology using a utility provided by KAoS. Inside the KAoS Grid service, the registration is handled through the associated Guard. This allows KAoS to distribute all applicable policies to the appropriate Guard and enforce them. We plan to continue to enhance this service and port it to GT4 when it is available.

---

[6] See *http://ontology.ihmc.us/applications.html* for more information about these applications.

7 Conclusions

Originally KAoS was not tailored for trust negotiation and management. However, from the very beginning the architecture of the framework architecture and its extensive use of ontologies ensured its versatility and adaptability. It already provides most of the generic mechanisms enumerated as required for the policy system to be integrated with a trust system, as enumerated in [7].[7] Current work in the area of Semantic Web Services [9] will fill the gaps in the area of negotiation, necessary ontologies for credentials, and integration with existing PKI infrastructure. Our current prototypes integrating KAoS with grid computing security and credential mechanisms, as presented above, gives us confidence in the promise of future work in this same direction.

Acknowledgments. The authors gratefully acknowledge the sponsorship of this research by the NASA Cross-Enterprise and Intelligent Systems Programs, and a joint NASA-DARPA ITAC grant. Additional support was provided by DARPA's CoABS, Ultra*Log, and CoSAR-TS programs. Thanks to the other members of the KAoS project team: Maggie Breedy, Larry Bunch, Matthew Johnson, Hyuckchul Jung, Shri Kulkarni, James Lott, William Taysom, and Gianluca Tonti. We are also grateful for the contributions of Austin Tate, Pat Hayes, Niranjan Suri, Paul Feltovich, Richard Fikes, Jessica Jenkins, Rich Feiertag, Timothy Redmond, Sue Rho, Ken Ford, Mark Greaves, Jack Hansen, James Allen, and Robert Hoffman.

References

[1] Baader, F., Calvanese, D., McGuinness, D., Nardi, D. & Patel-Schneider, P. (Ed.) (2003). The Description Logic Handbook. Cambridge University Press,

[2] Bradshaw, J. M., Beautement, P., Breedy, M. R., Bunch, L., Drakunov, S. V., Feltovich, P., Hoffman, R. R., Jeffers, R., Johnson, M., Kulkarni, S., Lott, J., Raj, A. K., Suri, N., & Uszok, A. (2003). Making agents acceptable to people. In N. Zhong and J. Liu (Eds.), Handbook of Intelligent Information Technology. Amsterdam: IOS Press, in press.

[3] Bradshaw, J. M., Dutfield, S., Benoit, P., & Woolley, J. D. (1997). KAoS: Toward an industrial-strength generic agent architecture. In J. M. Bradshaw (Ed.), Software Agents. (pp. 375-418). Cambridge, MA: AAAI Press/The MIT Press.

[4] Damianou, N., Dulay, N., Lupu, E. C., & Sloman, M. S. (2000). Ponder: A Language for Specifying Security and Management Policies for Distributed Systems, Version 2.3., Imperial College, London,

[5] Kahn, M., & Cicalese, C. (2001). CoABS Grid Scalability Experiments. O. F. Rana (Ed.), Second International Workshop on Infrastructure for Scalable Multi-Agent Systems at the Fifth International Conference on Autonomous Agents. ACM Press,

[6] Sierhuis, M. (2002). Brahms - Modeling and Simulating Work Practice. Univ. of Amsterdam Press,

[7] Seamons, K., Winslett, M., Yu, T., Smith, B., Child, E., Jacobson, J., Mills, H. and Yu L. (2002). Requirements for Policy Languages for Trust Negotiation. In Proceedings of IEEE Workshop on Policy 2002.

---

[7] We hope to be able to integrate with Seamons' work on TrustBuilder in the future.

[8]   Uszok, A., Bradshaw, J., Jeffers, R., Suri, N., Hayes, P., Breedy, M., Bunch, L., Johnson, M., Kulkarni, S. and Lott, J. (2003). KAoS Policy and Domain Services: Toward a Description-Logic Approach to Policy Representation, Deconfliction and Enforcement. In Proceedings of IEEE Workshop on Policy 2003.

[9]   Uszok, A., Bradshaw, J., Jeffers, R., Johnson, M., Tate A., Dalton, J., Aitken, S. (2004). Policy and Contract Management for Semantic Web Services. In Proceedings of the AAAI Spring Symposium on Semantic Web Services.

[10]   Johnson, M., Chang, P., Jeffers, R., Bradshaw, J.M., Soo, V-W., Breedy, M. R., Bunch, L., Kulkarni, S., Lott, J., Suri, N., & Uszok, A. (2003). KAoS semantic policy and domain services: An application of DAML to Web services-based grid architectures. In Proceedings of the AAMAS 03 Workshop on Web Services and Agent-Based Engineering. Melbourne, Australia, July. (To appear in a forthcoming volume from Kluwer.)

[11]   Tonti, G., Bradshaw, J. M., Jeffers, R., Montanari, R., Suri, N., & Uszok, A. (2003). Semantic Web languages for policy representation and reasoning: A comparison of KAoS, Rei, and Ponder. In D. Fensel, K. Sycara, & J. Mylopoulos (Ed.), The Semantic Web-ISWC 2003. Proceedings of the Second International Semantic Web Conference, Sanibel Island, Florida, USA, October 2003, LNCS 2870. (pp. 419-437). Berlin: Springer.

[12]   Sierhuis, M., Bradshaw, J. M., Acquisti, A., Van Hoof, R., Jeffers, R., & Uszok, A. (2003). Human-agent teamwork and adjustable autonomy in practice. Proceedings of the Seventh International Symposium on Artificial Intelligence, Robotics and Automation in Space (i-SAIRAS). Nara, Japan, 19-23 May.

W5: The Five W's of the World Wide Web

Massimo Marchiori[1,2,3]

[1] The World Wide Web Consortium (W3C)
[2] MIT Lab for Computer Science, Cambridge (USA)
[3] University of Venice, Italy
massimo@w3.org

Keywords: WWW, Trust, Semantic Web, HTTP.

1 The Five W's

The World Wide Web is a Web of information. Information can be more or less qualified, more or less usable, more or less usable by automatic processors. Information of the most different kinds, that can be reused for a lot of purposes. So how do we treat this information, how do we give some order, and possibly help its intelligent reuse?

Journalism has had the same problem since its inception: you have to report and classify a bit of information, but here "information" is as wide as the information we have nowadays in the WWW. So, what's the way out? One way out, which proved to be quite successful, is to use the so-called five W's, which are five axes that somehow identify the information event. These are the well-known and self-explanatory:

- WHAT
- WHERE
- WHO
- WHEN
- WHY

So, what about reusing this five W concept for the information present in the Web?

Historically, the five W's have already been used explicitly inside some application, for instance in XML dialects (cf. [5]), but what about reasoning about them at the most abstract level? Can they help, for instance in building a better Semantic Web?

2 Trust

The problem of Trust is a fundamental one in computer science, and in practice in the WWW. In order to talk about trust, we can try to give a more or less formal definition that we can later reuse to define some terminology. So, in general we can define:

C.D. Jensen et al. (Eds.): iTrust 2004, LNCS 2995, pp. 27–32, 2004.

Definition 1. *(Trust Scenario)*
A trust scenario *is a quintuple* $(\mathcal{T}, \mathcal{R}, \mathcal{U}, \mathcal{S}, \tau)$ *so defined:*

- *A "trust property"* $\mathcal{T}$ *(that can be computationally intractable).*
- *A "test property",* τ *(that is usually computationally tractable).*
- *A "universe"* $\mathcal{U}$ *of entities (e.g., software agents, persons, etc.).*
- *A number* $\mathcal{R}$ *($\in [0,1]$), indicating the "real" probability that* τ *implies* $\mathcal{T}$.
- *A mapping* $\mathcal{S}$ *from* $\mathcal{U}$ *to* $[0,1]$, *indicating that the "subjective" probability for an entity* $e \in \mathcal{U}$ *that* τ *implies* $\mathcal{T}$ *is* $\mathcal{S}(e)$.

Note that a trust scenario usually is not fixed but depends on an *environment* $\mathcal{E}$, which can contain the information on how to compute the probabilities, and that can be itself dependant on a number of factors, like time for instance.

In the following, when talking individually about entities and test properties, we shall always mean them within an understood environment and trust scenario (an "$\mathcal{E}$-$\mathcal{TRUST}$").

Having defined what a trust scenario is, we can now use it to somehow formally define when problems with trust occur, i.e., when we have deception:

Definition 2. *(Deception)*
Deception occurs for an entity e *when*

$$\mathcal{R} \ll \mathcal{S}(e)$$

So, in general, we can say that in a trust scenario deception occurs when there is an entity such that deception occurs for it.

The severity of a deception could of course be quantified in various degrees, both locally for an entity e (e.g. by using the gap measure $\mathcal{S}(e) - \mathcal{R}$), and globally by measuring its diffusion in the universe $\mathcal{U}$ (e.g., in case of a finite universe, by averaging the local gap measure, or by fixing a threshold and measuring how much of the universe has a deception higher than that).

3   The Cost/Benefit

In the WWW, resources do not come for free, but there is a cost for creation and modification. Every solution for the WWW may bring some *benefits*, but usually also implies new creation/modification of information, and this *cost* must be taken into account, because that could be a big obstacle to the widespread adoption of such solution. Therefore, the parameter to take into consideration for success is the ratio *cost/benefit*. The cost/benefit (for instance, to diminish deception of some trust scenario), must be sufficiently high for users to adopt the solution and to build critical mass, so to create a possible network effect.

4   The WWW

We consider the World Wide Web in its approximation of "universal information space" where there are certain resources that are retrieved by dereferencing a certain URL. In other words, more technically, we just consider the Web under the assumption that the HTTP GET method is the only one to be used[1]

So, we can view the WWW as a "dereference map" δ from URLs $\to$ byte streams, with the intended meaning that $\delta(u) = s$ if and only if, in the real WWW, there is a machine such that retrieving (GET) the URI u gives as a result the byte stream s.

When we later add semantics and meaning (depending on the particular application we use), we are essentially using an interpretation (let's say $\mathcal{I}$) of such web objects, that can give us more knowledge. That is the one that can allow, in trust scenarios, to lower deception.

Most of the times W3C sets up a standard (for example, for the Semantic Web), $\mathcal{I}$ is refined.

5   The Light Five W's

It is of utmost importance to minimize the cost of representing additional information in the WWW. This means that we should strive to obtain the information given by the five W's in the most economical possible way, almost "zero-cost" if possible. Is there such a way? The answer is yes, at least for four or the five axes:

zero-cost WHAT == the resource (at least the message-body)

zero-cost WHERE = yes, the URI of the resource (Content-Location or Request-URI)

zero-cost WHO = yes, the URI authority (Host)

zero-cost WHEN = yes, the time when the resource was transmitted (Date)

zero-cost WHY = no.

In the following, when applicable, zero-cost W's are understood.

6   The W1

What does it mean for a standard or for an application to be "Web"? In many cases, such standard/application doesn't take into account the mapping δ, but just takes into consideration the *message-body* (cf. [2]) of the image of δ, in some cases integrated with the information about their MIME type. Simply speaking, this is tantamount to considering "web pages".

Restated, such standards/applications are posing the WHAT axis equal to such web pages.

---

[1] In fact, this approximation gathers, at least architecturally, a good part of the WWW, as GET is architecturally a "universal operator" (in the sense of category theory) for most of the HTTP methods that collect information.

This is the starting point, and we can therefore define a first kind of World Wide Web:

$$W1 = WHAT$$

The current architecture of the Semantic Web stays in the W1 (where WHAT = message-body).

The problem is that, to build a reasonably effective Semantic Web (or in any case, to increase the semantic content, therefore diminishing deception) can have a very high cost.

7   W2 to W5

Another possible approach is to extend the W1 using the information provided by the other W axes.

Therefore, $\mathcal{I}$ (the W1) can be increasingly integrated with the zero-cost WHERE, WHO and WHEN, giving three flavors of W2 ((WHAT, WHERE), (WHAT, WHO), (WHAT, WHEN)), two flavors of W3 ((WHAT, WHERE, WHO), (WHAT, WHERE, WHEN), (WHAT, WHO, WHEN)), and one W4 (WHAT, WHERE, WHO, WHEN).

8   Into Action

The W's give a kind of temporal modal logic: WHERE == world , WHO == world, WHEN == time. As common to modal logics, statements expressed in the same world can usually combine seamlessly, using the operators that the interpretation $\mathcal{I}$ provides; as WHERE specializes WHO, this means that choosing a W2 or W3 with a WHO (and without a WHERE) will generally allow many more inferences than choosing a W2 or W3 with a WHERE.

On the other hand, the WHEN component is troublesome, as it represents a time instant, and so in general composition becomes practically impossible. Therefore, in order to allow a more useful use of WHEN, we can relax the composition rules, which is equivalent to change our interpretation of the timed logic.

For instance, one possible choice could be to employ some assumption of *local time consistency* (cf. [4]), therefore assuming that web resources stay somehow stable within some time intervals. This changes the interpretation of WHEN from a single instant to a time interval, allowing more inferences to take place. The price is that the approximation given in the choice of the stable time interval will likely make the deception increase, so there is a tradeoff. However, this tradeoff can be mitigated by using appropriate probability distributions of the "local stability" of a resource (therefore, passing to fuzzy/probabilistic reasoning).

Another choice is change the definition of WHEN, which is now rather simplistic (Date), and add for example the information about cacheability of the resource, and the expiration date: this gives right away a timed interval structure, which can be quite useful. The price to pay is that appropriate cache information can have a cost. However, the benefits are quite high, because this information not only can help produce many more useful inferences in a W2, W3 or W4, but help in general the performance of the WWW (the primary reason in fact why cache information is present...). So, this approach might be worth exploiting,

Finally, of course, more sophisticated approaches are possible, where some or all of the information in the WHERE/WHO/WHEN/WHY axes is refined by integration with the information in $\mathcal{I}$. This intermediate solution can be the right way to overcome the limitations of the simplest W2, W3 and W4 solutions, while still keeping reasonably low the cost/benefit ratio.

9   Skews

The approach that we have seen so far is based on principles, but it has to be noted that other complementary views must be taken into consideration, when analyzing for instance trust scenario. Problems may occur, coming from malicious attempts to increase deception over time: in such cases, it is not uncommon to use all possible means: many trust problems on the Web usually occur because of so-called *information-flow skews*. A skew occurs when there is a treatment of the information flow in the WWW that departs from the high-level standard architecture of the Web, and that the user cannot see. There are at least three main skews that we can categorize:

− The *Visual Skew*
− The *Navigation Skew*
− The *Protocol Skew*

The *Visual Skew* occurs when not all the data flow goes back to the user, and can be synthesized with the slogan

"What you see is not what you get"

In practice, this skew exploits the possibility that how a resource is rendered on the screen/medium (and so, what the user perceives) can be much different from what is actually in the resource.

One of the classic cases where Visual Skew shows its appearance is the so-called *search engine persuasion (sep)* (cf. [3]), also sometimes known (improperly) as search engine spam. Sep is the phenomenon of artificially "pumping up" the ranking of a resource in search engines, so to get a higher position (with all that means in terms of visibility and advertisement). Most of the techniques used in sep just profit in various ways of the visual skew, so to apparently present to the user a certain resource, which is quite different under the surface.

The *Navigation Skew* occurs when not all the WWW navigation is specified by the user. For instance, if we click on a link (i.e., request a resource on the WWW), we expect that we are just fetching the corresponding page. But this is not true: for example, frames and images are automatically loaded for us. This apparent facility, however, leaves the door open for the navigation skew, as it means essentially that the authors of a resource can make us click on the page they want (!). Well-known examples of use of the navigation skew are banner ads and pop-up windows, all employing this skew in its various flavors. But even worst, the navigation skew makes possible applications that are potentially quite dangerous for users, like *tracking systems* (a la DoubleClick and Engage). Typically, such privacy-risky applications might employ a combination of skews (for instance, using so-called "web bugs", images that use the navigation skew to send data, and the visual skew to hide, therefore resulting invisible).

The *Protocol Skew* occurs when the WWW protocols (e.g. HTTP) are abused (for instance, turning a stateless connection into a connection with state). For instance, the HTTP information flow in some cases should be from server to user (i.e., if we request a page, it's only the server that gives us information). But this architectural principle is not always followed in reality, as for example many sites tend to collect so-called "clickstream" information (what you requested, when you did it, what is your computer internet address, etc). Again, this skew allows to collect information "under the rug", and can therefore become quite a problem for the user's privacy. Such problem can be worsened a lot when abuse of this skew is performed via aggregation: for instance, use of dynamic links (URIs that are generated on the fly) together with appropriate use of other clickstream information can make such tracking easily work not just for a single click, but for an entire session.

Therefore, every practical use of W1, W2, W3 or W4 have to take into account the potential danger, that "light" solutions can be necessarily prone to a higher risk in terms of possible deception

References

1. T.Berners-Lee, R.Fielding, L.Masinter, *Uniform Resource Identifiers (URI): Generic Syntax*, IETF RFC, 1998.
2. R.Fielding, J.Gettys, J.Mogul, H.Frystyk, L.Masinter, P.Leach, T.Berners-Lee, *Hypertext Transfer Protocol – HTTP/1.1*, IETF RFC, 1999.
3. M.Marchiori, *Security of World Wide Web Search Engines*, Proceedings of the Third International Conference on Reliability, Quality and Safety of Software-Intensive Systems (ENCRESS'97), Chapman & Hall, 1997.
4. M.Marchiori, *The Quest for Correct Information on the Web: Hyper Search Engines*, Proceedings of the Sixth International World Wide Web Conference (WWW6), 1997.
5. M.Marchiori, The XML Documentation Markup, W3C, 1999.

A Case for Evidence-Aware Distributed Reputation Systems*

Overcoming the Limitations of Plausibility Considerations

Philipp Obreiter

Institute for Program Structures and Data Organization
Universität Karlsruhe (TH)
D-76128 Karlsruhe, Germany
obreiter@ipd.uni-karlsruhe.de

Abstract. Reputation systems support trust formation in artificial societies by keeping track of the behavior of autonomous entities. In the absence of any commonly trusted entity, the reputation system has to be distributed to the autonomous entities themselves. They may cooperate by issuing recommendations of other entities' trustworthiness. At the time being, distributed reputation systems rely on plausibility for assessing the truthfulness and consistency of such recommendations. In this paper, we point out the limitations of such plausibility considerations and present an alternative concept that is based on evidences. The concept combines the strengths of non-repudiability and distributed reputation systems. We analyze the issues that are related to the issuance and gathering of evidences. In this regard, we identify four patterns of how evidence-awareness overcomes the limitations of plausibility considerations.

1 Introduction

The past years have witnessed an increasing interest in trust for the conception of open artificial societies. Trust is a substitute for complete information regarding the entities that participate in such societies [1]. By this means, the behavior of autonomous entities may be pre-estimated. For the formation of trust, it seems promising to also consider the experiences made by other entities [2]. Such experiences are disseminated as recommendations in the context of a reputation system. The major challenge for reputation systems consists in assessing the truthfulness of such recommendations. In this regard, a recommendation is truthful if it corresponds to the experiences made by its issuer.

Self-organization is a central paradigm for P2P networks, ad hoc networks, open multi-agent systems, and autonomic computing. The application of reputation systems to such self-organized systems appears especially challenging.

* The work done for this paper is funded by the German Research Community (DFG) in the context of the priority program (SPP) no. 1140. The author would like to thank Michael Klein, Georgios Papadopoulos, Michael Christoffel, Birgitta König-Ries, Sokshee Goh and the anonymous reviewers for their comments on this paper.

C.D. Jensen et al. (Eds.): iTrust 2004, LNCS 2995, pp. 33–47, 2004.

In the absence of any commonly trusted entity, the reputation system has to be distributed to the autonomous entities themselves. Consequently, recommendations cannot be gathered and correlated by a central component. Hence, an entity may issue inconsistent recommendations, i.e., recommendations that contradict each other. As a result, distributed reputation systems have to be robust against both untruthful and inconsistent recommendations.

The existing approaches for distributed reputation systems [2,3,4,5,6,7] make use of plausibility considerations in order to provide such robustness. This means that the impact of a recommendation is contingent upon its plausibility which, in turn, depends on its compatibility with prior beliefs. Such schemes are vulnerable to misbehavior that is aimed at influencing the plausibility considerations themselves. The introduction of objective facts would strongly increase the effectiveness of such distributed reputation systems. In this paper, we introduce objective facts by making use of non-repudiable tokens that we call *evidences*.

The paper is organized as follows: In Section 2, the limitations of plausibility considerations are pointed out. The concept of evidences is introduced in Section 3 and their issuance is analyzed in Section 4. This builds the foundation for pointing out how evidences overcome the limitations of plausibility considerations in Section 5. We show the contribution of this paper with regard to the related work in Section 6 before concluding it in Section 7.

2   Distributed Reputation Systems

In this section, we present a model that facilitates the concise discussion of distributed reputation systems. We identify the requirements for such systems and point out the limitations of plausibility considerations.

2.1   System Model

We assume a system as it is described in [8,9]. It consists of *entities* that may enter into *transactions* at any time. Each transaction occurs between a pair of entities (*transaction peers*). The autonomy of the entities implies that an entity may *defect* in the course of a transaction. In this regard, defection refers to the premature abandonment of a transaction. Take for example two entities of a P2P network that agree on exchanging a pair of files. After having received the file of the transaction partner, a transaction peer may defect by refusing to transmit the promised file. The *reputation system* keeps track of defections in order to caution the entities about the defectors. By this means, the reputation system provides an incentive for adhering to one's own promises [8].

In the absence of any central component, the reputation system is distributed to the entities themselves. More specifically, each entity runs a *local instance* of the reputation system. These instances may cooperate by exchanging *recommendations*[1]. The considered system is illustrated for two entities in Figure 1.

---

[1] Hence, this notion of recommendations also includes disrecommendations that communicate distrust. In the following, if we want to stress that a recommendation communicates trust, it will be referred to as *positive* recommendation.

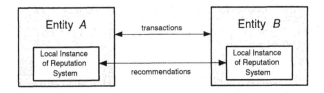

Fig. 1. Model of a distributed reputation system

The issuer of a recommendation (*recommender*) communicates the trustworthiness of a certain entity (*recommendee*) to the *recipient* of the recommendation. The autonomy of the entities implies that recommendations may be untruthful. Therefore, before taking a recommendation into account, the recipient has to *assess* the truthfulness of the recommendation. In the following, an entity that performs such assessment will be referred to as *assessor*. The roles of the entities that participate in the reputation system are interrelated in Figure 2.

As a prerequisite for the operation of a distributed reputation system, the entities have to be able to send *authenticated messages*. This means that the recipient of a message knows which entity has sent it. However, this does not mean that the recipient can prove to other entities that the message originated from the sender [10]. For example, messages may be authenticated but repudiable if symmetric key cryptography [11] is applied.

2.2 Requirements for the Reputation System

The reputation system should not only keep track of *transactional* behavior. In addition, it has to consider untruthful recommendations which represent misbehavior targeted at itself. Such untruthful recommendations either overstate the trustworthiness of an entity (*praising*) or they understate it (*defamation*) [9]. As a result, *recommendational* behavior has also to be tracked [12]. Apparently, such meta-tracking can only be performed by the reputation system itself. We conclude that the reputation system has to comply with the *demand for closure* with respect to misbehavior. In this regard, the mechanism that the reputation system introduces (i.e., the exchange of recommendations) has to protect itself against misbehavior.

2.3 Limitations of Plausibility Considerations

Plausibility considerations are contingent upon prior beliefs. More specifically, the considerations comprise two parts. On the one hand, a recommendation is assessed as rather trustworthy if it is compatible to the first hand experiences made by the assessor itself. On the other hand, the more the recommender is trusted[2] the more the recommendation is regarded as truthful. In the following, we give an in depth analysis of the limitations from the perspective of the recommender, the recommendee, and the assessor.

---

[2] Such *recommender trust* [12] may be confined to recommendational behavior.

Fig. 2. Roles regarding a recommendation

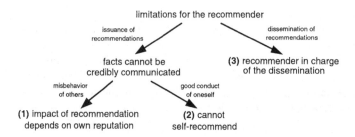

Fig. 3. Limitations of plausibility considerations from the recommender's point of view

Limitations from the recommender's point of view. In Figure 3, we illustrate the limitations of plausibility considerations from the recommender's point of view.

The recommender has to be aware that the credibility of the issued recommendation is contingent upon its plausibility. Hence, a correct observation of implausible behavior (*implausible fact*) cannot be credibly communicated to other entities. There are two types of such implausible facts. In the first place, the behavior of an entity may be contradicted by its reputation. For example, it is difficult to credibly communicate the defection of an entity that has a good reputation. The only means for doing so is to have a good reputation oneself. As a result, the impact of the issued recommendation depends on one's own reputation (**1**). This limitation restricts the issuance of credible recommendations by entities that lack good reputation, as it is true for newcomers. The second type of implausible facts consists of truthful self-recommendations. The plausibility of a self-recommendation depends on the trust in the self-recommender. More specifically, a self-recommendation can only be credibly communicated if its issuer has a good reputation. However, in such a case, the other entities would already be aware of the good conduct of the self-recommender so that the self-recommendation becomes dispensable. Consequently, good conduct cannot be usefully communicated by the well-behaving entity itself (**2**). The need for self-recommendations arises in situations in which the entities that are aware of the good conduct are offline and, thus, cannot recommend the respective entity.

Apart from the issuance of recommendations, there is a further limitation regarding their dissemination. Recommendations can only be credibly passed on by commonly trusted entities. If the system lacks such entities, the recommender is solely in charge of the dissemination of the issued recommendation (**3**). The ensuing costs represent a disincentive for issuing recommendations.

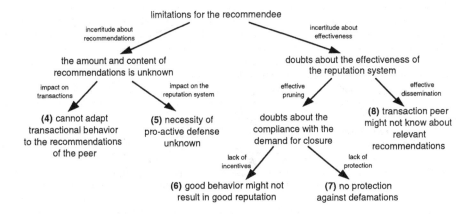

Fig. 4. Limitations of plausibility considerations from the recommendee's point of view

Limitations from the recommendee's point of view. In Figure 4, the limitations of plausibility considerations are shown from the recommendee's point of view.

Each entity is uncertain about which recommendations regarding itself are issued. However, it is important to know about the amount and content of such recommendations in order to adapt one's own behavior. In accordance with the system model, such adaption comprises two types of behavior, i.e., transactional and recommendational behavior. Transactional behavior should be adapted depending on the worthiness of good behavior. Take for example a transaction that is performed without any defection. A transaction peer may still defame the other one by disrecommending it to a third entity. In such a case, the defamed entity might want to refrain from participating in further transactions that are only beneficial to the defamer. Yet, the incertitude about recommendations that are issued by other entities does not allow for such adaption (**4**). The same applies to the adaption of recommendational behavior. Under certain circumstances, the defamed entity has to pro-actively defend itself by disrecommending the defamer. By this means, the impact of the defamation would be decreased. Yet, the incertitude about recommendations of other entities does not allow for such pro-active defense (**5**).

The limitations of plausibility considerations may result in doubts about the effectiveness of the reputation system. In this context, effectiveness refers to the effective pruning of untruthful recommendations and to the effective dissemination of recommendations respectively. The pruning of untruthful recommendations is stipulated by the demand for closure. If there are doubts about the effectiveness of such pruning, the entities lack incentives for good behavior (**6**). In addition, it may be postulated that the system lacks protection against misbehavior (**7**). In the eye of such doubts, it does not appear incentive compatible to participate and behave well in transactions and in the reputation system. The same consideration applies to doubts about the effective dissemination of recommendations (**8**). Even if good conduct is always honored by positive rec-

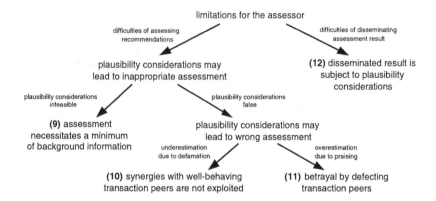

Fig. 5. Limitations of plausibility considerations from the assessor's point of view

ommendations, there is no guarantee that such recommendations are available to specific entities, e.g., future transaction partners. This occurs if the recommender is offline or, due to the arising costs, it is reluctant to disseminate the recommendation to many entities.

Limitations from the assessor's point of view. In Figure 5, we illustrate the limitations of plausibility considerations from the assessor's point of view.

Upon receival of a recommendation, an entity has to assess its truthfulness before taking it into account. Such assessment brings forth several difficulties that might lead to an inappropriate assessment. On the one hand, plausibility considerations may be infeasible due to the lack of background information (**9**). If there are no first hand experiences with the recommendee and the recommendational behavior of the recommender is unknown, the assessor cannot apply plausibility considerations. Apparently, this limitation is especially important for newcomers. On the other hand, plausibility considerations may be false and result in a wrong assessment. Such wrong assessment accrues from not being able to prune untruthful recommendations. If an assessor underestimates the trustworthiness of a well-behaving entity due to defamations, the synergies are not exploited since the assessor refrains from transacting with the entity (**10**). The other way round, due to praising, an assessor may overestimate the trustworthiness of a misbehaving entity that defects in the course of a subsequent transaction with the assessor (**11**). In any case, wrong assessments incur opportunity costs or costs that arise from being defected.

There is a further limitation that goes beyond the aforementioned difficulties of assessing recommendations. The assessment result represents a recommendation. Hence, other entities would assess the trustworthiness of the assessment result depending on its plausibility. Consequently, the assessor has to be trusted by other entities in order to be able to credibly disseminate the assessment result to them (**12**). This limitation is especially important for costly assessment methods.

3   The Basics of the Concept

The aforementioned limitations of plausibility considerations demand for an alternative concept. Therefore, in this section, we introduce a concept that allows for the verifiability of recommendations. We take a closer look at the central notion of this concept, i.e., evidences. In addition, we discuss the impact of evidences on the assessment of recommendations.

Introductory example. Before proposing and discussing the concept, we illustrate the key terms in an introductory example.

Let us assume two transaction peers that assume a provider-consumer relationship [8]. During the transaction, the provider transmits a document to the consumer that, in turn, hands over a receipt back to provider. In this context, the receipt represents an *evidence*. If the consumer subsequently defames the provider by stating that no document has been transmitted, the provider should be able to *refute* the defamation by showing the receipt. Even if the consumer goes offline immediately after handing over the receipt, the provider may self-recommend by stating that it has behaved well during a transaction with the consumer. Such self-recommendation should be *provable* if the receipt is attached to it.

Evidences. An *evidence*[3] is a non-repudiable token [14] that may be arbitrarily transferred. This means that, upon receival, an evidence may be credibly passed on to other entities. Digital signatures [11] provide a means for the implementation of evidences. In the remainder of the paper, we assume that every entity is able to issue evidences and to verify the validity of evidences that have been issued by other entities[4].

An evidence describes the behavior of a specific entity in a *statement*. In the following, we will call the issuer of an evidence the *evidencer*. In addition, the entity the behavior of which is described in the statement will be referred to as the *evidencee*. For instance, in the introductory example, the receipt is an evidence. The consumer represents the evidencer since it issues the receipt. Furthermore, the statement of the receipt is the confirmation of the transmission. Finally, the provider is the evidencee since the receipt describes its behavior.

Recommendations and verification. The introduction of evidences has an effect on the reputation system. Recommendations may contain evidences and become *verifiable*. In this context, verifiability refers to the ability to prove or refute a recommendation based on a set of evidences. A recommendation only has to be

---

[3] We are aware that the term evidence has been used differently in reputation systems. In [2,13,7], it depicts witnessed circumstances, i.e., first hand experiences and recommendations. In contrast, this paper's notion of evidences is based on non-repudiability.

[4] This means that the public key of the issuer of the evidence has to be available for the verification of the evidence's validity. A trivial solution to this problem is to attach the certificate of the issuer's identity and public key to the evidence.

assessed if it is not verifiable. In this regard, the assessor does not have to resort to plausibility considerations for every recommendation. During the process of constructing a proof or a refutation, the assessor becomes a *verifier*. Nevertheless, we retain the term assessor for reasons of clarity.

As a prerequisite for coupling recommendations and evidences, the granularity of recommendations has to match the one of evidences[5]. For instance, in the context of the introductory example, the provider cannot issue a provable self-recommendation that states that it always behaves well. The self-recommendation has to clearly relate to the transaction in order to match the granularity of the evidences and, thus, to be provable.

4   Issuance of Evidences

The concept that has been presented in the previous section is based upon the availability of evidences. Therefore, in this section, we take a closer look at the issuance of evidences. For this purpose, different types of evidences are identified. In addition, we point out the inherent restrictions of the issuance of evidences.

4.1   Different Types of Evidences

In the following, different types of evidences are introduced according to the division of behavior into transactional and recommendational behavior. More specifically, we show which types of evidences are issued during transactions and which ones are issued in the scope of the reputation system. The necessity of issuing evidences for both kinds of behavior is pointed out by the demand for closure.

Issuance during transactions. The processing of a transaction typically consists of the exchange of items. A desirable yet generally infeasible property of such exchanges is atomicity [9]. Therefore, weaker conditions of atomicity have been proposed, notably fairness [15]. Several exchange protocols [15,16] make use of evidences in order to assert such fairness. In the following, we introduce different types of evidences that are issued during the execution of such exchange protocols. A *receipt* is an evidence that confirms some action of the transaction partner. In Section 3, we have presented an exemplary exchange protocol that applies receipts. Non-repudiable actions and *bonds* represent further types of evidences that are handed over to the transaction partner. In this context, a bond is a non-repudiable promise of providing a service in return [8]. An *affidavit* is an evidence that attests the defection or good behavior of a transaction peer. A third party may issue an affidavit if it is able to observe the peers' transactional behavior, e.g., by overhearing their communication [8]. Alternatively, some exchange protocols [15,16] demand for the explicit involvement of a third party in

---

[5] Several recommendations may still be grouped into an aggregated one. For the sake of clarity, we will refrain from considering this possibility for the remainder of this paper.

order to arbiter an exchange. In general, affidavits are issued in the context of such arbitration. The application of exchange protocols is not only confined to the processing phase of transactions. After having negotiated the terms of the processing phase, the transaction peers may commit to the terms by entering in a contract signing phase. This phase consists of exchanging non-repudiable commitments (*contracts*).

Issuance in context of the reputation system. The introduction of recommendations in Section 3 does not demand for their non-repudiability. In order to capture recommendational behavior by evidences, a recommendation has to be rendered non-repudiable so that it represents an evidence. For such recommendations, the role of the recommendee coincides with the one of the evidencee.

From a broader point of view, receipts and affidavits may be regarded as non repudiable recommendations. For example, a receipt is a positive recommendation that is received by the recommendee. In case of defamation by the receipt's issuer, the recommendee is able to reveal the inconsistency of the defamer's recommendations, i.e., the inconsistency between the receipt and the defamation.

4.2 Inherent Restrictions of the Issuance

The issuance of evidences has to comply with the criterion of incentive compatibility. In the following, we examine the inherent restrictions that stem from this criterion. We show that these restrictions partially compromise the availability and truthfulness of the evidences.

Asymmetry of issuance. Each evidence causes an asymmetric relationship between the evidencer and the evidencee. Symmetric roles may only be asserted by superposing the issuance of two separate evidences such that the evidencer of one evidence is the evidencee of the other one and vice versa. Such superposing demands for atomicity with respect to the exchange of evidences. However, atomicity is impracticable for exchange protocols [16]. As a result, the asymmetry of roles cannot be overcome. The impact of this asymmetry is pointed out by the Coordinated Attack Problem [17]. It shows that evidences cannot completely capture transactional behavior. More specifically, behavior during the last step of the transaction protocol cannot be captured by the issuance of a further evidence. This is because the issuance of the evidence would represent a further step which yields a contradiction. For example, if the issuance of a receipt has to be attested, the only means for doing so consists of issuing a further receipt. Consequently, there exists a receipt the issuance of which is not attested.

Issuance of negative evidences. There exist inherent restrictions for the issuance of evidences that attest misbehavior (*negative evidences*). In the first place, the evidencee of a negative evidence refrains from storing and disseminating it. This is because a rational entity does not aim at convincing other entities of its misbehavior. Due to the same reason, an entity does not issue negative evidences about itself. We conclude that the dissemination of negative evidences always involves a third party. Hence, the only types of negative evidences are affidavits and non repudiable recommendations. In contrast to negative evidences, a positive evidence is readily stored and disseminated by the evidencee.

Untruthful evidences. In analogy to praising, an entity could issue an *untruthful* evidence that attests good behavior to a colluding entity. For example, the evidencer may attest good behavior in a transaction that actually has not taken place. Based on such an evidence, the evidencee is able to issue a provable self-recommendation. We conclude that the provability of a recommendation does not implicate its truthfulness. Hence, the concept of evidences does not deal with the problem of overestimation, as it is introduced in Section 2.3. We believe that the only remedy to overestimation consists in mechanisms that identify collusions. The thorough contextualization of behavior [18] is a promising mechanism for this purpose. Alternatively, evidencers could be held responsible for disappointed expectations.

In the following section, we will show that, despite the aforementioned restrictions, the application of evidences makes sense.

5   Overcoming the Limitations of Plausibility Considerations

The ability to verify certain recommendations provides the foundation for overcoming the limitations of plausibility considerations, as they are introduced in Section 2.3. In this section, we present the benefits that arise from the application of evidences. The benefits may be classified into four patterns. For each of them, we examine which limitations of plausibility considerations are overcome. In this regard, we demonstrate that virtually every limitation is overcome.

Transferability of evidences. Due to their non-repudiability, evidences may be credibly transferred to other entities. Hence, the dissemination of evidences can be performed by any entity. This opens up new opportunities for overcoming the limitations of plausibility considerations. On the one hand, the effectiveness of disseminating evidences is increased by relieving the evidencers of transferring them to every potentially interested entity. This is especially important if entities are frequently offline and, thus, cannot provide for dissemination of the evidences they issue. On the other hand, each entity may credibly reproduce the statement of an evidence on behalf of the evidencer simply by transferring it. In this respect, the evidencer loses control over which entities have access to the evidence. Consequently, each entity has to be aware that the issuance of inconsistent evidences may be proven and punished.

For the involved entities, the transferability of evidences translates as follows: The *recommender* is able to credibly communicate implausible facts. More specifically, the impact of a recommendation that is supported by evidences does not fully depend on the reputation of the recommender. The impact of verifiable recommendations does not depend on the recommender's reputation at all. By this means, an entity may self-recommend if it has gathered enough evidences that attest good behavior. For non repudiable recommendations, the recommender does not have to assume the costly task of disseminating the recommendation. In such a case, the *recommendee* should be in charge of disseminating positive recommendations. In this respect, each entity is able to contribute to the dissemination of positive recommendations about itself. The *assessor* does not necessarily require background information in order to assess the truthfulness of a recommendation. For instance, verifiable recommendations do not demand for any background information. Finally, the assessor is able to credibly disseminate the result of a verification. By this means, other entities do not have to re-assess the recommendation.

Screening of recommendational behavior. The transferability of evidences provides a means of identifying entities that issue inconsistent evidences. Due to the ensuing punishment in the context of the reputation system, each entity will generally refrain from issuing inconsistent evidences. This provides a means of anticipating recommendational behavior based on transactional behavior. In the context of the introductory example of Section 3, such screening [19] may be performed as follows: At the end of the exchange protocol, a transaction peer (*consumer*) is supposed to issue a receipt if it is pleased with the behavior of the transaction partner (*provider*). Upon receival of such receipt, the provider knows that the consumer will refrain from defaming it since such defamation would be inconsistent with the receipt. However, if the consumer falls short of issuing the receipt, the provider becomes suspicious of the consumer's motives and could refuse to transact with it anymore. The other way round, this means that the consumer is keen to issue the receipt[6] unless it prepares to defame later on. We conclude that the provider is able to anticipate the consumer's recommendational behavior.

Such anticipation facilitates the pro-active adaption of one's own behavior. There are two means of adapting to an anticipated defamation: On the one hand, one refrains from further transactions with the potential defamer. On the other hand, the impact of the anticipated defamation is further minimized by pro-actively disrecommending the potential defamer. More specifically, such disrecommendation states that the potential defamer has fallen short of issuing the receipt.

Policy based restriction of defamations. The assessor verifies recommendations according to a policy. Such a policy may define the procedure of gathering the evidences that are relevant to the verification. For example, the policy could demand that the recommendee is given the chance to refute negative recommendation. In addition, the assessor may apply the policy that suspicious recommendations are dropped without verification. For instance, a recommendation

---

[6] From a game theoretic point of view, such receipt is a signal [19].

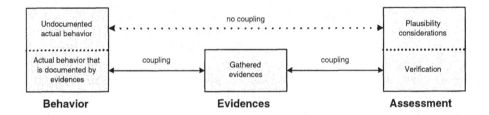

Fig. 6. Evidences as a means of coupling the assessment of recommendations with the actual underlying behavior

about transactional behavior is suspicious if it fails to enclose the contract of the transaction.

For the involved parties, the effect of policies is as follows: The *recommendee* does not have to pro-actively defend itself if it knows that assessors give the chance to refute negative recommendations. In addition, if contract-less recommendations are ignored, each entity is protected against defamations by entities it never transacted with. The other way round, the *assessor* is able to prune defamations. Hence, the underestimation of defamed entities is not as likely as without such pruning.

Coupling of behavior and evidences. Plausibility considerations are based on the assumption that present behavior may be deduced from past behavior. Yet, entities may change their behavior or they may have been perceived incorrectly. Consequently, present behavior may be implausible and, thus, result in false assessments about it. In contrast, we have seen in Section 4.1 that the issuance of evidences ensues from transactional and recommendational behavior. For example, if an entity issues a non repudiable recommendation, it exhibits recommendational behavior and, at the same time, provides an evidence about it. Still, the coupling of behavior and evidences is not perfect since there are inherent restrictions for the issuance of evidences, as shown in Section 4.2. Nevertheless, the partial coupling of behavior and evidences provides a sounder basis for assessing the truthfulness of recommendations. This principle is illustrated in Figure 6. Evidences provide a means of directly coupling actual behavior with the assessment of potentially untruthful recommendations about it. The part of the behavior that is not coupled with any evidences has still to be assessed by the means of plausibility considerations.

Such coupling provides the following advantages: Each entity is able to self-recommend if its behavior is documented with appropriate evidences. Furthermore, the sounder basis for the assessment of recommendations alleviates the doubts about the effective pruning of untruthful recommendations. This provides an incentive for good behavior and a protection against misbehavior. Finally, the assessor underestimates other entities more rarely since defamations are pruned more effectively.

Table 1. Overcoming the limitations of plausibility considerations

Limitations to overcome \ Patterns	Transfer-ability	Screening	Policies	Coupling
Recommender — impact depends on own reputation **(1)**	(✓)			
cannot self-recommend **(2)**	✓			(✓)
in charge of the dissemination **(3)**	✓			
Recommendee — cannot adapt to the peer's recommendations **(4)**		✓		
necessity of pro-active defense unknown **(5)**		✓	✓	
good behavior might not be rewarded **(6)**				(✓)
no protection against defamations **(7)**			(✓)	(✓)
peer unaware of positive recommendations **(8)**	✓			
Assessor — requires background information **(9)**	(✓)			
synergies with defamed entities unexploited **(10)**			(✓)	(✓)
betrayed by overestimated peers **(11)**				
cannot credibly share assessment result **(12)**	✓			

Summary. Table 1 illustrates which limitations of plausibility considerations are overcome by the application of evidences. The limitations that are fully overcome are identified by check marks. Due to the inherent restrictions regarding the issuance of evidences, some limitations are only partially overcome. In such a case, the respective check marks are parenthesized. Apparently, the overestimation of praised entities is the only limitation that is not overcome at all. This is because evidences do not allow for an effective pruning of praising. Possible remedies of this problem have been discussed in Section 4.2.

6   Related Work and Contribution

Non-repudiability is a key concept for exchange protocols and dispute resolution in the research field of electronic commerce. If desirable properties of the exchange cannot be directly asserted, the exchange protocols make use of evidences (so-called tokens) in order to retain or recover such properties [15]. For example, the definition of weak fairness makes explicit use of evidences by demanding that fairness may be recovered by presenting them. There exist several protocols that deal with the exchange of non-repudiable tokens [20]. The validity of evidences is discussed in [10]. If there is a dispute regarding an alleged defection, a commonly trusted third party is employed as verifier. It punishes misbehaving entities by blacklisting them. In this regard, the verifier is a central authority that provides a generally accepted resolution of the dispute. A framework for such dispute resolution is proposed in [15]. The disputes are always resolvable since the exchange protocols involve a trusted third party in case of defection. By this means, the recovery of fairness is based on a trustworthy affidavit.

On the other hand, distributed reputation systems provide a self-organized means of punishing misbehavior. For this purpose, each entity may issue recommendations and has to assess the truthfulness of the received recommendations.

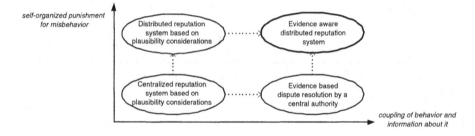

Fig. 7. Relating evidence-aware reputation systems to existing approaches

The existing approaches for distributed reputation systems [2,3,4,5,6,7] rely on plausibility considerations in order to perform such assessment. In this regard, the approaches fall short of basing the assessment on verifiable facts that are directly related to the transactional or recommendational behavior.

To our knowledge, the combination of evidence based dispute resolution and plausibility based distributed reputation systems has not been considered yet. Therefore, this paper does so by proposing and discussing the concept of evidence-aware distributed reputation systems. In Figure 7, it is shown that the proposed concept combines the strengths of two separate research fields. By this means, the limitations of plausibility considerations and centralized dispute resolution are overcome.

7   Conclusion

Distributed reputation systems provide a means for restricting misbehavior in self-organized systems of autonomous entities. The existing distributed reputation systems rely on plausibility considerations for the assessment of the truthfulness of recommendations. In this paper, we have pointed out the limitations of such plausibility considerations and have presented an alternative concept that is based on evidences. The general options and restrictions for the issuance of such evidences have been analyzed. We have identified four patterns of how the limitations of plausibility considerations are overcome by the application of evidences. In this regard, we have shown that virtually every limitation is overcome or partly overcome. Finally, we have pointed out that our concept combines the strengths of two separate research fields and, thus, renders distributed reputation systems more effective.

In the future, we aim at examining the verification process and the design space of policies in more detail. In this context, we plan to investigate whether there is a generic means of rendering existing distributed reputation systems evidence-aware or whether the specifics of the respective system have to be considered for such awareness.

References

1. Shionoya, Y., Yagi, K.: Competition, Trust, and Cooperation: A Comparative Study. Springer (2001)
2. English, C., Wagealla, W., Nixon, P., Terzis, S., Lowe, H., McGettrick, A.: Trusting collaboration in global computing systems. In: Proc. of the First Intl. Conf. on Trust Management (iTrust), Heraklion, Crete, Greece (2003) 136–149
3. Kinateder, M., Rothermel, K.: Architecture and algorithms for a distributed reputation system. In: Proceedings of the First Intl. Conf. on Trust Management (iTrust), Heraklion, Crete, Greece (2003) 1–16
4. Twigg, A.: A subjective approach to routing in P2P and ad hoc networks. In: Proc. of the First Intl. Conf. on Trust Management (iTrust), Heraklion, Crete, Greece (2003) 225–238
5. Buchegger, S., Le Boudec, J.Y.: Coping with false accusations in misbehavior reputation systems for mobile ad-hoc networks. Technical Report IC/2003/31, EPFL-DI-ICA (2003)
6. Michiardi, P., Molva, R.: Making greed work in mobile ad hoc networks. Technical report, Institut Eurécom (2002)
7. Yu, B., Singh, M.P.: An evidential model of distributed reputation management. In: Proceedings of the First International Joint Conference on Autonomous Agents and Multiagent Systems (AAMAS'02), Bologna, Italy (2002) 294–301
8. Obreiter, P., Nimis, J.: A taxonomy of incentive patterns - the design space of incentives for cooperation. In: Proceedings of the Second Intl. Workshop on Agents and P2P Computing (AP2PC'03), Springer LNCS 2872, Melbourne, Australia (2003)
9. Obreiter, P., König-Ries, B., Klein, M.: Stimulating cooperative behavior of autonomous devices - an analysis of requirements and existing approaches. In: Proceedings of the Second International Workshop on Wireless Information Systems (WIS2003), Angers, France (2003) 71–82
10. Zhou, J., Gollmann, D.: Evidence and non-repudiation. Journal of Network and Computer Applications, London: Academic Press (1997)
11. Kou, W.: Payment Technologies for E-Commerce. Springer (2003)
12. Abdul-Rahman, A., Hailes, S.: A distributed trust model. In: Proceedings of the ACM New Security Paradigms Workshop '97, Great Langdale, UK (1997) 48–60
13. Cahill, V., Shand, B., Gray, E., Bryce, C., Dimmock, N.: Using trust for secure collaboration in uncertain environments. IEEE Pervasive Computing 2 (2003) 52–61
14. ISO: ISO/IEC 13888 (1997)
15. Asokan, N.: Fairness in Electronic Commerce. PhD thesis, University of Waterloo (1998)
16. Pfitzmann, B., Schunter, M., Waidner, M.: Optimal efficiency of optimistic contract signing. In: Proceedings of the 7th Annual ACM Symposium on Principles of Distributed Computing (PODC), Puerto Vallarta, Mexico (1998) 113–122
17. Halpern, J.Y., Moses, Y.: Knowledge and common knowledge in a distributed environment. Symposium on Principles of Distributed Computing. (1984) 50–61
18. Mui, L., Halberstadt, A., Mohtashemi, M.: Notions of reputation in multi-agents systems: A review. In: Proceedings of the First International Joint Conference on Autonomous Agents and Multiagent Systems (AAMAS'02), Bologna, Italy (2002)
19. Fudenberg, D., Tirole, J.: Game Theory. MIT Press, Cambridge, Massachusetts (1991)
20. Kremer, S., Markowitch, O., Zhou, J.: An intensive survey of fair non-repudiation protocols. Elsevier Computer Communications 25 (2002) 1606–1621

Enhanced Reputation Mechanism for Mobile Ad Hoc Networks

Jinshan Liu and Valérie Issarny

INRIA - Rocquencourt,
Domaine de Voluceau, Rocquencourt, BP 105, 78153 Le Chesnay Cedex, France
Jinshan.Liu,Valerie.Issarny@inria.fr
http://www-rocq.inria.fr/arles/

Abstract. Interactions between entities unknown to each other are inevitable in the ambient intelligence vision of service access anytime, anywhere. Trust management through a reputation mechanism to facilitate such interactions is recognized as a vital part of mobile ad hoc networks, which features lack of infrastructure, autonomy, mobility and resource scarcity of composing light-weight terminals. However, the design of a reputation mechanism is faced by challenges of how to enforce reputation information sharing and honest recommendation elicitation. In this paper, we present a reputation model, which incorporates two essential dimensions, time and context, along with mechanisms supporting reputation formation, evolution and propagation. By introducing the notion of recommendation reputation, our reputation mechanism shows effectiveness in distinguishing truth-telling and lying agents, obtaining true reputation of an agent, and ensuring reliability against attacks of defame and collusion.

1 Introduction

The pervasiveness of lightweight terminals (e.g., handhelds, PDAs and cell phones) with integrated communication capabilities facilitates the ambient intelligence vision of service access anytime, anywhere. This necessitates interactions between terminals belonging to different authorities, which are marginally known or completely unknown to each other. Trust management to enable such interactions has thus been recognized as a vital part of mobile ad hoc networks (MANET), which features lack of infrastructure, openness, node mobility, and resource scarcity (e.g., network, energy and storage space) of composing light-weight terminals.

In closed networks, trust establishment is managed by an authentication mechanism that assigns roles to agents. By *agent*, we mean a software entity working for and representing a node in MANET; each agent also has some reachable neighbor agents named *peers*. In an open environment such as MANET, fixed role assignment has to be be replaced by dynamic decisions. An important factor affecting the decision making is an agent's *reputation*.

C.D. Jensen et al. (Eds.): iTrust 2004, LNCS 2995, pp. 48–62, 2004.

Reputation assessment requires knowledge, information and evidence about the evaluated agent, which can be derived from an agent's own experiences. However, openness implies significant opportunities of meeting with *strangers* an agent has never encountered before. Furthermore, more accurate estimation of an agent's reputation becomes possible with sharing of reputation information among peers. Reputation mechanism has been widely used and implemented in electronic market places [1,2] and online communities [3]. For example, visitors at "amazon.com" or eBay usually read previous customers' reviews and feedbacks before deciding whether to make transactions.

However, the design of a reputation mechanism is faced by a number of challenges, including: (i) the "free-rider" problem, i.e., agents do not share reputation information with peers; and (ii) the honest elicitation problem, i.e., agents may report false reputation information. There are multiple reasons for agents to be reluctant to report evaluations or to do so honestly [1]. Agents may withhold positive evaluations if a seller's capacity is limited, e.g., wise parents are reluctant to reveal the names of their favorite baby-sitters. Agents may be reluctant to give positive recommendations because it lifts the reputation of the evaluated agent, which is a potential competitor. Agents may wish to be considered "nice", or be afraid of retaliation for negative feedbacks. And last but not least, the reputation information agents provide only benefits other peers.

Therefore, it is necessary to build a reputation mechanism to enforce both active reputation information sharing and truthful recommendation elicitation, which are necessary for a reputation system to operate effectively [4]. Our target reputation mechanism aims to defend against the following three kinds of attacks:

- Inactivity: This refers to agents' free-ride activities by not sharing reputation information with peers.
- Defame: This refers to agents' activities of propagating a victim's reputation that is lowered on purpose.
- Collusion: This refers to agents' activities of propagating good reputation to promote each other.

Hence, the desired properties of a reputation system for MANET are:

1. Valid: The system is effective in the sense that agents are able to distinguish honest from dishonest agents through the reputation system.
2. Distributed: The system should not assume access to any trustworthy entity (e.g., Certificate Authority), or centralized storage of reputation values.
3. Robust: The system is robust to the attacks listed above.
4. Timely: The system should be dynamic and be able to reflect the trustworthiness of an entity in an up-to-date manner.
5. Resource-saving: The reputation system should take into account the limited computation power and storage space of each terminal in MANET.

Existing reputation systems either do not address the aforementioned incentive problems (e.g., [5,6]), or depend on some (centralized) trustworthy entity (e.g.,[1,7]). Our approach, which is targeted at mobile ad hoc networks, does not depend on any trustworthy entity or any centralized reputation storage, and possesses the aforementioned desired properties. Our contribution includes: (1) a reputation model that incorporates two dimensions, time and context, which captures reputation's time-sensitivity and context-dependence; (2) a simple yet effective reputation mechanism that enforces active and truthful reputation information sharing; (3) validation of the effectiveness and robustness of the proposed reputation mechanism via simulation tests. Our work targets service provision among agents in MANET. The *service* notion here is general[1], referring to not only services like Web services [8], packet forwarding services [6,5], but also activities like providing information (e.g., providing cuisine recipes) in online discussion forums.

In the following, Section 2 gives definitions and properties of reputation. Section 3 describes our reputation model, together with related mechanism supporting reputation formation, evolution and propagation. Section 4 presents results of simulation tests. Section 5 surveys related work. Finally, the paper finishes with conclusion and future work.

2   Reputation

Reputation is always associated, and often confused with *trust*. Therefore, in order to have a precise view of reputation, it is necessary to grasp the meaning of trust. Trust is a complex concept relating to belief in the honesty, truthfulness, competence, reliability, etc., of the trusted person or service [2]. Precisely defined, "...*trust (or, symmetrically, distrust) is a particular level of the subjective probability with which an agent assesses that another agent or group of agents will perform a particular action, both before he can monitor such action (or independently of his capacity ever to be able to monitor it) and in a context in which it affects his own action*" [9]. Trust towards an agent can been seen as a prediction on that agent's future action. An important factor affecting the prediction is then the reputation of the agent.

2.1   Defining Reputation

Mui *et al.* define reputation as "perception that an agent creates through past actions about its intentions and norms" [10]. This definition is precise except that it does not reflect the fact that reputation of an agent is created from the point of view of other agents. An agent can affect its own reputation by acting honestly or the other way, but it is unable to decide its reputation. To emphasize the "passive" property of reputation, we define reputation as follows:

> Reputation of an agent is a perception regarding its behavior norms, which is held by other agents, based on experiences and observation[2] of its past actions.

---

[1] Similar to the notion of *resource* in resource discovery

[2] As explained later, observation here refers to *indirect observation* through peers' recommendations.

The reputation assessment of an evaluated agent by an evaluator agent requires collecting related evidences beforehand. The sources of reputation include: (i) The evaluator's own interaction experiences with the evaluated agent; if the evaluator has first-hand experience of interacting with the evaluated agent, the interaction histories can serve as a strong reference for reputation evaluation. (ii) Recommendation from peers who have interacted with the evaluated agent before; note that recommendations of recommending agents are based on the agents' own experiences only, and do not include recommendations obtained from peers. This is necessary to prevent double counting that leads to rumors.

The node mobility and openness of MANET augment the opportunities for nodes to interact with nodes they never encountered before. This increases the agents' reliance on the latter source of reputation (i.e., recommendations from peers).

2.2   Properties of Reputation

Trust is widely deemed *subjective* [11,12]. Reputation, a perception of the trustworthiness of an agent based on experiences and recommendations, is also subjective [10] – because the same behavior can cause different impressions on different agents. It implies that one agent is likely to have different reputations in the view of different peers. We denote $Rep_a(o)$ as the reputation of the agent o, from the point of view of agent a. We represent reputation with a numeric value in the range $[-1.. + 1]$. The value of reputation ranges from *completely untrustworthy* (-1) to *completely trustworthy* $(+1)$. The larger the value is, the trustworthier the agent is. One value in the range that is worth mentioning is *ignorance*, which describes the reputation of agents about whom the evaluator has no knowledge. *Ignorance* bears the value 0^3. Also we define *very trustworthy* (0.8), *trustworthy* (0.2), *untrustworthy* (-0.2) and *very untrustworthy* (-0.8). These labels do not stand for the only possible values of reputation. Instead, they are used to attach semantic meanings to numeric values. For example, if an agent's reputation value is 0.5, it is then considered to be between very trustworthy and trustworthy.

Reputation is also *context-dependent* [13,14]. For example, David enjoys a reputation of being a very talented painter, but he may not have as high reputation as a cook. So *context* is an important dimension for reputation.

Reputation is also *dynamic* – disreputable agents should be able to improve their reputations by acting honest; reputable agents' reputation should get lower if they become deceitful. Dynamics of reputation is also reflected by its timeliness: reputation is aggregate in the time scale by taking into account recent behavior and past histories. Hence, *time* is also a necessary dimension for reputation.

In the next section, we present our reputation model to depict the aforementioned properties together with associated mechanism of reputation formation, evolution and propagation.

---

[3] As pointed out by [12,10] and discussed at the end of this paper, this assignment does not differentiate new comers from agents whose 0 reputation value results from previous behaviors.

3   Reputation Model

To build a reliable reputation mechanism that enforces reputation information sharing and honest recommendation elicitation, our model includes the following elements:

1. Separate reputation for expertise (providing good service) and reputation for helpfulness (providing fair recommendation), respectively denoted as *service reputation (SRep)* and *recommendation reputation (RRep)*.
2. Agents derive the *SRep* of another agent according to their experiences (*SExp*) and recommendations (*Rec*) of peers whom they consider trustworthy in service recommendation; the trustworthier a peer is, the more weight its recommendations are assigned.
3. Reputations are both timely (i.e., evolve with time) and dynamic (i.e., adjust with behaviors); especially, recommenders' *RRep* are adjusted according to the *SRep* value of the recommended agent.
4. Agents exchange reputation information, but only with peers they consider helpful (i.e., with good *RRep*).

The above elements motivate truthful recommendations because untruthful and inactive recommendations lead to low *RRep* and thus loss of peers' recommendations; peers' recommendations are an important knowledge source for evaluating an agent's *SRep*, especially a stranger's *SRep*.

3.1   Reputation Definition

Given reputation's properties of being time-sensitive and context-dependent, an accurate reputation model needs to capture the two dimensions by integrating them seamlessly into reputation's definition, formation, evolution and propagation.

Time-sensitive Reputation. Reputation builds with time. A reputation at time t can be very different from the reputation at another time t'. With respect to the time dimension, we denote reputation of agent o in the view of agent a at time t as $Rep_a(o)^t$. Reputation is aggregate in the sense that it integrates peers' recommendations and the evaluator's own experiences, which are also aggregate. The weights assigned to recent behavior and past histories decide how fast the reputation builds up. For example, if recent behavior is assigned a very high weight, an agent's reputation tears down very fast after a few misbehaviors. We assign more weight to recency, as suggested by the results of psychological studies in [15] and empirical studies of ebay feedback mechanism [16], by adopting a parameter named *fading factor* ρ_e:

$$Rep_a(o)^t = Rep_a(o)^{t'} * \rho_e^{t-t'} + \text{New Behavior} * (1 - \rho_e^{t-t'}) . \tag{1}$$

Value of ρ_e falls into range [0..1]: the lower value ρ_e has, the more quickly histories are forgotten. When ρ_e equals 0, histories are completely forgotten; while when ρ_e equals 1, the oldest history is forever remembered. This formula will be substantiated in the evolution of reputation (§3.3).

The representation of reputation assumes a single value with a timestamp stating the time of formation. More information is available if more history records (e.g., the last 10 reputation values) are kept. However, it consumes more space. Our representation with a single timestamped value saves storage space, which is a scarce resource for light-weight terminals, while still reflecting the time-sensitivity of reputation.

Context-dependent Reputation. As reputation is context-dependent, it is necessary to integrate context as a dimension into reputation. As stated, $SRep_a(o)^t$ in context C can be derived by information (i.e., a's experience and other peers' recommendation) in the context of C[4]. But, there are cases when there is no or not enough information in the context of C, but there are plenty in a related context of C'. It is good practice to be able to derive reputation from these related evidences. But, this is challenged by the question of how to capture the relevance of two contexts. This can be measured by the *distance* between two contexts, which is a quantitative parameter for describing the relation between the two contexts.

Context itself is a multi-dimensioned concept, it can include factors such as, importance and utility of a service [12] (e.g., transactions dealing with 10 euros vs. transactions of 10 thousand euros), service category (driving a car vs. flying a plane), and so on. We limit the context to service category in our work, which leads to the question: *how to measure the distance given two service categories?* For example, assuming an agent provides excellent service in providing cuisine recipes, but we need to know whether it is also as good in giving diet tips. The question becomes how far it is between providing cuisine recipes and giving diet tips.

The comparison of services can done in a syntactic way, e.g., comparison of interfaces, attributes and so on; or in a semantic way. The former is managed by comparing service signatures. The latter is currently undertaken by the Semantic Web activity of W3C[5], which proposes languages for service description such as Resource Description Framework (RDF), and Web Ontology Language (WOL). The DARPA Agent Markup Language (DAML), an extension of XML and RDF, is able to provide sophisticated classification and property definition of resources. We thus make use of an ontology tree of services using DAML-S[6], with each node in the tree representing a type of service. Each node is a subcategory (subclass) of its parent node. To save space, we assume each agent is able to obtain a part of the ontology tree that defines the services it is interested in. Given two nodes in the tree, the distance of the two nodes is defined as the least number of intermediate nodes for one node to traverse to another node. For example, in Fig. 1, service *s1* and *s2* has a distance of 3.

---

[4] For simplicity, we don't discuss context-dependent recommendation reputation here.

[5] http://www.w3.org/2001/sw/

[6] http://www.daml.org/services/

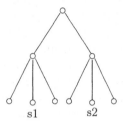

Fig. 1. A service ontology tree

Thus, reputation on context C can be calculated as:

$$SRep_a(o,C)^t = \frac{\sum_{C' \in Tree_a} SRep_a(o,C')^t * \rho_c^{|C'-C|}}{\sum_{C' \in Tree_a} \rho_c^{|C'-C|}} \quad . \tag{2}$$

Similar to (1), ρ_c is a fading factor reflecting an agent's reliance on context-related reputations. When ρ_c equals 0, it means the agent does not consider context-related reputations; while when ρ_c equals 1, the agent takes into account all context-related reputations, all of which have the same impact factor no matter how related or unrelated they are.

In the following, we denote $SRep$ of agent o held by agent a at time t as $SRep_a(o)^t$, instead of $SRep_a(o,C)^t$ for simplicity of denotation, except during discussions of context-dependent reputations. However, it always applies that reputation in a certain context can be derived from reputation in other related contexts according to Equation (2). Table 1 summarizes the notations we have introduced so far.

Table 1. Notations used in the model

Label	Value Range	Meaning
$SRep_a(o)^t$	$[-1..+1]$	service reputation of agent o held by agent a at time t
$RRep_a(o)^t$	$[-1..+1]$	recommendation reputation of agent o held by agent a at time t
$SExp_a(o)^t$	$[-1..+1]$	Reputation of o derived from a's interaction experiences with o
$Rec_a(o)^t$	$[-1..+1]$	Recommendation made by agent a regarding agent o's reputation at time t. For honest agent a, $Rec_a(o) = SRep_a(o)$
ρ_e, ρ_c	$[0..1]$	Fading factor, representing agent's reliance on recent behaviors or related contexts

Having integrated *time* and *context* dimensions into our reputation model, we explore the related mechanism supporting reputation formation, evolution and propagation.

3.2   Reputation Formation

Reputation formation is implemented by the following components running on each node: an experience manager, a recommendation manager and a reputation manager.

Experience Manager

The experience manager is in charge of recording the previous experiences of service provision with other peers. The records include the service category (i.e., context C), the timestamp of last experience (t), and an aggregate value of experience (i.e., $SExp_a(o,C)^t$). The aggregation process of experience value will be further explored in Sec. 3.3.

Recommendation Manager

The recommendation manager implements three functions: (1) storing recommendations from other peers, (2) exchanging reputation information with other peers, and (3) managing a table of $RReps$ of recommenders.

Recommendations from peers regarding an agent's reputation need to be combined together by some means. Dynamic Weight Majority (DWM) [17] is a learning algorithm for tracking *concept drift*, which predicts using a weighted-majority vote of "experts", and dynamically creates and deletes experts in response to changes in performance. Our approach tracks "an agent's reputation" by consulting recommendations (votes) from peers (experts), and dynamically changes their recommendation reputation according to their prediction accuracy. We do not delete peers from the recommender list, however, but we ignore a peer's recommendation if its $RRep$ falls below some threshold value.

Reputation Manager

The reputation manager administers and calculates the $SRep$ of a peer, taking into account inputs from both experience manager and recommendation manager. Reputation manager assigns different weights to experiences and recommendations, namely, greater weight for its own experience and less weight for recommendations from peers. This is due to the reason that agents tend to rely on their own experience more than on other peers' recommendation, as suggested by experimental studies of Kollock [18].

Consider agent a has recommendations regarding agent o from a group of peers P; the peers considered untrustworthy in service recommendation (i.e., with low $RRep$) have been excluded from P. We get the following formula for $SRep$ evaluation:

$$SRep_a(o)^t = \alpha * SExp_a(o)^t + (1 - \alpha) * \frac{\sum_{p \in P}(RRep_a(p) * Rec_p(o))}{\sum_{p \in P} RRep_a(p)} \; . \qquad (3)$$

where α is a parameter that reflects the agent's degree of reliance on its own experience. As discussed above, usually $\alpha > 0.5$.

3.3   Reputation Evolution

After every interaction, agents can give a score of satisfaction for the interaction. The score of satisfaction for a service in real world is so subjective that it can depend on factors such as provided service quality, service quality expectation, environment (place, weather) and even mood. In order to evaluate subjective degree of satisfaction, we apply a method of quantifying degree of satisfaction based on the Quality of Service (QoS)[7] an agent a receives from another agent o. Given n dimensions of QoS (e.g., availability, service latency) d_i ($i = 1..n$) which agent a cares about, a states in its request $(b_1, b_2,..,b_n)$ in which b_i is the value (either minimum or maximum) for dimension d_i. As a result of the service, the quality of service that a receives is represented by $(r_1, r_2,..,r_n)$, in which r_i is the value for dimension d_i. The degree of satisfaction of this interaction $(sat_a(o))$ can thus be obtained by:

$$sat_a(o) = \sum_{1 \leq i \leq n} \pi(r_i, b_i) * w_i \ . \tag{4}$$

where $\pi(r_i, b_i)$ is a function to calculate one-dimensioned degree of satisfaction with respect to requested and obtained QoS. It can take the following forms:

1. $\pi(r_i, b_i) = r_i/b_i$ when dimension i is quantitative and stronger with bigger values, for example, availability[8].
2. $\pi(r_i, b_i) = b_i/r_i$, when dimension i is quantitative and stronger with smaller values, for example, latency.
3. $\pi(r_i, b_i) = 1 - (r_i \otimes b_i)$ when dimension i is qualitative and bears boolean values, for example, confidentiality[9].
4. for dimensions whose value space is literals (e.g., *level of service* can have values of *deterministic, predictive* and *best-effort*), literals can be ordered from weak to strong and assign numeric values accordingly[10].

In the above equation, w_i refers to *relative importance* of a dimension to an agent (e.g., *availability* may be more important than *latency* to an agent) as defined in [19].

Experience Update

With the newest interaction, agents can update their experience value with each other. Similar to (1), updating of agent a's experience of agent o at time t (denoted as as $Exp_a(o)^t$) is as follows:

$$SExp_a(o)^t = SExp_a(o)^{t'} * \rho^{(t-t')} + sat_a(o) * (1 - \rho^{(t-t')}) \ . \tag{5}$$

where t' is the timestamp of last experience formation.

---

[7] If the provided service does not meet functionality requirement, it is considered completely unsatisfactory.

[8] Normalization is necessary here because r_i/b_i does not fall into $[-1, 1]$, one normalization way is to define a perfect value (i.e., 1), e.g., five times the requested value. All values higher than perfect is considered perfect.

[9] $\otimes$ represents XOR function, i.e., $x \otimes y = 0$ if x equals y, and 1 otherwise.

[10] For example, weakest value is mapped to 1, the second weakest to 2, and so on.

Reputation Update

With a new interaction, agent can then update the reputation value of the other according to (3), taking into account the newly updated experience.

Recommendation Update

Reputation varies with time. Hence, an agent's recommendation of another agent's trustworthiness also varies with time. It is thus possible for an agent a to receive recommendation from the same peer p regarding agent o (i.e., $Rec_p(o)$) again. It is necessary for agent a to update $Rec_p(o)$ with the new recommended value. Note that we do not apply (1) here because recommendations from peers (which is supposed to be based on their $SRep$) already take into account the past behaviors.

Recommendation Reputation Update

With a new experience available, agent a can update the $RRep$ of the recommender p who has recommended the newly interacted peer o.

Let us denote the difference between the newest experience value and the recommended value being $diff = |Rec_p(o) - SExp_a(o)|$. For an honest peer p, we have $Rec_p(o) = SExp_p(o)$. As stated above, reputation is subjective, but we argue that it is not arbitrary, i.e., although same kind of behavior may be of different experience to different agents, we do not expect the experience to be very contrastive. Therefore, similar to each agent's definition of threshold of trust and distrust, we propose definition of a threshold of recommendation tolerance for each agent, which defines the maximal tolerance of agent for recommendation bias (denoted δ_a in the following). The value of $diff$ reflects the accuracy of recommendations, which needs to be normalized: $diff = \frac{1-diff}{\delta_a}$.

Then the recommendation reputation is updated as follows:

$$RRep_a(o)^t = RRep_a(o)^{t'} * \rho^{(t-t')} + diff * (1 - \rho^{(t-t')}) . \qquad (6)$$

It can be seen that with false recommendation (i.e., negative $diff$), the $RRep$ tears down with time. In order to make it possible for a disreputable agent's $RRep$ to improve, we supplement the equation with an update method when $RRep_a(o)$ is already below σ_a, i.e., $RRep_a(o)^t = \sigma_a + \epsilon + diff * \rho^{(t-t')}$, where σ_a is an agent-defined reputation threshold value for being considered trustworthy in service recommendation, and ϵ is a small positive value.

With our reputation evaluation as shown above, it is possible that an honest recommender whose "taste" is very different from the evaluator agent a (i.e., $diff > \delta_a$) is mistaken as a dishonest agent. This does not affect our model's validity because those agents' recommendations are of little value to agent a anyway. The power of our reputation system to deter inactivity lies in the dynamics of agents' behavior (e.g., trustworthy agents become deceitful) . If an agent never recommends (i.e., never exchanges reputation information with other peers), its $RRep$ will remain as $ignorance$. Although ignorance bears the value of 0, it is highly possible that many agents are reluctant to exchange reputation information with agents whose $RRep$ bears the value of 0 (it is not considered trustworthy either way). If an inactive agent did recommend but stays lazy after, it is likely that its recommended agents change their behavior, which makes its recommendation inaccurate and its *RRep* low. Therefore, the only way to maintain decent *RRep* is to recommend actively and honestly.

Reputation Propagation

For every some period[11], the recommendation manager tries to contact peers – preferably the agents with good *RRep* – for reputation information exchange. In the mean time, if a recommendation manager receives a recommendation exchange request from a peer, it will first check the requester's *RRep*. The exchange proceeds only if the requester's *RRep* is above the agent-defined threshold value.

4   Reputation Mechanism Evaluation

In order to evaluate the effectiveness of our reputation mechanism to help agents distinguish honest and dishonest agents, and interact with unfamiliar agents, we carry out three sets of simulation tests.

Experiment Setting

Our experiment is set up with 100 agents including:

1. Agents A: it includes 30 agents which are trustworthy in both service provision and recommendation.
2. Agents B: it includes 30 agents which are trustworthy in service provision but untrustworthy in recommendation.
3. Agents C: it includes 40 agents which are untrustworthy in both service provision and recommendation.

We track agents' reputation in *nRound* rounds. For each round, $nInt * 2$ agents are randomly selected to interact with each other (before the interaction happens, they evaluate each other's *SRep* to decide whether to have the interaction); and $nRec * 2$ agents are randomly picked to exchange recommendation (similarly, they evaluate each other's *RRec* to decide whether to exchange).

RRec vs. SRec

The first experiment aims to show the advantages of having separate reputation for service provision and service recommendation. We set $nRound = 100, nInt = 30$, and set $nRec$ to 5, 10, 15,..,50. We are interested in the number of resulting mistakes during the interactions. A *mistake* occurs when one agent misjudges another agent and mistakenly interacts with an untrustworthy agent or avoids a trustworthy agent. To simulate the openness of the network, every agent evaluates another peer only by the recommendations obtained from

---

[11] The length of period depends on the agent's recent interactions. For example, if the agent meets strangers frequently in the recent period, it implies that it has to rely more on recommendations from peers. The need for reputation information from peers becomes stronger and the length is decreased accordingly.

its peers (otherwise most of the interactions are between agents who have encountered each other before). Figure 2 shows the different number of mistakes
occurred with or without using $RRep$ in the last 50 rounds[12].

We can see from the figure that, with increasing exchanges of reputation
information, mistakes are decreasing for both cases. However, mistakes are less
with the use of $RRep$, due to the impact of 30 agents (Agents B) which are honest
in service provision but deceitful in recommendation. And with full exchange of
reputation information (i.e., $nRec$=50, which means in each round, each agent
exchanges reputation information with another agent), the number of mistakes
decrease from 507 to 172 out of a total of 3000 interactions.

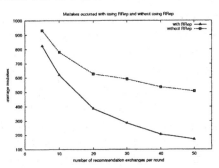

Fig. 2. Mistakes with and without RRep

Defense against Dynamic Behaviors

The second experiment aims to show the robustness of our reputation mechanism against dynamic behaviors of agents (e.g., some honest agents become
deceitful). It exhibits the power of our mechanism to incentivize active reputation information exchange.

$nRound$ is set to 500. In order to simulate the behavior dynamics, it is set
that at round 50, agents B become honest in service recommendation and agents
A become inactive and do not exchange reputation information with peers. We
benchmark the average $RRep$ of agents A, which indicates the trustworthiness in
service recommendation of agents A in the view of their peers. Figure 3 shows the
evolution of the average $RReps$ of agents A when they are active and inactive.
Although the average $RRep$ of agents A declines in both cases after agents B
change their behaviors at time 50, it can be seen that if agents A stay active
exchanging reputation information with other peers, their average $RRep$ picks
up after some time; otherwise, their average $RRep$ keeps dropping.

Defense against Dishonest Recommendation

The third experiment aims to show the robustness of our reputation mechanism against dishonest recommendations. It shows our mechanism's capability
to incentivize honest recommendation.

---

[12] In the initial phase, agents have no information of each other. Thus we only consider
the last 50 rounds when each agent has built up a knowledge base for reputation
evaluation.

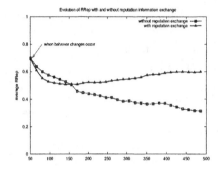
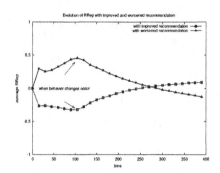

Fig. 3. Changes of RRep with active and inactive without exchange

Fig. 4. Changes of RRep with higher and lower trustworthiness of RRep

The experiment set includes 500 rounds (i.e., $nRound = 500$). At round 100, agents B become trustworthy in service recommendation. Similar to the above experiment set, we benchmark agents B's average $RRep$. It can be seen from Fig. 4 that agents B have established good service recommendation reputation by round 300. Similarly, suppose at round 100, agents A become deceitful in service recommendation (other agents stay unchanged). Figure 4 shows that the average $RRep$ of agents A falls below 0 by round 250. This proves the dynamics of reputation in our model: reputable recommenders' $RReps$ tear down if they recommend falsely and vice versa.

5   Related Work

Marsh [12] is among the first to present a formal trust model, incorporating properties of trust from psychology and sociology. It is well-founded yet complex model; it does not model reputation in the trust model. Mui, *et al*, [14] review the existing work on reputation across diverse disciplines and give a typology of reputation, classified by the source of reputation. Our reputation model incorporates two types of reputation: *interaction derived reputation* and *propagated reputation*.

Many reputation systems do not differentiate the reputation of service provision and recommendation [3,20,5], or assume the truthfulness of recommendations [6]. Some systems allow only positive recommendations [6] or only negative recommendations [5].

Abdul-Rahman and Hailes [21] present a trust model, incorporating direct trust based on interaction experiences and recommender trust, which is similar to our recommendation reputation. False recommendation are dealt by recording the difference between the recommended value and the experienced value. The difference is then applied to obtain a "true" value. The result is, however, uncertain when the difference is not fixed but varied. Additionally, their work does not provide incentives to give recommendations or punishment for those giving false information.

Pretty Good Privacy (PGP) [22] proposes a *Web of Trust* decentralized authentication scheme, by associating a public key (i.e., a recommender) with its trustworthiness of recommending name-public key binding. Agents can validate an unknown name-public key binding, or peers' credentials [23], through aggregate trust of recommendation (e.g., if a binding is recommended by a *completely trusted* key, it is considered valid). However, the degree of trustworthiness is static and assigned by users subjectively. Thus, it does not apply to dynamic scenarios. Reputation in our work evolves with behavior and time.

Jurca and Faltings [7] propose an incentive-compatible reputation system by introducing special broker agents named *R-agents*, which sell reputation information to and buy reputation information from agents. The payoff for an agent selling reputation information to an R-agent depends on whether its provided information coincides with the future reports on the same agent. The effectiveness of the proposed mechanism lies greatly on the integrity of R-agents, which assumely always exist in the system. In addition, collusion is not considered. Our mechanism defends against both collusion and defame attack by associating a reputation with each agent's recommendation behavior. Dishonest recommenders suffer low recommendation reputation, and thus their recommendations are either excluded or considered very trivial (i.e., assigned a small weight).

6 Conclusion and Future Work

In this paper, we have presented an enhanced reputation mechanism for mobile ad hoc networks by modeling reputation with two important dimensions, time and context, and incorporating reputation formation, evolution and propagation. Our scheme is distributed, effective and storage-saving without reliance on any trustworthy party or centralized storage.

Besides looking into incentive counterpart in sociology and psychology, our future work also includes a more formal analysis of context. As discussed, context is a multiple-facet notion, and can depend on many factors, whether subjective or objective.

We notice the problem of scalability issue with our approach. Although our mechanism does take care of the storage problem, it may still overload nodes given large distributed networks of tens of thousands of terminals. An intuitive approach is to incorporate a caching scheme with some replacement algorithm. However, discarding reputation information can be costly and requires careful tradeoff consideration.

Like most reputation systems, another unaddressed issue is changing of identities. Most online reputation systems protect privacy and each agent's identity is normally a pseudonym. It causes problems because pseudonym can be changed easily [3,10]. When a user ends up having a reputation lower than that of a new comer, the user is tempted to discard her initial identity and start from the beginning. This suggests the necessity of special treatments of new users. We plan to incorporate defense against this kind of attack in our future work.

References

1. Miller, N., Resnick, P., Zeckhauser, R.: Eliciting honest feedback in electronic markets. Working Paper (2002)
2. Grandison, T., Sloman, M.: A survey of trust in internet applications. IEEE Communication Surveys **3** (2000)
3. Zacharia, G., Maes, P.: Trust management through reputation mechanisms. Applied Artificial Intelligence **14** (2000) 881–907
4. Resnick, P., Zeckhauser, R., Friedman, E., Kuwabara, K.: Reputation systems. Communications of the ACM **43** (2000) 45–48
5. Buchegger, S., Boudec, J.Y.L.: Performance analysis of the CONFIDANT protocol. In: Proc. of MobiHOC. (June 2002)
6. Michiardi, P., Molva, R.: CORE: a collaborative reputation mechanism to enforce node cooperation in mobile ad hoc networks. In: CMS'2002. (August 2002)
7. Jurca, R., Faltings, B.: An incentive compatible reputation mechanism. In: Proceedings of IEEE International Conference on E-Commerce, CA, USA (2003)
8. Issarny, V., et al.: Developing Ambient Intelligence Systems: A Solution based on Web Services. JASE (2004, to appear)
9. Gambetta, D.: Can we trust trust? In: Trust, Making and Breaking Cooperative Relations. basil blackwell (1990) 213–237
10. Mui, L., Mohtashemi, M., Halberstadt, A.: A computational model of trust and reputation. In: Proceedings of the 35th HICSS. (2002)
11. Misztal, B.: Trust in Modern Societies. Polity Press, Cambridge, MA, USA (1996)
12. Marsh, S.P.: Formalising Trust as a Computational Concept. PhD thesis, University of Stirling (1994)
13. Cahill, V., Gray, E., Seigneur, J.M., et al.: Using trust for secure collaboration in uncertain environments. IEEE Pervasive Computing **2** (2003)
14. Mui, L., Halberstadt, A., Mohtashemi, M.: Notions of reputation in multi-agents systems: A review. In: Proceedings of AAMAS-02. (2002) 280–287
15. Karlins, M., Abelson, H.I.: Persuasion, how opinion and attitudes are changed. Crosby Lockwood & Son (1970)
16. Dellarocas, C.: The digitization of word-of-mouth: Promise and challenges of online feedback mechanisms. MIT Working Paper (2003)
17. Kolter, J.Z., Maloof, M.A.: Dynamic weighted majority: A new ensemble method for tracking concept drift. In: Proc. of the 3rd IEEE Int' Conf. on Data Mining. (2003)
18. Kollock, P.: The emergence of exchange structures: An experimented study of uncertainty, commitment, and trust. American Journal of sociology **100** (1994)
19. Liu, J., Issarny, V.: QoS-aware service location in mobile ad hoc networks. In: Proceedings of MDM 2004. (Jan. 2004, to appear)
20. Xiong, L., Liu, L.: Building trust in decentralized peer-to-peer electronic communities. In: Proc. of ICECR-5, Montreal, Canada (2002)
21. Abdul-Rahman, A., Hailes, S.: Supporting trust in virtual communities. In: Proc. Hawaii Int'l Conf. System Science HICSS-33. (2000)
22. Zimmermann, P.R.: The Official PGP User's Guide. MIT press (1995)
23. Keoh, S.L., Lupu, E.: Trust and the establishment of ad-hoc communitie. presentation in 2nd Internal iTrust Workshop (September, 2003)

Pinocchio: Incentives for Honest Participation in Distributed Trust Management

Alberto Fernandes, Evangelos Kotsovinos, Sven Östring, and Boris Dragovic

University of Cambridge Computer Laboratory
15 JJ Thomson Avenue
Cambridge CB3 0FD, UK
{firstname.lastname}@cl.cam.ac.uk

Abstract. In this paper, we introduce a framework for providing incentives for honest participation in global-scale distributed trust management infrastructures. Our system can improve the quality of information supplied by these systems by reducing free-riding and encouraging honesty. Our approach is twofold: (1) we provide rewards for participants that advertise their experiences to others, and (2) impose the credible threat of halting the rewards, for a substantial amount of time, for participants who consistently provide suspicious feedback. For this purpose we develop an honesty metric which can indicate the accuracy of feedback.

1 Introduction

Peer-to-peer systems, on-line auction sites and public computing platforms often employ trust management systems to allow users to share their experiences about the performance of other users in such settings [1,2]. However, the success of these trust management systems depends heavily on the willingness of users to provide feedback. These systems have no mechanisms to encourage users to participate by submitting honest information. Providing rewards is effective way to improve feedback, according to the widely recognised principle in economics which states that people respond to incentives.

Some of the most popular trust management systems in use currently operate without the promise of rewards for providing feedback, such as the eBay auction site or the used goods trading facility provided by the Amazon marketplace. Our view is that under these conditions the users who participate in the trust management scheme by submitting information about their interactions with others are, in fact, pursuing "hidden" rewards, often with unwanted effects. For instance, in the eBay case, there is strong empirical evidence to suggest that buyers and sellers advertise positive feedback regarding each other, seeking to increase in their reputation via mutual compliments [17]. In this case, the reward implicitly offered by the system is the possibility of getting a positive review about oneself.

Also, people who have had particularly bad experiences will be normally more inclined to advertise their experiences as a form of revenge against the

C.D. Jensen et al. (Eds.): iTrust 2004, LNCS 2995, pp. 63–77, 2004.

user that did not provide the desired service. Such hidden rewards bias the feedback system; users who have had average experiences with other users and are not aiming at increasing their reputation or seeking revenge against a bad service provider will have little reason to provide feedback. An explicit reward system has the advantage of attracting those users across the board.

Moreover, in other settings with different parameters, such as public computing environments, the inherent incentives for participation are very limited – as discussed later in the paper. In such cases, a component that will provide explicit incentives for participants to submit feedback about their experiences with others is crucial. However, incentives should not be provided for users that are likely to be dishonest or submit information that has little relevance to reality.

In this paper we introduce Pinocchio; a system which rewards participants that provide feedback that is likely to be accurate, while having mechanisms for protecting itself against dishonest participants. In Section 2, we define the environment in which Pinocchio is designed to operate. In Section 3, we describe how it is possible to spot cheats and use this knowledge to influence participation, and Section 5 summarises our conclusions.

2   Example Settings

To understand the operation of Pinocchio, it is important to set the scene in which our system is designed to operate. We will state the general parameters of the environment in which Pinocchio can fit, and then outline a few realistic examples of such environments in the area of trust management architectures operating with global public computing systems. The list of example settings is by no means exhaustive; there are several other similar environments in which our system could function.

2.1   Environmental Parameters

There is a group of *participants* that provide services to each other. Whether these participants are organised as peers or as clients and servers makes little difference. The participants are tied to semi-permanent identities – their identities can change but it is a costly operation and cannot happen very often. Obtaining an identity is a result of a *registration* process they had to go through in order to join the group. Participants are *authenticated*. We cannot make assumptions about the duration of each interaction between participants, but we expect participants to have a *long-term presence* in the system, even if they do not use the services provided by other participants or provide services themselves.

Participants are owned and administered by a number of independent organisations, and therefore are *autonomous*, in the sense that there is no central control or strict coordination on the services that these will provide. It can be assumed that some authority has the ultimate right to eject a participant from the platform in cases of serious offences, but the standard of service that each participant will deliver in each interaction is left to its discretion and cooperativeness. Also, each participant can valuate the services that other participants provide independently and subjectively, without any control on the correctness of its opinion. We term such systems *federated*. We outline a few typical examples of such systems in Section 2.2.

A number of analogies of federated systems can be drawn from the human society; restaurants are administered by different people, provide very diverse qualities of service, and there is little central control on the quality of the food that they provide, apart from making sure that they comply with the basic regulations of food hygiene. There is no control on how tasty the food will be, or on the size of portions. Accordingly, there is no control on the opinions that customers can voice. Each customer is allowed to express any opinion about any restaurant, even if she has never visited it.

A *trust management system*, as described in Section 2.3, is in place to allow participants to share their experiences about interactions with others – that is, to support facility similar to gossiping in the human society. Pinocchio intends to use opinions submitted by participants to the trust management system in order to automatically reward users who report information that is likely to be accurate.

2.2   Global Public Computing Systems

PlanetLab [16] is a global overlay network targeted to support the deployment and evaluation of large-scale distributed applications and services. Resource reservations – such as CPU time or memory space – are made through *resource brokers* that provide the tickets that users can submit to the servers to obtain resources. However, PlanetLab nodes are owned by several different organisations and administered by an even larger number of people. Whether a ticket will be honoured is in each node's discretion. While most nodes will behave as expected, some nodes may not honour slice reservations, and others may fail frequently. It is not hard to see that all nodes may not provide the same level of service. A similar setting is that of Grid computing systems [10].

The XenoServer Open Platform is building a global public infrastructure for distributed computing developing [12]. Clients can deploy untrusted tasks on servers that participate in the platform, and ultimately get charged for the resources their tasks consume. Servers are again owned and administered by a diverse set of organisational entities. The fact that users pay for the services promised by the servers – clients and servers agree on the resources to be provided by the server and the payment to be made by the user beforehand – makes the need for encouraging accurate feedback even more compelling. Some servers may overcharge clients or not deliver the expected service, and on the other side some clients may refuse to pay or abuse the resources given to them.

2.3   Distributed Trust Management

The overall experience of using the system can be improved if each participant shares her experiences about aspects of the level of services provided by the participants she interacts with. This is done by making quantitative statements about the level of services received. For instance, participant A rates B as 70% regarding property M.

Participants can share their experiences from interactions with other users by subscribing to a *trust management infrastructure* that is in place. Participants can make their opinions public by *advertising* them to the trust management infrastructure in the form of *statements*, and obtain information about others' opinions by *querying* the system. It is assumed that all supported queries have fairly similar complexity. The trust management system can be imagined as a pool, exporting unified interfaces for storing and retrieving statements.

A real-world system that follows the above properties is XenoTrust [9,8], the system we are developing to allow reputation dissemination in the XenoServer Open Platform. XenoTrust will act as a pool of statements, and export interfaces for submitting statements and querying the system to retrieve and combine them.

We assume that the trust management infrastructure will be able to charge for its services, in some sort of currency. One straightforward example where this would be possible is the XenoServer Open Platform, which encompasses charging and pricing mechanisms. Also, Grid computing projects have recently launched research on providing such functionality [11].

One of the problems that we seek to address is the common *free-riding* problem experienced in most open infrastructures [3], where in this case free-riding refers to the behaviour of participants who submit queries to the trust management system but who do not contribute to the system's knowledge base. The usefulness and reliability of the trust management scheme itself depends heavily on the amount of reputation feedback it receives from its participants. If few participants choose to advertise reputation statements, information in it will be significantly less accurate. Thus a policy that rewards active participation benefits the system.

However, rewarding participation will also provide an incentive for providing inaccurate information. Giving an honest account of a participant's experience takes more time than just feeding random reputation statements back to the system. If both approaches result to the same reward, our incentive for active participation becomes an incentive for inaccurate feedback.

To anticipate the above issues, we propose Pinocchio, a consultant component that can be attached to trust management infrastructures, designated to provide advice on who to reward, as shown in Figure 1, by applying an honesty metric to spot dishonest advertisements.

3   The Pinocchio Framework

Our approach for improving the quality of information in the trust management system is twofold; we encourage users to submit statements, reporting their

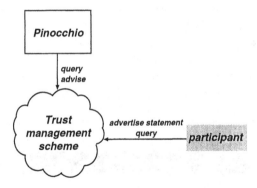

Fig. 1. Pinocchio in the envisaged trust management context

experiences about their interactions with other users, by providing a *reward* for each submitted statement. At the same time, to protect the reward system from users who may submit inaccurate or random statements to obtain rewards we use a probabilistic *honesty metric* to support spotting dishonest users and deprive them of their rewards.

This metric allows weeding out dishonest providers of information, but its main purpose is to prevent it, by the simple advertisement of its existence. Assuming that agents act on self-interest, they will not cheat if perception of risk of exposure and punishment for misbehaviour increases the cost of cheating sufficiently so that it outweighs its benefit.

Section 3.1 establishes a pricing and reward model and Section 3.2 shows how cheats can be detected.

3.1 Reward Model

Participants that have subscribed to the trust management scheme can advertise their experiences – in the form of statements – and perform queries that combine, weigh and retrieve statements, in order to obtain information about others' experiences. Each query will incur a fixed cost to the participant, as we expect that the complexity of evaluating individual queries will not vary significantly. To create incentives for participants to provide information regarding the performance of others, the trust management system will provide a reward for each statement submitted, provided that the user submitting it is deemed to be honest.

The trust management system will set up a credit balance for each participant, which will be credited with a reward for each statement advertised and debited for each query made by that user. The trust management system can set a maximum limit to the amount of credit given as rewards to a participant per minute.

If a participant's credit balance is positive, she can use it to get a discount on queries she will make in the future. There is no way to cash the credit for money.

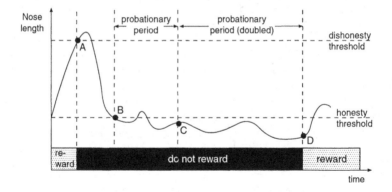

Fig. 2. Honesty and dishonesty thresholds, and probationary period

While the credit provides a tangible incentive to users to participate and submit information to the system, the system does not specifically reimburse the users with monetary repayments. We believe that this feature makes attacks against our system less attractive, as discussed in 3.3.

When Pinocchio determines, using the honesty metric described in the next section, that a participant has been dishonest, the behaviour of the system changes. If the honesty metric rises above a *dishonesty threshold*, then the trust management system will be advised not to reward statements advertised by this participant any more. If her behaviour reverses, with subsequent information being regarded as honest, then once her nose length metric falls below an *honesty threshold* and stays below that threshold until the *probationary period* is completed, the system will resume accumulating credits for the client.

We consider it necessary to have hysteresis in setting the dishonesty and honesty thresholds, as well as the adjustable probationary period, to ensure that participants cannot oscillate, with small amplitude, around a single threshold for their own gain. The probationary period can be doubled each time a participant is estimated to be dishonest, to be long enough to discourage participants from being dishonest several times, but not be too harsh and disappoint first-time cheaters.

An example is shown in Figure 2, where a participant, initially rewarded for every statement she provides, is deemed dishonest at point A. At that point the system stops providing rewards. Once the participant's nose length falls below the honesty threshold – at point B –, she enters a first probationary period, during which she has to remain honest in order to start receiving rewards again. However, her nose length rises above the honesty threshold during that period. Thus, after the end of the first probationary period she enters a second one of double length, starting at point C. The participant is only considered honest again at point D, after demonstrating honest behaviour for as long as the second probationary period required.

3.2   Honesty METRIC

The metric is based on an intuitive process used by human beings on an everyday basis. To illustrate it, let's introduce Joe. He has not tried out every single make of automobile in the market, but he interacts with his friends and colleagues and hears their opinions about the different brands. He builds in his head a first-level probabilistic model that tells him how likely it is that someone will be pleased by cars made by different brands. For instance, suppose most of the people he interacts with like cars made by ABC and dislike cars made by DEF. If his friend, Adam, buys an ABC and tells Joe he is disappointed, this surprises him, as in his probabilistic model the chance of an ABC being considered low-quality is low.

Joe makes similar intuitive estimates of probabilities for many different car brands. On the basis of these, he also constructs a second-level probabilistic model, built on top of the first, to judge the people he normally interacts with. If Adam always gives Joe opinions that seem bizarre, such as valuing DEF as great and ABC as poor, Joe may stop taking Adam's opinions into account. On the other extreme, there is Miss Sheep, whose opinions always agree with the average opinion about everything. Again, Miss Sheep may lose Joe's respect, because he thinks she does not offer him any new or useful information. Joe finds Mr Goody, who often follows the general opinion but sometimes contradicts it, a useful source of advice.

This is an instinctive self-defence mechanism present in the way humans operate, but not in existing trust management systems. Our approach follows the intuitive process that Joe uses. We build a first-level model that maps opinions to probabilities. In that model, "ABC is poor quality" would be mapped to low probability. The second-level model will look at the history of a participant to estimate how good he is at assessing car manufacturers in general, and whether he may be dishonest – like Adam – or always following the stream – like Ms Sheep. The translation of the very general observations of Joe's behaviour into mathematical models are detailed in the following section.

Our view is that augmenting trust management systems with a component that will be able to suggest which users are worth rewarding is necessary, although not sufficient, to improve the integrity of a trust management system. The main goal of our metric is to protect the reward system against a very specific threat, which is users that take the easiest route to the reward – sending random opinions instead of genuine ones.

Naturally, this threat may occur simultaneously with others; Pinocchio does not intend to protect against conspiracies among participants or bad mouthing. These could be addressed at the trust management system level or by other external consultant components, and there already exist tools that can deal with them, such as [7]. Such conspiracies are not expected to be affected by the existence of a small reward for accurate information providing.

Mathematical Model. In this section, we propose a probabilistic model that balances the need to get an accurate assessment of the honesty of information providers against limited computational resources. We devise an *estimator* of the probability of each participant being dishonest.

Our model fundamentally treats the *perceptions* that participants have about a certain subject as discrete random variables. A single interaction may give rise to many different subjects for opinions – for instance, beauty, safety and reliability of ABC cars or expediency of service and quality of product provided by a server.

All of these subjects are collected in a set of random variables R. When a user interacts with a participant X, she *observes* one sample from all random variables associated with X – i.e. all of X's properties. The user then reports the observed values for each of those random variables, by assigning scores to each property of X.

After collecting a sizable number of observations of each element of R, we fit a probability distribution to each of them. As in Bayesian theory, if we have little information about a variable – because few opinions have been collected about a certain subject –, the distribution will be closer to uniform and will have less weight in our final metric. The collection of the *assumed* probability distributions for all of our random variables forms a database that will be used to check on each user's credibility.

We introduce a new set S of random variables, whose elements are

$$S_{s,p} = ln(P(R_{s,p}))$$

where $P(\bullet)$ stands for *estimated probability*. This is the probability that a score about property p of user s is accurate.

For example, suppose user Bob assigns a score of 0.9 to the performance of user X. Pinocchio will consult the estimate of the probability distribution for the performance of user X, and get an estimate of the probability for a score of 0.9, say 10% probability. So $ln(0.10)$ would be one instantiation, associated with Bob, of $S_{x,performance}$.

At this point we have two values associated with Bob and the "performance of x" subject. The first one is the grade given by Bob, 0.9. The other one is the log-probability – $ln(0.10)$ – with which a score of 0.9 would be reported for X's performance. We are interested in the second value. For every opinion expressed by Bob, we'll have such a log-probability.

The data associated with Bob is limited to a small subset of S, as he quite likely did not provide information on every single participant in the system. So we define a subset of S, $B \subseteq S$, of all elements of S instantiated by Bob. We can further cut this set down by excluding elements of B where data is very sparse, such as where few users have expressed opinions about a particular participant.

Let us assume for the moment that all the variables in B are independent. We can then sum all of them to get a new random variable:

$$T_{Bob} = \sum_{s,p \in B} ln(P(R_{s,p})) \tag{1}$$

This is the log of the probability that our model assigns to a user submitting a particular set of statements about the participants and properties in B. A natural intuition would be to say that the higher the probability our R-distributions assign to Bob's statements, the stronger the evidence for these being true observations from our random variables. We would then choose T_{Bob} as our estimator.

This is not the best estimator, though. In an intuitive way, a typical honest user, when voicing his opinion about several properties of several participants, will in many cases be close to the average opinion in the community, and sometimes far from it. So this naive method would heavily punish honest users that frequently happen to disagree with the community.

Because T_{Bob} is defined as a sum of random variables, we know from the Central Limit Theorem [1] that if the set B is large enough, it will have a distribution close to Gaussian. So we can proceed to estimate its mean and variance via, for instance, Monte Carlo sampling. Our estimator for the honesty of the user, Bob's *Nose length* statements would be then how much the observed instance of T_{Bob} deviates from its mean, in terms of standard deviations: $Nose length = |Z|$, where

$$Z = (t_{Bob} - \hat{\mu})/\hat{\sigma}, \qquad (2)$$

and $\hat{\mu}, \hat{\sigma}$, are our estimates for mean and standard deviations of T_{Bob}; and t_{bob} is the observed sample.

An attentive reader could accuse us of an apparent contradiction. How can our most likely sequences, the ones with a high T_{Bob} score, be somehow considered less probable by *Nose length*? For exposition, let us imagine that in a foreign country, on every single day there is a 10% probability of raining. Every day Bob observes if it rained or not and take notes over a year. The single most likely sequence of events is no rain at all. But the expected number of days of rain is $365 \times 0.1 = 36.5$, and a report of zeros days of rain in the whole year would be very suspicious. In our analogy, a "rainy day" would correspond to some statement that is given a low R-probability and we would prefer to see Bob reporting roughly "36.5 rainy days" rather than zero.

Simulation. To illustrate this idea, we created 20 discrete random variables with random probability distributions to simulate the behaviour of the variables in set B. We simulated 50 thousand different users, all of them giving a set of 20 opinions, according to our underlying probability distributions. Using our previous knowledge of the distributions, we computed *Nose length*. Figure 3 shows that our simulated *Nose length* behaves like a Gaussian random variable.

In the figure, we show the nose lengths corresponding to sets of statements made by honest users, produced from the true R distributions. The nose lengths of these users cluster together very close to the average (zero), and all of them within a small number of standard deviations from the mean, varying between minus seven and plus three.

---

[1] Although the random variables are not identically distributed, the CLT still applies as they are bounded (see for instance [5])

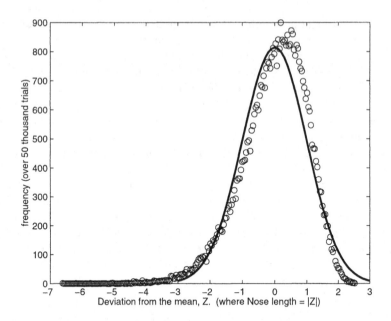

Fig. 3. Simulation of the behaviour of *Noselength*. The circles are a histogram obtained by Monte Carlo sampling. The continuous line is a Gaussian fitted to it. Points to the right of the x axis are those with high probability according to the R variables

Points to the right of the cluster of circles shown in the figure – deviation from the mean more than plus three – would correspond to sets of statements t_{bob} where every single statement is very close to the mean of the other users opinion – behaviour similar to Miss Sheep's. After a certain point, our estimator judges them "too good to be true".

The nose lengths of users whose sets of statements were generated without regard to the true distributions would be larger than seven, and fall way to the left of the circles, This would correspond to "lazy" users that try to obtain the reward by submitting random numbers instead of their true opinions. We simulated these users by assuming a uniform distribution of answers – that they users would be as likely to attribute a "1" as a "10" to any property. In 50 thousand simulations, every time the "dishonest" answers got *Nose length* values between 50 and 300, totally disjoint from the "honest" set. But these are overly optimistic results due to the fact that our R distributions are known and include some regions of very low probability.

Discussion. The accepted sets of statements cluster together in a small area of the range of T_{Bob}; completely random responses would be unlikely to fall in this area, and to successfully emulate an acceptable sequence. If we knew the true distributions and the malicious user did not, this probability in most cases – if the true distributions are distant from a uniform distribution – would be very small.

As we do not have access to the true probability distributions, we expect to use a Maximum Likelihood estimator of these distributions. Any such estimator will have wide error bars if data is sparse, so we propose only including in set B distributions with a sizable amount of data. Conversely, we cannot judge Bob before he provides a reasonable amount of information on several participants/criteria. And because our data is highly subjective, we propose using the estimator described above to cut off information from users only after a relatively high threshold, so that people with unusual opinions aren't punished.

An alternative to this estimator would be to estimate the probability distribution of T_{Bob} directly from Monte Carlo methods or by using convolution over the individual R distributions. The former would have to involve careful line fitting in zones of low probability and the later would have to follow a sensible approach of quantising over some common x-axis.

We assumed earlier that all properties give rise to independent distributions, but in some cases this may not be so. The same ideas still hold, with the difference that a joint probability distribution for those two would be computed and its log incorporated in the sum of logs T_{Bob}.

An additional limitation is the fact the data available is very subjective, because the same performance can lead to different evaluations from different participants.

Regarding a practical implementation of our model, small adjustments may easily be made, depending on the requirements of the particular setting; for instance, in a fast changing environment ageing of feedback should be used.

3.3   Statement Engineering

One can anticipate that some participants may try to deceive the system by submitting statements that appear to be honest but are not accurate, just to accumulate credit by collecting rewards. Is there something to prevent a participant from querying the system to find the current views of others on Bob's performance, and then issue statements that are consistent with that view? Alternatively, suppose that a participant asks the system about ABC cars' reliability. The participant is told that the average reliability rating is 90%. If she buys an ABC car that turns out to be broken, why should she report what she sees rather than just 90%?

That is exactly the behaviour that the system is designed to detect. Honest participants will normally agree with others but sometimes disagree, and – as shown in the previous section – our estimator takes that into account. If a participant's opinions are always consistent with the average – possibly as a result of him querying the system and then submitting an opinion based on the result –, our estimator will mark her as dishonest.

Other users may try to maximise their rewards by being as close to dishonest as possible, but without crossing the threshold, thus submitting as few honest statements as possible to remain marginally not dishonest. For instance, one may find that for every three honest statements she submits she can add another seven random ones without her nose length crossing the dishonesty threshold. However, participants do not have access to their nose length or to the algorithm based on which it is computed, or even to the thresholds themselves – these are all held in Pinocchio. No immediate information about how close or far they are from being regarded as dishonest is available to them.

Although it may be theoretically feasible to build intelligent software that will learn the behaviour of Pinocchio through a lengthy trial and error process – for instance, by incrementing the proportion of random statements until found dishonest, and repeating several times –, we believe that the cost of such an attack would significantly outweigh its potential benefit. The probationary period is doubled every time a participant is found to be dishonest, so after a few errors the punishment for each new error will be heavy. Also, as the value of the nose length for a participant depends not only on the opinions of that participant, but on the opinions of other participants as well, the system's behaviour may be less predictable.

At the same time, the system does not provide any monetary payments to the users. Rewards can only be cashed for discounts on future queries, and users who are not genuinely interested in obtaining useful information from the system – and more likely to be interested in obtaining short-term benefits by attacking it – will probably not be very interested in non-monetary rewards.

4   Research Context

To devise a viable rewards model we studied examples present in existing distributed systems [4,1,2] and auction sites, such as the amazon.co.uk marketplace and eBay.

Providing incentives for participation is a fairly general research avenue, not necessarily coupled with trust management. Recent studies have focused on providing incentives for cooperation between nodes in wireless ad hoc networks [6], rewarding users who participate in ad hoc routing by allowing them to generate more traffic.

Existing trust management systems operate mainly in three categories of settings: traditional anonymous and pseudonymous *peer to peer systems*, on-line *auction systems* and platforms for *public distributed computing*.

Peer to peer systems. In traditional peer to peer systems, free-riding is widely observed [13,3], as the fact that participants are anonymous or pseudonymous, and in any case not tied to a real-world identity, operates as a disincentive for active participation. While trust management systems for peer to peer infrastructures have been devised [14], we expect that similar free-riding behaviour would be observed in these systems as well. Users may try to obtain as much information as they can about others, without submitting any new information themselves. Users can escape bad reputations by creating new identities, and also operations are very frequent, therefore providing performance ratings for each one can be significant hassle for a user.

On-line auction sites. Auction systems differ considerably; participants in auction systems have semi-permanent identities, as they are usually somehow tied to a real-world identity – for instance, a credit card. This means that they are not indefinitely able to escape bad reputations easily by creating new identities. Participants care about their reputations more because these are more permanent, and often submit positive feedback about others because they expect reciprocity [15]. The incentive for submitting negative feedback is often a feeling of revenge.

Transactions in auction systems happen in much longer timescales than in peer to peer systems. A purchase of an item can take a few days until it is delivered, while an average download would rarely take more than a few hours. Also, interactions in on-line auction sites happen a lot less frequently; users download files from KaZaA much more often than buying a sandwich maker from eBay. Moreover, the process of purchasing items from auction systems is highly manual, and participants are identifiable. The overall relative overhead of rating a seller in eBay and similar environments is significantly smaller than the one for rating a KaZaA node after a file download.

Additionally, the difference between the level of service that a user expects and the level of service that she actually gets after an interaction plays a significant role in her decision to provide feedback or not. On-line auction sites are inherently risky environments, and clients normally are aware of the risks and are prepared to receive bad service. When the service turns up to be better than expected – which happens often because expectations are low –, clients provide feedback. Clients would provide feedback even for average service, just because it is far better than what they had expected. This provides another insight to why eBay users provide feedback so often.

We believe that the high participation observed in the eBay ratings scheme as [17] can be explained by the reasons mentioned above. Semi-permanent reputations lead to reciprocal behaviour, submitting opinions incurs a much smaller overhead, and clients are happy enough about an interaction to report it more often, as the level of their expectations is low.

Public computing systems. We have outlined some public computing settings in Section 2.2. Participants – peers, or users and servers – are identifiable, and their identities are not subject to very frequent changes. In public computing systems, as in on-line auction sites, users and servers are registered with an infrastructural authority, and this registration often requires binding them with real, legal identities or other forms of semi-permanent identification – for instance, credit cards.

In public computing systems, users take good service for granted. Computing resources are regarded as a *utility* by the users, and the expectations are bound to be high. An analogy can be drawn with other utilities; customers would expect to have electricity at home at any time and electricity providers always expect that customers will pay. The customer will almost exclusively report negative experiences and vary rarely positive ones. In another example, how often does a regular guest of high-end hotels provide spontaneous positive comments about the experienced quality of service unless it fails to meet his expectations?

One of the consequences is that trust management systems for public computing platforms can not rely on the high participation observed in the eBay ratings scheme and expect spontaneous feedback and Pollyanna-style behaviour. Quite the contrary, as interactions happen frequently and in short timescales – as in peer to peer systems – and the level of expectations is high. There are few inherent incentives for participants to submit feedback. We believe that devising a system to provide explicit incentives for honest participation is crucial for the quality of information held in the trust management system.

5   Conclusion

In this paper we have examined a system for providing incentives for active and honest participation of components in trust management schemes. We propose Pinocchio, a module that has an advisory role, complementary to trust management systems. We suggest rewarding the publication of information and charging for the retrieval, and show that it is possible to provide a credible threat of spotting dishonest behaviour.

Pinocchio is a system that is general enough to co-operate with a large number of trust management schemes in advising when feedback should be rewarded. We have focused more on trust management settings operating in global public computing, but our techniques are generic enough to be applied in other environments.

As an initial experimental setting, we envisage implementing and evaluating Pinocchio as a consultant component attached to XenoTrust [8], the trust management architecture we are developing in the context of our global public computing project, the XenoServer Open Platform [12].

Acknowledgements. We would like to thank Jon Crowcroft, Tim Harris and the anonymous reviewers for their valuable suggestions, as well as Marconi PLC and New Visual Inc for the financial support of Evangelos Kotsovinos' and Alberto Fernandes' research.

References

1. Alfarez Abdul-Rahman and Stephen Hailes. Supporting Trust in Virtual Communities. In *Proceedings of the Hawaii International Conference on System Sciences 33, Maui, Hawaii (HICSS)*, January 2000.
2. Karl Aberer and Zoran Despotovic. Managing Trust in a Peer-2-Peer Information System. In *CIKM*, pages 310–317, 2001.
3. E. Adar and B. Huberman. Free riding on gnutella, 2000.
4. A. Chavez and P. Maes. Kasbah: An agent marketplace for buying and selling goods. In *Proceedings of the First International Conference on the Practical Application of Intelligent Agents and Multi-Agent Technology (PAAM'96)*, pages 75–90, London, UK, 1996. Practical Application Company.

5. S. Snell C.M. Grinstead. Introduction to probability.
6. J. Crowcroft, R. Gibbens, F. Kelly, and S. Ostring. Modelling incentives for collaboration in mobile ad hoc networks. In *Proc. of WiOpt'03*, 2003.
7. Chrysanthos Dellarocas. Mechanisms for coping with unfair ratings and discriminatory behavior in online reputation reporting systems. In *ICIS*, pages 520–525, 2000.
8. Boris Dragovic, Steven Hand, Tim Harris, Evangelos Kotsovinos, and Andrew Twigg. Managing trust and reputation in the XenoServer Open Platform. In *Proceedings of the 1st International Conference on Trust Management*, May 2003.
9. Boris Dragovic, Evangelos Kotsovinos, Steven Hand, and Peter Pietzuch. XenoTrust: Event-based distributed trust management. In *Second IEEE International Workshop on Trust and Privacy in Digital Business*, September 2003.
10. Global Grid Forum, Distributed Resource Management Application API Working Group. Distributed resource management application api specification 1.0, September 2003. Available from
http://www.drmaa.org/.
11. Global Grid Forum, Grid Economic Services Architecture Working Group. Grid economic services, June 2003. Available from
http://www.doc.ic.ac.uk/ sjn5/GGF/gesa-wg.html.
12. Steven Hand, Timothy L Harris, Evangelos Kotsovinos, and Ian Pratt. Controlling the XenoServer Open Platform. In *Proceedings of the 6th International Conference on Open Architectures and Network Programming (OPENARCH)*, April 2003.
13. Ramayya Krishnan, Michael D. Smith, and Rahul Telang. The economics of peer-to-peer networks. Draft technical document, Carnegie Mellon University, 2002.
14. Seungjoon Lee, Rob Sherwood, and Bobby Bhattacharjee. Cooperative Peer Groups in NICE. In *Infocom*, 2003.
15. L. Mui, M. Mohtashemi, and A. Halberstadt. A Computational Model for Trust and Reputation. In *Proceedings of the 35th Hawaii International Conference on System Sciences*, 2002.
16. Larry Peterson, David Culler, Tom Anderson, and Timothy Roscoe. A blueprint for introducing disruptive technology into the internet. In *Proceedings of the 1st Workshop on Hot Topics in Networks (HotNets-I)*, Princeton, NJ, USA, October 2002.
17. Paul Resnick and Richard Zeckhauser. Trust among strangers in internet transactions: Empirical analysis of ebay's reputation system. In *The Economics of the Internet and E-Commerce*, volume 11 of *Advances in Applied Microeconomics*. Elsevier Science, 2002.

History-Based Signature or How to Trust Anonymous Documents

Laurent Bussard, Refik Molva, and Yves Roudier

Institut Eurécom[1]
Corporate Communications
2229, route des Crêtes BP 193
06904 Sophia Antipolis (France)
{bussard,molva,roudier}@eurecom.fr

Abstract. This paper tackles the following problem: how to decide whether data are trustworthy when their originator wants to remain anonymous? More and more documents are available digitally and it is necessary to have information about their author in order to evaluate the accuracy of those data. Digital signatures and identity certificates are generally used for this purpose. However, trust is not always about identity. In addition authors often want to remain anonymous in order to protect their privacy. This makes common signature schemes unsuitable. We suggest an extension of group signatures where some anonymous person can sign a document as a friend of Alice, as a French citizen, or as someone that was in Paris in December, without revealing any identity. We refer to such scheme as *history-based signatures*.

1 Introduction

Verifying the reliability of a piece of information without revealing the identity of its source is becoming an important privacy requirement. Anybody can easily broadcast inaccurate or even deliberately deceptive information like in the case of what is referred as urban legends or hoaxes. Author authentication thanks to the signature of that very document seems a natural way to check whether the author can be trusted and thus to determine whether the document is accurate or misleading. Furthermore, protecting the privacy of signers is necessary. When people are exchanging ideas in a public forum, anonymity may be a requirement in order to be able to state some disturbing fact or even simply not to be traced based on their opinions. When users have a way to attach comments to surrounding physical objects [10] (e.g. painting in a museum) the chance that statistics be made on their interests might simply refrain them from commenting at all.

---

[1] Institut Eurécom's research is partially supported by its members: Bouygues Télécom, Cegetel, France Télécom, Hasler Foundation, Hitachi, STMicroelectronics, Swisscom, Texas Instruments, and Thales.

C.D. Jensen et al. (Eds.): iTrust 2004, LNCS 2995, pp. 78–92, 2004.
© Springer-Verlag Berlin Heidelberg 2004

There are number of cases like pervasive computing or ad-hoc networks in which infrastructure is lacking: neither a public key infrastructure nor a web of trust is available which renders identity-based authentication impossible [13]. Even with an infrastructure, authenticating the author is often not sufficient and more information on the *context*, in which the document was created, is required. For instance, beginning of this year the mass media announced that a senior radio reporter in Swaziland pretending to be reporting live from the war front in Iraq had never left his country and was broadcasting from a broom closet. This case shows that the context (*being in some place*) is sometimes more important than the role or the identity of the author (*being who he pretends to be*). Group signature schemes [5] make one step forward towards such new requirements by assuring the anonymity of the signer when revealing some information on his relationships, i.e. group membership. This paper extends this concept using attributes embedded within each signature in order to enable the evaluation of trust information on any signed document without revealing the identity of the author.

Various attributes can be relevant to evaluate trust. When some clear hierarchy exists among entities, a public key infrastructure [8] is sufficient to define trust relationships. A *web of trust* [9] allows non-hierarchical trust relations similar to those formed in human communities. However, using a model based on human notions of trust is not straightforward. Three main sources of information are generally proposed to evaluate trust [7]: *personal observations* of the entity's behavior, *recommendations* from trusted third parties, and *reputation* of an entity. However, other sources of information exist: sometimes, the *physical context* is also taken into account in the trust evaluation [14,11]. In a simple example, any person present in a room can be authorized to turn on the light. In this paper, we add the notion of *proof of context*, which certifies that some entity has been to some location at some time. It provides evidence for trustworthiness based on contextual parameters such as location and history.

This paper suggests a new signature scheme that takes those sources of trust into account. The scheme ensures anonymity and untraceability of signers. When signing, authors choose which part of their history will be shown to readers. For instance, a report relating some event can be signed by *an employee who was there when this event occurred*; an e-mail can be signed by *an inhabitant of a given district of a town*; or an article could be signed by *a member of a trade union who attended a given demonstration*. Like this, the signature is not based anymore on the identity of the signer but rather on his history. Such a history is defined as a set of the context (time and location), group memberships (reporter, trade unionist), and recommendations (defined by Bob as a trusted party). The signer chooses the degree of accuracy of the details he wants to disclose, e.g. someone that can prove that he was in Paris on the 15th of January could choose to sign a document as someone who was in France in January.

The remaining of the paper is organized as follows: section 2 presents the requirements and some related work. Section 3 describes the group signature scheme that is modified in Section 4 to define a history-based signature scheme.

Section 5 introduces a mechanism to code context and relation so that these can only be modified in a controlled way. Finally, Section 6 evaluates the security of this scheme.

2 Problem Statement

This section gives an overview of the interactions necessary to build a provable history and to use this for history-based signatures. Related work is discussed with respect to the feasibility of a provable history scheme.

2.1 Principle

Users anonymously collect evidence of their activity and store it as a provable history. In Figure 1, a user gets a proof that he has been at a location. To ensure non-transferability of evidences, they are implemented as credentials attached to a valuable secret. Credentials can define group membership, location-and-time stamps, recommendations, etc.

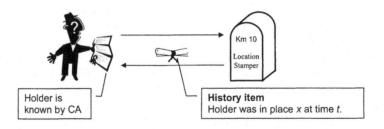

Fig. 1. Getting history items

When signing a document, the author chooses some credentials in his history, modifies them, and signs the document with those credentials. In Figure 2, a user is able to prove that he was at a location x at time t, that he is said reliable by some entity Z, that he is a member of group G, and that he has a given name and address (electronic id card). He chooses to sign the document as *someone that was at location x at time t*. The signature does not reveal more information on the signer and it is even not possible to link two signatures of the same signer. To ensure untraceability, it is necessary to avoid being too precise: it is indeed easier to identify a person that signed as having been in a given room at a precise time than to recognize this person based on the knowledge that he was in the building at some time.

Credentials have to fulfill the following requirements to build a provable yet anonymous history:

Fig. 2. History-based signature

- *Non-transferability*: credentials can only be used by the owner of some valuable secret (equivalent to the private key in public key infrastructures). This secret is critical and thus will not be transferred to another entity. As a result, credentials cannot be transferred.
- *Anonymity*: use of history-based credentials should not reveal the identity of the author.
- *Untraceability*: it is not possible to link different documents signed by a same person even when the same credential is used.

2.2 Related Work

Some existing work [4,2] already allow for privacy-preserving attribute verification. However, the target of those works is anonymous attribute certificates and untraceable access control. Credentials defined in [4] rely on pseudonyms and thus it is necessary to know the verifier before starting the challenge-response protocol. Credentials defined in [2] do not ensure non-transferability and have to be used only once to ensure untraceability. The one-time property of these credentials also does not suit multiple interactions as required by our scenario.

Using information on the user's context to evaluate trust or define rights is not new: [6] proposes a generalization of the role-based access control paradigm taking into account contextual information. Location verification techniques range from ultrasound-based challenge response [14] to distance bounding protocols [3], which forbid Mafia fraud attacks and thus defeat collusion of insiders. In this paper we assume that the location stamper implements one of those techniques to verify the presence of entities before delivering a proof of location.

3   Basic Mechanisms

This section presents the first group signature of Camenisch [5] that will be modified in the sequel of this paper in order to define a history-based signature scheme.

We define the following elements: $n = pq$ where p and q are two large primes; $\mathcal{Z}_n = \{0, 1, 2, \ldots, n-1\}$ is a ring of integers modulo n; $\mathcal{Z}_n^* = \{i \in \mathcal{Z}_n \mid \gcd(i, n) = 1\}$ is a multiplicative group; $G = \{1, g, g^2, \ldots, g^{n-1}\}$ is a cyclic group of order n; g is a generator of this group G; $a \in \mathcal{Z}_n^*$ is an element of the multiplicative group; and λ is a security parameter (see [5] for more details).

3.1   Interactive Proof of Knowledge

A *proof of knowledge* (PK) allows an entity to prove the knowledge of some secret without revealing this secret. For instance, the prover P claims to know the double discrete logarithm of y to the bases g and a. The verifier V tests if P indeed knows x. This is denoted $PK[\alpha \mid y = g^{(a^\alpha)}]$.

P sends a witness to V: $w = g^{(a^r)}$ where r is a random value and V returns a random challenge bit $c \in_R \{0, 1\}$. Finally P sends a response $s = r$ (if $c = 0$) or $s = r - x$ (if $c = 1$). The verifier checks that

$$c = 0 \; : \; w \stackrel{?}{=} g^{(a^s)} \quad = g^{(a^r)}$$
$$c = 1 \; : \; w \stackrel{?}{=} y^{(a^s)} \quad = \left(g^{(a^x)}\right)^{(a^s)} = g^{(a^{x+s})} = g^{(a^r)}$$

This protocol has to be run l times where l is a security parameter.

3.2   Signature Based on a Proof of Knowledge

A *signature based on a proof of knowledge* (or signature of knowledge) of a double discrete logarithm of z to the bases g and a, on message m, with security parameter l is denoted $SPK_l[\alpha \mid z = g^{(a^\alpha)}](m)$. It is a non-interactive version of the protocol depicted in Section 3.1. The signature is an $l+1$ tuple $(c, s_1, \ldots, s_l)$ satisfying the equation:

$$c = \mathcal{H}_l(m \parallel z \parallel g \parallel a \parallel P_1 \parallel \ldots \parallel P_l) \quad \text{where } P_i = \begin{cases} g^{(a^{s_i})} & \text{if } c[i] = 0 \\ z^{(a^{s_i})} & \text{otherwise} \end{cases}$$

It is computed as following:

1. For $1 \le i \le l$, generate random r_i.
2. Set $P_i = g^{(a^{r_i})}$ and compute $c = \mathcal{H}_l(m \parallel z \parallel g \parallel a \parallel P_1 \parallel \ldots \parallel P_l)$.
3. Set $s_i = \begin{cases} r_i & \text{if } c[i] = 0 \\ r_i - x & \text{otherwise} \end{cases}$

3.3   Camenisch's Group Signature

The group signature scheme in [5] is based on two signatures of knowledge: one that proves the signer knows some secret and another one that proves this secret is certified by the group manager. The scheme relies on the hardness of computing discrete logarithm, double discrete logarithm and e^{th} root of the discrete logarithm.

The public key of a group is (n, e, G, g, a, λ) where e is chosen so that $\gcd(e, \phi(n)) = 1$ where $n = pq$. The private key of the manager is (p, q, d) where $de = 1 \bmod \phi(n)$. When Alice *joins* the group, i.e. becomes a member, she uses her secret x to compute a membership key (y, z) where $y = a^x \bmod n$ and $z = g^y$. A sends (y, z) to the group manager, proves that she knows x and receives a group certificate $(y+1)^d \bmod n$ corresponding to her secret x. In order to sign a message m, A chooses $r \in_R Z_n$ and computes $\tilde{g} = g^r$, $\tilde{z} = \tilde{g}^y$ ($= z^r$), and two signatures:

$$V_1 = \text{SPK}[\alpha \mid \tilde{z} = \tilde{g}^{(a^{\alpha})}](m)$$
$$V_2 = \text{SPK}[\beta \mid \tilde{z}\tilde{g} = \tilde{g}^{(\beta^e)}](m)$$

V_1 is a signature of knowledge of a double discrete logarithm that can be computed when knowing some secret x. Similarly, V_2 is a signature of knowledge of an eth root of the discrete logarithm that can be computed using the certificate $(y+1)^d \bmod n$. The group signature of message m is $(\tilde{g}, \tilde{z}, V_1, V_2)$.

The verifier checks that V_1 and V_2 are valid signatures of m. Both signatures together mean that $\tilde{g}^{(\beta^e)} = \tilde{z}\tilde{g} = \tilde{g}^{(a^{\alpha}+1)}$ and thus $\beta = (a^{\alpha} + 1)^d \bmod n$. The verifier knows that the signer holds a certified secret x. However, the verifier cannot get any information on x. In other words, the identity of the signer is preserved: this is a group signature.

4 Solution: History-Based Signature Scheme

History-based signature is an extension of the group signature scheme described in Section 3. Alice (A) is the signer. She collects some credentials to subsequently prove some history. For instance, A holds credentials to prove that she has been in some place. When A is traveling or visiting partners, she collects location stamps. A has credentials to prove some membership, e.g. employee of a company, member of ieee computer society, partner of some project, member of a golf club, citizen of some state, client of some bank, customer of some airline. A can show some recommendations: when she collaborates with other entities, she receives credentials. All those credentials define her provable history. Each credential can be used as a proof during a challenge-response protocol or as an attribute of a signature.

4.1 Certification by a CA or Group Manager

To initiate the system, each entity has to get some certificate proving that he/she has a valid secret, i.e. a secret linked to his/her identity. This part is similar to the join protocol of the Camenisch's scheme. However, we use a modified version because a coalition attack exists against the initial scheme [1,12].

In Table 1, A generates some secret x with the help of a CA or group manager B. Moreover, A receives a certificate on this secret x: $\text{cert}_{1b} = (a_b^x + 1)^{d_b} \bmod n_b$. Now, A is certified and can act anonymously as a member of group or as an entity certified by a given CA in order to get credentials and build a provable history.

4.2 Obtaining Context Proofs or Recommendations

Once certified, A can visit different entities that will provide proofs of location, proofs of interaction, recommendations, etc. A provable history is a set of such

Table 1. Creation and first certification of A's secret x

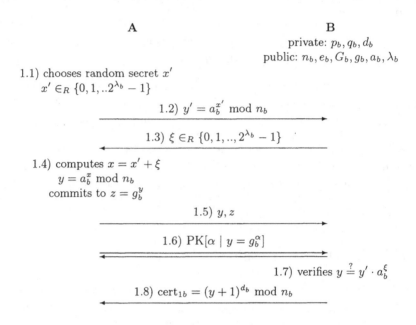

proofs. Table 2 shows how A can get a credential from C. The identity of A is not known but C verifies that this entity is certified by some known CA or Group manager. It is always necessary to have some trust relationship with previous signers when providing credentials or when verifying history. In this example, C has to trust B otherwise the previous protocol has to be done once more. However, when an entity D needs to verify the signature of A on some document, D only has to know C.

Two proofs of knowledge are done in step 2.3). The first one proves that y_2 is based on some secret. The second shows that this secret has been certified by B. Indeed, $\tilde{z}\tilde{g}_b = \tilde{g}_b^{(\beta^{e_b})} = \tilde{g}_b^{(a_b^\alpha)}\tilde{g}_b = \tilde{g}_b^{(1+a_b^\alpha)}$ and thus $1 + a_b^\alpha = \beta^{e_b}$. It means that A knows $\beta = (1+a_b^\alpha)^{d_b}$ that is a certification of α, which is also the discrete logarithm of y_2 to the base a_c. In other words, y_2 has been computed from the same secret x.

In step 2.4) A receives a new credential $\text{cert}_{2c} = (a_c^x + b_c^t)^{d_h} \bmod n_c$ from C that will be used to prove some history. b_c as well as a_c are elements of $\mathbb{Z}_{n_c}^*$, x prevents the transferability of credentials, and t is different for each credential to forbid a user from combining multiple credentials (see Section 6). The attribute value, be it a location or a recommendation, is defined using a technique that comes from electronic cash: $d_h = \prod_{i \in S} d_{c_i}$ where S is a set that defines the amount or any attribute. Construction of d_h is given in Section 5. Two other credentials can be provided: $\text{cert}_{1c} = (a_c^x + 1)^{d_c} \bmod n_c$ is a certification of the secret that can replace cert_{1b}. To avoid a potential attack (see Section 6), we add $\text{cert}_{3c} = (b_c^t + 1)^{d_c} \bmod n_c$.

Table 2. Obtaining some credential to build history

A
private: $x, (a_b^x + 1)^{d_b}$

C
private: $p_c, q_c, d_c, d_{c_1}, \ldots d_{c_k}$
public: $n_c, e_c, e_{c_1}, \ldots e_{c_k},$
$G_c, g_c, a_c, b_c, \lambda_c$

2.1) $y_2 = a_c^x \bmod n_c$
$\tilde{g}_b = g_b^r$ for $r \in_R \mathcal{Z}_{n_b}$
$\tilde{z} = \tilde{g}_b{}^y$ (i.e. $\tilde{z} = z^r$)

2.2) y_2

——————————————————————————————————————→

2.3) pk_2: $\text{PK}[\alpha \mid y_2 = a_c^\alpha \wedge \tilde{z} = \tilde{g}_b{}^{(a_b^\alpha)}]$
pk_3: $\text{PK}[\beta \mid \tilde{z}\tilde{g}_b = \tilde{g}_b{}^{(\beta^{e_b})}]$

←——————————————————————————————————————

2.4) $t \in_R \{0, 1, \ldots, 2^\lambda - 1\}$
$\text{cert}_{1c} = (a_c^x + 1)^{d_c}$
$\text{cert}_{2c} = (a_c^x + b_c^t)^{d_h}$
$\text{cert}_{3c} = (b_c^t + 1)^{d_c}$
where $d_h = \prod_{i \in S} d_i$

2.5) t, cert_{1c}, cert_{2c}, cert_{3c}, S

←——————————————————————————————————————

4.3   Using History for Signing

This section shows how Alice can sign a document as the holder of a set of credentials. A knows a secret x, the certification of this secret (cert_{1c}), and some credential that is part of her history (cert_{2c}). Using these credentials, she can compute a signature on some message m. A generates a random number $r_1 \in_R \mathcal{Z}_{n_c}$ and computes:

$\hat{g}_c = g_c^{r_1}$, $\hat{z}_2 = \hat{g}_c{}^{y_2}$, and $\hat{z}_3 = \hat{g}_c{}^{(b_c^t)}$
$spk_1 = \text{SPK}[\alpha \mid \hat{z}_2 = \hat{g}_c{}^{(a_c^\alpha)}](m)$
$spk_2 = \text{SPK}[\beta \mid \hat{z}_2 \hat{g}_c = \hat{g}_c{}^{(\beta^{e_c})}](m)$
$spk_3 = \text{SPK}[\delta \mid \hat{z}_3 = \hat{g}_c{}^{(b_c^\delta)}](m)$
$spk_4 = \text{SPK}[\gamma \mid \hat{z}_2 \hat{z}_3 = \hat{g}_c{}^{(\gamma^{e_{h'}})}](m)$ where $e_{h'} = \prod_{i \in S'} e_i$ and $S' \subseteq S$
$spk_5 = \text{SPK}[\epsilon \mid \hat{z}_3 \hat{g}_c = \hat{g}_c{}^{(\epsilon^{e_c})}](m)$

The signature of message m is $\{spk_1, spk_2, spk_3, spk_4, spk_5, \hat{g}_c, \hat{z}_2, \hat{z}_3, S'\}$. The signatures of knowledge spk_1 and spk_2 prove that the signer knows cert_{1c}: $\beta = (1 + a_c^\alpha)^{d_c} \bmod n_c$. The signatures of knowledge spk_1, spk_3 and spk_4 prove that the signer knows cert'_{2c}: $\gamma = (a_c^\alpha + b_c^\delta)^{d_{h'}} \bmod n_c$. To avoid some potential attack (see Section 6), we added spk_5 to prove the knowledge of cert_{3c}. spk_3 and spk_5 prove that t was generated by C: $\epsilon = (1 + b_c^\delta)^{d_c} \bmod n_c$.

When credentials from different entities (e.g. B and C) have to be used together, it is necessary that A generate a random number $r_2 \in_R \mathcal{Z}_{n_b}$ and compute $\hat{g}_b = g_b^{r_2}$ and $\hat{z} = \hat{g}_b{}^y$ ($= z^{r_2}$). spk_1 and spk_2 are modified as follows:

$$spk_1' = \text{SPK}[\alpha \mid \hat{z}_2 = \hat{g}_c^{(a_c^\alpha)} \wedge \hat{z} = \hat{g}_b^{(a_b^\alpha)}](m)$$
$$spk_2' = \text{SPK}[\beta \mid \hat{z}\hat{g}_b = \hat{g}_b^{(\beta^{e_b})}](m)$$

spk_1' and spk_2' prove that the signer knows cert_{1b}: $\beta = (a_b^\alpha + 1)^{d_b} \bmod n_b$ and spk_1' proves that cert_{1b} and cert_{2c} are linked to the same secret x. spk_1' is a signature based on a proof of equality of two double discrete logarithms (see Appendix A). The new signature of message m is $\{spk_1', spk_2', spk_3, spk_4, spk_5, \hat{g}_b, \hat{z}, \hat{g}_c, \hat{z}_2, \hat{z}_3, S'\}$.

5   Encoding Attribute Values

In Section 4, the user receives cert_{2c} and signs with cert_{2c}' to hide part of the attributes when signing. This section presents a flexible mechanism for atteibute encoding that allows the user to choose the granularity of attributes.

A straightforward solution to define attributes with various levels of granularity would be based on multiple credentials. For instance, a location stamper would provide credentials defining room, building, quarter, town, state, etc. The holder would thus be able to choose the granularity of the proof of location. Unfortunately, this requires too much credentials when transversal attributes have different granularities (longitude, latitude, time, etc.).

5.1   Principle

Each authority that delivers certificates (time stamper, location stamper, group manager, etc.) has a public key: a RSA modulo (n), and a set of small primes $e_1, \ldots, e_m$ where $\forall i \in \{1, \ldots, m\} \mid \gcd(e_i, \phi(n)) = 1$. The meaning of each e_i is public as well. Each authority also has a private key: p, q, and $\{d_1, \ldots, d_m\}$ where $pq = n$ and $\forall i \in \{1, \ldots, m\} \mid e_i \cdot d_i = 1 \bmod \phi(n)$.

A signature $SIGN_{(S,n)}(m) = m^{d_h} \bmod n$, where S is a set and $d_h = \prod_{i \in S} d_i$, can then be transformed into a signature $SIGN_{(S',n)}(m) = m^{d_{h'}} \bmod n$, where S' is a subset of S and $d_{h'} = \prod_{i \in S'} d_i$. The the attribute value is coded as a set S corresponding to its bits equal to one. This signature based on set S can be reduced to any subset $S' \subseteq S$:

$$SIGN_{(S',n)}(m) = \left(SIGN_{(S,n)}(m)\right)^{\left(\prod_{i \in \{S \setminus S'\}} e_i\right)} = m^{\left(\prod_{i \in S'} d_i \bmod \phi(n)\right)} \bmod n$$

Thus, an entity that received some credential cert_{2c} is able to compute cert_{2c}' and to sign a document with this new credential.

$$\text{cert}_{2c}' = (\text{cert}_{2c})^{\prod_{j \in \{S \setminus S'\}} e_j} = \left(\left(a_c^x + b_c^t\right)^{\prod_{i \in S} d_i}\right)^{\prod_{j \in \{S \setminus S'\}} e_j} = \left(a_c^x + b_c^t\right)^{\prod_{i \in S'} d_i}$$

This technique ensures that part of the signed attributes can be modified. For instance, the attribute value $v = 13_d$ is equivalent to the binary string 01101_b and can be encoded as $S = \{4, 3, 1\}$, i.e. 4th, 3rd, and 1st bits set to one. $d_h = d_4 \cdot d_3 \cdot d_1 \mod \phi(n)$. Knowing $\{e_i \mid i \in S\}$, the following transformations are possible: $S' \in \{\{4,3,1\}; \{3,1\}; \{4,3\}; \{4,1\}; \{4\}; \{3\}; \{1\}\}$ and thus $v' \in \{13,5,12,9,8,4,1\}$. Any bit i equal to one can be replaced by a zero (by using e_i) but any bit j equal to zero cannot be replaced by a one (because d_j is private).

5.2 Possible Codes

Choosing different ways to encode data enables to define which transformations of the attribute values are authorized:

- *more-or-equal*: values are encoded so that they can only be reduced. For instance, $v = 13_d \rightarrow 01101_b \rightarrow S = \{1,3,4\}$. Because bits equal to one can be replaced by zeros, it can be transformed into $v' \in \{13,12,9,8,5,4,1\}$.
- *less-or-equal*: values are encoded so that they can only be increased. For instance, $v = 13_d \rightarrow 10010_b \rightarrow S = \{2,5\}$. It can be transformed into $v' \in \{13,15,29,31\}$.
- *unary more-or-equal*: the problem with binary encoding is that they cannot be reduced to any value. For instance, $7_d = 111_b$ can be shown as 7, 6, 5, 4, 3, 2, 1, or 0 but $6_d = 110_b$ can only be shown as 6, 4, 2, or 0. This limitation can be solved by using a binary representation of unary: $v = 6_d = 111111_u \rightarrow 0111111_b \rightarrow S = \{1,2,3,4,5,6\}$ can be shown as $v' \in \{6,5,4,3,2,1,0\}$. The overhead is important (l bits data is encoded with 2^l bits) and thus unary has to be restricted to small values.
- *unary less-or-equal*: unary representation a similar approach can be used for less-or-equal too: $v = 2_d \rightarrow 1111100_b \rightarrow S = \{3,4,5,6,7\}$ can be transformed in $v' \in \{2,3,4,5,6,7\}$.
- *frozen*: values are encoded so that they cannot be changed. In this case, the number of bits have to be larger: l bits becomes $l + \lfloor \log_2(l) \rfloor + 1$ bits. For instance, $13_d \rightarrow 0001101_b, c = 100_b \rightarrow 0001101|100_b \rightarrow S = \{7,6,4,3\}$. The checksum c represents the number of bits equal to zero, any modification of the value increase the number of zero but the checksum can only be decreased. It is not possible to change frozen values.
- *blocks*: data are cut into blocks. Each block is encoded with one of the previous schemes.

5.3 Example: Location-and-Time Stamper

This section describes how the previous encoding schemes can be used. Let us define a location and time stamper (LTS) that certifies that some entity has been in a given place at a given time. The proof can be provided by a cell-phone operator that locates subscribers, by a beacon in a building, or even by using some distance bounding protocol. A LTS can define logical location (e.g. continent, country, department, town, quarter, building, room) or geographic location (longitude, latitude). We only focus on the latter case because it does not require the definition of a complex data structure.

A location-and-time stamper company can deploy a network of public terminals and sensors. When Alice plugs her smart card in a terminal or when she passes a wireless sensor, she receives a location-and-time stamp with the following attributes: time (UTC, date) and location (latitude, longitude). Table 3 shows an example of the attributes that could be delivered by some LTS in Eurecom Institute.

Table 3. Context data: location and time

Value	Meaning
180432	UTC in hhmmss format (18 hours, 4 minutes and 32 seconds)
24112003	Date in ddmmyyyy format (November 24, 2003)
43.6265	Geographic latitude in dd.dddd format (43.6265 degrees)
N	Direction of latitude (N - North, S - South)
007.0470	Geographic longitude in ddd.dddd format (7.047 degrees)
E	Direction of longitude (E - East, W - West)

It can be represented by four attributes [180432, 24112003, 436265, -0070470] that can be divided into frozen blocks: [18|04|32, 24|11|2003, 43|62|65, -007|04|70] the meaning of each block is publicly known: LTS defines his public key as n and a set of e. For instance, e_1 is the least significant bit of the time in seconds (0-59 : 6 bits), e_6 is the most significant bit of the time in seconds, e_7 is the LSB of checksum of time in seconds, etc. If a location and time stamper provides the following credential to Alice: [18|04|32, 24|11|2003, 43|62|65, -007|04|70], she can sign a document with a subset of this credential.
[18|XX|XX, XX|XX|XXXX, 43|62|65, -007|04|70], i.e. the document is signed by *someone that was in the building someday around six o'clock*. Or [XX|XX|XX, 24|11|2003, 43|XX|XX, -007|XX|XX], i.e. *someone who was in the South of France the 24th of November.*

Hidden attributes are different than zero values (XXX $\neq$ 000). Indeed, XXX is represented as 000|00 and is not equal to 000 that is defined as 000|11. Thus it is not possible to convert 09:08:30 into 09:00:30. The only way to suppress minutes is to remove seconds as well: 09:XX:XX. This value does not mean that some action occurred at nine o'clock but that it occurred between nine and ten o'clock.

Similarly, a company can qualify customers as *Platinum, Gold, or Silver*; a state can provide digital Id cards to citizen to certify gender, name; a company can provide credentials that define role, access rights; and a partner can define recommendations. In all those cases, the ability of selecting which attribute is displayed is very important to protect privacy when enabling trust evaluation.

6   Security Evaluation

The security of the scheme is based on the assumptions that the discrete logarithm, the double discrete logarithm and the roots of discrete logarithm problems are hard. In addition it is based on the security of Schnorr and RSA signature schemes and on the additional assumption of [5] that computing membership certificates is hard.

Our proposal is based on the group signature scheme of [5], whose join protocol is subject to a collusion attack [1]. Modifications suggested in [12] and that prevent this attack have been taken into account (see Table 1). Even with this modification, there is no proof that the scheme is secure. The security does, however, rest on a well-defined number-theoretic conjecture.

6.1   Unforgeability of Signature

The signature produced by the above protocol is not forgeable. Specifically, only an entity having received a given credential could have issued this signature. This holds because, in the random oracle model, spk_1 proves that the signer knows his secret, spk_3 proves that the signer knows a credential's secret, and spk_4 proves that the signer knows a credential corresponding to both secrets. That is, spk_1 and spk_3 respectively show that

$$\hat{z}_2 = \hat{g}^{(a^\alpha)} \quad \text{and} \quad \hat{z}_3 = \hat{g}^{(b^\delta)}$$

and therefore:

$$\hat{z}_2 \hat{z}_3 = \hat{g}^{(a^\alpha + b^\delta)}$$

Whereby integers α and δ are known by the signer. On the other hand, spk_4 proves that

$$(a^\alpha + b^\delta) = \gamma^{e_h h'}$$

for some γ that the signer knows. Under the hardness assumption on the unforgeability of credentials, this can only happen if the signer received a credential.

6.2   Unforgeability and Integrity of Credentials

In order to code attribute values, a set of different e_i and d_i are used with the same modulo n. However, the common modulus attack does not apply here because each d_i is kept secret and each modulo n is known by a single entity as with the standard RSA. Because there are multiple valid signatures for a given message, this scheme seems to make easier brute force attacks that aim at creating a valid signature for a given message: an attacker can choose a message m and a random $d_R \in_R \mathcal{Z}_n$ and compute a signature $m^{d'} \bmod n$. If e_i and d_i are defined for $i \in \{1, \ldots, k\}$, there are 2^k valid $d = \prod_{i \in S' \subseteq S} d_i$. The probability that a random d_R be acceptable is 2^k times higher than with standard RSA where $k = 1$. However, even if the number of possible signatures for a given message increases, it is necessary to find out the set S corresponding to the randomly chosen signature. In other words, the attacker has to test whether $\forall S' \subseteq S \mid m \overset{?}{=} (m^{d'})^{\Pi_{i \in S'} e_i} \bmod n$. There are 2^k possible sets S' to check and thus the security of this scheme is equivalent to RSA.

In some cases, the signature scheme can allow combining attributes of two credentials in order to create a new one: naive credentials $(a^x + 1)^{d_{h_1}}$ and $(a^x + 1)^{d_{h_2}}$ could be used to create $(a^x + 1)^{d_{h'}}$ where $S' \subseteq S_1 \cup S_2$. If h_1 states that Alice was present from 8 a.m. to 10 a.m. and h_2 states that she was present from 4 p.m. to 6 p.m., it is necessary to forbid that Alice could create a h' stating that she was present from 8 a.m. to 6 p.m. To avoid this attack, a unique secret t is associated to each credential. Hence $(a^x + b^{t_1})^{d_{h_1}}$ cannot be combined with $(a^x + b^{t_2})^{d_{h_2}}$.

6.3   Non-transferability of History

Even when the signature of a message cannot be forged, a desirable goal is to be able to assure that it is not possible to find another message with the same signature. Violation of this property with our protocol would require the generation of two pairs (x, t) and (x', t') so that $a^x + b^t = a^{x'} + b^{t'}$. In order to prevent transferability based on such generation of equivalent pairs, cert_{3c} and spk_5 were included in the protocol. Computing (x', t') from a credential based on (x, t) would thus require computing $x' = \log_a(a^x + b^t - b^{t'})$ which is equivalent to solving the discrete logarithm problem. Our protocol thus assures that the credential received as a proof of context or as a recommendation cannot be transferred. A proof that the generation of equivalent pairs is equivalent to a difficult problem (e.g. the discrete logarithm problem) would allow for important simplifications of the history-based signature scheme.

7   Conclusions and Future Work

This paper introduces a *history-based signature* scheme that makes it possible to sign data with one's history. In this scheme, signers collect credentials (proof of location, recommendation, etc.) in order to build a provable history. This scheme preserves the privacy of authors and makes a large variety of attributes possible for defining trust: recommendations, contextual proofs, reputation, and even hierarchical relationships.

This scheme can be useful in different situations. For instance, any visitor of a pervasive computing museum could be allowed to attach digital comments to painting and to read comments of previous visitors. Notes could be signed by an *art critic that visited the museum one week ago*. In this example, we assume that the critic received some credential to prove that he is an expert (e.g. electronic diploma when completing study) and that he can prove that he visited the gallery. Each visitor will filter the numerous notes according to some parameters defining trustworthiness, i.e. art critic, location, or recommended by the museum. The authors of note have a guarantee that they cannot be traced. In another situation, the signature of an article written by a journalist could require one credential to prove that the author was where the event occurred and another credential to prove that he is a reporter.

There are two main limitations to this scheme. First, it is well-known that signatures based on the proof of knowledge of a double discrete logarithm are not efficient in terms of computational complexity. It could be interesting to study other approaches to define more efficient history-based signatures. Second, the deployment of the scheme is easy when some authorities (CA, TTP, group manager, LTS, etc.) provide proofs of context and recommendations and some users collect those credentials in order to sign. Peer-to-peer frameworks where each entity acts as a signer and as a credential provider would require the binding of members' secrets with the group manager's keys.

References

1. G. Ateniese and G. Tsudik. *Some open issues and new directions in group signatures.* In Proceedings of Financial Cryptography'99, volume 1648 of LNCS, pages 196–211. Springer-Verlag, 1999.
2. S. Brands. *A technical Overview of Digital Credentials.* Research Report, February 2002.
3. L. Bussard and Y. Roudier, *Embedding Distance-Bounding Protocols within Intuitive Interactions,* in Proceedings of Conference on Security in Pervasive Computing (SPC'2003), Boppard, Germany, March, 2003.
4. J. Camenisch and A. Lysyanskaya, *An Efficient System for Non-transferable Anonymous Credentials with Optional Anonymity Revocation,* LNCS 2045, 2001.
5. J. Camenisch and M. Stadler. *Efficient group signature schemes for large groups.* In Advances in Cryptology, CRYPTO '97 Proceedings, LLNCS 1294, pages 410–424, Santa Barbara, CA, August 1997.
6. M.J.Covington, M.J.Moyer, and M.Ahamad, *Generalized Role-Based Access Control for Securing Future Applications.* In 23rd National Information Systems Security Conference (2000).
7. Nathan Dimmock. *How much is 'enough'? risk in trust-based access control,* In IEEE International Workshops on Enabling Technologies (Special Session on Trust Management), June 2003.
8. C. Ellison, B. Frantz, B. Lampson, R. Rivest, B. Thomas, and T. Ylonen. *Rfc 2693 – spki certificate theory,* 1999.
9. Simson Garfinkel. *PGP : Pretty Good Privacy.* International Thomson Publishing, 1995.
10. D. Ingram. *Trust-based filtering for augmented reality.* In Proceedings of the First International Conference on Trust Management, volume 2692. LNCS, May 2003.
11. T.Kindberg, K.Zhang, and N.Shankar, *Context authentication using constrained channels,* in Proceedings of the IEEE Workshop on Mobile Computing Systems and Applications (WMCSA), pages 14–21, June 2002.
12. Zulfikar Amin Ramzan. *Group blind digital signatures: Theory and applications,* Master Thesis, MIT, 1999.

13. J.M. Seigneur, S. Farrell, C.D. Jensen, E. Gray, and Y. Chen *End-to-end Trust Starts with Recognition*, in Proceedings of Conference on Security in Pervasive Computing (SPC'2003), Boppard, Germany, March, 2003.
14. N. Sastry, U. Shankar, and D. Wagner. *Secure verification of location claims*, In Proceedings of the 2003 ACM workshop on Wireless security, 2003.

A   Signature Based on a Proof of Equality of Double Discrete Logarithms

Section 4.3 uses a signature based on a proof of equality of two double discrete logarithms (SPKEQLOGLOG).

$$\mathrm{SPK}_l[\alpha \mid y_1 = g_1^{(a_1^{\alpha})} \wedge \cdots \wedge y_k = g_k^{(a_k^{\alpha})}](m)$$

where l is a security parameter. The signature is an $l + 1$ tuple $(c, s_1, \ldots, s_l)$ satisfying the equation

$$c = \mathcal{H}\left(m\|k\|\{y_1 \ldots y_k\}\|\{g_1 \ldots g_k\}\|\{a_1 \ldots a_k\}\|\{P_{1,1} \ldots P_{1,l}\}\| \cdots \|\{P_{k,1} \ldots P_{k,l}\}\right)$$

where $P_{i,j} = \begin{cases} g_i^{(a_i^{s_j})} & \text{if } c[j] = 0 \\ y_i^{(a_i^{s_j})} & \text{otherwise} \end{cases}$

The signature can be computed as following:

1. For $1 \leq j \leq l$, generate random r_j where $r_j \geq x$.
2. For $1 \leq i \leq k$, for $1 \leq j \leq l$, set $P_{i,j} = g_i^{(a_i^{r_j})}$
3. Compute $c = \mathcal{H}\left(m\|k\|\{y_1 \ldots y_k\}\|\{g_1 \ldots g_k\}\|\{a_1 \ldots a_k\}\|\{P_{1,1} \ldots P_{1,l}\}\| \cdots\right)$
4. Set $s_j = \begin{cases} r_j & \text{if } c[j] = 0 \\ r_j - x & \text{otherwise} \end{cases}$

The verification works as following:

if $c[j] = 0$: $P_{i,j} = g_i^{(a_i^{r_j})} = g_i^{(a_i^{s_j})}$

if $c[j] = 1$: $P_{i,j} = g_i^{(a_i^{r_j})} = \left(y_i^{(a_i^{-x})}\right)^{(a_i^{s_j+x})} = y_i^{(a_i^{-x}a_i^{s_j+x})} = y_i^{(a_i^{s_j})}$

It is not possible to reduce s_j modulo because the order of $a_1 \in \mathcal{Z}_{n_1}^*$ is different than the order of $a_2 \in \mathcal{Z}_{n_2}^*$.

Trading Privacy for Trust

Jean-Marc Seigneur[1] and Christian Damsgaard Jensen[2]

[1]Trinity College Dublin
Jean-Marc.Seigneur@cs.tcd.ie
[2]Technical University of Denmark
Christian.Jensen@imm.dtu.dk

Abstract. Both privacy and trust relate to knowledge about an entity. However, there is an inherent conflict between trust and privacy: the more knowledge a first entity knows about a second entity, the more accurate should be the trustworthiness assessment; the more knowledge is known about this second entity, the less privacy is left to this entity. This conflict needs to be addressed because both trust and privacy are essential elements for a smart working world. The solution should allow the benefit of adjunct trust when entities interact without too much privacy loss. We propose to achieve the right trade-off between trust and privacy by ensuring minimal trade of privacy for the required trust. We demonstrate how transactions made under different pseudonyms can be linked and careful disclosure of such links fulfils this right trade-off.

1 Introduction

Privacy can be seen as a fundamental human right "to be left alone" [2] or a basic need (according to Maslow's hierarchy of needs [12]) for a private sphere protected against others. Regardless of the definition, different mechanisms have been proposed to protect the privacy of people in the online world. The most common mechanisms are either legislative or technological, depending on whether privacy is seen a right which should be protected by law or a need which should be supported by the devices that are used to access the online world. In this paper we focus on the technological aspects of privacy protection, especially techniques to control the dissemination of personal information.

Information becomes personal when it can be linked back to an individual or when it, in some way, allows two individuals to be linked together. This means that control of the dissemination of personal information can be exercised through preventing, or at least limiting, linkability of information to individuals. This is illustrated in Fig. , where a user Alice performs some transactions with another user Bob (neither Alice nor Bob needs to be actual users, but could be clients, servers or part of the computing infrastructure).

In Fig. 1, Alice performs two transactions tr_1 and tr_2 with Bob. In order to protect the privacy of Alice[1], it is important that Bob, or anyone who eavesdrops on their

---

[1] The rights/needs to privacy of Alice and Bob are symmetrical, so it may be equally important to prevent Alice from knowing that the two transactions were performed with the same entity.

C.D. Jensen et al. (Eds.): iTrust 2004, LNCS 2995, pp. 93–107, 2004.
© Springer-Verlag Berlin Heidelberg 2004

Fig. 1. Linkability of transactions

communication, is unable to link either transaction tr_1 or tr_2 directly to Alice's real-world identity. However, it is equally important to prevent Bob from linking the two transactions to each other, since this would allow him to compile a comprehensive profile of the other party, which could eventually identify Alice. Moreover, the violation of Alice's privacy would be increased dramatically if any future transaction tr_x can be linked to Alice, since this would allow Bob to link the full profile to Alice and not just tr_x. However, trust is based on knowledge about the other party [7], which directly contradicts the prevention of linkability of information to users, so perfect privacy protection, i.e., preventing actions to be linked to users, prevents the formation, evolution and exploitation of trust in the online world.

In the human world, trust exists between two interacting entities and is very useful when there is uncertainty in result of the interaction. The requested entity uses the level of trust[2] in the requesting entity as a mean to cope with uncertainty, to engage in an action in spite of the risk of a harmful outcome. Trust can be seen as a complex predictor of the entity's future behaviour based on past evidence. In the literature, divergent trust definitions are proposed but it is argued that they can fit together [13].

Interactions with uncertain result between entities also happen in the online world. So, it would be useful to rely on trust in the online world as well. The goal of a computational trust/risk-based security framework (TSF) is to provide trust in the online world. Researchers are working both theoretically and practically towards the latter goal. Others have shown how trust can be formalized as a computational concept [7, 11]. The aim of the SECURE project [1, 14] is an advanced TSF formally grounded and usable. The basic components of a TSF (depicted in Figure 2) should expose a decision-making component that is called when a requested entity has to decide what action should be taken due to a request made by another entity, the requesting entity.

In order to take this decision, two sub-components are used:
- a trust engine that can dynamically assess the trustworthiness of the requesting entity based on pieces of evidence (e.g., observation or recommendation [19])
- a risk engine that can dynamically evaluate the risk involved in the interaction and choose the action that would maintain the appropriate cost/benefit

In the background, another component is in charge of gathering evidence (e.g., recommendations, comparisons between expected outcomes of the chosen actions and real outcomes...) This evidence is used to update risk and trust information. Thus, trust and risk follow a managed life-cycle. In the remainder of the paper, we use TSF in its broad sense: any TSF can be used (even though the TSF being developed in the SECURE project is an example of an advanced TSF).

---

[2] In this paper, we use the following terms as synonyms: *level of trust* and *trustworthiness*. In a TSF, they are represented as a trust value. This is different than *trust*, which is the concept.

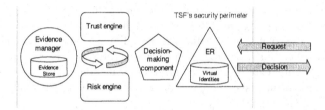

Fig. 2. High-level view of a TSF

Recalling the process of trust formation makes apparent the fact that privacy is at stake in trust-based systems. In order to be able to trust another entity, the first step is to establish the level of trust in that entity, which is the result of an analysis of the existing knowledge and evidence. Thus, trust relies on profiling, where more information is better, because it allows the likely behaviour of the other entity to be more accurately predicted. Any link with the real-world identity of the user changes this information into sensitive personally identifiable information (PII). From a privacy point of view, a first technological line of defence may be to use virtual identities – pseudonyms (mapping to principals in SECURE). The ordinary definition of a pseudonym is "a fictitious name used when the person performs a particular social role"[3]. Ian Goldberg underlined that any transaction engaged by a person reveals meta-content, especially information about the identity of the person. He defined "the nymity of a transaction to be the amount of information about the identity of the participants that is revealed" and gave a continuum, called the "Nymity Slider", with different levels of nymity: verynimity (e.g., government id), persistent pseudonymity (e.g., pen names), linkable anonymity (e.g., prepaid phone cards), unlinkable anonymity (e.g., anonymous remailers). He also pointed out that it makes sense to associate reputation with persistent pseudonyms. In a TSF, the minimum requirement is a local reference for the formation of trust, which is in turn managed by other components in the TSF. According to the privacy protection principle of "collection limitation" [10], data collection should be strictly restricted to mandatory required data for the purpose of the collection.

Our requirement is to establish the trustworthiness of entities and not their real-world identity. This is why pseudonymity, the level of indirection between trust and the real-world entity, is necessary. Transaction pseudonyms [8] (i.e., a pseudonym used for only one transaction) and anonymity cannot be effectively used because they do not allow linkability between transactions as required when building trust. In the following, we consider a model where linkability of different transactions with a specific pseudonym is achieved by using the APER [15] Entity Recognition (ER) scheme for transactions between the two principals. There are two roles distinguished in APER, the recogniser and the claimant (though any party can take on any role). The approach is for the claimant to send claims, i.e., digitally signed messages, and for the recogniser to be able to recognise the claimant on the basis of correctly signed claims. A principal, i.e., a pseudonym, is an APER claimant who is recognised using a digital signature and who sends APER claims. When an entity makes a request,

---

[3] Definition from WordNet Dictionary:
http://www.hyperdictionary.com/search.aspx?define=pseudonym

which requires a trusting decision from another entity, the requesting entity sends an APER claim that tells the requested entity which pseudonym is claimed. So, transactions are linked through asymmetric key digital signature validation (which provides a level of confidence in recognition called APERLevel1) using the same key. The requested entity can refer to a specific pseudonym (e.g., in order to get recommendations about a specific pseudonym) by specifying the public key (Pub) claimed by the requesting pseudonym.

The next section describes a scenario where it makes sense to trade privacy for trust. A model for privacy/trust trade is given in Section 3. This model is applied at the level of virtual identities in Section 4. Section 5 surveys related work and we draw conclusions.

2 Scenario

As an example, the following figure depicts the scenario where Alice plans to spend her holidays in SunnyVillage. Normally Alice works and lives in RainyTown. She will take the plane and relax for two weeks in this village where she has never been but that some of her friends recommended.

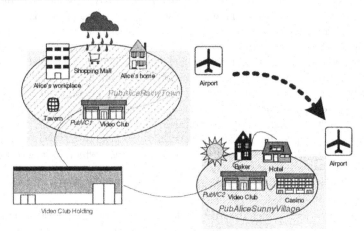

Fig. 3. Alice's smart world

She will have to pay to enjoy some of her leisure activities, which could be enhanced if collaboration with other local entities is allowed. We assume that Alice uses an e-purse. So, an e-purse is associated with public key (Pub) / private key (Pri) pairs: a Pub becoming a pseudonym for Alice. An e-purse has also an embedded TSF, which takes care of trust decision-making and management. Similarly, a vendor's cashier-machine can be recognised with a Pub and run a TSF. For example, exchange of Alice's trustworthiness in being a good payer in the neighbourhood would let her pay without being asked real-world credentials (e.g., a passport); credit may also become viable. Vendors would also benefit from trust calculation adjunct. The video shop of SunnyVillage, having to deal with passing customers, would be reassured to take a lower risk if payment with electronic coins is combined with the level of trust in the customer. Nevertheless, Alice also wishes to be left alone and have different social profiles in different places. Alice has indeed two pseudonyms automatically selected according to location: one in RainyTown (PubAliceRainyTown) and one in SunnyVillage (PubAliceSunnyVillage). This offers better protection for her privacy than having one pseudonym. Even though the video club holding spans both domains, SunnyVillage's video club cannot obviously link PubAliceRainyTown and PubAliceSunnyVillage by comparing keys known by RainyTown's video club. The latter would not be true with a unique Pub for Alice's e-purse.

However, trust, as with privacy, is dynamic and evolving interaction after interaction. Privacy is a constant interaction where information flows between parties [5, 17]. Privacy expectations vary [5, 17] and depend on context [8]. We have demonstrated a prototype where privacy disclosure policies can be based on context [17], especially location. Depending on what people can get based on their trustworthiness, they may be willing to disclose more of their private data in order to increase trust. There is a need for contextual privacy/trust trade. Let us assume that the trustworthiness of people for being good payers is managed by the TSF of the vendor's cashier-machine. Recalling the scenario in Fig. , if Alice arrives in SunnyVillage's video club for the first time, her e-purse will exhibit PubAliceSunnyVillage when she wants to pay for the large video display that she wants to rent. Since no direct observation, i.e., a previous experience with PubAliceSunnyVillage, is available, PubVC2 (the SunnyVillage video club cashier's Pub) will ask for recommendations from its neighbors (e.g., PubBaker). However, Alice's trust obtained through recommendations is not enough to commit the renting transaction. Alice really wants the display, so she is now disposed to give up some of her privacy in order to exhibit enough trust. In fact, SunnyVillage's video club is held by a holding of video clubs, which has a video club in RainyTown. The following example of contextual privacy/trust trade is started. The list of Pubs owned by the holding is sent to Alice's e-purse, which finds that PubVC1 of RainyTown's video club is a known entity. Alice has noticed that she could link PubAliceRainyTown and PubAliceSunnyVillage in order to reach the necessary level of trust. Although Alice now knows that what she has done in RainyTown is potentially exposed to both areas, i.e., RainyTown and SunnyVillage, she agrees to present herself as the owner of both keys (i.e., pseudonyms).

3 Privacy/Trust Trade Model

We start by an informal summary of the model. When true knowledge[4] about an entity increases:

- The evaluation of its trustworthiness is more accurate and if this entity is indeed truly trustworthy, its trustworthiness increases[5].

---

[4] By true knowledge, we mean knowledge which cannot be refuted (i.e., it cannot be a lie, noise information or revised).

[5] We do not mean that the trustworthiness increases in all possible trust dimensions (but at least it increases in the dimension where the knowledge is useful/relevant, e.g., propensity to be a good payer).

- Its privacy decreases and it is almost a one-way function[6] because privacy recovery is hard to achieve [16].

Knowledge is composed of evidence. A piece of evidence ev may be any statement about some entity(ies), especially: a transaction tr, an observation[7] obs (i.e., evaluated outcome of a transaction [6]), a recommendation rec (i.e., locally discounted[8] observation of a recommending external entity)... The nymity of evidence is the amount of information about the identity of the entity that is revealed. The trustworthiness assessment impact, called tai of evidence, is the amount of information that can be used for assessing the trustworthiness of the entity, which is represented as a trust value.

There are different levels of nymity. So we assume that there is a partial order between nymity levels, called Privacy Asset Order (PAO). The Nymity Slider is one example of such ordering. We present another example of PAO below:

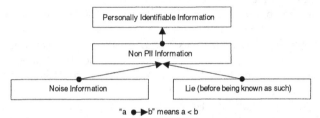

"a ●▶b" means a < b

Fig. 4. Privacy Asset Order example

Similarly, evidence may be more or less useful for trustworthiness assessment. So we assume that there is a partial order between tai levels, called Trustworthiness Assessment Impact Order (TAIO). An example of TAIO is:

A piece of evidence of PII nymity is more likely to have a strong positive impact tai, especially when it is assumed that the real-world identity can be sued. However, one non-PII evidence may have low positive impact and another one strong positive impact.

We provide a mechanism that can link n pieces of evidence ev_i for $i=1,...,n$ and represented by:

$$link\left(ev_1, ev_2,..., ev_n\right)$$

---

[6] On Goldberg's Nymity Slider, it is "easy to change the transaction to have a higher position on the slider" and "extremely difficult to move a transaction down the slider (towards unlinkable anonymity)" [4].

[7] It is sometime difficult to find out when the observation should be made because it is not clear whether the action is finished or not. It may be solved by having a kind of dynamic observation, i.e., a piece of evidence which varies through time as well.

[8] By discounted, we mean that the trustworthiness of the recommender is taken into account. The final value, which is used locally, may be different than the recommended one. For example, a recommender with trust value of 0.6 on a [0,1] scale giving a recommendation of 0.8 provides the discounted trust value: 0.6*0.8.

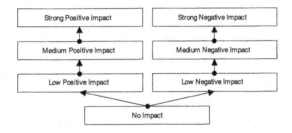

Fig. 5. Trustworthiness Assessment Impact Order example

The result of link is a new piece of evidence with a new tai level as well as a new nymity level. Sometimes, linking of evidence is implicit (i.e., the requesting entity cannot keep secret that two pieces of evidence are linked) and it is redundant to make it explicit (i.e., the requesting entity discloses to other entities that two pieces of evidence are indeed linked). For example, if two events ev_2 and ev_3 are implicitly linked, then explicitly linking ev_1 and ev_2 is equivalent to explicitly linking ev_1, ev_2 and ev_3: $link(ev_1,ev_2) = link(ev_1,ev_2,ev_3)$.

It is needed to recognise entities and it is useful to know what piece of evidence is linked to a specific entity for the recognition of entities. An APER virtual identity vi (i.e., pseudonym) is recognised by a public key Pub, which can be seen as evidence. However, presenting a public-key is meaningless until you link it to the current (or a previous) transaction by signing something with it, i.e., providing linkability. In our case, after the first transaction, the requested entity links the transaction with the pseudonym Pub: $link(tr_1,Pub)$. Then, after the second transaction, the requested entity does: $link(tr_1, Pub, tr_2)$ and so on. Thus, the pseudonym links a set of pieces of evidence together. If each transaction is non-PII/low positive impact and Pub considered as non-PII/no impact, the resulting evidence is: two low positive impacts from a tai point of view and three non-PII from a nymity point of view.

If not enough evidence is available under the chosen pseudonym, evidence not linked to this pseudonym may improve trustworthiness and allow the requesting entity to be granted the request. The entity may be willing to disclose further evidence to the requested entity in spite of potential increased privacy loss. So, a protocol for disclosing to the requested entity that some evidence can be linked is needed. We present such a protocol, called the privacy/trust trade process (depicted in Fig. 6). In this process, the requested entity makes the decision that not enough evidence is available for granting and this fact should be disclosed to the requesting entity. So, after step 2, the requesting entity knows the tai of evidence that should be obtained.

In step 2.1, different potential evidence can be envisaged to be linked by the requesting entity. The choice of evidence should be based on the following principle:

The Minimal Linkability principle: No more evidence than needed should be linked.

The latter principle is a variant of the "Need-To-Know" principle. One of the reasons is that more trust implies more knowledge given out, thus less chance for privacy.

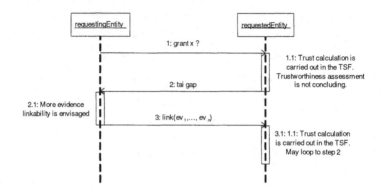

Fig. 6. Privacy/trust trade sequence diagram

Some thresholds should be set concerning the acceptable evidence that should be disclosed in step 3. Without such thresholds, an attacker may ask to retrieve all evidence (i.e., knowledge), which is what we want to prevent by using pseudonyms. If the user must confirm that some evidence can be linked, more care has to be taken into account. It is known that users can easily agree to sell privacy in stressed circumstances without thinking of the consequences [18], which are often irrevocable since privacy recovery is hard [16]. Alice, in order to get quick access to the large video display, may regret to present her full profile to the video club due to this small benefit compared to life-long spam messages. One way to prevent such abuse may be the existence of a broker where reasonable trades are listed (this also reduces interoperability issues). In practice, it may require an exchange of messages with trusted third parties to decide whether the trade is fair (within the current market price) or not. We propose to introduce another partial order to cope with such abusive trade attack. The utility of a transaction is represented on a utility partial order (UO). An example UO may be:

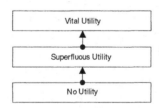

Fig. 7. Utility Order example

During a trade process, tai, nymity and utility must be balanced. Alice under the pseudonym Pub requests Bob to grant the transaction tr_x of utility u from Alice's point of view. In step 1.1, if Pub had done two previous transactions tr_1 and tr_2 with Bob, Bob's TSF checks if the trustworthiness given by this previous evidence is enough to grant tr_x. In this case, the trustworthiness assessment is not concluding, so the TSF computes the z tai of evidence missing, called tai gap. Alice's TSF is noticed that z tai of evidence is missing.

In step 2.1, Alice's TSF does the following 2-step algorithm, called link selection engagement (liseng) algorithm:

1. *Search link of evidence expected to fill the tai gap but minimizing nymity*: As an example, we assume that the TSF cannot guarantee that all recommenders of Pub can exhaustively be found and queried in a timely manner. All transactions directly done between Alice and Bob should have been taken into account by Bob's TSF. However, Alice has done 2 transactions with Charles, tr_{1r} and tr_{2r}. We assume that these two transactions may not have been recommended by Charles to Bob in the first round. We end up with one set[9]: link(tr_{1r}, tr_{2r}, Pub). Alice has done transactions with other people than Charles and Bob but tr_{1r} and tr_{2r} fills the tai gap and adding more transactions would increase nymity.

2. *Check that nymity of the selected link of evidence is reasonable compared to the utility*: if yes engage in further trade steps; else abort the trade. We assume that each utility level is associated with a maximum nymity threshold. This check corresponds to a cost/benefit analysis. So, the risk engine of the TSF should be responsible for carrying out this analysis. The tai gap message may be treated as a request from the requested entity to the requesting entity. If the trustworthiness of the requesting entity in keeping private information for personal use only is available, it is possible to have finer PAO. A level may be: PII-information kept for personal use. For example, this level happens when users subscribe to privacy policies specifying that their private information will not be disclosed to third parties. The consequence of detecting breached privacy policies is lower trustworthiness. In this case, the check also uses the trust engine as in the standard decision-making process of a TSF.

A difficult aspect of the liseng algorithm is to take into account the sequencing of interactions. Pieces of evidence revealed before the current interaction can impact the selection as well as future pieces of evidence due to the combination of pieces of evidence. For example, for two candidates ev_1 and ev_2 with same tai but different nymity ($nymity_1 < nymity_2$), in the scope of this specific interaction, ev_1 should be chosen. However, if a future interaction links ev_3 with $nymity_{link(ev1,ev3)} > nymity_{link(ev2,ev3)}$, the choice becomes more difficult.

By allowing any entity to make recommendations we directly support a change of identity, where evidence can be transferred and linked to the new identity through a recommendation, without explicitly linking the two identities. This limits the extent of the profile that can be built for a given virtual identity, thereby reducing the violation of privacy resulting from a single transaction being linked to the real-world identity of a user. So, in step 3, a list of pseudonyms owned by the requesting entity could be sent back as potential new recommenders. If the requested entity has not already used

---

[9] There are two choices to retrieve the recommendations rec_1 and rec_2 associated with tr_{1r} and tr_{2r}: either Alice's TSF contacts Charles to get the signed recommendations and passes them back to Alice, or Bob's TSF contacts Charles to get the signed recommendations.

these pseudonyms as recommenders, it would do so. However, the tai of evidence provided by these entities would be discounted by the recommendation process. This is why it may be more beneficial to make the link between some pseudonyms explicit as explained in the next section.

4 Linking Evidence on Multiple Virtual Identities

In the above privacy/trust trade model, we said that a virtual identity vi is a set of linked pieces of evidence, indeed vi is the result of linking evidence with its own nymity and tai. In our example implementation, evidence is linked through digital signature validation. In this case, it is possible to link virtual identities as it is possible to link any other piece of evidence. For example, we may have link(Pub', vi) = link(Pub', tr_1, ..., tr_i, ..., tr_n, Pub) with tr_i being all n transactions linked to Pub. It is worth noticing that we also implicitly link all m transactions tr'$_j$ linked to Pub': link(Pub', vi) = link(tr'$_1$, ..., tr'$_j$, ..., tr'$_m$, Pub', tr_1, ..., tr_i, ..., tr_n, Pub) = link(vi', vi). In our payment scenario [17], customers are given the possibility to generate pseudonyms on demand in order to protect their privacy. However, due to the resulting division of evidence between virtual entities, it takes more time for these virtual entities to reach the same trustworthiness than for a unique virtual identity. So, customers can link virtual identities during trust calculation in the privacy/trust trade process (depicted in Fig. 6).

This new prospect for linking evidence allows us to envisage new linked evidence in step 2.1 of Fig. 6). So, in step 3, a list of pseudonyms owned by the requesting entity could be sent back as potential new evidence of the form: link(Pub_1,..., Pub_i,...,Pub_n) with Pri_i known by the requesting entity for all i. In step 1 of the liseng algorithm (using the example we presented in Section 3 when describing this algorithm), another choice may be to use two transactions, tr_3 and tr_4, that Alice under the pseudonym Pub' did with Bob: the resulting link can be specified with more or less explicit linked evidence depending on what can be implicitly linked. For example, if the TSF does not guarantee that all transactions done under a specific pseudonym can be available in a timely manner (especially for recommendations), the explicit link should be longer: link(tr_3, tr_4, Pub', Pub). If any transaction is guaranteed to be known by all entities[10], it would be sufficient with a link of this type: link(Pub', Pub). Anyway, the first choice that we had, link(tr_{1r}, tr_{2r}, Pub) has low nymity because the implicit link appears somewhere in clear and can be established if other legitimate means are used. From a tai point of view, both give the same tai if each transaction gives the same tai and linking two keys is not acknowledged further. However, link(tr_3, tr_4, Pub', Pub) has potentially high nymity (it is intuitively higher than link(tr_{1r}, tr_{2r}, Pub) because Pub' could be used in another context and/or in the future whilst still being linked). Then, the link between two virtual identities is permanent and cannot be easily undone (e.g., as explained at the end of this section, when we link two keys, we use the fact that an entity cryptographically shows the ownership of both private keys of the two pseudonyms). It is important to note that transactions are

---

[10] It is a strong assumption to guarantee global propagation of information. This assumption is not realistic in most scenarios (e.g., when random disconnection is possible).

often temporary, while linking transaction and/or virtual identities is permanent. This must be taken into account when estimating the utility of a given transaction.

We emphasize that care should be taken when linked evidence on multiple virtual identities is assessed. The most important requirement is to avoid counting the same evidence twice when it is presented as part of two different pseudonyms or overcounting overlapping evidence. In some cases, passing recommendations in the form of a simple trust value, instead of all supporting information[11], does not fulfil the later requirement. Assessing evidence may require analysis and comparison of each piece of evidence to other pieces of evidence. For example, let us assume that we have the relation depicted in Fig. 8 and two trust values tv_1 and tv_2.

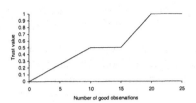

Fig. 8. Example relation between observations and trust values

If $tv_1 = 0.5$, whatever value tv_2 is, we cannot compute the combined trust value without knowing the number of good observations, which is at a level of evidence deeper than the level of trust values. In fact, assessing linked evidence requires great care and implementations may vary depending on the complexity of trust-lifecycle [19] and trust dynamics [6]. When recommendations are used, previous self-recommendations (i.e., recommendations from virtual identities belonging to the same entity) are also not easy to take into account. If this is part of a low cost mechanism for introducing new pseudonyms, it may be correct to simply discard the recommendations in the calculation. Another choice might be to consider such recommendations as evidence of untrustworthiness. Let vi_1 and vi_2 be two pseudonyms of the same entity. At the first interaction with the requested entity, vi_2 is used as a recommender for vi_1 due to the recommendation rec_{21}. So, the entity has now link(vi_1,tr_1,rec_{21}) for trustworthiness assessment of vi_1. At the second interaction, vi_1 discloses link(vi_1,vi_2). Logically, the tai of rec_{21} needs to be revised, e.g., by discarding rec_{21} in the tai of the resulting evidence.

We shortly propose our view for a group of entities. A group may consist of a number of entities, the exact number of entities being unknown as well as the virtual identities of the entities part of this group. In this case, it is valid to assume that trust should be formed and built as if the group of entities would be indeed one conceptual virtual identity. For example, if a group signature scheme is used to sign and send messages

---

[11] We agree that only passing the trust value may improve performance and may be better from a privacy point of view than all evidence information but it may also decrease interoperability as highlighted here, may show how another entity computes trust from evidence which may help to mount attacks and may reveal feelings towards other entities which may not be welcome.

on behalf of the entire team. In addition to the fact that powerful entity recognition could discern entities from such conceptual virtual identity, we see another case where a different approach would be welcome, especially when collaboration is from many-to-one entities. If two or more already known virtual identities make a specific request under an explicit group (i.e., the different members are known), the group should not be considered as a completely new virtual identity for several reasons (e.g., past history may show untrustworthiness or it may simply be unfair and inefficient to rebuild trust from scratch). Thus, a mechanism is needed to assess evidence from many virtual identities.

Combining levels of trust in entities is also very important when the ER process is used. The outcome of ER [15] can be a set of n principals p (i.e., virtual entity or pseudonym) associated with a level of confidence in recognition lcr:

$$\sum_{i=0}^{n}(p_i, lcr_i), e.g.\{(Pub_1, APERLevel1), (Pub_2, APERLevel1)\}$$

The previous example occurs when an APER claim is signed by two keys[12] and both signatures are valid. It may be because both keys are indeed pseudonyms for the same entity or two entities decided to form a group and sign the claim as one entity. However, we envision that ER can be more proactive and uses evidence not directly provided by the requesting entities to compute a probability distribution of recognised entities. A range of methods can be used to compute this distribution (e.g., using fuzzy logic or Bayes). A person among n persons enters a building which is equipped with a biometric ER scheme. The outcome of recognition demonstrates hesitation between two persons: p_2 and p_3 are recognized at 45% and 55% respectively. So, all other principals are given 0%. We have:

$$OutcomeOfRecognition= \sum_{i=0}^{n}lcr_i\,p_i =0*p_1+0,45*p_2+0,55*p_3+...+0*p_i+...+0*p_n$$

If the level of trust in an entity is given by a value between [0,1], let say that p_2 is 0.5 and p_3 is 0.6. We then apply our simplest end-to-end trust model [15]:

    End-to-end trust = aFunctionOf(Confidence In Recognition, Level of Trust In Entity)
    End-to-end trust = Level Of Confidence * Level of Trust In Entity
    End-to-end trust = 0.45 * 0.5 + 0.55 * 0.6

Once again, we assess evidence on different entities and care should be taken during the assessment.

Finally, we propose the following implementation[13] to carry out the privacy/trust trade process when pseudonyms are linked. Let p_1 be the requesting entity and p_2 the requested entity, they exchange APER claims with special keywords in Ctxt:

1: $p_1 \rightarrow p_2$: [GRANTX]p_1
2: $p_2 \rightarrow p_1$: [TAIGAP,HINT]p_2
3: $p_1 \rightarrow p_2$: [LINK]p_1,...,p_i,...

In step 2, HINT is optional and may contain hints for optimizing the liseng on the requesting entity's side. In fact, it may say which recommenders have been used for

---

[12] We restrain from using other technical trust clues (e.g., key length and algorithm).

[13] We use the notation: X is the special keyword used in the Ctxt of a claim, p is a principal; $p_1 \rightarrow p_2$ means that an APER Claim is sent from p_1 to p_2; [X]p_1,...,p_i,...,p_n means that X is signed by several private keys, e.g., p_i's Pri.

the first round of the trustworthiness assessment. It would then be known that it is useless to send back a link for the same recommenders. In our scenario, the HINT consists of a list of other pseudonyms (video clubs) owned by the video club holding company. Then, the liseng should try to link evidence to these pseudonyms. In step 3, the LINK lists other Pubs that are linked to p_1 and the claim must be signed by the Pri of each listed Pub. For example, in Alice's scenario, we have:

1: $p_1 \rightarrow p_2$: [GRANTX("rent large video display")]PubAliceSunnyVillage
2: $p_2 \rightarrow p_1$: [TAIGAP("strong positive impact"),HINT("PubVC1")]PubVC2
3: $p_1 \rightarrow p_2$: [LINK("PubAliceSunnyVillage,PubAliceRainyTown")]PubAliceSunny Village,PubAliceRainyTown

Concerning the liseng, the provided hint allows the requesting entity's TSF to search straightaway evidence that can be linked to PubVC1 and find the link with PubAliceRainyTown.

5 Related Work

Although automated trust negotiation (ATN) [20] is argued to establish trust between strangers, the approach considerably differs from the TSF's approach described in Section 1 (e.g., as used in SECURE). The method consists of iteratively disclosing digital credentials between two entities. Through this sequence of bilateral credential disclosures, trust is incrementally founded. The notion of trust formation and assessment based on past experience does not explicitly appear in ATN. However, the notion of negotiation underlined the importance of the Minimal Linkability principle and that care should be taken when more trust is asked before choosing to disclose linked evidence. In ATN, revocation is based on certificate revocation whereas in TSF-like approach the trustworthiness may be decreased without the use of certificates. In fact, certificates could be seen as another type of evidence and included in the list of evidence of our privacy/trust model. Revocation implies that a piece of evidence based on a credential also varies over time. It is beyond the scope of the paper to fully study credentials but the following points are worth mentioning. First of all, credentials can be redundant. The issue appears when virtual identities are combined. Patient ID could be linked with another credential (e.g., Driver License) as well as Employee ID. However, when Patient ID is linked to Employee ID, the logic would be that Driver License should be counted once. Winslett encourages more work on the issue of multiple virtual identities and this paper is a contribution on this topic. Also, ATN is known to have not fully resolved privacy issues [21]. In our approach, it is possible to use pseudonyms and to stop using a specific pseudonym. This has the effect to break too much evidence accumulation.

Another type of evidence that can be used in our privacy/trust trade model is reputation. By reputation, we mean that a piece of evidence on the trustworthiness of another entity is given by a supposed large number of entities but unknown. Again, it is not clear how reputation should be combined if the goal is to avoid overcounting overlapping evidence.

Wagella et al. [19] use trustworthiness of an information receiver to make the decision on whether private information should be disclosed or not, which is another way to envisage the relation between trust and privacy. However, as highlighted in this paper, it may be difficult to evaluate trustworthiness in first place without enough evidence linked with the receiving entity.

The work on modelling unlinkability [9] and pseudonymity [4, 8] is valuable towards founding privacy/trust trade. Previous work on pseudonym credential system should be useful to formally prove (in future work) that an entity really owns different private keys. The Sybil attack [3], which challenges the use of recommendations, is also worth keeping in mind when providing means to create virtual identities at will without centralized authority.

6 Conclusion

There is an inherent conflict between trust and privacy because both depend on knowledge about an entity but in the opposite ways. Although trust allows us to accept risk and engage in actions with a potential harmful outcome, a computational TSF must take into account that humans need (or have the right to) privacy. Trust is based on knowledge about the other entity: the more evidence about past behaviour is known, the better the prediction of future behaviour will be. This is why we propose to use pseudonymity as a level of indirection, which allows the formation of trust without exposing the real-world identity.

However, depending on what benefits can be reaped through trustworthiness, people may be willing to trade part of their privacy for increased trustworthiness: hence, contextual privacy/trust trade is needed. We propose a model for privacy/trust trade based on linkability of pieces of evidence. If insufficient evidence is available under the chosen pseudonym, more evidence may be linked to this pseudonym in order to improve trustworthiness and grant the request. We present a protocol for explicitly disclosing to the requested entity that some evidence can be linked. Some thresholds should be set concerning the acceptable evidence that should be disclosed. This is why we introduce the liseng algorithm to ensure that the Minimal Linkability principle is taken into account. During a trade process, tai, nymity and utility must be balanced.

We then explain that it may be more beneficial to make the link between some pseudonyms explicit (e.g., to avoid discounted evidence or reduce the time to reach trustworthiness due to division of evidence between virtual identities). We show how we implemented this on top of the APER scheme.

We emphasize that care should be taken when linked evidence on multiple virtual identities is assessed, especially when pseudonyms are linked during the privacy trade/process but also when groups and the outcome of entity recognition result in a set of possible principals (as defined in ER).

As levels of privacy asset, trust assessment impact and utility are key metrics to carry out minimal linkability, we are trying to enhance the trade in our prototype with real metrics on privacy loss and trust gain extracted from localized payment transactions.

Acknowledgments. This work is sponsored by the European Union, which funds the IST-2001-32486 SECURE project and the IST-2001-34910 iTrust Working Group.

References

[1]   V. Cahill, et al., "Using Trust for Secure Collaboration in Uncertain Environments", in *Pervasive Computing*, vol. 2(3), IEEE, 2003.

[2]   T. M. Cooley, "A Treatise on the Law of Torts", Callaghan, Chicago, 1888.

[3]   J. R. Douceur, "The Sybil Attack", in *Proceedings of the 1st International Workshop on Peer-to-Peer Systems*, 2002.

[4]   I. Goldberg, "A Pseudonymous Communications Infrastructure for the Internet", PhD Thesis, University of California at Berkeley, 2000.

[5]   X. Jiang, J. I. Hong, and J. A. Landay, "Approximate Information Flows: Socially Based Modeling of Privacy in Ubiquitous Computing", in *Proceedings of Ubicomp 2002*, pp. 176-193, Springer-Verlag, 2002.

[6]   C. M. Jonker and J. Treur, "Formal Analysis of Models for the Dynamics of Trust based on Experiences", in *Proceedings of the Workshop on Modelling Autonomous Agents in a Multi-Agent World*, 1999.

[7]   A. Jøsang, "The right type of trust for distributed systems", in *Proceedings of the 1996 New Security Paradigms Workshop*, ACM, 1996.

[8]   A. Kobsa and J. Schreck, "Privacy through Pseudonymity in User-Adaptive Systems", in *ACM Transactions on Internet Technology*, vol. 3 (2), 2003.

[9]   S. Köpsell and S. Steinbrecher, "Modeling Unlinkability", in *Proceedings of the Third Workshop on Privacy Enhancing Technologies*, 2003.

[10]   M. Langheinrich, "Privacy by Design - Principles of Privacy-Aware Ubiquitous Systems", in *Proceedings of Ubicomp 2001*, Springer, 2001.

[11]   S. Marsh, "Formalising Trust as a Computational Concept", PhD Thesis, Department of Mathematics, University of Stirling, 1994.

[12]   A. H. Maslow, "Motivation and Personality", Harper, 1954.

[13]   D. McKnight and N. L. Chervany, "The Meanings of Trust", MISRC 96-04, University of Minnesota, 1996.

[14]   SECURE project, Website, http://secure.dsg.cs.tcd.ie.

[15]   J.-M. Seigneur, S. Farrell, C. D. Jensen, E. Gray, and Y. Chen, "End-to-end Trust Starts with Recognition", in *Proceedings of the First International Conference on Security in Pervasive Computing*, LNCS, Springer, 2003.

[16]   J.-M. Seigneur and C. D. Jensen, "Privacy Recovery with Disposable Email Addresses", in *Special Issue on "Understanding Privacy", December 2003*, vol. 1(6), IEEE Security&Privacy, 2003.

[17]   J.-M. Seigneur and C. D. Jensen, "Trust Enhanced Ubiquitous Payment without Too Much Privacy Loss", in *Proceedings of SAC 2004*, ACM, 2004.

[18]   S. Spiekermann, J. Grossklags, and B. Berendt, "E-privacy in 2nd Generation E-Commerce: Privacy Preferences versus actual Behavior", in *Proceedings of the 3rd Conference on Electronic Commerce*, ACM, 2001.

[19]   W. Wagealla, M. Carbone, C. English, S. Terzis, and P. Nixon, "A Formal Model of Trust Lifecycle Management", in *Proceedings of FAST2003*, 2003.

[20]   M. Winslett, "An Introduction to Trust Negotiation", Proceedings of the First International Conference on Trust Management, LNCS, Springer, 2003.

[21]   T. Yu and M. Winslett, "A Unified Scheme for Resource Protection in Automated Trust Negotiation", in *Proceedings of the IEEE Symposium on Security and Privacy*, 2003.

Supporting Privacy in Decentralized Additive Reputation Systems

Elan Pavlov, Jeffrey S. Rosenschein, and Zvi Topol

Hebrew University, Givat Ram, Jerusalem 91904, Israel,
{elan, jeff, zvit}@cs.huji.ac.il,
http://www.cs.huji.ac.il/~{elan,jeff, zvit}

Abstract. Previous studies have been suggestive of the fact that reputation ratings may be provided in a strategic manner for reasons of reciprocation and retaliation, and therefore may not properly reflect the trustworthiness of rated parties. It thus appears that supporting privacy of feedback providers could improve the quality of their ratings. We argue that supporting perfect privacy in decentralized reputation systems is impossible, but as an alternative present three probabilistic schemes that support partial privacy. On the basis of these schemes, we offer three protocols that allow ratings to be privately provided with high probability in decentralized additive reputation systems.

1 Introduction

In recent years, reputation systems have emerged as a way to reduce the risk entailed in interactions among total strangers in electronic marketplaces. Such systems collect and aggregate feedback about past behavior of participants in electronic transactions, so as to derive reputation scores assumed to predict likely future behavior.

Centralized reputation systems, such as the system in use by the electronic auction site eBay [1], collect and store reputation ratings from feedback providers in a centralized reputation database. These ratings are then processed to produce a publicly available reputation measure that can be obtained by querying the database. In eBay, for example, both buyers and sellers participating in a transaction may provide one of three possible feedbacks: positive (+1), neutral (0), and negative (-1). The reputation score of a user is simply the sum of his accumulated ratings over a period of six months.

Decentralized reputation systems, on the other hand, do not make use of a central repository to collect and report reputation ratings [2]. In this type of system, participants help one another with the provision of reputation ratings in order to evaluate the trustworthiness of potential transaction partners. Each participant is responsible for his own local repository of reputation through the collection and propagation of feedback when needed.

One concern about reputation systems (which has received relatively little attention in the trust and reputation management literature), is that of feedback

C.D. Jensen et al. (Eds.): iTrust 2004, LNCS 2995, pp. 108–119, 2004.

providers' privacy. An empirical study conducted by Resnick *et al.* [3] on data sets extracted from eBay's reputation system reported a high correlation between buyer and seller ratings. Moreover, more than 99% of the feedback provided was positive.

This might be due to the fact that mutually satisfying transactions are simply the (overwhelming) norm. However, it might also be the case that when feedback providers' identities are publicly known, reputation ratings can be provided in a strategic manner for reasons of reciprocation and retaliation, not properly reflecting the trustworthiness of the rated parties. For example, a user may have an incentive to provide a high rating because he expects the user he rates to reciprocate, and provide a high rating for either the current interaction or possible future ones.

This type of strategic manipulation in the process of feedback provision is likely to occur also in decentralized reputation systems. There too, agents providing feedback would like to ensure that the ratings they provide cannot be abused by malicious agents in a way that can affect them negatively in the future. An example of such malicious behavior might occur if individual ratings were first reported to the rated agent, who can then retaliate or reciprocate on his turn (when he is given an opportunity to rate the feedback providers).

The logic of anonymous feedback to a reputation system is thus analogous to the logic of anonymous voting in a political system. It potentially encourages truthfulness by guaranteeing secrecy and freedom from explicit or implicit influence. Although this freedom might be exploited by dishonest feedback providers, who tend to report exaggerated feedbacks, it seems highly beneficial for honest ones, protecting the latter from being influenced by strategic manipulation issues as described above.

1.1   Structure of Paper

The rest of the paper is organized as follows. Section 2 describes the problem setting with which we are dealing, while Section 3 presents the notion of Decentralized Additive Reputation Systems and gives an example of one — the Beta Reputation system. Section 4 proves an impossibility result and suggests methods of partially circumventing it. Section 5 then suggests three protocols achieving probabilistic privacy in decentralized additive reputation systems. Section 6 surveys related work, and Section 7 concludes by summarizing our results and suggesting directions for future research.

2   Problem Setting

We assume that each user in the system is represented by an *agent*, which performs necessary computations and communication activities with other agents, on behalf of the user. We also assume authenticated, secure channels between every two users. Such channels can be achieved via standard technologies such as SSL (Secure Sockets Layer).

We are concerned with the following problem: a *querying agent* A_q has to decide whether to interact with a potential partner, the *target agent* A_t. A_q has incomplete information about A_t. It either has no prior knowledge about A_t's past behavior at all, since both agents do not have a common history of interactions, or its experience with A_t is too limited or outdated, so that it cannot derive a meaningful reputation measure regarding the trustworthiness of the target agent.

In a decentralized reputation system, A_q consults a group of agents, or *witnesses*, $\{W_1, W_2, ..., W_n\}$, considered to have a reputation score regarding A_t. One way to obtain such a set of witnesses is through a series of referrals from agents residing in the same social network of A_t (see [2] for further details about how to obtain such a set of witnesses). We denote the reputation rating of witness i by r_i. Although r_i is generally represented by a vector of finite dimension (measuring reputation over different contexts of interest), we will assume without loss of generality throughout the paper that r_i is a scalar. We are interested in a method assuring that whenever feedbacks received from the witnesses are combined in an additive manner, their privacy is properly maintained, i.e., feedbacks are not revealed to any other agent in the system, nor to possible third parties.

We divide agents participating in the feedback provision process into two types: *curious but non-malicious agents* (which we call "curious agents") and *malicious agents*. Curious agents follow the protocol; that is, curious witnesses provide honest feedback about the target agent, and do not try to interfere with the correct flow of the protocol in order to change or corrupt the result obtained at the end of the process (the combined reputation rating). The main concern about such agents is that they might try to reveal reputation ratings in different ways, including collusion with other agents.

Malicious agents, on the other hand, might try to actually tamper with the protocols, provide dishonest feedback in order to bias the combined reputation rating according to their interests, or even render the resulting rating unusable.

In our scenario, the querying agent can act only as a curious agent. Clearly, it would not be in its interest to interfere with the rating calculation in any way. An example of a querying agent acting curiously would be if the target agent itself masquerades as a querying agent in order to reveal the reputation ratings of witnesses.

3   Decentralized Additive Reputation Systems

We here define Decentralized Additive Reputation Systems, and follow with an example of such a reputation system, the Beta Reputation system.[1]

Definition 1. *Reputation System R is said to be a Decentralized Additive Reputation System if it satisfies two requirements:*

---

[1] Our approach in this paper is broadly applicable to Decentralized Additive Reputation Systems, but we specifically present the Beta Reputation system as one example.

1. *Feedback collection, combination, and propagation are implemented in a decentralized way.*
2. *Combination of feedbacks provided by agents is calculated in an additive manner.*

The Beta Reputation system presented in [4] and described in the next subsection is an example of a reputation system satisfying both requirements. eBay's reputation system, on the other hand, satisfies only the second requirement, i.e., it is additive but centralized.

3.1   The Beta Reputation System

The Beta Reputation system is based on the beta-family of probability density functions which are typically used to represent a posteriori probability distributions of binary events. The beta functions are continuous functions of the form $f(p|a, b)$ which can be expressed as:

$$f(p|a, b) = \frac{\Gamma(a + b)}{\Gamma(a)\Gamma(b)} p^{(a-1)} (1 - p)^{(b-1)} \tag{1}$$

where Γ is the gamma function, a generalization of the factorial function to real values, $0 \le p \le 1$, $a > 0$, $b > 0$, $p \ne 0$ if $a < 1$ and $p \ne 1$ if $b < 1$. The expectation of the beta distribution can be shown to be:

$$E(p) = \frac{a}{a + b} \tag{2}$$

Given a binary stochastic process with two possible outcomes $\{o_1, o_2\}$, the probability p of observing o_1 in the future as a function of past observations of r_1 instances of o_1 and r_2 instances of o_2 is given by: $a = r_1 + 1$, $b = r_2 + 1$, where $r_1 \ge 0$ and $r_2 \ge 0$. The expectation can now be written as:

$$E(p) = \frac{r_1 + 1}{r_1 + r_2 + 2} \tag{3}$$

Letting o_1 be a positive outcome of an interaction between two agents and o_2 be a negative one from the point of view of the rating agent, r_1 and r_2 could be seen as the degree of satisfaction and dissatisfaction respectively. Since the agent's satisfaction after a transaction is not necessarily binary, (r_1, r_2) is represented as a pair of continuous values. The expectation value is then defined to be the reputation rating about the target agent:

$$Rep(r_1, r_2) = \frac{r_1 + 1}{r_1 + r_2 + 2} \tag{4}$$

Let A_t be the target agent and let A_1 and A_2 be two agents that interacted with A_t in the past. Let $Rep^1(r_1^1, r_2^1)$ be A_1's reputation rating about A_t and let $Rep^2(r_1^2, r_2^2)$ be the reputation rating of A_2. The combined reputation value is then obtained by calculating:

$$r_1^* = r_1^1 + r_1^2 \tag{5}$$

$$r_2^* = r_2^1 + r_2^2 \tag{6}$$

and plugging the results into (4), to obtain $Rep^*(r_1^*, r_2^*)$. This additive property of the Beta Reputation system, which is both commutative and associative, could be generalized to any number of agents.

4   Witness Selection

An inherent problem with decentralized reputation systems is the collusion of $n - 1$ witnesses along with a dishonest (either curious or malicious) querying agent in order to reveal the reputation information of an honest witness. The querying agent can *choose* $n - 1$ dishonest agents and a single honest agent. If the function calculating reputation is reversible, then there is no protocol that can anonymously calculate reputation. This yields the following lemma:

Lemma 1. *For a reversible reputation function F that accepts n witnesses and outputs a reputation, if there are $n - 1$ dishonest witnesses, there is no protocol that deterministically anonymously calculates reputation.*

Proof. For any protocol there might be $n-1$ dishonest witnesses and one honest one. If the querying agent is malicious then he can create such a set deterministically. Thus, collusion between the n dishonest agents would expose the reputation score of the honest witness.

To circumvent this inherent limitation, we look at probabilistic methods of ensuring that there is a large number of honest witnesses.

Lemma 2. *Let $N > 1$ be the number of potential witnesses and let $n > 0$, $n < N$ be the number of witnesses participating in the process. Let $b < N$ be the number of dishonest agents in N. If honest agents are uniformly distributed over N, then there exists a witness selection scheme that guarantees at least two honest witnesses with probability greater than $(1 - \frac{1}{n})(\frac{N-b-1}{N-1})$.*

Proof. Consider the following witness selection scheme: A_q chooses the first witness W_1. Each witness chosen, with probability $1 - \frac{1}{n}$, chooses another witness to participate in the feedback collection process and with probability $\frac{1}{n}$ does not invite additional witnesses. At some point, an honest witness is chosen. Let W_h be the first honest witness to be chosen. If b' dishonest witnesses were chosen before W_h, then W_h chooses another honest witness with probability $P_r \geq (1 - \frac{1}{n})(\frac{N-b-1}{N-b'-1}) \geq (1 - \frac{1}{n})(\frac{N-b-1}{N-1})$.

Similar witness selection schemes can be implemented using protocols for leader selection resilient to linear size coalitions, such as the one described in [5]. Witness selection is equivalent to leader selection; thus, n witnesses are selected by n activations of the leader selection protocol. It is also possible to use the same instance of the protocol to select more than one witness.

Sometimes it is not enough to ensure that there is a large number of honest witnesses in the group; we might also need to make sure that there is a predefined proportion between the size of the group and the number of honest witnesses in it, as in the case of Section 5.3. This is achieved by the following lemma, provided that A_q is honest.

Lemma 3. *Let $N > 0$ be the number of potential witnesses and let $n > 0$, $n < N$ be the number of witnesses participating in the process. Let $b < N$ be the number of dishonest agents in N. If honest agents are uniformly distributed over N, then there exists a witness selection scheme that guarantees at least $n(\frac{N-b-n}{N})$ honest witnesses in the group of witnesses participating in the process, with high probability.*

Proof. Consider the following witness selection scheme: A_q chooses the first witness W_1. At this point, the size of the group of witnesses participating in the process k is 2. Given a group of size k, the agents in the group collectively flip a weighted coin in order to decide whether to extend the group. With probability $1 - \frac{1}{n}$ they choose at random another agent from N to join the group, and with probability $\frac{1}{n}$ they stop. The expected number of coin tosses until the group stops is n. At each coin toss, the probability of choosing an honest witness to join the group is greater than $\frac{N-b-n}{N}$; thus, the expected number of honest witnesses in the group is greater than $n(\frac{N-b-n}{N})$. If we denote $\mu = n(\frac{N-b-n}{N})$, then by Chernoff bounds (see for example [6]), the probability that the number of honest witnesses is substantially smaller than μ, namely $(1-\delta)\mu$, is less than $e^{-\frac{\mu\delta^2}{2}}$.

This type of collective coin flipping scheme can be implemented as follows: the agents agree on value v, $0 \leq v \leq n$. Every agent i chooses at random and independently $log_2(n)$ bits, x_i, and sends them to the other agents in the group. Each agent calculates $x = x_1 \oplus x_2 \oplus \ldots \oplus x_n$. If $x = v$ the agents stop, otherwise the agents continue. The decision about which new witness is to join the group could be rendered random in a similar way. Note that if at least one honest witness is present, then the value of x is guaranteed to be random. This scheme requires $\sum_{k=2}^{n+1} k^2 = O(n^3)$ messages among the agents.

5   Privacy in Decentralized Additive Reputation Systems

In this section, we present three different protocols achieving privacy in Decentralized Additive Reputation Systems. The basic idea behind the protocols is to consider the feedback provided by each witness to be his private information, or *secret*. The sum of secrets represents the combined reputation rating, and should be constructed without revealing the secrets.

5.1   Towards Achieving Privacy

One protocol achieving privacy in the presence of curious but non-malicious agents is the following:

1. Initialization Step: the querying agent, A_q, orders the agents in a circle: $A_q \rightarrow W_1 \rightarrow W_2 \rightarrow \ldots \rightarrow W_n \rightarrow A_q$ and sends each witness i the identity of his successor in the circle, i.e., witness $i+1$. W_n is sent the identity of A_q.
2. A_q chooses $r_q \neq 0$ at random and sends it to W_1.
3. Upon reception of r_p from his predecessor in the circle, each agent W_i $i = 1 \ldots n$ calculates $r_p + r_i$, where r_i is the reputation score of W_i about the target agent, and sends it to his successor in the circle.
4. Upon reception of the feedback from W_n, A_q subtracts r_q from it and plugs the result into the additive reputation system engine, that calculates the combined reputation rating.

Lemma 4. *If agents do not collude, then at the end of the protocol the querying agent obtains the sum of the feedbacks, such that feedbacks are not revealed to any of the agents.*

Proof. Every witness i adds in stage 3 his reputation rating to the number he previously received from his predecessor in the circle, so W_n sends to A_q the sum $\sum_{i=1}^{n}(r_i) + r_q$. Therefore, in stage 4, when A_q subtracts from this sum his random number r_q, he obtains the sum of the feedbacks. The random number r_q that A_q contributes at stage 2 masks the feedback provided by W_1, as it is different from zero, so W_2 doesn't reveal it. From this point in the protocol, no agent can guess any of the feedbacks provided by his predecessors.

If we consider transmissions of r_p between two adjacent agents in the circle as a single message, we can see that in this scheme $O(n)$ messages are passed among the agents.

A prominent drawback of this approach is its lack of resilience to collusion among agents. Two witnesses, W_{i-1} and W_{i+1}, $i = 2 \ldots n-1$, separated by a single link in the circle, namely W_i, could collude against W_i and reveal its private information, i.e., his feedback, by subtracting the rating transmitted by W_{i-1} from the one transmitted to W_{i+1}.

In the following subsections we will provide a way to overcome this vulnerability through the description of two protocols resilient to collusion of up to $n-1$ witnesses with high probability.

5.2   Privacy through Secret Splitting

In this subsection, we present a simple protocol that provides privacy for curious agents, yet is resilient with high probability to collusion of up to $n-1$ agents, if witnesses are selected as described in the first witness selection scheme proposed in Section 4.

1. Initialization Step: A_q sends to the witnesses $\{W_1, ..., W_n\}$ the details of all agents participating in the process, i.e., identities of the n witnesses and itself, and chooses r_q at random.

2. Each of the $n + 1$ agents participating in the protocol splits its secret, i.e., its reputation score, into $n+1$ shares in the following way: agent i chooses n random numbers $s_{i,1}, ..., s_{i,n}$, and calculates $s_i = r_i - \sum_{k=1}^{n}(s_{i,k})$. He keeps s_i and sends $s_{i,1}, ..., s_{i,n}$ to the n other agents, such that each agent j receives share $s_{i,j}$.
3. Each agent j calculates $val_j = \sum_{i=1}^{n}(s_{i,j}) + s_j$, and sends val_j to the querying agent.
4. The querying agent calculates, upon reception of val_i $i = 1 \ldots n$ from the n witnesses, $r = \sum_{j=1}^{n+1}(val_j) - r_q$ and provides r to the reputation engine.

Lemma 5. *If the agents participating in the protocol are curious, then at the end of the last stage, the querying agent obtains the sum of the feedbacks, such that feedbacks are not revealed to any of the agents with probability greater than* $(1 - \frac{1}{n})(\frac{N-b-1}{N-1})$.

Proof. At stage 2 of the protocol, each agent i distributes n random shares, but keeps in private a share s_i, that along with the distributed shares uniquely defines his secret. At stage 3, each agent sums his private share along with n random numbers he receives from the other agents, masking his private share, such that when he sends this sum to the querying agent, his private share cannot be revealed, unless the other $n-1$ witnesses and the querying agent form a coalition against him. The latter case occurs with probability less than $1 - (1 - \frac{1}{n})(\frac{N-b-1}{N-1})$, if agents are self-ordered as suggested in the first witness selection scheme in Section 4. At stage 4, the querying agent calculates: $r = \sum_{j=1}^{n+1}(val_j) - r_q = \sum_{j=1}^{n+1}(\sum_{i=1}^{n}(s_{i,j}) + s_j) - r_q = \sum_{j=1}^{n+1}(r_j - s_j + s_j) - r_q = \sum_{j=1}^{n} r_j$ and thus obtains the sum of feedbacks.

This protocol requires $O(n^2)$ messages among the agents participating in the process, as opposed to $O(n)$ messages in the protocol from the previous subsection. On the other hand, the current protocol is resilient against collusion of up to $n - 1$ agents with high probability.

This protocol works well in the presence of curious agents, but malicious agents can tamper with it in various ways. A simple yet effective attack is the provision of reputation ratings out of range, such that the resulting reputation score is affected in an extreme way or is even rendered unusable. For example, if the reputation ratings should be positive integers in the range [1, 100] and there are 5 witnesses, one of the witnesses providing a reputation rating of 500 renders the resulting sum greater than 500, hence unusable. The following subsection presents another protocol that ensures that the provided reputation ratings lie within a predefined range.

5.3   Achieving Privacy Using Verifiable Secret Sharing

In this subsection, we suggest a protocol that achieves privacy in Decentralized Additive Reputation Systems, resilient with high probability to collusion of up to $n-1$ curious agents participating in the process, and supports validity checking of the feedback provided. We use the Pederson Verifiable Secret Sharing scheme [7], which is based on Shamir Secret Sharing [8] and a discrete-log commitment method, in a manner similar to what is described in [9]. Both the Shamir Secret Sharing scheme and the discrete logarithm commitment are homomorphic in nature, making them suitable building blocks to use with additive reputation systems.

One of the properties of the Shamir Secret Sharing scheme is its resilience to up to $n/2$ malicious agents. Thus, the presence of more than $n/2$ such agents might be problematic for an honest querying-agent. If witnesses are selected as described in the second witness selection scheme proposed in Section 4 and if $b < \frac{N}{2} - n$, then with high probability, there are less than $n/2$ malicious agents.

For the purpose of this protocol, we assume that the reputation rating provided by W_i, r_i, is an integer in the group G_q of prime order q. The protocol is as follows:

1. Initialization Step: A_q selects a group G_q of a large prime order q with generators g and h, where $log_g h$ is hard to find. He sends to the witnesses $\{W_1, \ldots, W_n\}$, g and h and the details of all agents participating in the process, i.e., the n witnesses and itself.

2. Witness i chooses two polynomials of degree n: $p^i(x) = p_0^i + p_1^i x + p_2^i x^2 + \ldots + p_n^i x^n$ and $q^i(x) = q_0^i + q_1^i x + q_2^i x^2 + \ldots + q_n^i x^n$. The witness then sets r_i as p_0^i. The other coefficients of the polynomials are chosen at random uniformly from G_q.

3. W_i sends to each agent j, $j = 1, \ldots, i-1, i+1, \ldots, n+1$, from the set $\{W_1, \ldots, W_{i-1}, W_{i+1}, \ldots, W_n, A_q\}$ the point j on his polynomials, i.e., $p^i(j)$ and $q^i(j)$ along with commitments on the coefficients of its polynomials of the form: $g^{p_0^i} h^{q_0^i}, \ldots, g^{p_n^i} h^{q_n^i}$.

4. Witness m, upon reception of $p^1(m), p^2(m), \ldots, p^{m-1}(m), p^{m+1}(m), \ldots, p^n(m)$ and $q^1(m), q^2(m), \ldots, q^{m-1}(m), q^{m+1}(m), \ldots, q^n(m)$, calculates $p^m(m), q^m(m), s_m = \sum_{i=1}^{n} p^i(m)$ and $t_m = \sum_{i=1}^{n} q^i(m)$, and sends s_m and t_m to A_q. A_q calculates $s_{n+1} = \sum_{i=1}^{n} p^i(n+1)$ and $t_{n+1} = \sum_{i=1}^{n} q^i(n+1)$.

5. Upon reception of $s_1, \ldots, s_n$ and $t_1, \ldots t_n$, A_q obtains $s(0)$, the reputation rating, where $s(x) = \sum_{i=1}^{n} p^i(x)$ in the following manner: it computes $\sum_{i=1}^{n+1} s_i L_i(0)$, where $L_i(0)$ is the Lagrange polynomial at 0, and in this case could be expressed by: $L_i(0) = \Pi_{j=1, j \neq i}^{n+1} \frac{j}{j-i}$.

At the end of the last stage of the protocol, A_q holds the sum of the reputation ratings provided, as required. At stages 4 and 5, agents can verify that the shares they received from the other agents are valid using the homomorphic property of the commitments received at the end of stage 3. Complaints about invalid shares may be resolved by the accused agent sending the disputed point on the polynomial to A_q, since A_q cannot use it to reconstruct his secret.

For stage 3 we need a practical zero knowledge proof for the validity of the reputation ratings to be conducted between the witnesses and the querying agent; such a proof is provided, e.g., by [9].

This protocol requires $O(n^3)$ messages to be passed among the agents (due to the witness selection scheme) and does not reveal the reputation ratings of the witnesses involved since no less than $n + 1$ different points on a polynomial of degree n are required for interpolation. It also requires linear work on the part of the agents.

6 Related Work

Much research concerning trust and reputation management has been conducted in recent years. Researchers have suggested different models of trust and reputation, both for centralized and decentralized systems. Most of the work on decentralized reputation systems, including [10,11,12], focus on efficient algorithms for distributed storage, collection and aggregation of feedbacks, but not on manipulative feedback provision.

Bin and Singh [2] propose a distributed reputation management system, where trust is modelled based on the Dempster-Shafer theory of evidence. In [13], they suggest a method for detection of deceptive feedback provision in their system, by applying a weighted majority algorithm adapted to belief functions. It is not clear, however, that their suggested scheme is efficient against wide-scale reciprocation and retaliation in the feedback provision process.

Dellarocas suggests in [14] a collaborative filtering-based method to deal with the problem of unfair ratings in reputation systems. His method is applicable to centralized reputation systems. It is not clear whether this method could be efficiently applied in the decentralized case.

There has been little work on privacy and anonymity concerns related to reputation management systems. Ismail *et al.* [15,16] propose a security architecture based on electronic cash technology and designated verifier proofs. Their suggested architecture is targeted at centralized reputation systems and does not seem suitable for decentralized systems, on which we focus our attention.

Kinateder and Pearson [17] suggest a privacy-enhanced peer-to-peer reputation system on top of a *Trusted Computing Platform* (TCP); see [18] for more details on TCP. The platform's functionality along with the use of pseudonymous identities allow the platform to prove that it is a trusted platform, yet to conceal the real identity of the feedback provider. A possible privacy-breach in the IP layer is handled by the use of MIX cascades or anonymous web-posting. As opposed to our scheme, this approach is dependent on a specific platform, which is currently arousing controversy in the computing community. Further details on this issue can be found in [19].

7 Conclusions and Future Work

Decentralized reputation systems do not make use of a central repository to collect and report reputation ratings; participants help one another with the provision of reputation ratings in order to evaluate the trustworthiness of potential transaction partners. This kind of reputation system is a natural match for many kinds of distributed environments, including popular peer-to-peer systems. Systems are being used not only for content sharing (e.g., KaZaA, Gnutella), but for social and business interactions (e.g., Friendster, LinkedIn), classified advertising (e.g., Tribe Networks), and ecommerce (CraigsList), and while not all of these have a peer-to-peer architecture, they are all potentially modelled by peer-to-peer alternatives. Reliable distributed reputation systems in these settings would provide an important service to these communities.

Additive Reputation systems are those in which the combination of feedbacks provided by agents is calculated in an additive manner. They are a particular class of reputation systems with the attractive property of simplicity in the calculation of results.

In this paper, we have shown that there are limits to supporting perfect privacy in decentralized reputation systems. In particular, a scenario where $n-1$ dishonest witnesses collude with the querying agent to reveal the reputation rating of the remaining honest witness demonstrates that perfect privacy is not feasible. As an alternative, we have suggested a probabilistic scheme for witness selection to ensure that such a scenario occurs with small probability.

We have offered three protocols that allow ratings to be privately provided in decentralized additive reputation systems. The first protocol is not resilient against collusion of agents, yet is linear in communication and simple to implement, and might be used when dishonest witnesses are not an issue. The other two protocols are based on our probabilistic witness selection scheme, and are thus probabilistically resistant to collusion of up to $n-1$ witnesses. The second protocol achieves privacy through secret splitting and requires $O(n^2)$ messages among the agents. Its main drawback is its inability to ensure that ratings are provided correctly within the predefined range. The third protocol, based on Pederson Verifiable Secret Sharing, makes use of zero knowledge proofs to circumvent this vulnerability. It requires $O(n^3)$ messages among the agents and some computation on the part of the agents, compared to the second protocol.

In future work, we plan to study schemes and protocols achieving privacy in the general case, i.e., in decentralized reputation systems which are not necessarily additive. In addition, we plan to study other approaches to improve the feedback provided in reputation systems, such as through the design of mechanisms inducing agents to reveal their honest feedback. The combination of privacy and complementary mechanisms promoting truthful feedback revelation will make reputation systems more robust than ever. We believe that such reputation systems would provide solid ground for ecommerce to prosper.

References

1. eBay auction site: http://www.ebay.com (2003)
2. Yu, B., Singh, M.: Distributed reputation management for electronic commerce. Computational Intelligence **18** (2002) 535–549
3. Resnick, P., Zeckhauser, R.: Trust among strangers in internet transactions: Empirical analysis of ebay's reputation system. In: Working paper for the NBER Workshop on Emprical Studies of Electronic Commerce. (2000)

4. Josang, A., Ismail, R.: The beta reputation system. In: The Proceedings of the 15th Bled Conference on Electronic Commerce, Bled, Slovenia (2002)
5. Saks, M.: A robust noncryptographic protocol for collective coin flipping. SIAM Journal on Discrete Mathematics **2** (1989) 240–244
6. Motwani, R., Raghavan, P.: Randomized Algorithms. Cambridge University Press (1995)
7. Pederson, T.: Non-interactive and information secure veriable secret sharing. In: Advances in Cryptology - Crypto '91. (1991) 129–140
8. Shamir, A.: How to share a secret. Communications of the ACM **22** (1979) 612–613
9. R. Cramer, M. Franklin, L.S., Yung, M.: Multi-authority secret ballot elections with linear work. Technical Report CS-R9571, Centrum voor Wiskunde en Informatica (1995)
10. Aberer, K., Despotovic, Z.: Managing trust in a peer-2-peer information system. In: Proceedings of 9th International Conference on Information and Knowledge Management, Atlanta (2001)
11. Abdul-Rahman, A., Hailes, S.: Supporting trust in virtual communities. In: Proceedings of the 33rd Hawaii International Conference on System Sciences, Maui, Hawaii (2000)
12. Kinateder, M., Rothermel, K.: Architecture and algorithms for a distributed reputation system. In: Proceedings of the First International Conference on Trust Management, Crete, Greece (2003)
13. Yu, B., Singh, M.: Detecting deception in reputation management. In: Proceedings of the Second International Joint Conference on Autonomous Agents and Multi-Agent Systems. (2003) 73–80
14. Dellarocas, C.: Immunizing online reputation reporting systems against unfair ratings and discriminatory behavior. In: Proceedings of the 2nd ACM Conference on Electronic Commerce, Minneapolis, MN (2000)
15. Ismail, R., Boyd, C., Josang, A., Russel, S.: Strong privacy in reputation systems (preliminary version). In: the proceedings of WISA 2003. (2003)
16. Ismail, R., Boyd, C., Josang, A., Russel, S.: A security architecture for reputation systems. In: The Proceedings of EC-WEB 2003. (2003)
17. Kinateder, M., Pearson, S.: A privacy-enhanced peer-to-peer reputation system. In: Proceedings of the 4th International Conference on Electronic Commerce and Web Technologies (EC-Web 2003), Prague, Czech Republic (2003)
18. tcpa homepage: http://www.trustedcomputing.org (2003)
19. againsttcpa homepage: http://www.againsttcpa.com (2003)

Engineering Trust Based Collaborations in a Global Computing Environment

Colin English, Sotirios Terzis, and Waleed Wagealla

The Global and Pervasive Computing Group
Dept. of Computer and Information Sciences
University of Strathclyde
FirstName.LastName@cis.strath.ac.uk

Abstract. Trust management seems a promising approach for dealing with security concerns in collaborative applications in a global computing environment. However, the characteristics of this environment require a move from reliable identification to mechanisms for the recognition of entities. Furthermore, they require explicit reasoning about the risks of interactions, and a notion of uncertainty in the underlying trust model. From our experience of engineering collaborative applications in such an environment, we found that the relationship between trust and risk is a fundamental issue. In this paper, as an initial step towards an engineering approach for the development of trust based collaborative applications, we focus on the relationship between trust and risk, and explore alternative views of this relationship. We also exemplify how particular views can be exploited in two particular application scenarios. This paper builds upon our previous work in developing a general model for trust based collaborations.

1 Introduction

Global computing is characterised by large numbers of roaming entities and the absence of a globally available fixed infrastructure [11]. In such an environment entities meet and need to collaborate with little known or even unknown entities. Entering any kind of collaboration requires entities to make security decisions about the type and level of access to their resources they provide to collaborators. In traditional environments with clearly defined administrative boundaries and limited entity movement security decisions are usually delegated to a centralised administrative authority [13,15,16]. In the global computing environment no single entity can play this role and as a result traditional techniques that statically determine the access rights of entities are not an option. Entities are required to make their own security decisions. Moreover, the absence of a globally available security infrastructure means that these decisions need to be made autonomously. The sheer number of roaming entities means, however, that it is not feasible to gather and maintain information about all of them. Consequently, in the global computing environment decisions have to be made in the absence of complete knowledge of the operating environment.

C.D. Jensen et al. (Eds.): iTrust 2004, LNCS 2995, pp. 120–134, 2004.
© Springer-Verlag Berlin Heidelberg 2004

Autonomous decision making with partial information is something that humans have to deal with on a day-to-day basis. To help them with the complexity of such a task humans have developed the notion of trust [9]. Although trust is an elusive concept, a number of definitions have been proposed and it is our belief that it can be modelled in adequate detail to facilitate security decision making in global computing. This belief is shared by others, as is demonstrated by research in Trust Management systems [1,2,3,5,12,14,17,21,22].

The purpose of this paper is to give a high level description of our experiences of trying to engineer trusting collaborations in a global computing environment. Rather than suggest a unified model of trust and risk, we show how applications can be engineered by combining two models. Our experience emanates from engineering two scenarios, a smart space with sensitive location information and an electronic purse. A central issue in both scenarios is modelling the relationship between trust and risk, which is the main focus of this paper. Section 2 gives a brief insight into trust and risk for global computing, prior to outlining the scenarios in section 3. The relationship between trust and risk is discussed in section 4, before examining the modelling and exploitation of the relationship in the two scenarios in section 5. Section 6 concludes the paper.

2 Trust and Risk in Global Computing

In recent years, research in Trust Management has moved away from what was essentially credential based distributed policy management [2,3,12,14,17]. These approaches fail to address fundamental characteristics of trust such as what trust is made of and consequently the related issue of how trust can be formed. Furthermore they provide only limited support for the evolution of trust between entities in the form of credential revocation. As a result, early trust management systems lack support for autonomous decision-making and the dynamism in trust evolution necessary for global computing.

Novel approaches have been proposed to address these weaknesses [1,5,21,22] by modelling explicitly the trustworthiness of entities and supporting its formation and evolution based on information gathered through personal interactions. A key difference in these approaches is the shift from attempting to provide absolute protection against potential dangers, to accepting that dangers are an intrinsic part of any global computing system. Such dangers necessitate explicit reasoning about risk. Trust is therefore used as a mechanism for managing risk and learning from past interactions in order to reduce risk exposure. This fundamental change is reflected in the shift in discussion from security decisions to trusting decisions.

However, even these approaches have certain weaknesses in light of the characteristics of global computing. First, they assume a global identification system for entities. This is a very strong assumption to make in the context of global computing. Schemes based on entity recognition, an extension of authentication, have been proposed to remove this assumption. We do not examine this point any further in this paper, but refer the interested reader to [18]. Second, in the few cases where risk is explicitly considered [6,10], the relationship between trust and risk is not satisfactorily addressed. Trust and risk are intrinsically related in the sense that there is no need for a trusting decision unless there is risk involved. Any model of trust and risk should reflect this relationship. Third, very few of these approaches model explicitly uncertainty, a consequence of decision making in the absence of complete information.

Consequently, in a global computing setting, it is necessary to model trust in a manner that allows comparisons within a domain of trust values in terms of both which value expresses "more trust" and which expresses "more certainty". This model should also be able to represent complete uncertainty for the case where interactions with completely unknown or unrecognised entities are possible. The manner in which trust is updated based on evidence must also take this into account, as evidence which indicates different trends in behaviour emerging may make us less certain about our opinion rather than merely changing in terms of trustworthiness. An example of such a trust model has been provided by the SECURE project [4]. Note that this model allows the definition of application specific trust domains, provided they have certain properties.

Moreover, in terms of risk, we consider actions, which have a set of possible results or outcomes. Each outcome has an associated risk, defined as the likelihood of an outcome occurring and the cost or benefit of this outcome if it occurs. The overall risk of an action is a combination of the risks of all its outcomes.

3   Overview of Scenarios

In this section we will introduce the two scenarios, focussing on the specific aspects of trust based interactions of relevance to the previous discussion. We simplify the scenarios and outcomes due to space constraints. Both scenarios use intervals as trust values, and as such enable uncertainty comparisons using the set or interval inclusion operator. Thus interval I_1 is more uncertain than interval I_2, $I_2 \sqsubseteq I_1$, if the corresponding sets $I_2' \subseteq I_1'$.

3.1   Smart Space Scenario

In the smart space scenario, we consider the case of a smart environment equipped with sensors in rooms and offices to enable the collection of data such as the location of the smart space inhabitants. In this particular scenario, there exists a context information server (CIS) that collects, stores and interprets user contextual information, such as location. Users can request the information that the CIS collects for other users. The way information is exchanged between users classifies them as *information owners*, those whose contextual information is managed by the CIS, or *information receivers*, those who would like to use the managed contextual information. In particular, we consider the case of a CIS that is able to track certain users, the information owners, as they move within the smart space. Any user can play the role of information receiver, requesting from the CIS location information about other users with the intention to meet them. Note that for simplicity, we consider that all trust reasoning is performed by the central CIS for the domain, but in line with global computing, each information owner may possess a device which manages their own trust information, with the domain adopting some form of distributed context management. However, this would complicate the scenario greatly, thus it is outside the scope of this paper.

The concern in such systems is about the privacy of their users, due to the vast amounts of personal information collected. Users concerned about their private information are likely to refuse participation in such systems. At the same time, information owners may be willing to disclose their contextual information if this disclosure is potentially beneficial. Accordingly, for any context information system to be acceptable to the users, it must provide mechanisms for the fine-grained control of access to their personal contextual information. In this scenario, trust-risk based access control constitutes this mechanism.

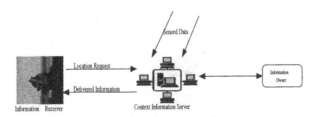

Fig. 1. A user requests location information from the context information server.

As depicted in Figure 1, first, the information receiver sends a request to the CIS for location information regarding a particular information owner. We assume that all users are registered with the system, and as a result, the identification by the CIS of both the information receiver and the information owner is trivial. On receipt of the request the CIS needs to decide whether to permit the tracking of the information owner, based on trust-risk evaluation. If the CIS decides to provide the requested information it starts sending location notifications to the information receiver. This will cease either when the allocated tracking time expires or when the sensors detect the information receiver and information owner in proximity of 1 meter to each other, indicating that the purpose of the request has been fulfilled, i.e. a meeting between the information receiver and the information owner is taking place. Moreover, the CIS sends messages to the information owners when the allocated meeting time is due to expire.

Here, we take the approach of defining a set of basic trust values (FD,D,N,T,FT) representing *fully distrusted, distrusted, neutral, trusted* and *fully trusted*. From this, we follow the constructive approach described in [4] to construct intervals for the actual trust values. For example [FD,N] means that we know this principal is either FD, D or N, but are uncertain which exact value is the case.

A trust value, coupled with parameters (for specific groups of users) reflecting the information owner's willingness to trade privacy for a potentially beneficial meeting, allows reasoning about the risk of information disclosure for a decision.

3.2   E-purse Scenario

The e-purse scenario involves the use of an electronic purse when a user interacts with a bus company. The purpose of the e-purse is to hold a relatively small amount of e-cash (in this scenario the e-purse is limited to 100 euro) that the owner can use as if it were real cash for buying bus tickets (see figure 2).

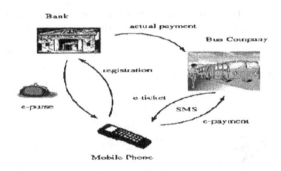

Fig. 2. E-purse scenario interaction.

Users can refill their e-purse by contacting their bank provided that there is enough cash in their account. There are three different principals involved in this scenario: the user (owner) of the e-purse, the bus company and the bank. We focus on modelling the interaction between the bus company and the user, where users want to purchase tickets using their e-purse.

E-cash is based on a protocol that although it protects user anonymity during normal transactions, enables identification of guilty parties in fraudulent transactions. Although there are some guarantees of fraud compensation by the bank, we assume that the bank requires that the bus company takes measures to reduce the incidents of fraud (e.g. some kind of financial penalty for a high percentage of fraudulent transactions). In the extreme case it could even pass the whole cost of the fraudulent transactions to the bus company. Therefore, every time the bus company accepts e-cash in a transaction it takes the risk of losing money due to fraud. For the bus company to decide how to respond to a purchasing request, it needs to determine the trustworthiness of the user. Principals can assign different levels of trust to different users based on the available information, to allow a decision to consider the risk that transactions involving the user entail. The trust values in this case are intervals from 0 to 100 in line with the maximum amount of e-cash. The question for the bus company is: given this trust value, what is the cut off point for accepting e-cash for the ticket?

4 Relationship of Trust and Risk

This section discusses the relationship between trust and risk, aiming to high-light considerations for developers rather than propose a definitive approach. We assume that an entity, the *decision maker*, receives a request for an interaction from another entity, the *requester*. We assume a model where before each inter-action the decision maker has to make a trusting decision, termed the decision process. This process is based on the combined reasoning about the trustwor-thiness of the requester and the risk of the interaction (see figure 3). After a decision to proceed with an interaction has been taken, the decision maker has to evaluate this decision in terms of both trust and risk. We term these feedback process, *trust evaluation* and *risk evaluation* respectively.

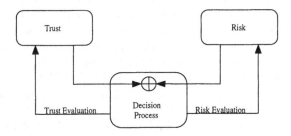

Fig. 3. Relationship of Trust and Risk in Decisions and Evaluation

4.1 Trust and Risk in Decision Making

In general, there are two alternative views of the relationship between trust and risk. On one hand, we can view risk "driving" trust. According to this view, risk reflects how vulnerable we are in a particular situation, or in other words how likely is our current situation to lead to an accident, combined with the severity or cost of the accident. In this case, our aim is to protect ourselves by only exposing serious vulnerabilities to highly trusted collaborators. In this context the trusting decision we have to make can be expressed as: in a particular situation s, or a particular action a which entails a level of risk r, how trustworthy should a principal be in order to be allowed to enter situation s or carry out action a? In this view the level of risk determines the level of required trustworthiness, i.e. risk drives the decision making.

On the other hand, we can view trust "driving" risk. According to this view, trust reflects the likelihood of a principal behaving well in a particular situation. In this case, our aim is to protect ourselves by only collaborating with principals that are likely to behave well and as a result an interaction with them is not very risky. In this context the trusting decision we have to make can be expressed as: in a particular situation s, or a particular action a, involving a particular principal p, how much risk are we willing to accept by allowing principal p to enter situation s or carry out action a? In this view the level of trustworthiness determines the level of perceived risk, i.e. trust drives the decision making.

It seems to be the case that the former view is more natural in a safety critical systems setting, while the latter in a financial systems setting. Supposing that costs and benefits are quantifiable, the latter view seems more appropriate. For this reason we concentrate on it for the remainder of the paper. Looking at this decision making process, combined with the adopted view of risk, it is clear that the decision-maker requires the ability to associate each principal to a risk profile, described by the combination of the risks of individual outcomes of an interaction. This profile can also be seen as a profile of how good or bad the behaviour of a principal is expected to be in the context of the requested action. In this sense, the trust values can be viewed as classifiers of principals, where principals are classified according to their expected behaviour in a number of groups, one for each trust value. This has significant benefits for the scalability of the decision making process. It allows the decision-maker to keep a relatively small number of risk profiles, which is independent of the number of principals in the system. This is particularly important in a global computing setting, where the number of principals is expected to be particularly high.

This approach dictates a very close relation between trust values and risk profiles. In fact, every trust value must be associated to a single risk profile. Additionally, two different trust values should be associated to different risk profiles. This approach requires that the mapping between trust values and risk profiles is not only a function but an *injective* or *one-to-one* function. As a result of this, the number of trust values and consequently risk profiles is dependent on the required granularity of the decision making process. The larger the number of trust values the more able the decision-maker is to discern variations in the expected behaviour of principals, allowing finer differentiation on the way principals are treated. However, there is a tradeoff between the granularity and the complexity of the decision making process. Finer differentiation in the treatment of principals requires a more complicated process. Therefore,in most cases we would expect a relatively small number of risk profiles.

4.2   Trust and Risk in Evaluation of Decisions

In a global computing environment characterised by the lack of complete information about principals, their classification into similarly behaving groups cannot be final. As additional information about the behaviour of individual principals becomes available the classification needs to be re-evaluated. The results of this process may be twofold. It may either lead to the re-classification of the principal into a different group whose associated risk profile is a more accurate predictor of the principal's behaviour. Or, it may even lead to a reconfiguration of the classification scheme by updating the risk profiles associated to each group. In this context, the two aspects of evaluation process can be captured by the following questions:

- Has each principal been classified to the correct group, i.e. is the trust value for each principal correct?
- Is the risk.profile associated to each group correct, i.e. is the risk profile for each trust value correct?

The former aspect of the evaluation process can be associated to the feedback of evidence from completed collaborations. We refer to this aspect of the process as *trust evaluation*. Moreover, it becomes clear that a second form of feedback is necessary to represent the latter aspect of evaluation. We refer to this aspect of the process as *risk evaluation*. In the remainder of this paper, we focus on the dynamic aspects of trust (i.e. trust evaluation). Within this context, we can view the feedback collected from the multiple cases of an action as a profile of observed behaviour for the requester with respect to the action. Likelihood in this profile represents the proportion of the total occurrences where an outcome occurred. Then, we could rephrase the above trust evaluation question as follows:

- Which of the risk profiles predicts principal behaviour reflecting most closely the observed behaviour?

Being able to use the answer to this question to determine the appropriate trust value for the user requires an even stronger relationship between trust values and risk profiles. Not only should we be able given any trust value to select a risk profile, but we should also be able given any risk profile to select a trust value. This requirement implies that mapping from trust values to risk profiles should also be *surjective* or *onto* function. As a result, this function must be a *bijection*.

4.3   Structure of the Risk Domain for Decision Making and Trust Evaluation

So far in the discussion of the relationship between trust and risk, we have ignored the structure of the trust value domain. According to the discussion in section 2 this domain must allow the comparison of values in terms of "more trust" and "more uncertainty". This, in combination with the fact that both the decision making and trust evaluation processes require a very close relationship between trust values and risk profiles, implies that the set of the risk profiles should reflect the structure to the trust domain.

In the case of comparison in terms of trust (represented by the $\preceq$ operator), if we consider two trust values t_1, t_2 with respective risk profiles r_1, r_2 such that $t_1 \preceq t_2$ then r_2 must represent less risk than r_1. Given that risk consists of both likelihood and cost, two views can be taken. One view is that outcomes with lower costs and/or higher benefits are more likely in profile r_2 than in profile r_1. There is also the alternative view, according to which it also means that if the corresponding outcomes are equally likely then their associated costs are lower in profile r_2 than in profile r_1. Therefore, we can take the general view that the trustworthiness of a principal can affect both the likelihood and/or the associated costs of the outcomes.

In the case of comparison of uncertainty of trust values, and the effect of this on risk, there are three alternatives:

1. Ignore the uncertainty dimension of the trust values in both the decision making and trust evaluation processes. In this approach, if the trustworthiness of two principals differs only in terms of certainty then both principals will be treated the same. At the same time, the trust evaluation process will only affect the trust dimension of the trust values leaving the uncertainty aspects either completely unaffected or managed through external procedures.
2. Consider the uncertainty dimension of the trust values only in the decision making process and not in the trust evaluation process. Following this approach the risk profiles reflect only the trust dimension of the trust values. As a result, the decision making process cannot rely exclusively on the risk profiles. Instead it also requires the trust values themselves in order to consider their information dimension. At the same time, the trust evaluation process still only affects the trust dimension of the trust values. Similarly to the first approach, this leaves the uncertainty aspects either completely unaffected or managed through external procedures.
3. Introduce a notion of uncertainty to the risk model, which will allow consideration of both trust dimensions in both processes. In this approach in contrast to the second one, the risk profiles reflect both trust dimensions. As a result, the decision making process can rely exclusively on the risk profiles, rather than requiring trust information to facilitate reasoning about uncertainty. At the same time, the trust evaluation process considers and affects both trust dimensions. For example, as a result of the trust evaluation process the new trust value may be different only in terms of uncertainty and not in terms of trustworthiness.

The first approach is the least desirable of the three since it does not fully utilise the structure of the trust domain in both processes. The second approach is a half way between the other two. On one hand, it does not ignore the uncertainty of the trust values during decision making as the first one does. On the other hand, it still considers the uncertainty aspect as external to the trust evaluation process. As a result is still does not fully utilise the structure of the trust domain in the trust evaluation process. The third approach fully utilises the structure provided of the trust domain in both process. Moreover, it requires that the risk profiles reflect relationships between the respective trust values both in terms of trustworthiness and uncertainty. This requires a risk model which is able to capture uncertainty.

From the three approaches we consider the third one as the most desirable, mainly because of the requirements it places on the risk model. We believe that a risk model incorporating uncertainty is more in tune with the global computing setting that is characterised by high degrees of uncertainty about the collaborators. Consequently, we focus the discussion on the third approach in section 4.4.

4.4   Uncertainty in Risk Modelling

Our aim in this section is not to describe a full model for uncertain risks. It is more to suggest ways in which uncertainty may be designed into a risk model, bearing in mind the definition in section 2, where we pointed out that risk is the combination of the likelihood of an outcome occurring and the cost it incurs.

We can introduce uncertainty by considering risk ranges instead of specific risk values, in a constructive approach similar to that used for constructing intervals from basic trust values in [4], and also demonstrated in the smart space scenario. A risk range can be seen as either a set containing a number of distinct risk values or a notion of ordering on the risk values as an interval containing all the values between an upper and a lower bound. In either case, the higher the number of included risk values the more uncertain we are about the risk. As the number of included risk values is reduced our certainty about risk increases reaching complete certainty at the point when we have a specific risk value. In other words, we can compare risk ranges in terms of uncertainty using the set or interval inclusion operator. Thus a risk range RR_1 is more uncertain than risk range RR_2, $RR_2 \sqsubseteq RR_1$, if the corresponding sets $RR_2' \subseteq RR_1'$.

Regarding the exact meaning of a risk range we could consider it to be that all the included risk values are equally likely while all other risk values are considered totally unlikely. This is the same as the intervals of trust in the scenarios, i.e. considering all included trust values as equally likely. In this way we can now easily reflect the full structure of the trust domain on the risk domain. We can see the certainty dimension of the trust domain as defining an inverse uncertainty dimension on the risk domain.

Following this approach results in some changes in the decision making and the trust evaluation processes. In the decision making process instead of considering a single risk profile for a principal we will have to consider a range of likely profiles. Any decision taken must acknowledge this fact. Furthermore, the trust evaluation process will have to decide on the appropriateness of the current trust value not only in terms of trustworthiness but also in terms of uncertainty. In terms of uncertainty the issues are whether any of the risk profiles of the range can be safely excluded (uncertainty reduction) or if additional profiles need to be included (uncertainty increase).

Taking into consideration the above discussion, we can define two special cases:

- The case where the uncertainty is limited to the costs of the outcomes while their likelihoods are certain. The smart space scenario is an example of this case.
- The case where the uncertainty is limited to the likelihoods of the outcomes while their costs are certain. The e-purse scenario is an example of this case.

5   Engineering Trust and Risk in the Scenarios

In this section we elaborate on how the discussion in section 4 affects decision making and trust evaluation in the scenarios. This discussion builds upon our previous work on the dynamic evolution of trust [8,7,20,19]. In this work, the observations made after an interaction are evaluated in terms of their *attraction*, which represents the influence they exert on the current trust value T_{curr}. The interested reader can find more details of these and other trust evolutionary concerns in [19].

5.1   Case 1: Smart Space Scenario

This scenario represents the case where the uncertainty is limited to the costs of the outcomes while their likelihoods are certain. More specifically, we consider a single interaction, a request for location information, that has a single certain outcome, loss of user privacy, with a range of costs and benefits determined by the cost or benefit of meeting with the information receiver (requester). To facilitate risk assessment, information owners specify a privacy policy that determines under which circumstances the CIS should disclose their location information. The privacy policies sets boundaries on the acceptable expected costs/benefits of interactions, expressed as limits on both the tracking and meeting duration. Different privacy policies can be defined for different groups of users, and can be configured in terms of *Maximum tracking duration units, (mtdu), Maximum meeting duration units, (mmdu), Value of time, (vt)* for the information owner, and *Privacy sensitivity level, (psl)*, which determines the degree to which information owners are concerned about their privacy.

Making a decision. The requester's trustworthiness determines the likelihood of the various costs/benefits. We assume a mapping from the basic trust values (FD,D,N,T,FT), to probability distributions of costs, representing the range of likely costs for each trust value. As there is only one outcome (loss of privacy), this probability distribution represents the risk profile. The associated risk profiles of the trust value intervals are constructed by considering the corresponding risk profiles of the included basic trust values as equally likely, averaging the respective distributions. To simplify this construction, the range of cost/benefit is divided into 5 intervals and the value on top of each column represents the likelihood of this interval of cost/benefit. For example, the constructed risk profile for the interval [FD,N] is the average of the distributions for [FD,FD], [D,D] and [N,N] and is depicted in figure 4(a).

   To make a decision, the CIS knows the identity and group of the requester from the interaction request, and can select the corresponding privacy policy. This, coupled with the risk profile for the requester, enables the decision making process. Access policies are described as functions that given the risk profile determine how many units of tracking and meeting duration should be provided to the requester. These policies in fact describe the risk that the information owner is willing to take. For example, if the risk profile predicts high benefits from an interaction, then the access control policy will assign more units for both tracking duration and meeting duration, up to a limit defined by privacy policy.

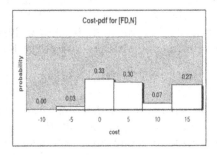 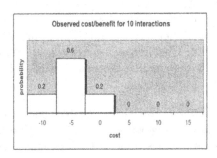

(a) [FD,N] Risk profile   (b) Risk profile from observations

Fig. 4. An example risk profile and observed behaviour profile

Trust evaluation. In order to determine the range of possible costs/benefits for each outcome, we calculate first the maximum costs/benefits, again using the privacy policy factors. In calculating the total maximum benefit, we only consider the maximum benefit of a meeting since there is no direct benefit from tracking. When a meeting has taken place, the information owner provides feedback, reflecting the observed cost/benefit of it. The actual cost/benefit is combination of both the cost of tracking duration and the cost/benefit of the meeting based on the privacy policy factors mentioned above.

The evidence evaluation function, *eval()*, determines the attraction that a piece of evidence conveys. The evaluation is relative to the current trust value and attempts to determine which trust value would have been a more accurate predictor of the observed outcome. This calculation utilises the reverse of the mapping from the risk profiles to trust values used during decision making. More specifically, let us suppose that figure 4(b) depicts the observed cost/benefit of ten interactions. A comparison of this risk profile to the set of profiles provided by the risk analysis would show that the closest one is the profile for the [T,T] trust value. Therefore, the *eval()* function should produce an attraction which would evolve T_{curr} towards [T,T].

5.2   Case 2: E-Purse Scenario

This scenario demonstrates the case where the uncertainty is limited to the likelihoods of the outcomes while their costs are certain. More specifically, we consider a single interaction, e-cash payment for a bus ticket, that has two outcomes, valid and invalid e-cash, each with a specific cost determined by the amount of the transaction. Users are considered reliable up to a certain transaction amount, no chance of invalid e-cash, and unreliable above a certain transaction amount, no chance of valid e-cash. Trust value intervals on the range [0, 100] reflect the amount of e-cash that the bus company is willing to accept from the requesting

user. An interval $[d_1, d_2]$ indicates that the bus company is quite certain about
the validity of amounts up to d_1 of e-cash , fairly uncertain about the validity of
amounts between d_1 and d_2 and fairly certain that any amount above d_2 will be
invalid. Risk in the E-purse scenario is rather simple, with the cost of the bus
ticket determining the cost part of risk.

Making a decision. Again, the trust interval is used to determine the risk
of interacting with a particular principal. The assumption is that the user's
trustworthiness reflects the expected loss or gain during a transaction involving
him or her. The costs involved in an interaction range from -100 to 100, denoting
the maximum gain or loss for the bus company. The calculated risk allows entities
to decide whether or not to proceed with an interaction. In this scenario, a
simplified view is taken, whereby the trust value directly determines the amount
of e-cash a bus company is willing to accept. The decision making process for a
ticket of value x regarding a user with trust value $[d_1, d_2]$ is as follows:

- If $x < d1$ then the whole amount of the transaction can be paid in e-cash.
- If $x > d2$ then the option of paying in e-cash is not available and the full
  amount has to be paid in cash.
- If $d_1 < x < d_2$ then the likelihoods of the possible outcomes are examined.
  Note that there are only two possible outcomes, the e-cash provided by the
  user will be either valid or invalid. For the calculations of the likelihoods,
  we divide the range from d1 to d2 into a number of units, n. For example n
  could be equal to the price of the cheapest ticket, say 5 euro. In this case,
  the number of units is determined by dividing the whole range over five
  $(d_1 - d_2)/5$. The likelihood of invalid e-cash for each unit is *(m/n)*, where
  m=0,1, .., n (see figure 5).

Fig. 5. Risk Analysis.

Note that the likelihood of invalid e-cash increases in ascending order from
d_1(with a probability of 0 for invalid e-cash) to d_2 (with a probability of 1 for
invalid e-cash). This represents the risk profile of each outcome of each action for
each trust value as an interval of likelihoods combined with the certain cost, while
the level of uncertainty is represented by the size of the interval. Considering
these likelihoods for the possible outcomes the bus company can place a threshold
on acceptable risk. It will only accept e-cash for transaction with risk below the
threshold.

Trust Evaluation. Observations about the outcome of an interaction in this scenario are straightforward, as they are just the observed payment of valid e-cash, or the lack thereof. Due to the simple mapping from cost/benefit to the trust value domain, the evaluation of this observation is simple. The attraction produced by the evaluation process merely raises or drops the bounds of the current trust value. Moreover, if the outcome was expected, i.e. its likelihood was more than 50%, then the attraction reflects this. The details of this, however, will not be discussed here due to space limitations, but are provided in [19].

6   Conclusions and Future Work

In conclusion, engineering trust based collaborative applications in a global computing environment requires explicit reasoning about risk, and a trust model that encodes uncertainty. The decision making process in such applications should combine both trust and risk. As a result the relationship between the underlying risk and trust models is central. There is a vast space of alternative views of this relationship. This paper is an attempt to chart this space, as a first step towards an engineering methodology for such applications. Moreover, the presentation of the two scenarios gives an insight into the tradeoffs that engineers must make in selecting the most appropriate view for the needs of their application.

We are currently validating the described scenarios through simulations. We are planning to develop a simulation framework for general purpose experimentation in trust based collaborative applications in global computing. Furthermore, there are clearly a number of issues that remain to be addressed. For example, it is not currently clear under which circumstances alternative approaches are more applicable. This is an important step in developing engineering guidelines for such applications.

Finally, our investigation so far has omitted the important issue of context in the interpretation of trust values during the decision making process. Exploration of this issue is at the top of our agenda for research in the near future.

Acknowledgements. The work is this paper is supported by the EU project SECURE: Secure Environments for Collaboration among Ubiquitous Roaming Entities (IST-2001-32486).

References

1. A. Abdul-Rahman and S. Hailes. Supporting trust in virtual communities. In *Hawaii International Conference on System Sciences*, January 2000.
2. Matt Blaze, Joan Feigenbaum, and Angelos D. Keromytis. Keynote: Trust management for public-key infrastructures. In *Secure Internet Programming: Issues in Distributed and Mobile Object Systems*, Lecture Notes in Computer Science: State-of-the-Art. Springer-Verlag, 1998.
3. Matt Blaze, Joan Feigenbaum, and Jack Lacy. Decentralized trust management. In *IEEE Conference on Security and Privacy*. AT&T, May 1996.

4. Marco Carbone, Mogens Nielsen, and Vladimiro Sassone. A formal model for trust in dynamic networks. In *International Conference on Software Engineering and Formal Methods*, September 2003.
5. Rita Chen and William Yeager. Poblano - a distributed trust model for peer-to-peer networks. 2001.
6. Theo Dimitrakos. System models, e-risks and e-trust. towards bridging the gap? In *1st IFIP Conference on e-Commerce, e-Business, e-Government*. Kluwer Academic Publishers, October 2001.
7. Colin English, Sotirios Terzis, Waleed Wagealla, Paddy Nixon, Helen Lowe, and Andrew McGettrick. Trust dynamics for collaborative global computing. In *IEEE International Workshops on Enabling Technologies: Infrastructure for Collaborative Enterprises: Enterprise Security (Special Session on Trust Management)*, 2003.
8. Colin English, Waleed Wagealla, Paddy Nixon, Sotirios Terzis, Andrew McGettrick, and Helen Lowe. Trusting collaboration in global computing. In *First International Conference on Trust Management*, May 2003.
9. Diego Gambetta. Can we trust trust? In Diego Gambetta, editor, *Trust: Making and Breaking Cooperative Relations*, pages 213–237, Oxford, 1990. Basil Blackwell.
10. Tyrone Grandison and Morris Sloman. Trust management tools for internet applications. In *First International Conference on Trust Management*, May 2003.
11. Global Computing Initiative. Website. *http://www.cordis.lu/ist/fet/gc.htm*, 2002.
12. Lalana Kagal, Jeffrey L Undercoffer, Filip Perich, Anupam Joshi, and Tim Finin. A security architecture based on trust management for pervasive computing systems. In *Grace Hopper Celebration of Women in Computing*, October 2002.
13. Kerberos. Website. *http://web.mit.edu/kerberos/www/*.
14. Ninghui Li and John C. Mitchell. RT: A role based trust management framework. In *3rd DARPA Information Survivability Conference and Exposition (DISCEX III)*. IEEE Computer Society Press, April 2003.
15. John McLean. Security models. In J. Marciniak, editor, *Encyclopedia of Software Engineering*. John Wiley & Sons, 1994.
16. Ravi Sandhu. Access control: The neglected frontier. In *First Australian Conference on Information Security and Privacy*, 1996.
17. K. E. Seamons, M. Winslett, T. Yu, B. Smith, E. Child, J. Jacobson, H. Mills, and L. Yu. Requirements for policy languages for trust negotiation. In *3rd International Workshop on Policies for Distributed Systems and Networks (POLICY 2002)*, June 2002.
18. J.-M. Seigneur, S. Farrell, C. Jensen, E. Gray, and C. Yong. End-to-end trust starts with recognition. In *First International Conference on Security in Pervasive Computing*, 2003.
19. Sotirios Terzis, Waleed Wagealla, Colin English, and Paddy Nixon. The secure collaboration model. Technical Report 03, University of Strathclyde, Computer and Information Sciences, December 2003.
20. Waleed Wagealla, Marco Carbone, Colin English, Sotirios Terzis, and Paddy Nixon. A formal model of trust lifecycle management. In *Workshop on Formal Aspects of Security and Trust (FAST2003) at FM2003*, September 2003.
21. Li Xiong and Ling Liu. A reputation-based trust model for peer-to-peer ecommerce communities. In *ACM Conference on Electronic Commerce*, 2003.
22. Bin Yu and Munindar P. Singh. An evidential model of distributed reputation management. In *1st International Joint Conference on Autonomous Agents and MultiAgent Systems*, 2002.

Analysing the Relationship between Risk and Trust

Audun Jøsang[1] and Stéphane Lo Presti[2]

[1] DSTC ***, Queensland University of Technology, GPO Box 2434, Brisbane Qld 4001,
Australia.
ajosang@dstc.edu.au
[2] University of Southampton †, School of Electronics and Computer Science,
Southampton SO17 1BJ, United Kingdom.
splp@ecs.soton.ac.uk

Abstract. Among the various human factors impinging upon making a decision in an uncertain environment, risk and trust are surely crucial ones. Several models for trust have been proposed in the literature but few explicitly take risk into account. This paper analyses the relationship between the two concepts by first looking at how a decision is made to enter into a transaction based on the risk information. We then draw a model of the invested fraction of the capital function of a decision surface. We finally define a model of trust composed of a *reliability trust* as the probability of transaction success and a *decision trust* derived from the decision surface.

1 Introduction

Manifestations of trust are easy to recognise because we experience and rely on it every day. At the same time it is quite challenging to define the term because it is being used with a variety of meanings and in many different contexts [12], what usually lead to confusion. For the purpose of this study the following working definition inspired by McKnight and Chervany's work [12] will be used:

Definition 1 (Trust). *Trust is the extent to which one party is willing to depend on somebody, or something, in a given situation with a feeling of relative security, even though negative consequences are possible.*

Although relatively general, this definition explicitly and implicitly includes the basic ingredients of trust. The term *situation* enables this definition to be adapted to most needs, and thus be general enough to be used in uncertain and changing environments. The definition acknowledges the subjective nature of trust by relying on one's *willingness* and *relative* security. The aspect of dependence is implicitly complemented by uncertainty through *possibility* and by risk through *negative consequences*.

*** The work reported in this paper has been funded in part by the Co-operative Research Centre for Enterprise Distributed Systems Technology (DSTC) through the Australian Federal Government's CRC Programme (Department of Industry, Science & Resources).

† This work has been funded in part by the T-SAS (Trusted Software Agents and Services in Pervasive Information Environment) project of the UK Department of Trade and Industry's Next Wave Technologies and Markets Programme.

C.D. Jensen et al. (Eds.): iTrust 2004, LNCS 2995, pp. 135–145, 2004.

Risk emerges for example when the value at stake in a transaction is high, or when this transaction has a critical role in the security or the safety of a system. It can be seen as the anticipated hazard following from a fault in or an attack of the system and can be measured by the consequences of this event.

The question regarding whether adequate models of risk and trust can be designed is still open at the present time. This ensues from the fact that these two notions encompass so many aspects of our life that their understanding is made difficult by the scale and the subjectivity of the task. Furthermore, these notions intrinsically rely on uncertainty and unpredictability, what complicates even more their modelling. Nevertheless, many models and approaches have been proposed to delimit, to reason and to solve a part of the problem that trust and risk constitute.

There are at the moment few trust systems and models that explicitly take the risk factor into account [8]. In most trust systems considering risk, the user must explicitly handle the relationship between risk and trust by combining the various ingredients that the system provides. At the same time, all those systems acknowledge the intuitive observation that the two notions are in an inverse relationship, i.e. low value transactions are associated to high risk and low trust levels and vice versa, or, similarly, risk and trust pull in opposite directions to determine a user's acceptance of a partner [13].

Falcone and Castelfranchi (2001) [6] recognise that having high trust in a person is not necessarily enough to decide to enter into a situation of dependence on that person. In [6] they write: *"For example it is possible that the value of the damage per se (in case of failure) is too high to choose a given decision branch, and this independently either from the probability of the failure (even if it is very low) or from the possible payoff (even if it is very high). In other words, that danger might seem to the agent an intolerable risk."*

Povey (1999) [14] introduces the concept of risk in McKnight and Chervany's work. Risk is exposed by the Trusting Behaviour and influences the Trusting Intentions and possibly the Situational Decision to Trust. Dimitrakos (2002) [5] presents this schema with a slightly different, and corrected, point of view. Trust metrics, costs and utility functions are introduced as parameters of an algorithm that produces the trust policy for a given trusting decision. Nevertheless, this work lacks a quantitative definition of the various involved measures and lacks examples of application of this generic algorithm.

The SECURE project [4] analyses a notion of trust that is *"inherently linked to risk"*. Risk is evaluated on every possible outcome of a particular action and is represented as a family of cost-PDFs (Probability Density Function) parameterized by the outcome's intrinsic cost. The considered action is then analysed by a trust engine to compute multidimensional trust information which is then used by a risk engine to select one cost-PDF. The decision to take the action is then made by applying a user-defined policy to select one of the possible outcomes' cost-PDFs.

The system described by Manchala (1998) [10] avoids expressing measures of trust directly, and instead develops a model based on trust-related variables such as the cost of the transaction and its history, and defines risk-trust decision matrices as illustrated in Figure 1. The risk-trust matrices are then used together with fuzzy logic inference rules to determine whether or not to transact with a particular party.

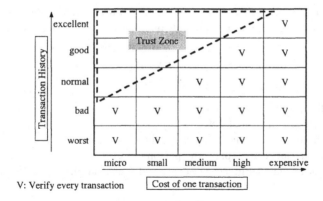

Fig. 1. Risk-trust matrix (from Manchala (1998) [10]).

In this paper, we expand on Manchala's model of trust with the intention of refining the relationship between trust and risk. Section 2 analyses how risk influences the decision-making process by calculating some of the factors impinging upon the outcome of the transaction. These factors are the expected gain and the fraction of the capital that is invested. Section 3 follows by deriving two trust factors from the previous elements: reliability and decision trust. In Section 4, we conclude by summarising our approach and discussing further work.

2   Decisions and Risk

Risk and trust are two tools for making decisions in an uncertain environment. Though central to many works, these two indicators only have semantics in the context of a decision that an agent is taking. An agent, here, can equivalently be a human being (e.g. a stockbroker) or a program (e.g. a software agent), whose owner (another agent) has delegated the decision-making process for a particular kind of interaction.

We focus on transactions rather than general interactions. This abstraction is not a limitation but rather a point of view on interactions, since most interactions can be modelled by transactions. Collaborations can be viewed as a group of transactions, one for each collaborator. The case of an attack by a malicious agent is a degenerated case where the transaction is abused by the attacker who invests fake income. Lastly, dependability can be considered as a combination of the various transactions between the agents so that the transactions' history and their overall effect are summarized.

Since risk is involved, we assume that numerical information is available from the transaction context to compute the level of risk. Practically these values may be hard to determine, since many factors of the transaction need to be taken into account [7,1], and financial modelling may not be suited to all the transaction contexts. For the sake of simplicity, we will limit ourselves to simple financial transaction contexts, but without loss of generality in our explorative approach.

In classical gambling theory the *expected monetary value* EV of a gamble with n mutually exclusive and exhaustive possible outcomes can be expressed as:

$$EV = I \sum_{i=1}^{n} p_i G_i \qquad (1)$$

where p_i is the probability of outcome i and G_i is the gain factor on the monetary investment (or bet) I in case of outcome i.

However in many cases the utility is not the same as monetary value, and *expected utility EU* is introduced to express the personal preferences of the agent. In classical utility theory the expected utility can be expressed as a linear function of the probabilities:

$$EU = \sum_{i=1}^{n} p_i u(IG_i) \qquad (2)$$

where u is an *a priori* non-linear function of monetary value. In traditional EU theory the shape of the utility function determines risk attitudes. For example, the agent would be risk averse if u is a concave function, meaning that, at a particular moment, utility gain from a certain transaction outcome is less that the actual monetary value of the same outcome. Considering that a utility function is identified only up to two constants (origin and units) [11], the concavity condition can be simplified to: $u(IG) < IG$ for risk aversion behaviour; and $u(IG) > IG$ for risk seeking behaviour.

However, studies (e.g. [2]) show that people tend to be risk seeking for small values of p, except if they face suffering large losses in which case they will be risk averse (e.g. buy insurance). On the contrary, people accept risk for moderate to large values of p or to avoid certain or highly probable losses. The later case can be illustrated by a situation of trust under pressure or necessity: if the agent finds himself in an environment where he faces an immediate high danger (e.g. a fire) and has to quickly decide whether or not to use an insecure means (e.g. a damaged rope) to get out of this environment, he will chose to take this risk, thus implicitly trusting the insecure means, since it is a better alternative than death.

These studies show that risk attitudes are not determined by the utility function alone. We will not attempt to formally describe and model risk attitudes. Instead we will simply assume that risk attitudes are individual and context dependent, and based on this attempt to describe some elements of the relationship between trust and risk attitudes. For an overview of alternative approaches to utility theory see Luce (2000) [9] for example.

When analysing the relationship between risk and trust, we will limit ourselves to the case of transactions with two possible outcomes, by associating a gain factor $G_s \in [0, \infty]$ to the outcome of a successful transaction and a loss factor $G_f \in [-1, 0]$ to the outcome of a failed transaction. This can be interpreted as saying that a gain on an investment can be arbitrarily large and that the loss can be at most equal to the investment.

A purely rational and risk-neutral (in the sense that it has no particular propensity to take or avoid risks) agent will decide to enter into a transaction as long as the expected utility is positive. Since risk-neutrality means that $u(IG) = IG$, we use an expression for expected gain without a factor I to determine whether the expected utility will be positive or negative. Given an investment I the return will be IG_s in the case of a successful transaction, and the loss will be IG_f in case the transaction fails. If we denote by p the probability of success, the *expected gain EG* can then be expressed as:

$$EG = pG_s + (1-p)G_f$$
$$= p(G_s - G_f) + G_f \tag{3}$$

The expected value, which is the same as the expected utility in the case of a risk-neutral attitude, resulting from an investment I can in turn be expressed as:

$$EV = EU = I \cdot EG \tag{4}$$

The parameters G_s, G_f and p determine whether the expected gain is positive or negative. If we assume that a transaction failure causes the total investment to be lost, which can be expressed by setting $G_f = -1$, the expected gain EG is equal to $p(G_s + 1) - 1$, as illustrated in Figure 2.

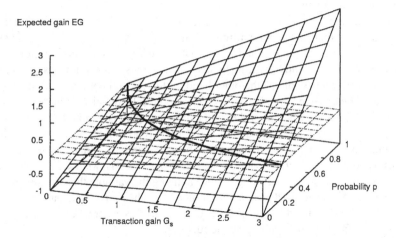

Fig. 2. Expected gain as a function of transaction gain and probability of success.

In Figure 2, the sloping surface (squared and solid line) represents the expected gain for given values of G_s and p, whereas the horizontal surface (squared and dotted line) represents the cut-off surface for zero expected gain. The intersection between the two surfaces is marked with a bold line. Points on the sloping surface above this line represent positive expected gain, whereas points below the line represent negative expected gain.

Figure 2 covers expected gains in the range $[-1, 3]$ (-100% + 300%) but in general the expected gain can be from -1 to any positive value depending on G_s. For example, public lottery can provide gains G_s in the order of several millions although the probability of success is so low that the expected gain is usually negative. An expected gain $EG = -1$ occurs for example when lending money to a con-artist ($p = 0$ and $G_f = -1$).

However, it is not enough to consider whether a transaction has a positive expected gain when making a decision to transact. How much the relying party can afford to loose also plays a role. We examine two examples in order to illustrate this behaviour.

In the first example, an agent deposits amount C in a bank. The transaction consists of keeping the money in the bank for one year in order to earn some interests. The transaction gain G_s is simply the bank's interest rate on savings. The probability of success p is the probability that the money will be secure in the bank. Although money kept in a bank is usually very secure, p can never realistically be equal to 1, so there is a remote possibility that C might be lost. Given that the transaction gain for bank deposits are relatively low, the decision of the relying party to keep his money in the bank can be explained by the perception that there is no safer option easily available.

As another example, let the transaction be to buy a $1 ticket in a lottery where there are 1,000,000 tickets issued and the price to be won is valued at $900,000. In this case, according to Equation 3 $G_s = 900,000$, $G_f = -1$ and $p = \frac{1}{1,000,000}$, so that $EG = -\$0.10$. The fact that people still buy lottery tickets can be explained by allocating a value to the thrill of participating in the hope to win the price. By assuming the utility of the thrill to be valued at $0.11, the expected gain becomes $0.01, or close to neutral gain. Buying two tickets would not double the thrill and therefore puts the expected gain in negative.

These examples, as well as the case of trust under pressure or necessity previously illustrated, show that people are willing to put different amounts of money at risk depending on the transaction gain and the probability of success. A purely rational agent (in the classic sense) would be willing to invest in any transaction as long as the expected gain is positive. Real people on the other hand will in general not invest all their capital even though the expected gain is positive. More precisely, the higher the probability of success, the higher the fraction of the total capital an agent is willing to put at risk. Let C represent an agent's total capital and $F_C \in [0,1]$ represent the fraction of capital C it is willing to invest in a given transaction. The actual amount I that a person is willing to invest is determined as $I = F_C C$. In the following analysis, we use F_C rather than I because it abstracts the capital value, by normalising the variable that we are studying.

In general F_C varies in the same direction as G_s when p is fixed, and similarly F_C varies like p when G_s fixed. As an example to illustrate this general behaviour let a given agent's risk attitude be determined by the function:

$$F_C(p, G_s) = p^{\frac{\lambda}{G_s}} \tag{5}$$

where $\lambda \in [1, \infty]$ is a factor moderating the influence of the transaction gain G_s on the fraction of total capital that the relying party is willing to put at risk. We will use the term *decision surface* to describe the type of surface illustrated in Figure 3.

λ is interpreted as a factor of the relying party's risk aversion in the given transaction context, and in Fig.3 $\lambda = 10000$. . Independently from the utility function (propensity towards risk), λ represents the contextual component of the risk attitude. A low λ value is representative of a risk-taking behaviour because it increases the volume under the surface delimited by F_C (pushes the decision surface up in Figure 3), whereas a high λ value represents risk aversion because it reduces the volume under the surface (pushes the decision surface down).

Risk attitudes are relative to each individual, so the shape of the surface in Figure 3 only represents an example and will differ for each agent. In this example, we assumed a relatively complex function to represent a non-linear investment behaviour. We do

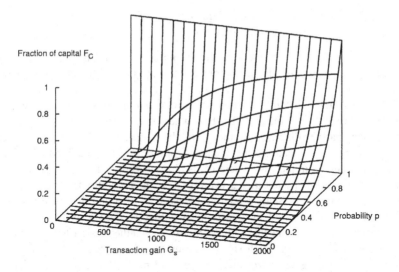

Fig. 3. Example of an agent's risk attitude expressed as a decision surface.

not address here the issue of user modelling, but simply choose a non-trivial example. The surface shape depends as much on the personal preferences of the agent as on its mood in the particular context, but this does not preclude that in unusual situations agent may behave out of the norm, even irrationally. The risk attitude also depends on the total capital C an agent possesses and can change as a function of past experience, notably via the agent's confidence. As already mentioned, we will not try to define general expressions for individual risk attitudes. The expression of Equation 5, with the corresponding surface in Figure 3, only illustrates an example.

A particular transaction will be represented by a point in the 3D space of Figure 3 with coordinates (G_s, p, F_C). Because the surface represents an agent's risk attitude the agent will per definition accept a transaction for which the point is located underneath the decision surface, and will reject a transaction for which the point is located above the decision surface.

3   Balancing Trust and Risk

We now move our point of view on the situation from risk to trust. Whereas in Section 2 the situation was modelled as a transaction, here it revolves around the concepts of dependence and uncertainty. By this we mean that the outcome of the transaction depends on somebody or something and that the relying party is uncertain about the outcome of the transaction.

We assume that transactions can either be successful or failures and that the outcome of a transaction depends on a party x. Furthermore we will let the uncertainty about the outcome of the transaction be represented by the probability p used in Section 2. We can deduce from these hypotheses that p in fact represents the reliability of x for producing a successful outcome, and that p thereby partly represents the trustworthiness of x.

Definition 2 (Reliability Trust). *Reliability trust is defined as the trusting party's probability estimate p of success of the transaction.*

As shown in Section 2, the specific value of p that will make the relying party enter into a transaction also depends on the transaction gain G_s and the invested fraction of the capital F_C

The idea is that, for all combination of values of G_s, p and F_C underneath the decision surface in Figure 3, the relying party trusts x, whereas values above the decision surface lead the relying party to distrust x for this particular transaction. The degree to which the relying party trusts x depends on the distance from the current situation to the decision surface. For example, in the case where G_s is close to zero and F_C is close to one, the relying party will normally not trust x even if p (i.e. the reliability trust) is high.

Since in reality p represents a relative measure of trust and that even agents with high p values can be distrusted, the question is whether it would be useful to determine a better measure of trust, i.e. one that actually measures whether x is trusted for a particular transaction in a given context. Such a measure must necessarily be more complex because of its dependence on gains, investment values and possibly other context-dependent parameters. Although it strictly speaking constitutes an abuse of language to interpret p as a measure of trust, it is commonly being done in the literature. We will therefore not dismiss this interpretation of p as trust, but rather explicitly use the term *reliability trust* to describe it.

Another question which arises when interpreting p as trust is whether it would be better to simply use the concepts of reliability or outcome probability for modelling choice because trust does not add any new information. In fact it has been claimed that the concept of trust is void of semantic meaning in economic theory [17]. We believe that this is an exaggeration and that the notion of trust carries important semantics. The concept of trust is particularly useful in a context of relative uncertainty where a relying party depends on another party to avoid harm and to achieve a successful outcome.

As an attempt to define a measure that adequately represents trusting decisions, we propose to use the normalized difference between x's reliability p and the cut-off probability on an agent's decision surface, what we will call *decision trust*.

Definition 3 (Decision Trust). *Let us assume that: 1) the relying party's risk attitude is defined by a specific decision surface D; 2) a transaction X with party x is characterised by the probability p of x producing a successful outcome, by the transaction gain G_s, and by the fraction of the relying party's capital F_C to be invested in the transaction; 3) p_D is the cut-off probability on the decision surface D for the same values of G_s and F_C. The decision trust T, where $T \in [-1, 1]$, is then defined as:*

$$
\begin{cases}
For\ p < p_D : T = \frac{p - p_D}{p_D} \\
For\ p = p_D : T = 0 \\
For\ p > p_D : T = \frac{p - p_D}{1 - p_D}
\end{cases}
\tag{6}
$$

This decision trust is first defined by its three extreme points: $(0, -1)$, $(p_D, 0)$, and $(1, 1)$. The next constraint is that the decision trust must explicitly depend on a distance between the current probability p and the cut-off probability p_D. We then choose the most simple functions, given that we have no *a priori* knowledge or experimental data, i.e. a linear function from the distance $\delta = p - p_D$.

A positive decision trust is interpreted as saying that the relying party trusts x for this transaction in this context. A zero decision trust is interpreted as saying that the relying party is undecided as to whether he or she trusts x for this transaction because x's reliability trust is at the cut-off value on the decision surface. Finally, a negative decision trust corresponds to the relying party not trusting x for the transaction in this context.

As an example, Figure 4 illustrates the case of two possible transactions X_1 and X_2. This figure is a section of the decision surface D in Figure 3 for a given value of G_s. The probability difference δ is illustrated for the two transactions X_1 and X_2, as δ_1 and δ_2 respectively. The figure illustrates the case of positive (T_1) and negative (T_2) decision trust, although the actual transaction probability p (i.e. reliability trust) is the same for both situations.

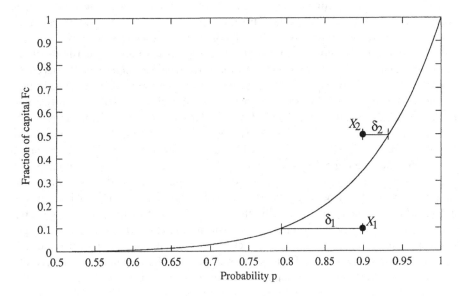

Fig. 4. Illustrating decision trust by difference between reliability and decision cut-off probability.

Finally, one can ask what the relying party should do in the case when the decision trust is negative. Povey (1999) [14] argues that, if the trusting decision is not made, the relying party can treat the risk by: 1) adding countermeasures; 2) deferring risk; 3) or re-computing trust with more or better metrics. Options 1 and 2 aim at increasing the reliability trust p by, respectively, increasing the cost I for the transacting opponent, and hoping that time will soften the relying party's investment. Option 3 confirms our idea that complex trust measures which are introduced early may sap an interaction. The two interacting parties would then need to re-negotiate the terms of the interaction.

Traditional risk management [15,3] provides us with even more solutions, like risk diversification or risk control, but that falls outside the subject of this study.

4 Conclusion

Risk and trust are two facets of decision-making through which we view the world and choose to act. In an attempt to shape the relationship between risk and trust, this paper tries to refine Manchala's model in order to derive a computational model integrating the two notions. We first compute the transaction's expected gain and illustrate it on several examples. But this transaction factor is not enough to determine the choice of whether to transact or not. We complete this model by introducing the fraction of the capital that an agent is willing to risk.

The intuitive parallel with trust of the first part of our approach is to use the probability of success of the transaction as a measure of trust, what we called *reliability trust*. The decision surface which defines an agent's risk attitude is then taken into account in order to derive a more complete definition of trust, the *decision trust*. This approach provides a more meaningful notion of trust because it combines trust with risk attitudes.

This work is a first step at integrating the two important aspects of decision-making that are risk and trust. We explored their relationship by trying to define a model that could be applied to various examples. Although there is no universal mathematical definition of several aspects of our model (utility function, decision surface) [16], we showed how agent's risk attitudes can be modelled and evaluated in the case of a particular transaction.

As further work, the model needs to be tested with various utility function shapes and decision surfaces, and extended to cope with multiple outcomes. Several other variables can also be integrated into this model. First, we could incorporate more economics and legal information. For example, insurances would consider contractual transactions or the influence of the law, and they could take the form of basic outcomes, minimal investments and specific risk thresholds. Secondly, the temporal aspects should be explored, for example via reinforcement learning or planning techniques to model how an agent adapts to a sequence of transactions. This research activity should tie together trust and risk dynamics. As a continuation of this work, research will be conducted to analyse the situation where trust decision is not made after risk evaluation.

References

1. Bachmann, R. Trust, Power and Control in Trans-Organizational Relations. *Organization Studies*, 2:341–369, 2001.
2. M.H. Birnbaum. Decision and Choice: Paradoxes of Choice. In N.J. Smelser et al., editors, *International Encyclopedia of the Social and Behavioral Sciences*, pages 3286–3291. Elsevier, 2001.
3. D. Borge. *The Book of Risk*. John Wiley & Sons, 2001.
4. Cahill, V. and al. Using Trust for Secure Collaboration in Uncertain Environment. *IEEE Pervasive Computing*, 2(3):52–61, July-September 2003.

5. T. Dimitrakos. A Service-Oriented Trust Management Framework. In R. Falcone, S. Barber, L. Korba, and M. Singh, editors, *Trust, Reputation, and Security: Theories and Practice*, LNAI 2631, pages 53–72. Springer, 2002.

6. R. Falcone and C. Castelfranchi. *Social Trust: A Cognitive Approach*, pages 55–99. Kluwer, 2001.

7. T Grandison. *Trust Management for Internet Applications*. PhD thesis, University of London, July 2003.

8. Grandison, T. and Sloman, M. A Survey of Trust in Internet Applications. *IEEE Communications Surveys*, 3(4):2–16, Fourth Quarter 2000.

9. R.D. Luce. *Utility of Gains and Losses: Measurement-Theoretical and Experimental Approaches*. New Jersey: Lawrence Erlbaum Associates, Inc., 2000.

10. D.W. Manchala. Trust Metrics, Models and Protocols for Electronic Commerce Transactions. In *Proc. of the 18th International Conference on Distributed Computing Systems*, pages 312–321. IEEE Computer Society, 1998.

11. A. Mas-Colell, M. Whinston, and J. Green. *Microeconomic Theory*. Oxford University Press, 1995.

12. D. H. McKnight and N. L. Chervany. The Meanings of Trust. Technical Report MISRC Working Paper Series 96-04, University of Minnesota, Management Information Systems Reseach Center, 1996. http://www.misrc.umn.edu/wpaper/wp96-04.htm.

13. Patrick, A. Building Trustworthy Software Agents. *IEEE Internet Computing*, 6(6):46–53, November-December 2002.

14. Povey, D. Developing Electronic Trust Policies Using a Risk Management Model. In *Proc. of the Secure Networking - CQRE (Secure)'99, International Exhibition and Congress*, LNCS 1740, pages 1–16, Düsseldorf, Germany, November 30 - December 2 1999. Springer.

15. E. J. Vaughan. *Risk Management*. John Wiley & Sons, 1997.

16. D. Vose. *Risk Analysis (2nd edition)*. John Wiley & Sons, 2001.

17. O.E. Williamson. *The Economic Institutions of Capitalism*. The Free Press, New York, 1985.

Using Risk Analysis to Assess User Trust
– A Net-Bank Scenario –

Gyrd Brændeland[1] and Ketil Stølen[1,2]

[1] Department of Informatics, University of Oslo, Norway
[2] SINTEF ICT, Norway

Abstract. The paper advocates asset-oriented risk analysis as a means to help defend user trust. The paper focuses on a net-bank scenario, and addresses the issue of analysing trust from the perspective of the bank. The proposed approach defines user trust as an asset and makes use of asset-oriented risk analysis to identify treats, vulnerabilities and unwanted incidents that may reduce user trust.

1 Introduction

There is no generally accepted definition of the term "trust". One obvious reason for this is that the meaning of "trust" as the meaning of most other natural language terms depends on the context in which it is used. In this paper we restrict our investigation of trust to a scenario involving a net-bank (online banking), the bank that owns the net-bank, and the net-bank users. We argue that risk analysis is suited to help defend existing user trust. The term "defend" is taken from asset-oriented risk analysis where vulnerabilities of a system are analysed with regard to identified assets. We claim that the user trust is a major asset to the bank. Furthermore, we argue that risk analysis is well-suited to find strategies to defend user trust and prevent unwanted incidents that may reduce user trust.

In order to use risk analysis to asses user trust, we need a way to measure trust in a quantitative or qualitative manner. We argue that it is not the trust itself, but its consequences, such as the number of net-bank users, that is important to the bank. Such observable consequences are often easy to measure and may provide a firm basis for risk analysis.

The paper is divided into six sections. Section 2 introduces a basic terminology with emphasis on factors that affect trust. Section 3 gives a short introduction to asset-oriented risk analysis. Section 4 describes a net-bank scenario on which much of this paper focuses. Section 5 argues the suitability of risk analysis to help defend existing user trust. The evaluation is angled towards the scenario introduced in Section 4. Section 6 summarises our findings, presents the main conclusions and outlines related work.

C.D. Jensen et al. (Eds.): iTrust 2004, LNCS 2995, pp. 146–160, 2004.
© Springer-Verlag Berlin Heidelberg 2004

2   Trust and Trust Affecting Factors

It is generally accepted that trust is a more general issue than security in particular and dependability in general. Jones et al. [15] argue that "although businesses and consumers may consider underlying systems to be completely dependable in the traditional sense, they may not trust these systems with their business or personal interests unless there exists a suitable legal framework they can fall back on, should problems arise." An analysis of trust will therefore encompass a number of issues like legal, sociological and psychological aspects that are not directly related to security.

2.1   Basic Terminology

Studies of trust distinguish between the trustor, that is, the agent that trusts another agent, and the trustee; the agent being trusted. Trust is a property of the trustor, whereas credibility and trustworthiness are properties of the trustee. Trust can also be seen as a binary relation, from the trustor to the trustee.

Mayer et al. [19] defines trust as "the willingness of a party to be vulnerable to the actions of another party based on the expectation that the other will perform a particular action important to the trustor, irrespective of the agility to monitor or control that other party." Koufaris and Hampton-Sosa [17] use Mayer's definition of trust in their survey of user trust in a web site, which is not so different from our net-bank scenario.

Attributes of the trustee, such as credibility and trustworthiness are considered important factors influencing an agent's trust in another party [19]. In a recent book on the role of computers in influencing peoples attitudes, Fogg [9] is concerned with what constitutes computer credibility. In accordance with existing literature, Fogg defines credibility as "a perceived quality, that has two dimensions: trustworthiness and expertise" (Figure 1).

Fig. 1. Fogg – The two key dimensions of credibility

Fogg decomposes the concept of trustworthiness further into the terms *well-intentioned, truthful* and *unbiased*, and expertise into *knowledgeable, experienced* and *competent*. Fogg and Tseng [10] argue that users' evaluation of computer trustworthiness and credibility is a function of both system design features and psychological factors ascribed to the entity behind a system.

2.2   Factors That Affect Trust

Egger [6] has developed a model of trust-relevant factors in e-business that encompasses such features as those discussed by Fogg and Tseng. Egger's model,

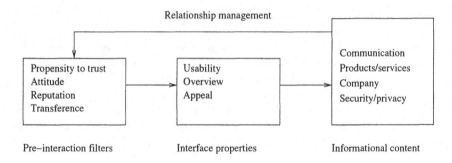

Fig. 2. Egger – Model of trust in e-commerce

shown in Figure 2, identifies factors that affect user trust in a system. *Pre-interaction filters* are factors that may affect a user's trust in a system prior to any interaction. An individual's general *propensity* to trust affects the degree to which she is willing to trust any agent. A user's general *attitude* towards an industry may affect her trust in particular members of that industry. *Reputation* concerns such factors as the strength of a company's brand name and the user's experience with the system through earlier interaction. *Transference* of trust covers the situation where a user trusts a company because a trusted third party has reported that the company is trustworthy.

Interface properties concern the impression that a system gives through its design interface. The significance of such factors are well documented in the literature. An empirical study performed by Stanford Web Credibility Project [8] discovered that users had more trust in a web site with a picture of a nice car in the upper right corner, than the same web site where the picture of the car was replaced by a dollar sign.

Informational content concerns other properties of a system such as security and privacy and how they are conveyed to the user. It is not enough that a system is properly evaluated and certified with regard to security. The user must also be informed that the system has undergone such evaluations. The provider of a web service may for example include information in its web site that the system has undergone a security evaluation that is certified by a licensed certifier.

Egger's model includes factors that are encompassed by both the terms "trust" and "credibility", as introduced in the previous section. In fact, Egger views user trust as perceived trustworthiness. Egger's model is a practical tool for assessing user trust, and has already been tried out in a few cases discussed in Egger's PhD thesis [7].

3   Risk Analysis – The CORAS Approach

The Australian/New Zealand standard for risk management [1] defines risk analysis as the systematic use of available information to determine how often specified risks may occur and the magnitude of their consequences. Furthermore, as illustrated by Figure 3, risk analysis is one of seven risk management processes.

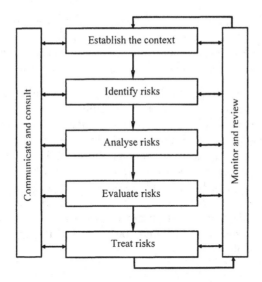

Fig. 3. Risk management overview

In practise, however, the term "risk analysis" normally has a broader meaning covering the five sequentially ordered processes that the Australian/New Zealand standard refers to as: establish the context, identify risk, analyse risk, evaluate risk and treat risk. In this paper we use this broader definition. We refer to what the standard [1] calls "risk analysis" as consequence and frequency analysis.

There are many forms and variations of risk analysis. Asset-oriented risk analysis where system vulnerabilities and unwanted incidents are analysed with regard to identified assets, is a kind of risk analysis often used within the security domain. One such approach to risk analysis is the CORAS [5,2] methodology that will be used in the following.

CORAS is characterised by tight integration of state-of-the-art systems modelling methodology based on UML2.0 with leading methodologies for risk analysis as Hazard and Operability (HazOp) analysis [20], Failure Mode Effect Analysis (FMEA) [4], and Fault Tree Analysis (FTA) [12]. In fact, CORAS comes with its own specialisation of UML, a so-called UML profile for security analysis that has recently become a recommended OMG (Object Management Group) standard integrated in the UML Profile for Modeling Quality of Service and Fault Tolerance [18].

Hence, an important aspect of the CORAS methodology is the practical use of UML to support risk management in general, and risk analysis with respect to security (in the following referred to as security risk analysis) in particular. The CORAS risk analysis methodology makes use of UML models for three different purposes:

– To describe the target of evaluation in a uniform manner at the right level of abstraction.

- To facilitate communication and interaction between different groups of stakeholders, experts and users involved in a risk analysis.
- To document risk analysis results and the assumptions on which these results depend to support reuse and maintenance.

The former two are particularly relevant in the case of trust. To analyse trust, technical system documentation is not sufficient; a clear understanding of system usage and its role in the surrounding organisation, enterprise and society is just as important. UML is well-suited to describe technical aspects as well as human behaviour in the form of work-processes. One major challenge when performing a risk analysis is to establish a common understanding of the target of evaluation, threats, vulnerabilities and risks among the stakeholders, experts and users participating in the analysis. The CORAS UML profile has been designed to facilitate improved communication during risk analysis, by making the UML diagrams easier to understand for non-experts, and at the same time preserving the well-definedness of UML.

4   A Net-Bank Scenario

Figure 4 presents a simple UML class diagram that specifies the overall context of our net-bank scenario. There is a web-service exemplified by the net-bank, the net-bank is owned by a bank, and the net-bank users are account holders performing net-bank transactions via the Internet. The bank, the net-bank, the net-bank users and the Internet exist in an overall context known as Society.

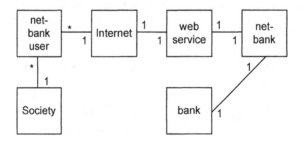

Fig. 4. A net-bank scenario: The main actors

When interacting with a net-bank, a user normally knows very little about the actual design of the bank, but is nevertheless willing to make herself vulnerable, by entrusting her money and personal data with the net-bank. If asked why, the user may answer that she expects the net-bank to perform several actions, such as safe handling of her money, confidential handling of personal data, legislative insurance in the case something goes wrong, and so on.

Figure 5 outlines the relationship between the notions introduced in Section 2.1 and the entities of our net-bank scenario.

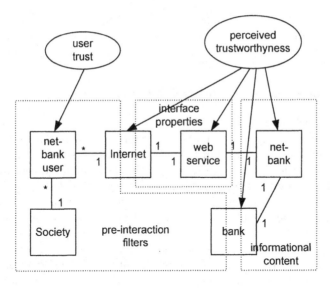

Fig. 5. Trust and trustworthiness in a net-bank scenario

Since this paper restricts its attention to user trust, we consider trust only as a property of the net-bank user. It is in the interest of the net-bank owner that it, as well as the net-bank and the Internet, is viewed as trustworthy by the net-bank users. As explained in Section 2.2, both trust and trustworthiness are influenced by several factors, categorised as pre-interaction filters, interface properties and informational content, respectively. The pre-interaction filter "user's propensity to trust" is clearly a property of the user. The same holds for attitude. The bank's reputation as well as the reputation of the Internet as a medium for interaction has impact on user trust. Transference takes place between actors in society. Properties of the web-service, such as user appeal, are part of the interface properties. Informational content concerns such factors as the net-bank's security and privacy policy.

5 Analysing User Trust in the Net-Bank Scenario

In the following we sketch how the model-based risk analysis approach of CORAS can be used to identify treats, vulnerabilities and unwanted incidents that may reduce user trust. We focus on those aspects where a risk analysis targetting trust differs from an ordinary security risk analysis. An important observation is that there is a difference between perceived security, which is a basis for user trust, and well-founded security, which is the target of conventional security risk analysis. The security of a system may be perceived to be worse than the actual security, if the latter is not properly conveyed to the user, as discussed with regard to informational content in Section 2.2. It may be perceived to be better than the actual security, through for example an appealing interface that gives a sound impression of the system, regardless of implementation. The presentation is structured into the five main sub processes of risk analysis described in Section 3.

5.1   Subprocess I: Establish the Context

To conduct a risk analysis we need a characterisation of the target of analysis. This target may be a system, a part of a system or a system aspect. The term "system" should be understood in the broadest sense. A system is not just technology, but also the humans interacting with the technology, and all relevant aspects of the surrounding organisation and society. In the following we take the net-bank scenario specified in the previous section as our target of analysis. A risk analysis is always conducted on behalf of one or several customers. In the following we view the bank owning the net-bank as our only customer.

The CORAS risk analysis process is asset-oriented. An *asset* is a part or feature of a system that has a value for one of the stakeholders on behalf of which the risk analysis is conducted, in our case, the bank. A risk analysis makes sense only if there are some assets to be protected. If there are no assets, there is no risk and no need for a risk analysis. Let us therefore identify and value assets from the perspective of the bank. When analysing users' trust in the net-bank, it is not the trust as such, but its direct impact on the market share that the bank is interested in. User trust has impact on the number of users and the amount of time and money they are willing to invest in a system. These are precise factors that are easy to measure. A user's willingness to risk time and money on for example web gambling may also be triggered by other factors than trust, such as addiction to gambling. User trust, however, is clearly one important factor that affects observable customer behaviour, and may therefore be viewed as an asset on its own. Figure 6 makes use of an asset-diagram expressed in the CORAS UML profile to specify that the market share asset depends on other assets like users' trust in the net-bank.

Confidentiality is the property that information is not made available or disclosed to unauthorised individuals, entities or processes [13]. Confidentiality of the customer database is clearly important for the market share since such information could be used by competitors to "steal" customers. That the market share may depend on the confidentiality of the net-bank technology should also be obvious. Furthermore, there are also dependencies between user trust and the confidentiality of the net-bank technology and customer database. We may use Egger's model (see Figure 2) to decompose user trust in more specialised assets. We consider only those factors that the bank can directly influence, leaving reputation as the only asset under pre-interaction filters.

The risk evaluation criteria specify what the customer may tolerate with respect to risk. The risks that do not satisfy the risk evaluation criteria must be treated. Table 1 presents two examples of risk evaluation criteria. In order to assign a quantitative risk acceptance value to user trust, we need a way to measure user trust. We may for example use Jøsang and Knapskog's [16] metric for trusted systems, based on their subjective logic approach. They define trust

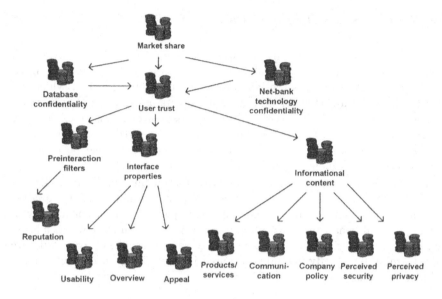

Fig. 6. Hierarchy of trust-related assets

as a subjective belief consisting of three probability values; belief, disbelief and uncertainty that together equal 1. If a person's belief value for a given proposition is 1, she has full trust in the proposition. A decrease in the belief value is a decrease in the trust. Jøsang and Knapskog give guidelines to determine opinions when evidence can only be analysed intuitively, as in the case of trust. Their proposal involves formulating a questionnaire to guide people in expressing their belief as valued opinions. An agent's trust is computed from the value of several beliefs about the trustee, that together constitute the total trust.

Table 1. Risk evaluation criteria

Id	Stakeholder	Asset	Criteria description
1	bank	user trust	if risk impact ¡ "0.15 decrease in user trust within a week" then "accept risk" else "assign priority and treatment"
2	bank	market share	if risk impact ¡ "loss of 500 customers within a week" then "accept risk" else "assign priority and treatment"

For this to make sense, we need an understanding of the effect of reduced user trust on the market share. For example, it seems reasonable to require that any risk that satisfies Criteria 1 also satisfies Criteria 2. Such an understanding may for example be based on statistical data, or be acquired through user surveys.

5.2   Subprocess II: Identify Risks

Identifying risks includes identifying threats to assets, identifying vulnerabilities of assets, and documenting unwanted incidents caused by threats exploiting vulnerabilities. A *threat* is a potential cause of an unwanted incident which may result in harm to a system or organisation and its assets. A *vulnerability* is a weakness with respect to an asset or group of assets which can be exploited by one or more threats. An *unwanted incident* is an undesired event that may reduce the value of an asset. A risk is an unwanted incident that has been assigned consequence and frequency values.

Conventional approaches to risk identification include checklists, judgement based on experience and records, flow charts, brainstorming, systems analysis, scenario analysis and systems engineering techniques. A UML sequence diagram showing normal behaviour of a system in combination with guidewords addressing the various security and trust aspects may be used as a basis for a structured brainstorming to identify possible unwanted incidents. Figure 7 specifies a normal login session.

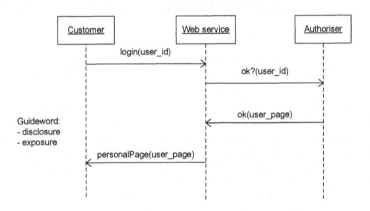

Fig. 7. User login session

Disclosure of personal customer data to outsiders is an example of a security related unwanted incident, during a normal login session. This is what happened in 2000 when it was reported that the net-bank of the Norwegian company Gjensidige NOR made web pages containing confidential customer data accessible to outsiders [3]. This incident was caused by a weakness in the security technology. When analysing trust we may be interested in other types of unwanted incidents than typical security incidents. Whether such an incident is a threat to customer trust depends on public exposure. In our risk assessment we therefore identify exposure of a security incident in media, as the unwanted incident, and disclosure of personal customer data as a threat that may cause the incident, see Table 2.

Table 2. HazOp table: Unwanted incidents

Id	Stakeholder	Asset	Guideword	Threat	Unwanted incident
1	bank	perceived security	disclosure	disclosure of confidential customer data	incident reported to media
2	bank	perceived security	disclosure	security weakness revealed	weakness reported to media
3	bank	user trust	exposure	negative press coverage	loss of user trust
4	bank	market share	exposure	loss of user trust	loss of regular customers

The user trust asset may also be affected by unwanted incidents that are not directly related to security. Lack of support and non-appealing web-sites are two examples.

To model a full scenario corresponding to an unwanted incident we may use the CORAS UML profile as demonstrated in Figure 8. The unwanted incident that a security incident is reported to media, from Table 2, is modelled as a use case including the threat that confidential customer data is disclosed. The threat scenario is caused by a threat agent; in this case an eavesdropper. Each threat scenario and each unwanted incident may be further specified by UML sequence and activity diagrams as in the case of an ordinary UML use case.

5.3 Subprocess III: Determine Consequence and Frequency

A *risk* in the CORAS terminology is an unwanted incident that has been assigned a consequence, in terms of reduced asset value, and frequency values. If the frequency of an incident is not known we can use a fault tree to document the possible routes that can lead to the incident. The objective of a fault tree analysis is to document in a structured way the possible routes that can lead to the violations of security requirements identified by for example HazOp. The unwanted incidents identified in the HazOp table, Table 2, are inserted in a fault tree, see Figure 9, based on abstraction level and the relationship between the incidents. Through the fault tree analysis, the incident is broken down into smaller causes for which we have better estimates of the frequency. The top event of the fault tree in Figure 9, negative press coverage on security leakage, may lead to reduced user trust which may lead to loss of market share. Historical data from similar incidents in the past can be used to estimate the consequences in the form of reduced asset value.

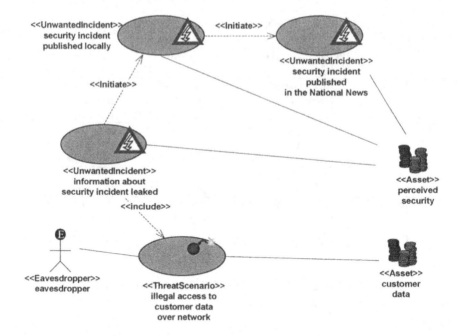

Fig. 8. Specification of threat scenario

5.4 Subprocess IV: Evaluate Risks

Evaluating risks includes determining level of risk, prioritising risks, categorising risks, determining interrelationships among risk themes and prioritising the resulting risk themes and risks. A *risk theme* is a categorisation of similar risks, assigned its own risk value.

When trust relevant risks have been assigned frequency and consequence they can be evaluated in the same manner as any other risk.

5.5 Subprocess V: Treat Risks

Treating risks includes identifying treatment options and assessing alternative treatment approaches. A *treatment* is a way of reducing the risk value of a risk or a risk theme. The Australian/New Zealand standard for risk management [1] identifies five options for treating risks: acceptance, avoidance, reduce likelihood, reduce consequences, and transfer to another party.

Risks having impact on user trust may require other types of treatment than security related risks. In Section 5.2 we identified media coverage of a security incident as an unwanted incident (Table 2) and in Section 5.3 we proposed fault tree analysis to estimate the frequency of such an event. In order to treat this type of risk it may not be enough to fix a programming error. It may also be necessary to do some public relations work, or to prevent information on

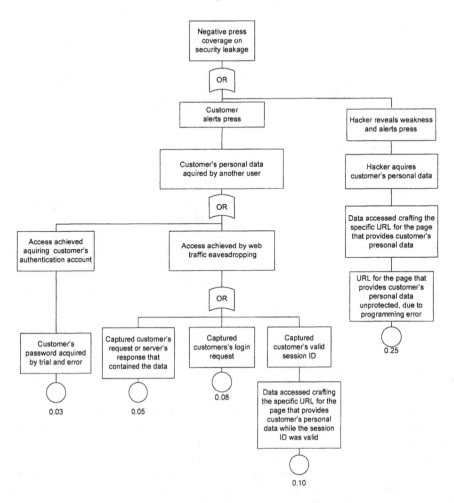

Fig. 9. A fault tree for revealing weak security

the security breach to reach the public. The CORAS UML profile can be used to document security treatments as use case diagrams. As indicated by Figure 10, we may use the CORAS UML profile to document treatments with regard to trust in the same way. We have identified the treatment "public relations work" to reduce the consequences of negative press coverage, and the treatment "authentication" to reduce the likelihood of an intruder obtaining illegal access to customer data.

6   Conclusions

The paper has advocated asset-oriented risk analysis as a means to help defend existing user trust. The proposed approach defines user trust as an asset and makes use of asset-oriented risk analysis to identify threats, vulnerabilities and

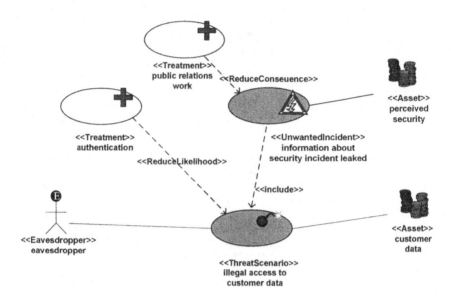

Fig. 10. Documentation of treatments

unwanted incidents that may cause a reduction in user trust. Risk analysis targetting user-trust may be based on the same overall process as risk analysis in the security domain.

Herrmann [11] distinguishes between two principal approaches to integrate trust values into the process of security risk analysis. In the first approach, the auditing process is extended by considering trust values in the risk level computation. Simply said, the higher the trust in the good-naturedness of the involved parties, the lower the likelihood of a successful attack. In the other approach, the auditing process is kept unchanged and the decision about which risk can be run and which not, is made dependent on the trust in the parties. In that case, "an asset owner should be willing to take as greater risks as higher the belief in the benevolent behaviour of the involved parties is."

Herrmann's focus on integrating trust values in the auditing process is clearly different from our use of risk analysis as a means to analyse user trust by interpreting user trust as an asset. Herrmann proposes to express trust relations by so-called trust values, that were first introduced by Jøsang and Knapskog [16].

To accept asset-oriented risk analysis as a means to help defend user-trust entails accepting asset-oriented risk analysis as means to help build new user trust or increase already existing user trust. The same techniques that are used to identify factors that may cause loss of asset value may also be used to identify factors that may increase the value of assets. In that case, a trust incident is wanted and may have positive impact mirroring the negative impact in the "hazard" risk analysis used in this paper.

An interesting issue for further research is the use of modal logic, as for example in [14], in combination with UML to gain the expressiveness that may be required to describe certain trust relevant scenarios. Furthermore, to estimate frequencies and consequences, we may need a tight integration of methods from decision psychology, or social science. The methods may vary from user surveys, to technical assessments and lab experiments.

Acknowledgements. The research on which this paper reports has partly been funded by the Research Council of Norway project SECURIS (152839/220). It is influenced by discussions and interaction within the EU working group iTrust (IST-2001-34910). The authors thank Asbjørn Følstad and Ida Solheim for valuable input.

References

1. Australian/New Zealand Standard for Risk Management 4360:1999.
2. J. Ø. Aagedal, F. den Braber, T. Dimitrakos, B. A. Gran, D. Raptis, and K. Stølen. Model-based risk assessment to improve enterprise security. In *EDOC2002*, pages 51–62. IEEE Computer Society, 2002.
3. P. K. Bjørkeng, C. Haraldsen, and S. Stenseng. Strykkarakter til internett-bank. Aftenposten, August 2000.
4. A. Bouti and D. A. Kadi. A state-of-the-art review of FMEA/FMECA. *International journal of reliability, quality and safety engineering*, 1:515–543, 1994.
5. T. Dimitrakos, B. Ritchie, D. Raptis, J. Ø. Aagedal, F. den Braber, K. Stølen, and S.-H. Houmb. Integrating model-based security risk managament into ebusiness systems development: The coras approach. In *I3E2002*, pages 159–175. Kluwer, 2002.
6. F. N. Egger. Towards a model of trust for e-commerce system design. In *CHI 2000: Workshop Designing Interactive Systems for 1-to-1 E-commerce*, April 2000. http://www.zurich.ibm.com/~mrs/chi2000/contributions/egger.html.
7. F. N. Egger. *From Interactions to Transactions: Designing the Trust Experience for Business-to-Consumer Electronic Commerce*. PhD thesis, Eindhoven University of Technology, 2003.
8. B. Fogg, C. Soohoo, D. Danielson, L. Marable, J. Stanford, and E. R. Tauber. How do people evaluate a web sites credibility? Technical report, Stanford Persuasive Technology Lab, October 2002. http://www.consumerwebwatch.org/news/report3_credibilityresearch/ stanfordPTL_abstract.htm.
9. B. J. Fogg. *Persuasive Technology. Using Computers to Change What We Think and Do*. Morgan Kaufman Publishers, December 2002.
10. B. J. Fogg and H. Tseng. The elements of computer credibility. In *Proceedings of the SIGCHI conference on Human factors in computing systems*, pages 80–87. ACM Press, 1999.
11. P. Herrmann. How to integrate trust management into a risk analysis process. Second Internal iTrust Workshop On Trust Management In Dynamic Open Systems, September 2003.
12. IEC 1025. *Fault Tree Analysis (FTA)*, 1990.
13. ISO/IEC TR 13335-1. *Information Technology - Guidelines for the management of IT Security - Part 1: Concepts and models for IT security*, 2001.

14. A. J. I. Jones. *The open agent society*, chapter 3; A logical framework. John Wiley & Sons, Chichester, UK, 2004. To be published.
15. S. Jones, M. Wilikens, P. Morris, and M. Masera. Trust requirements in e-business. *Communications of the ACM*, 43(12):81–87, 2000.
16. A. Jøsang and S. Knapskog. A metric for trusted systems. In *21st National Security Conference*, 1998.
    http://csrc.nist.gov/nissc/1998/proceedings/paperA2.pdf.
17. M. Koufaris and W. Hampton-Sosa. Customer trust online: Examening the role of the experience with the web site. Technical Report #CIS-2002-05, Department of Statistics & Computer informations systems. Zicklin school of business, Baruch college, May 2002. CIS Working paper series.
18. M. S. Lund, I. Hogganvik, F. Seehusen, and K. Stølen. UML profile for security assessment. Technical Report STF40 A03066, SINTEF Telecom and informatics, December 2003.
19. R. C. Mayer, J. H. Davis, and F. D. Schoorman. An integrative model of organizational trust. *Academy of management review*, 20(3):709–734, 1995.
20. F. Redmill, M.Chudleigh, and J. Catmur. *Hazop and software hazop*. Wiley, 1999.

E-notebook Middleware for Accountability and Reputation Based Trust in Distributed Data Sharing Communities

Paul Ruth*, Dongyan Xu*†, Bharat Bhargava*†, and Fred Regnier‡

Purdue University, West Lafayette, IN 47907. USA,
{ruth, dxu, bb}@cs.purdue.edu, fregnier@purdue.edu

Abstract. This paper presents the design of a new middleware which provides support for trust and accountability in distributed data sharing communities. One application is in the context of scientific collaborations. Multiple researchers share individually collected data, who in turn create new data sets by performing transformations on existing shared data sets. In data sharing communities building trust for the data obtained from others is crucial. However, the field of data provenance does not consider malicious or untrustworthy users. By adding accountability to the provenance of each data set, this middlware ensures data integrity insofar as any errors can be identified and corrected. The user is further protected from faulty data by a *trust view* created from past experiences and second-hand recommendations. A *trust view* is based on real world social interactions and reflects each user's own experiences within the community. By identifying the providers of faulty data and removing them from a *trust view*, the integrity of all data is enhanced

1 Introduction

In scientific research, scientists rely on experimental data to demonstrate their findings. The accuracy of the data is critical not only for the validity of the research results but also for the reputation of the scientist. Currently, a scientist's professional reputation is determined by peer review of papers submitted to conferences and journals for publication. Frequently, results obtained are based on complete data that does not accompany the paper. It is assumed that the integrity of the data has been maintained throughout.

To complicate matters even more, the recent growth in processing power and storage capacity along with the ease of communication through the Internet, has allowed scientists to create and process very large data sets based on locally derived data as well as data obtained from other scientists. Although a large data set can provide better results because of larger and more diverse sampling,

---

* Department of Computer Science

† The Center for Education and Research in Information Assurance and Security (CERIAS)

‡ Department of Chemistry and The Bindley Bioscience Center at Purdue University

C.D. Jensen et al. (Eds.): iTrust 2004, LNCS 2995, pp. 161–175, 2004.

in order to be confident with the results, the origin of all data in the set must be known. In most scientific communities there is no standardized method for collecting and sharing data, which makes it difficult to achieve global data consistency, validity, and credibility. More specifically heterogeneity between labs may lay in the following:

- The condition and calibration of experimental instruments in different labs, and the condition and configuration of lab environments.
- The context of different experiments, such as the time, location, temperature of the experiments, and in the case of medical or social experiments, the age and ethnic group of human subjects.
- The protocol (and the strictness of its enforcement) of data generation, transformation, and derivation. For example, different labs may use different sampling rates, precision, and number of repetitions.
- The capacity, version, and configuration of computing platforms (both software and hardware) in different labs.
- Non-uniform data formats adopted by different labs, due to their formatting conventions and differences in software/hardware/instruments.

There is a need for a distributed environment that allows researchers to collaborate by sharing data while maintaining the complete history and source of all data sets. This by necessity would include those smaller sets which constitute the greater accumulation of data and the transformations from which they were combined. The field of data provenance is evolving out of this concern [2,4,6,7, 8,10,11,12,14,16,17,20,25,27]. Data provenance is the description of the origins of a piece of data and the process by which it arrived in a database [7]. Data provenance is often used to validate data or re-execute a derivation with different input parameters. Currently the field of data provenance is working on how to annotate large ad-hoc data sets in order to identify and correct erroneous data or rederive data sets based on new input. However, the existence of malicious and incompetent users has not been considered. To date, data provenance projects have considered all participants to be trustworthy and meta-data to be correct.

We have determined that data provenance schemes can also be used to store information regarding the validity of data sets. Similar to how the scientific community performs peer reviews on scientific research, shared data sets can be subjected to peer review before they are widely accepted. Users of the shared data set will be able to assess the set's integrity through a similar analytic process as that employed in the peer review process and malicious or incompetent users will be exposed.

In most fields of science, instruments for collecting data and the algorithms to operate on data are constantly advancing. Ideally, any system which expedites the communal sharing of data should record all of the context information related to the data's collection and transformation. By using our system, an individual scientist may investigate the history of a particular data set to determine if s/he disagrees with any collection techniques or transformation algorithms used to construct it. The scientist could then explore whether users with a previously determined low reputation collected or derived any part of the data. Thus, by allowing the examiner to asses the product as a sum of its parts, s/he can produce a thorough peer review of the data.

It is important to investigate the source of collaborative data. Errors made at very low levels may never be seen once the data is integrated and replicated multiple times. One might consider the affect a misconfigured instrument may have on data obtained in any given data set. Unless the configuration/calibration of each instrument used to collect the data is recorded, it may never be possible to identify the problem at a later stage.

A more specific example is found in bioinfomatics. Here the functional annotation of proteins by genome sequencing projects is often inferred from similar, previously annotated proteins. The source of the annotation is often not recorded so annotation errors can propagate throughout much of the data base [5,9,13, 15,21]. In extreme cases, data may be faked intentionally. In 2002, an external committee concluded that former Bell Labs researcher Hendrik Schön. manipulated and misrepresented data in 16 papers involving 20 co-authors [3]. These co-authors and an unknown number of scientists who have used parts of the 16 falsified papers all blindly trusted the integrity of Schön's data. It has been suggested, in the wake of this incident that the research community adopt a data auditing and validation system which can help verify the integrity of data and results independently.

We have designed a system that records the history of a data set similar to other data provenance systems which use a directed acyclic graph (DAG). However, our system establishes a cryptographic signature for each data set and its history. A user will then be accountable for the validity of each signed data set. If a data set contains material contributed by many other sources, the identity of those sources will be included in the history of the larger set. In this way, not only can the original faulty data set be found, but the researcher who made the mistake can be held accountable.

Once a system of accountability is in place, a trust management system based on real world notions of trust and reputation can be implemented. This will go a long way towards increasing the probability that an individual data set is valid and increase the integrity of the data in the entire community. Users will interact with each other and record their experiences. Each user will individually evaluate the probable integrity of each piece of data based on the unforgeable and irrefutable information contained in the signed histories, his or her personal experiences, and the recommendations of others.

The remainder of this paper is organized as follows: section 2 gives a brief summary of current related work, section 3 provides an overview of our project goals, section 4 shows the basic architecture of the system, section 5 provides the data history data structure, section 6 gives a detailed description of how *trust views* are determined and implemented, and the final sections talk about future work and our conclusions.

2   Related Work

Recently there has been increased activity in the area of data provenance. Research is focused on providing the correct annotations for recording the history of data. What follows is a very brief description of several data provenance projects.

The Chimera project [2,10,11] is is a system developed as part of the Grid Physics Network (GriPhyN) project. Chimera provides for ad-hoc sharing and creation of distributed data sets while recording the history of each data set. The purpose of Chimera is to play the role of a makefile for large systems comprised of many data sets distributed across a network. This distributed makefile allows for the recreation of large data sets when a smaller sub-data set is changed. However, Chimera neither provides accountability for the shared data, nor helps users determine which data sets are most likely to consist of valid information.

Earth System Science Workbench (ESSW) [4,12] is for data centers studying earth sciences. The goal of the project is to allow participating data centers to search and obtain data while publishing their own data. This project does not consider malicious or incompetent users in the system.

The ^{my}Grid project [16,25,27] has more capabilities. ^{my}Grid is a complete e-Science system in which not only data will be shared but all electronic resources including: instruments, sensors, data, and computational methods. In essence, ^{my}Grid provides for an experiment to be done completely *in silico*. However the data in the system is assumed to be correct and of high integrity.

ESP2Net [20] is developing a Scientific Experiment Markup Language (SEML). SEML is based on XML and is a language which requires data provenance information be stored with all data. SEML is aimed at scientific data sharing.

The PENN Database Research Group led by Peter Bunemen [7] has done significant work at the lower levels of data provenance. Their work is focused on how to record data provenance within a database and does not consider the peer-to-peer relationships formed by the various data providers.

Audun Jøsang [18,19,24] has concentrated his research on the theoretical side of trust. Most of his work in the logic of trust relationships. More recently he has studied the trust relationship between agents in e-commerce.

Alfarez Abdul-Rahman [1] proposed a model of trust that mimics the real world trust each of us exhibits everyday when dealing with other people. His trust model allows for each participant to form their own opinion of other peers based on his or her own experiences with the system. Each user will independently form this opinion and the opinion with change as more experiences are created. We use Abdula-Rahman's trust model in our system.

RAID lab [26] has developed an approach to establish the trust of a principal, *Alice*, based on her history (i.e. a sequence of trust establishment events that involved *Alice*). They assume that *Alice* obtains a rating for each event that characterizes her behavior. Their approach is context-sensitive in that it considers the ratings and attributes associated with trust establishment events such as risk and event sequence patterns.

3   Overview

The goal of our research is to design and prototype an accountable, trust-aware, and data-centric e-notebook middleware. This e-notebook middleware is distributed, running on machines in individual research labs and possibly on larger servers (for example a campus-wide e-notebook that could be created at a university or large company). The e-notebook will record (1) the context in which raw data is generated (by communicating with on-board software) and (2) the history of curated data including data transformation, derivation, and validation. The individual, through his or her e-notebook, will digitally sign and be accountable for the result of every process performed. Based on the information recorded and experiences with others participating in the network, the distributed e-notebook will establish and maintain *trust views* for scientists sharing scientific data. We contend that these *trust views* and accountability for each data item will provide a measure of confidence in the shared data similar to the trust gained by the peer review process.

The e-notebook will change the way scientific data is compared and correlated. With the proposed e-notebook, a user will not only judge the value of a data set, the context in which the data was collected and the history (organized as a directed acyclic graph recording the steps of data collection and transformation from the very beginning) of how the data came to be can be used, improving the trustworthiness of scientific discoveries based on such comparison.

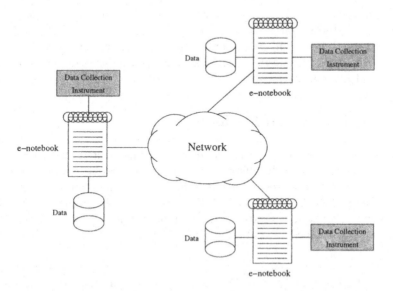

Fig. 1. High level view of the architecture. Users will participate in the community through an e-notebook. Each e-notebook will store some amount of data and participate in the querying for and sharing of data. In addition, each e-notebook will digitally sign and claim responsibility for data sets which it creates.

4   Architecture

The middleware architecture (figure 1) of the proposed system will be highly distributed and flexible. The key element of the system is the e-notebook. Each user will create his or her own notebook and through it collaborate with other users by querying for and retrieving data published on their e-notebooks. The access is also provided to instruments for collecting raw data. The e-notebook will do more than simply collect raw data from the instruments. It will also collect all contextual data (instrument settings, temperature, time, researcher's name, etc.) that the researcher might not think are important. Similar to other data provenance research projects the desired way to accomplish this is for the e-notebook to be connected directly to the instrument's on-board software. It will also be possible for a researcher to input data manually. It should be noted, however, that human error and the common desire to exclude seemingly irrelevant data demonstrates the benefit of automating this process. The e-notebook will also record all applications of transformations on a data set.

In addition to e-notebooks which belong to individual scientist, there may be e-notebooks that reside on servers for the purpose of sharing large amounts of data. An e-notebook of this type will be identical to a regular one and provide a sharing and storage facility for a group of users. Ideal sites for a server e-notebook may include universities and large companies. The only differences between a user e-notebook and a server e-notebook will be the size and the way that it is used. Server e-notebooks will have a larger storage capacity and higher bandwidth capabilities. A server e-notebook's intent is to provide a large repository for storing data that regular users might not want to store locally. The server e-notebook will query for and download any and all data which is to be shared. It may be desirable for the owner of a server e-notebook to allow other users to upload data to the server themselves.

5   Data History and Evidence

When data is collected, transformed, and combined in a distributed ad-hoc manner by different people with different agendas, the temporal history of the data is often lost. Data provenance is the recording of meta-data which describes the history of a data set. Our design of the data provenance system not only records the history of the data, but extends the current systems to include unforgeable and irrefutable evidence of what happened to the data and who performed those actions.

We use a data provenance scheme, similar to current data provenance systems [2,4,6,7,8,10,11,12,14,16,17,20,25,27] in which a directed acyclic graph (DAG) is used to describe a data set's history (figure 2). In our design, a data set's DAG is a digitally signed claim of the history of a data set made by the user of the e-notebook from which it was created. Each node in the DAG contains a single data set and information describing how it was created. Some data sets are collected directly from instruments while others are created by performing transformations on one or more existing data sets. For each data set created through transformations there will be a directed edge from the data set's node to each node used as input to the transformation. In figure 2, data sets 1-3 were collected directly from instruments while data sets 4-6 were the results of transformations.

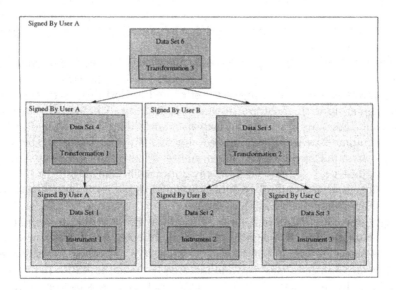

Fig. 2. Each data sets has a directed acyclic graph (DAG) that stores its history. Each DAG is created and digitally signed by a user. A user's digital signature is unforgeable and irrefutable evidence of how the data was created and who created it. Within each DAG a signed sub-DAGs can provide the histories of any data sets that contributed to the larger data set. Signed DAGs create accountability that can be used to form reputations.

When a user collects or derives a new data set, s/he creates a new node with directed edges to a copy of each node used to create the new one. The entire DAG is digitally signed by its creator. It is worth mentioning that within the signed DAG each sub-DAG remains digitally signed by and accountable to its original creator.

The purpose of digitally signing the DAG is to establish accountability. When a user signs a DAG, s/he claims creative responsibility and credit for the data. All sub-DAGs will remain signed by and accountable to their creators. The DAG is then published through the e-notebook for download and use by other users.

When a user downloads a data set, that user may wish to investigate its history by searching the DAG. In this manner, s/he can know all transformations which were applied, all users who were involved, and the context in which the data was collected. It can be known if any of the transformations, users, or contexts are inadequate for the intended use of the data set and if necessary, the material may be avoided.

In some cases, downloaded data sets may contain errors (intentional or otherwise). If an error is found, the digitally signed DAG is unforgeable and irrefutable evidence of what happened and who is responsible. At the very least, the evidence of errors in data sets should be used to adjust the reputation of the careless or malicious user, while at the most the evidence can be made public (possible in a court case) to prove malice. Although, the intent of the system is to increase the integrity of all data in the system by discouraging inappropriate use of the system, the evidence of carelessness and malice must be strong enough to present in court for this to be effective.

Figure 2 shows an example DAG for data set 6, which was created and signed by user A. With his signature A is claiming that he created data set 6 using transformation 3 and input data sets 4 and 5. Both data sets 4 and 5 are in turn signed by their creators. In this case data set 4 happens to have been created and signed by A who performed the transformation to create data set 6. The other input data set, 5 was created and signed by B. Because data set 5 is signed by B, A makes no claims to its validity. A only claims that he agreed to the use of data set 5. If data set 5, or any data which went into it, is discovered to be faulty, user A should disband the use of that data set and the creator of the first faulty data set is held accountable.

If any user were to obtain data set 2 and 3 along with transformation 2, s/he can validate user A's claim by recreating data set 5. If it is not possible to recreate data set 5 by applying transformation 2 to data sets 2 and 3, user A did not create data set 5 this way and incorrectly made the claim that s/he did. Once user A digitally signs data set 5's DAG and releases it to the community, user A can never assert s/he did not make this claim. If it can be shown that data set 5 was not created in the way user A claimed it was, the signed DAG is evidence that A released incorrect data to the community. Evidence of malice cannot be shown with the DAG and must be determined in some other way.

6   Trust Views

One novel technique used by our system is the formation of *trust views* resulting from the reputation of an e-notebook user. Using previous, first-hand experience and second-hand recommendations each user will decide how to trust other e-notebook users. As in real world situations involving trust, there is no universal value assigned to the integrity of each user. No person necessarily judges integrity in the same way as someone else. Each user may have his own algorithm for determining the integrity of others. We propose that using the signed history DAGs described in section 5 users have enough information to make value judgments. This will increase the probability of an individual obtaining valid data and raise the integrity of all the data in the system.

6.1   Trust Judgments

In order to create a *trust view*, each user must make judgments of how much and what kind of trust to assign other users. E-notebook users can make trust judgments in any way they wish. At first, users might rely on off-line relationships. However, as experiences with the community increases, it becomes possible to use accountability information obtained from the signed data histories to make judgments about other's findings. There are endless possibilities in which to use signed histories to make trust judgments. Describing them all would be impossible. Listed below are a few properties which might lead to an increase in the level of trust assigned to a user:

- Consistently producing mistake free data sets.
- Quickly modifying data when mistakes are found in lower level data sets.
- Recommending users who provide quality data sets.

Alternatively, the next list of properties might lead to a reduction of a user's trust:

- Creating and signing a data set which is known to be intentionally fraudulent.
- Consistently making unintentional mistakes in the creation of new data sets.
- Using data which are known to be faulty in the creation of new data sets.
- Recommending users who provide faulty data sets.

In addition to personal experiences, trust judgments can be made using second hand recommendations. Building trust in recommendations can initially be done by accepting the positive assessments of other users who are known outside of the system. Once a base of trust has been established, one may trust the recommendation of users who are unknown outside the system.

Abdul-Rahman describes one social model for supporting trust in virtual communities [1]. In this research, agents trust each other by ranking all first-hand experiences into discrete categories (for example: very good, good, bad, very bad). If only first-hand experiences were considered, when deciding on the trust to award another agent the trust category with the most experiences in it is used. However, Abdul-Rahman provides for trusting through recommendations as well. Recommendations are made by sharing assessments based on first hand-experiences. However, an agent cannot use recommended experiences in the same way as first-hand experiences. The technique used is to calculate the semantic difference between recommendations received and first-hand experiences using those recommendations. Future recommendations can be modified by the semantic difference seen in the past to more accurately suggest amounts of trust to award. In other words, for each user who makes recommendations, the receiving users will calculate the typical difference between the recommendation and personally observed outcome. The typical difference can then be applied to adjust future recommendation from that user.

We have designed a similar model of social trust for users to determine the probability that a given data set is valid. In our system, agents are users and the categories are *very trustworthy*, *trustworthy*, *untrustworthy*, and *very untrustworthy*. It should be noted that any finite number of categories will work and we chose four categories to mirror Abdul-Rahman's work. Each user will record all first hand experiences and determine which category each experience should belong to. At any given time, the trust level determined by first hand experience is the level associated with the category containing the most experiences. For example, if user A has 4 *very trustworthy* experiences and 5 *trustworthy* experiences with user B, then A applies the category *trustworthy* to B.

Recommendations are made by incorporating the experiences of others into one's rating. Each user has his or her own experiences and techniques for categorizing the experiences. For this reason, another user's recommendation must be adjusted to approximately fit his or her categorizations. To do this the past recommendations and the user's resulting experiences are used to find the semantic difference between the recommendations and his or her experiences. This is done as described in Abdul-Rahman's paper [1]. The semantic difference is then used to adjust each future recommendation. To complete the example, remember that user A determined that user B deserves the trust category of *trustworthy*. If user C has determined (from previous experiences) that when user A recommends *trustworthy*, C's personal experience has shown that a *untrustworthy* experience usually occurs. In this case the semantic difference says to reduce A's recommendation by one category. Therefore, C would adjust A's *trustworthy* recommendation to that of *untrustworthy*.

6.2   Trust Implementation

We propose a novel application of Role-based Trust-management language (RT_0) [22] to implement the social trust model described above. RT_0 uses *credentials* to delegate trust roles from one entity to another. Determining if an entity can have a particular role relies on finding a *credential chain* between the entity and the ultimate authority on that role. What follows is some background on RT_0 and credential chains.

Background on RT_0 and Credential Chains. In RT_0 entities (users) declare *roles* of the form $U.r$, where U is a user and r is a role. Users can issue four types of *credentials*:

- Type 1: $U_1.r \longleftarrow U_2$
  Entity U_2 is a member of U_1's role $U_1.r$. U_1 and U_2 may be the same user.
- Type 2: $U_1.r_1 \longleftarrow U_2.r_2$
  All members of $U_2.r_2$ are to be included as members of $U_1.r_1$. U_1 and U_2 may be the same users. r_1 and r_2 may be the same roles.
- Type 3: $U_1.r_1 \longleftarrow U_1.r_2.r_3$
  Any member of $U_1.r_2$ (say U_2) is allowed to determine members of $U_1.r_1$ by adding a credential $U_2.r_3 \longleftarrow U_3$.
- Type 4: $U_1.r \longleftarrow f_1 \cap f_2 \cap ... \cap f_k$
  The intersection of any number of roles and users.

As an example we present a naive, but valid, strategy for the creation of *credential chains* for the purpose of recommending trust.

Each user i creates a role $U_i.trusted$. For each other user U_j that U_i trusts, U_i issues the credential:

$$U_i.trusted \longleftarrow U_j \qquad (1)$$

In this simple case, determining if U_a trusts U_b is done be finding the. credential chain (the number over the arrow refers back to the credential number as labeled in the paper):

$$Chain : U_a.trusted \overset{1}{\longleftarrow} U_b$$

User U_c can be indirectly trusted by U_a by the appropriate users issuing the credentials as follows:

$$U_a.trusted \longleftarrow U_b \qquad (2)$$
$$U_a.trusted \longleftarrow U_b.trusted \qquad (3)$$
$$U_b \longleftarrow U_c \qquad (4)$$

The credential chain that allows U_c to have the role $U_a.trusted$ is:

$$Chain : U_a.trusted \overset{3}{\longleftarrow} U_b.trusted \overset{4}{\longleftarrow} U_c$$

Although this set of credentials is useful it has a draw back. All users who are directly or indirectly trusted by U_b are trusted by U_a. Since U_a might trust U_c's data sets, but not trust U_c's recommendations, we need a more powerful set of credentials.

This example has shown the basic features of RT_0. Users in our system will be able to use any strategy they wish for creating roles and credential. The next section describes a better suggested strategy for creating roles and credentials.

Credential Chain Strategy. We have created a strategy for creating roles and credential rules that allow for the implementation of the social trust model described in section 6.1. The trust model, as presented, provides four categories of trust: *very trustworthy*, *trustworthy*, *untrustworthy*, and *very untrustworthy*. Again, these categories were chosen because of their similarity to Abdul-Rahman's examples. However, any finite number of categories can be chosen.

Any user i subscribing to our strategy will first create four basic trust roles:

$U_i.vt$: very trustworthy
$U_i.t$: trustworthy
$U_i.ut$: untrustworthy
$U_i.vut$: very untrustworthy

A user j is awarded a certain amount of trust depending on which of four roles applies to that user. Credentials are needed to assign these roles to users. This set of credentials has to do with the first-hand experiences a user has had. These credentials require the creation of four additional roles.

$U_i.exp\_vt$: Users awarded *very trustworthy* by first-hand experiences
$U_i.exp\_t$: Users awarded *trustworthy* by first-hand experiences
$U_i.exp\_ut$: Users awarded *untrustworthy* by first-hand experiences
$U_i.exp\_vut$: Users awarded *very untrustworthy* by first-hand experiences

Because personal experience is always more important than recommendations the first-hand experience roles will directly linked to the basic roles by the *credentials*:

$$U_i.vt \longleftarrow U_i.exp\_vt \qquad (5)$$

$$U_i.t \longleftarrow U_i.exp\_t \qquad (6)$$

$$U_i.ut \longleftarrow U_i.exp\_ut \qquad (7)$$

$$U_i.vut \longleftarrow U_i.exp\_vut \qquad (8)$$

If most of U_i's first-hand experiences with U_j are good experiences, U_i will create a credential rule $U_i.exp\_t \longleftarrow U_j$. The role $U_i.t$ is given to U_j by the *credential chain*:

$$Chain : U_i.t \xleftarrow{5} U_i.exp\_t \longleftarrow U_j$$

Next, *credentials* need to be created to incorporate second hand recommendation of other users. If the other user subscribes to this strategy, s/he will record his or her first-hand experiences and create *credentials* according to these experiences.. A user will link to his or her first-hand experience roles in a manner consistent with the trust model. In the model, a user must record recommendations of other users and compare these recommendations with his or her own first-hand experiences. The difference between the recommended values and the observed values will be applied to all new recommendations as an adjustment. The effect on *credential* will be that a recommendation by U_j of role $U_j.t$ may be, in U_i's eyes, equivalent to $U_i.ut$. This will be the case when U_j rates others higher than U_i, possible because his or her standards are lower. U_i may adjust U_j's recommendations by submitting the *credentials*:

$$U_i.t \longleftarrow U_j.exp\_vt \qquad (9)$$

$$U_i.ut \longleftarrow U_j.exp\_t \qquad (10)$$

$$U_i.vut \longleftarrow U_j.exp\_ut \qquad (11)$$

$$U_i.vut \longleftarrow U_j.exp\_vut \qquad (12)$$

If U_j had first-hand experiences with U_k which produced the *credential* $U_j.exp\_t \longleftarrow U_k$, the *credential chain* from U_k to U_i would grant U_k the role $U_i.ut$ and would be:

$$Chain : U_i.ut \xleftarrow{10} U_j.exp\_t \longleftarrow U_k$$

In this case U_i has determined that U_j usually recommends at one level higher than U_i's personal experience shows to be true. All of the recommendations have been adjusted down by one level. Notice that U_i will not except any of U_j's recommendation to the *role* $U_i.vt$. In general, the transformation from U_j's recommendations to U_i's trust values does not have to adjust all levels in the same direction or by the same about. As an example. U_i's experience with U_k may l produce the *credentials*:

$$U_i.vt \longleftarrow U_k.exp\_ut \qquad (13)$$

$$U_i.t \longleftarrow U_k.exp\_t \qquad (14)$$

$$U_i.ut \longleftarrow U_k.exp\_vut \qquad (15)$$

$$U_i.vut \longleftarrow U_k.exp\_vt \qquad (16)$$

This situation probably would not happen, but is still acceptable.

If there are a significant number of users making recommendations, there may be conflicting results of the *credential chains* (more than one basic role may be applied to a single user). For this reason the final decision on the appropriate role to apply to the user is made by counting the number of times each *role* is applied. In a similar fashion to the model, the *role* that was applied most is chosen. A user may even weight recommendation to achieve a weighted sum.

For the trust model to work each user should follow this strategy for creating *credentials* based on the semantic differences between his or her own experiences and the recommendations of others. However, if any user accidentally or maliciously creates faulty *credential chains*, the semantic differences applied to that user will adjust the recommendations accordingly.

There are many other possible strategies using RT_0 and *credential chains*. We plan on developing more and studying how different strategies interact with each other.

7 Future Work

We have many ideas for increasing the capabilities of our system. First, we would like to look at how much of the credential creation can be automated. Currently, validation of data sets must be done manually and rating of first-hand experiences must be done by a human. We think that some decisions about experiences can be automated and the credential chains can be updated accordingly.

Second, we would like to look at different strategies that users may use in determining trust and creating credential chains. We expect to find that not all strategies work well together and would like to answer these questions: Which strategies do work together? Is there a best strategy? If so, what is the best strategy?

Li [22] has proposed algorithms for distributed credential chain discovery. We would like to extend Li's work by discovering not just credential chains, but also directed credential graphs. It may be that a user trusts data using several different credential chains that form a directed graph. This graph could be used to find the chain that provides the greatest amount of trust.

We would also like to find credential chains or graphs with which we can find data that is trusted by some set of users. This could be used by the community to find the data sets which the community as a whole tends to trust. This data would be the best to use when drawing results to be presented to the community.

8   Conclusion

This paper proposes an e-notebook data sharing middleware for scientific collaboration. The aim of the system is to create a virtual community where scientists sharing files are accountable for the files they share. We would also like to encourage the formation of natural *trust views* among these scientists. Accountability for shared data and the repercussions of obtaining a negative reputation will not only help scientists identify valid data but raise the integrity of the data in the entire system. Future research will refine the trust model as well as the data history with the goal of creating distributed community file sharing systems with integrity similar to the professional peer review process in which malicious or incompetent users are exposed and there contributions are removed.

Acknowledgments. This work is supported in part by a grant from the e-Enterprise Center at Purdue University, a gift from Microsoft Research, and grants from the National Science Foundation IIS0209059 and IIS0242840.

References

1. Abdul-Rahman, A., Hailes, S.: Supporting trust in virtual communities. In: Proceedings of the 33rd Hawaii International Conference on Systems Sciences. (2000)
2. Annis, J., Zhao, Y., Vockler, J., Wilde, M., Kent, S., Foster, I.: Applying chimera virtual data concepts to cluster finding in the sloan sky survey. (2002)
3. Beasley, M., Datta, S., Kogelnik, H., Kroemer, H., Monroe, D.: Report of the investigation committee on the possibility of scientific misconduct in the work of Hendrik Schön and co-authors. Technical report (2002)
4. Bose, R.: A conceptual framework for composing and managing scientific data lineage. In: 4th International Conference on Scientific and Statistical Database Management. (2002) 15–19
5. Brenner, S.E.: Errors in genome annotation. Trends in Genetics **15** (1999) 132–133
6. Buneman, P., Khanna, S., Tajima, K.: Data archiving. In: Workshop on Data Derivation and Provenance. (2002)
7. Buneman, P., Khanna, S., Tan, W.C.: Why and where: A characterization of data provenance. In: International Conference on Database Theory (ICDT). (2001)
8. Cavanaugh, R., Graham, G.E.: Apples and apple-shaped oranges: Equivalence of data returned on subsequent queries with provenance information. In: Workshop on Data Derivation and Provenance. (2002)
9. Devos, D., Valencia, A.: Intrinsic errors in genome annotation. Trends in Genetics **17** (2001) 429–431

10. Foster, I., Vockler, J., Wilde, M., Zhao, Y.: Chimera: A virtual data system for representing, querying, and automating data derivation. In: Proceedings of the 14th International Conference on Scientific and Statistical Database Management. (2002)
11. Foster, I., Vockler, J., Wilde, M., Zhao, Y.: The virtual data grid: A new model and architecture for data-intensive collaboration. In: Proceedings of the 2003 CIDR Conference. (2003)
12. Frew, J., Bose, R.: Earth system science workbench: A data management infrastructure for earth science products. In: SSDBM 2001 Thirteenth International Conference on Scientific and Statistical Database Management. (2001) 180–189
13. Galperin, M., Koonin, E.: Sources of systematic error in functional annotation of genomes: domain rearrangement, non-orthologous gene displacement and operon disruption. Silico Biol. 1 (1998) 55–67
14. Gertz, M.: Data annotation in collaborative research environments. In: Workshop on Data Derivation and Provenance. (2002)
15. R.Gilks, W., Audit, B., Angelis, D.D., Tsoka, S., Ouzounis, C.A.: Modeling the percolation of annotation errors in a database of protein sequences. Bioinformatics 18 (2002) 1641–1649
16. Greenwood, M., Goble, C., Stevens, R., Zhao, J., Addis, M., Marvin, D., Moreau, L., Oinn, T.: Provenance of e-science experiments - experience from bioinformatics. In: Proceedings UK e-Science All Hands Meeting 2003 Editors. (2003)
17. Howe, B., Maier, D.: Modeling data product generation. In: Workshop on Data Derivation and Provenance. (2002)
18. Jøsang, A.J.: The right type of trust for distributed systems. Proceedings of the 1996 New Security Paradigms Workshop (1996)
19. Jøsang, A.J., Hird, S., Faccer, E.: Simulating the effect of reputation systems on e-markets. Proceedings of the First International Conference on Trust Management (2003)
20. Kaestle, G., Shek, E.C., Dao, S.K.: Sharing experiences from scientific experiments. In: Proceedings of the 11th International Conference on Scientific and Statistical Database Management (SSDBM). (1999)
21. Karp, P.D.: What we do not know about sequence analysis and sequence databases. Bioinformatics 14 (1998) 753–754
22. Li, N., Winsborough, W.H., Mitchell, J.C.: Distributed credential chain discovery in trust management: extended abstract. In: ACM Conference on Computer and Communications Security. (2001) 156–165
23. Mann, B.: Some data derivation and provenance issues in astronomy. In: Workshop on Data Derivation and Provenance. (2002)
24. Patton, M.A., Jøsang, A.: Technologies for trust in electronic commerce. Electronic Commerce Research Journal 4 (2004)
25. Stevens, R.D., Robinson, A.J., Goble, C.A.: myGrid: Personalized bioinformatics on the information grid. Bioinformatics 19 (2003) i302–i304
26. Zhong, Y., Lu, Y., Bhargava, B.: Dynamic trust production based on interaction sequence. Technical Report CSD TR 03-006, Department of Computer Sciences, Purdue University (2003)
27. Zhao, J., Goble, C., Greenwood, M., Wroe, C., Stevens, R.: Annotating, linking and browsing provenance logs for e-science. In: Proceedings of the Workshop on Semantic Web Technologies for Searching and Retrieving Scientific Data. (2003)

Requirements Engineering Meets Trust Management[*]
Model, Methodology, and Reasoning

Paolo Giorgini[1], Fabio Massacci[1], John Mylopoulos[1,2], and Nicola Zannone[1]

[1] Department of Information and Communication Technology
University of Trento - Italy
{massacci,giorgini,zannone}@dit.unitn.it
[2] Department of Computer Science
University of Toronto - Canada
jm@cs.toronto.edu

Abstract. The last years have seen a number of proposals to incorporate Security Engineering into mainstream Software Requirements Engineering. However, capturing trust and security requirements at an organizational level (as opposed to a design level) is still an open problem.
This paper presents a formal framework for modeling and analyzing security and trust requirements. It extends the Tropos methodology, an agent-oriented software engineering methodology. The key intuition is that in modeling security and trust, we need to distinguish between the actors that manipulate resources, accomplish goals or execute tasks, and actors that own the resources or the goals. To analyze an organization and its information systems, we proceed in two steps. First, we built a trust model, determining the trust relationships among actors, and then we give a functional model, where we analyze the actual delegations against the trust model, checking whether an actor that offers a service is authorized to have it.
The formal framework allows for the automatic verification of security and trust requirements by using a suitable delegation logic that can be mechanized within Datalog. To make the discussion more concrete, we illustrate the proposal with a Health Care case study.

Keywords: Requirements Engineering for Security and Trust, Agent-Oriented Technologies, Security Engineering, Trust Models for Modeling Business and Organizations

1 Introduction

Trust Management is one of the main challenges in the development of distributed open information systems (IS). Not surprisingly, Security Engineering

[*] This work has been partially funded by the IST programme of the EU Commission, FET under the IST-2001-37004 WASP project and by the FIRB programme of MIUR under the RBNE0195K5 ASTRO Project. We would like to thank the anonymous reviewers for useful comments.

C.D. Jensen et al. (Eds.): iTrust 2004, LNCS 2995, pp. 176–190, 2004.
© Springer-Verlag Berlin Heidelberg 2004

has received substantial attention in the last years [3,7,10]. Looking at traditional approaches to software requirements engineering, we find that security is treated as a non-functional requirement [6] which introduces quality constraints under which the system must operate [24,26]. Software designers have recognized the need to integrate most non-functional requirements (such as reliability and performance) into the software development processes [8], but security still remains an afterthought. Worse still, trust is often left entirely outside the picture.

This often means that security mechanisms have to be fitted into a pre-existing design which may not be able to accommodate them due to potential conflicts with functional requirements or usability. Moreover, the implementation of the software system may assume trust relationships among users or between users and the system that are simply not there. Alternatively, the implementation may introduce protection mechanisms that just hinder operation in a trusted domain that was not perceived as a trusted domain by the software engineer. In a nutshell, current methodologies for IS development do not resolve security- and trust-related concerns early on [25].

This has spurred a number of researchers to model security and trust requirements into "standard" software engineering methodologies. Jürjens proposes UMLsec [16], an extension of the Unified Modelling Language (UML), for modeling security related features, such as confidentiality and access control. Lodderstedt et al. present a modeling language, based on UML, called SecureUML [21]. Their approach is focused on modeling access control policies and how these (policies) can be integrated into a model-driven software development process. McDermott and Fox adapt use cases [22] to analyze security requirements, by introducing the abuse case model: a specification of complete interaction between a system and one or more actors, where the result of the interaction is harmful to the system, one of the actors, or one of the stakeholders of the system. Guttorm and Opdahl [15] model security by defining the concept of a misuse case as the inverse of a use case, which describes a function that the system should not allow.

One of the major limitations of all these proposals is that they treat security and trust in system-oriented terms, and do not support the modeling and analysis of trust and trust relationships at an organizational level. In other words, they are targeted to *model a computer system* and the policies and access control mechanisms it supports. In contrast, to understand the problem of trust management and security engineering we need to *model* the organization and the relationships between all involved actors, the system being just one possible actor. For instance, Jürjens introduce cryptographic functions which represent a particular implementation of some trust-protection mechanism at the digital level. However, an analysis of operational Health Care systems suggests that (for better or worse) most medical data are still only available in paper form. In such a setting, cryptographic mechanisms are largely irrelevant, whereas physical locks are very useful in avoiding untrusted access to sensitive medical data[1]. Yet,

---

[1] For example, the file of a patient waiting for a kidney transplant in a high-profile nephrology center contains many paper documents that are copies of reports from surgeons or clinicians from the referring hospitals of the patient. These documents

once we focus on the digital solution, we end up having little room to specify physical protection requirements at the organizational (as opposed to IS) level.

Thus, we need to focus on requirement engineering methodologies that allow for modeling organizations and actors, and enhance these with notions of trust and trust relationships. To this extent, Tropos - an agent-based software engineering methodology [4,5] are particularly well suited. For example, in [19, 20] Liu et al. have shown how to use Tropos to model privacy and security concerns of an organization. However, in [13] the authors have shown that Tropos lacks the ability to capture at the same time the functional and security features of the organization. In [23] a structured process integrate security and system engineering has been proposed. However, a formal framework for modeling and analyzing security requirements within Tropos is still missing.

In this paper we introduce a process that integrates trust, security and system engineering, using the same concepts and notations used during "traditional" requirements specification. Building upon [23], we propose a solution that is based on augmenting the i*/Tropos framework to take trust into account. The key intuition is to distinguish and make explicit the notion of offering a service and owning a service[2] and the notions of functional dependency and trust dependency. A functional dependency can lead to the delegation of tasks, whereas a trust dependency can lead to the delegation of permissions.

Next (§2) we provide an brief description of the Tropos methodology and introduce a simple Health Care information system that will be used as case study throughout the paper. Then we describe the basic concepts and diagrams that we use for modeling trust (§3), followed by their formalization (§4), and implementation, along with some experimental results (§5). Finally, we conclude the paper with some directions for future work (§6).

2   Case Study

This section presents a simple health care IS to illustrate our approach. Security and trust are key issues for health care information systems, with privacy, integrity and availability of health information being the major security concerns [2].

The Tropos methodology [4,5] strives to model both the organizational environment of a system and the system itself. It uses the concepts of actor, goal, task, resource and social dependency for defining obligations of actors (dependees) to other actors (dependers). Actors have strategic goals within the system or the organization and represent (social) agents (organizational, human or software), roles etc. A goal represents some strategic interest of an actor. A task

---

are by far more sensitive than the patient's date and place of birth or waiting list registration number in the medical information system.

[2] Here it is an example derived from EU privacy legislation: a citizen's personal data is processed by an information system (which offer a data access service) but it is owned by the citizen himself whose consent is necessary for the service to be delivered to 3rd parties.

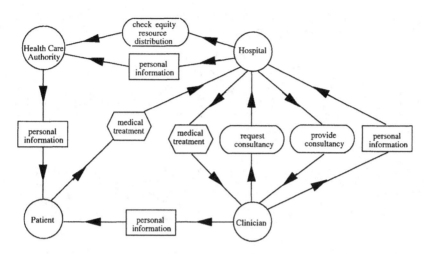

Fig. 1. The first Health Care System dependency model (without the Medical Information System actor)

represents a way of doing something (in particular, a task can be executed to satisfy a goal). A resource represents a physical or an informational entity. In the rest of the paper, we say service for goal, task, or resource. Finally, a dependency between two actors indicates that one actor depends on another to accomplish a goal, execute a task, or deliver a resource.

We start the Health Care example by considering the following actors:

- *Patient*, that depends on the hospital for receiving appropriate health care;
- *Hospital*, that provides medical treatment and depends on the patients for having their personal information.
- *Clinician*, physician of the hospital that provides medical health advice and, whenever needed, provide accurate medical treatment;
- *Health Care Authority* (HCA) that control and guarantee the fair resources allocation and a good quality of the delivered services.

Figure 1 shows the dependency model among these actors. Actors are represented as circles; dependums - goals, tasks and resources - are respectively represented as ovals, hexagons and rectangles; and dependencies have the form *depender* → *dependum* → *dependee*. The *Patient* depends on the *Hospital* for receiving medical treatments, and in turn, the *Hospital* depends on the *Clinician* for providing such treatments. *Clinician* depends on *Patients* for their personal information and on the *Hospital* for specific professional consultancies and for patient personal information. The *Hospital* depends on other *Clinicians* for providing professional consultancies and on *HCA* for checking equity resource distribution. Finally, *HCA* depends on *Patient* for personal information.

Finally we introduce the *Medical Information System* as another actor who, according the current privacy legislation, can share patient medical data if and only if consent is obtained from the patient in question. The *Medical Information*

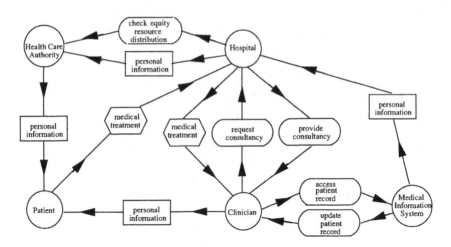

Fig. 2. The final Health Care System dependency model (with the Medical Information System actor)

System manages patients information, including information about the medical treatments they have received. Figure 2 shows the final dependency model.

3   Security-Aware Tropos

The Tropos models so far say nothing about security requirements. Loosely speaking, the dependee is a server and the depender is a client. There is an implicit trust and delegation relationship between the two. In our extended modeling framework, we identify four relationships:

Trust (among two agents and a service), so that A trust B on a certain goal G;

Delegation (among two agents and a service), whenever A explicitly delegates to B a goal, or the permission to execute a task or access a resource;

Offer (between an agent and a service), so that A can offer to other agents the possibility of fulfilling a goal, executing a task or delivering a resource;

Ownership (between an agent and a service), whenever an agent is the legitemate owner of a goal, task or resource.

Note the difference between owning a service and offering a service. For example, a patient is the legitemate owner of his personal data. However the data may be stored on a Medical Information System that offers access to the data. This distinction explains clearly why IS managers need the consent of the patient for data processing. Also note the difference between trust and delegation. Delegation marks a formal passage in the requirements modeling: a TM certificate will have to be eventually issued for the delegatee when implementing the system. Such certificate needs not to be digital, but it marks presence of a transaction. In contrast, trust marks simply a social relationship that is not formalized by a

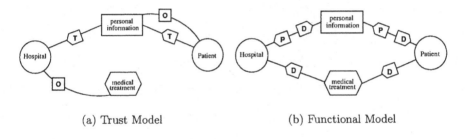

(a) Trust Model   (b) Functional Model

Fig. 3. Patient-Hospital Basic Dependencies

"contract" (such as digital credential). There might be cases (e.g. because it is impractical or too costly), where we might be happy with a "social" protection, and other cases in which security is essential. Such decision must be taken by the designer and the formal model just offers support to spot inconsistencies. The basic effect of delegation is augmenting the number of permission holders.

Intuitively, we have split the trust and delegation aspects of the dependency relation. Moreover, we do not assume that a delegation implies a trust. Using this extension of the modeling framework, we can now refine the methodology:

1. design a trust model among the actors of the systems;
2. identify who owns goals, tasks, or resources and who is able to fulfill goals, execute tasks or deliver resources;
3. define functional dependencies and delegations of goals among agents building a functional model.

The basic idea is that the owner of an object has full authority concerning access and disposition of his object, and he can also delegate it to other actors. We represent this relationship as an edge labelled by **O**. We use trust (**T**) to model the basic trust relationship between agents and permission (**P**) to model the actual transfer of rights in some form (e.g. a digital certificate, a signed paper, etc.), and **D** for a Tropos dependency. There are other relations in Tropos, but we do not use them here.

The new constructs and the methodology make it possible to analyze the trust relationship between actors and the consequent integrated security and functional requirements. Figure 3-a and Figure 3-b show, respectively, the trust model and the functional model with just *Patient* and *Hospital*, as a first modeling attempt. Here, the *Hospital* owns medical treatments, the *Patient* owns his own personal information and trusts the *Hospital* for his personal data. In the functional model, *Patient* depends on *Hospital* for medical treatments. Since *Hospital* needs personal information to provide accurate medical treatment, *Patient* permits the use of his personal information to *Hospital*.

We refine the system building the trust model (Figure 4) corresponding to the original Tropos model of Figure 1. *Clinician* owns medical treatments. *Patient* trusts *HCA* and *Clinician* for his personal information, and *HCA* trusts *Hospital* for it. Further, *Hospital* trusts *HCA* for checking equity resource distribution.

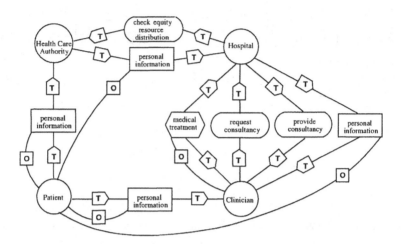

Fig. 4. Health Care System-2 trust model

Clinician trusts *Hospital* for medical treatment and for requesting specific professional consulting, and *Hospital* trusts *Clinician* for providing such consulting and for patient personal information. Notice at top of Figure 4 that there is a trust relationship between two actors (HCA and Hospital) on a resource that is owned by neither of them.

The next step is to add the *Medical Information System* and its relationship with other actors. Figure 5 and Figure 6 corresponding to the dependencies model in Figure 2, show respectively the trust model and the functional model. In the trust model we consider the trust relationship between *Hospital* and *Medical System Information* for patient personal information, and in the functional model the dependency between *Clinician* and *Medical Information System* to access patient record and to update patient record.

An interesting feature of Tropos is the refinement analysis and the usage of rationale diagrams that explain relationships among actors. Specifically, the goal of accessing a patient record introduced in Figure 2, can be and-decomposed in three subgoals: request patient personal data, check authorization and send medical information. To save on space, we merge the trust model and the functional model for the rationale diagram in Figure 7. We can see that after *Medical Information System* requests patient personal information to *Clinician*, it requests also an authorization to send patient medical information to *Clinician*. It can get it directly by the *Patient* or by the *Clinician* through delegation.

4   Formalization

In the "trust-management" approach to distributed authorization, a "requester" submits a request, possibly supported by a set of "credentials" issued by other parties, to an "authorizer", who controls the requested resources. To this end, we consider some features of delegation logics to model security requirements.

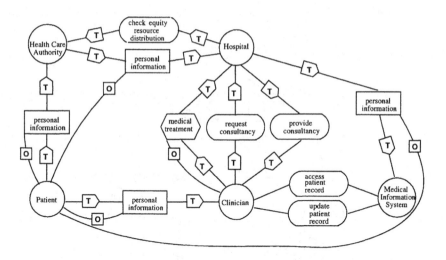

Fig. 5. Health Care System-3 trust model

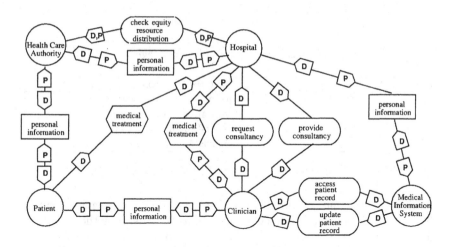

Fig. 6. Health Care System-3 functional model

Particularly, we follow Li et al [18] that provides a logical framework for representing security policies and credentials for authorization in large-scale, open, distributed systems. To simplify authorization in a decentralized environment, Li, Grosof and Feigenbaum use a system where access-control decisions are based on authenticated attributes of the subjects, and attribute authority is decentralized. They then develop a logic-based language, called *Delegation Logic* (DL) [17], to represent policies, credentials, and requests in distributed authorization that satisfy the above requirements. Note that they use the term *authorization* to denote the process of "authentication + access control".

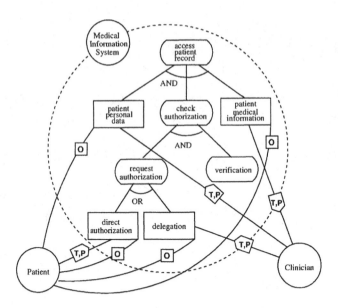

Fig. 7. Rationale Diagram

Table 1. Properties for the single agent

Formal Tropos	Secure Tropos
fulfilled(Service : s)	owns(Actor : a, Service : s)
	has(Actor : a, Service : s)
	offers(Actor : a, Service : s)
	fulfills(Actor : a, Service : s)

At first we introduce the predicates used for modeling properties of an actor (Table 1) and relationships between actors (Table 2). In defining these predicates, we don't distinguish between goals, tasks and resources, and treat them all as services, instead. Thus, we say "fulfill a service" for "accomplish a goal", "execute a task", or "deliver a resource". The intuition behind predicate *owns* is that owns(a, s) holds if the agent a owns the service s. The owner of a service has full authority concerning access and disposition of his service, and he can also delegate this authority to other actors. The basic idea of has is that when someone has a service, he has authority concerning access and disposition of the service, and he can also delegate this authority to other actors if the owner of the service agrees. When an actor has the capabilities to fulfill a service, he offers it. This means that offers(a, s) holds if a offers s. We assume that a can offer the service if he has it. The predicates fulfilled and fulfills are true when the service are fulfilled by an actor. Particularly, predicate fulfills(a, s) holds if actor a fulfills the service s, and predicate fulfilled(s) holds if s has been fulfilled. Formal Tropos already includes the predicate fulfilled [12].

Table 2. Relationship between actors

Formal Tropos
depends(Actor : a, Service : s, Actor : b)

Secure Tropos
trustBL$\big($Actor : a, Service : s, Actor : b, $\mathcal{N}^+ \cup \{*\}$: n, ActorSet : $\mathcal{B}\big)$
delegBL$\big($id : idC, Actor : a, Service : s, Actor : b, $\mathcal{N}^+ \cup \{*\}$: n, ActorSet : $\mathcal{B}\big)$

Example 1. The patient owns his data and he has full authority concerning its access and disposition. In particular, the owner of the service has the service. In our framework we model these notions, respectively, as owns($patient1, record1$) and has($patient1, record1$).

Example 2. Once the Health Care Authority has the patient records and the hospital gives it the goal to check behavior of patients and of the doctors, the HCA offers the goal and then fulfills it. Following we show as we model this in Secure Tropos offers($hca, check$) and fulfills($hca, check$).

As for trust, we present predicate trustBL: trustBL$(a, s, b, n, \mathcal{B})$ holds is actor a trusts actor b for service s; n is called the *trust depth* ("*" means unlimited depth); and $\mathcal{B}$ is called *black list*. As suggest by Li et al. [17] for their delegation logics, trust has depth, which is either a positive integer or "*" ("*" means unlimited depth). One way to view trust depth is the number of re-delegation of permission steps that are allowed, where depth 1 means that no re-delegation of permission is allowed, depth 2 means that one further step is allowed, depth 3 means that two further steps are allowed, and depth * means that unlimited re-delegation of permission is allowed. The black list is the set that the actor a distrusts at least for what concerns this permission. delegBL$(idC, a, s, b, n, \mathcal{B})$ holds is actor a delegates the service s to actor b. The actor a is called the *delegater*; the actor b is called the *delegatee*; idC is the certificate identifier; n is the *delegation depth*; and $\mathcal{B}$ is called *black list*. The latter represents the set of actors that the delegater doesn't want to have the object. The idea behind black-lists in trust and delegation is modeling exceptions along the chain of trust. For example, a patient may want to delegate the permission to read his personal data to his general practitioner and to all agents trusted by him (delegation with depth 1). However, he may want to restrict such blank transfer of rights to avoid that the information goes to somebody he distrusts (e.g. his previous general practitioner). A delegation has depth, as for trust. We can also define an abbreviation for a delegation chain as

$$\text{delegBLChain}(a, o, b) \equiv \begin{cases} \exists k \;\; \text{s.t.} \;\; \exists a_1 \ldots a_k \;\; \exists n_1 \ldots n_{k-1} \;\; \exists \mathcal{B}_1 \ldots \mathcal{B}_{k-1} \\ \forall i \in [1 \ldots k-1] \;\; \text{delegBL}(id_i, a_i, o, a_{i+1}, n_i, \mathcal{B}_i) \; \wedge \\ \qquad a_1 = a \wedge a_k = b \end{cases}$$

Table 3. Axioms for trust model and functional model

Trust model
Ax1: $\mathsf{has}(A, S) \leftarrow \mathsf{owns}(A, S)$
Ax2: $\mathsf{trustBL}(A, S, B, N-1, \mathcal{B}) \leftarrow \mathsf{trustBL}(A, S, B, N, \mathcal{B}) \wedge N > 2$
Ax3: $\mathsf{trustBL}(A, S, C, P, \mathcal{B}_1 \cup \mathcal{B}_2) \leftarrow \mathsf{trustBL}(A, S, B, N, \mathcal{B}_1) \wedge$
$\mathsf{trustBL}(B, S, C, M, \mathcal{B}_2) \wedge$
$N > 2 \wedge P = min\{N-1, M\}$
Functional model
Ax4: $\mathsf{has}(B, S) \leftarrow \mathsf{delegBL}(ID, A, S, B, N, \mathcal{B})$
Ax5: $\mathsf{fulfilled}(S) \leftarrow \mathsf{fulfills}(A, S)$
Ax6: $\mathsf{fulfills}(A, S) \leftarrow \mathsf{has}(A, S) \wedge \mathsf{offers}(A, S)$

Example 3. Patient trusts Clinician on his medical data.

$$\mathsf{trustBL}(patient1, record1, clinician1, 1, \emptyset)$$

When the Clinician visits his patient he requests to the Medical Information System the patient record. The Medical Information System delegates patient record to the patient's clinician. The clinician cannot delegate the record to others actors. Formally this is $\mathsf{delegBL}(m1, medicalIS, record1, clinician1, 1, \emptyset)$.

In Table 3 we present the axiom for the trust model and for the functional model. As mentioned earlier, the owner of a service has full authority concerning access and disposition of it. Thus, Ax1 states that if an actor owns a service, he has it. Ax2 states that if someone trusts with depth N, then he also trusts with smaller depth. Ax3 describes the trust relationship, i.e, it completes the trust relationship between actors. Ax4 says that a delegatee has the service he was delegated. Ax5 states that an actor fulfills a service, then the service is (eventually) fulfilled. Ax6 states that if an actor has a service and offers it, then he (eventually) fulfills it.

Properties are different from axioms: they are constraints that must be checked. It is up to designer to choose which properties his own design should respect. If the set of constraints is not consistent, i.e. they cannot all be simultaneously satisfied, the system is inconsistent, and hence it is not secure. In Table 4 we use the $A \Rightarrow? B$ to mean that one must check that each time A holds, it is desirable that B also holds. Pr1 and Pr2 state that if an agent offers or delegates, he should have the object. Pr3 says that to fulfill a goal an actor must be able to use and offer it. Pr4, Pr5 and Pr6 state that if an actor has, offers, or fulfills a goal and this goal belongs to another actor, the last has to trust the first one. Pr7, Pr8 are used to verify whether the delegatee is not in the black list. Pr9 and Pr10 state that an actor who delegates something to an other, has to trust him. Rights or privileges can be given to trusted agents that are then accountable for the agents to whom may further delegate this right to. So the agents should only delegate to agents that they trust. This forms a delegation chain. If any agent along this chain fails to meet the requirements associated with a delegated

Table 4. Desirable Properties of a Design

Pr1:	offers$(A, S) \Rightarrow?$ has(A, S)
Pr2:	delegBL$(ID, A, S, B, N, \mathcal{B}) \Rightarrow?$ has(A, S)
Pr3:	fulfills$(A, S) \Rightarrow?$ offers(A, S)
Pr4:	has$(B, S) \wedge$ owns$(A, S) \Rightarrow? \exists N \exists \mathcal{B}$ trustBL$(A, S, B, N, \mathcal{B})$
Pr5:	offers$(B, S) \wedge$ owns$(A, S) \Rightarrow? \exists N \exists \mathcal{B}$ trustBL$(A, S, B, N, \mathcal{B})$
Pr6:	fulfills$(B, S) \wedge$ owns$(A, S) \Rightarrow? \exists N \exists \mathcal{B}$ trustBL$(A, S, B, N, \mathcal{B})$
Pr7:	delegBL$(ID, A, S, B, N, \mathcal{B}) \wedge$ owns$(A, S) \Rightarrow? \forall X \in \mathcal{B} \neg$has$(X, S)$
Pr8:	delegBL$(ID, A, S, B, N, \mathcal{B}) \Rightarrow? B \notin \mathcal{B}$
Pr9:	delegBL$(ID, A, S, B, N, \mathcal{B}_1) \Rightarrow? \dfrac{\exists M \geq N \ \exists \mathcal{B}_2 \ \text{trustBL}(A, S, B, M, \mathcal{B}_2) \wedge}{B \notin \mathcal{B}_1 \cup \mathcal{B}_2}$
Pr10:	delegBLChain$(A, S, B) \Rightarrow? \exists N \exists \mathcal{B}$ trustBL$(A, S, B, N, \mathcal{B}) \wedge B \notin \mathcal{B}$
Pr11:	delegBLChain$(A, S, B) \Rightarrow? \exists M \ \exists A_1 \ldots A_M \ \exists N_1 \ldots N_{M-1} \ \exists \mathcal{B}_1 \ldots \mathcal{B}_{M-1}$ $\forall i \in [1 \ldots M-1]$ delegBL$(ID_i, A_i, S, A_{i+1}, N_i, \mathcal{B}_i) \wedge$ $A_1 = A \wedge A_M = B \wedge N_i > N_{i+1} \wedge \mathcal{B}_i \subseteq \mathcal{B}_{i+1} \wedge A_{i+1} \notin \mathcal{B}_i$

right, the chain is broken and all agents following the failure are not permitted to perform the action associated with the right. Thus, Pr11 is used to verify if the delegate chain is valid.

There are additional properties that we have not listed due to a lack of space, such as checking delegation to actors that cannot have a service directly.

5 Implementation and Experimental Results

In order to illustrate our approach we formalize the case study and check-model it in Datalog [1]. A datalog logic program is a set of rules of the form $L:-L_1 \wedge \ldots \wedge L_n$ where L, called head, is a positive literal and $L_1, \ldots, L_n$ are literals and they are called body. Intuitively, if $L_1, \ldots, L_n$ are true in the model then L must be true in the model. The definition can be recursive, so defined relations can also occur in bodies of rules. Axioms of the form $A \leftarrow B \wedge C$ can be represented as $A:-B, C$. In Datalog properties can be represented as the constraint :-A, not B.

We use the DLV system [9] for the actual analysis. Consistency checks are standard checks to guarantee that the security specification is not self-contradictory. Inconsistent specifications are due to unexpected interactions among constraints in the specifications. The consistency checks are performed automatically by DLV. The simplest consistency check verifies whether there is any valid scenario that respects all the constraints of the security specification.

Example 4. For model checking purposes we consider two patients, three clinicians, and one HCA. Patients trust completely the HCA for their personal information. Then we rapresent the relation between Patient and Clinician shown in Figure 4, that is, the Patient trusts his clinicians with depth 1. Further, HCA trusts completely Hospital for patients personal informations. Finally, we present the relationship between Hospital and Clinician on patient personal information.

Table 5. Axioms in Datalog

```
has(A,S) :- owns(A,S).
has(B,S) :- delegate(ID,A,S,B,N).
fulfill(A,S) :- has(A,S), offer(A,S).
fulfilled(S) :- fulfill(A,S).
trustBL(A,S,B,N) :- #succ(N,M), trustBL(A,S,B,M), N>0.
trustBL(A,S,C,P) :- -bL(C), #succ(P,N), trustBL(A,S,B,N),
                    trustBL(B,S,C,M), M>=N, N>1.
trustBL(A,S,C,M) :- -bL(C), trustBL(A,S,B,N), trustBL(B,S,C,M), N>M, N>1.
```

Table 6. Some properties in Datalog

```
:- offer(A,S), not has(A,S).
:- delegate(ID,A,S,B,N), not has(A,S).
:- offer(B,S), owns(A,S), not trustNP(A,S,B), A<>B.
:- fulfill(B,S), owns(A,S), not trustNP(A,S,B), A<>B.
:- delegateChain(A,S,C,N), not trustBL(A,S,C,N).
```

Table 7. Health Care System-3 trust relationship in Datalog

```
trustFull(Pat,Rec,X) :- isHCA(X), owns(Pat,Rec).
trust(Pat,Rec,Cli,1) :- isClinicianOf(Cli,Pat), owns(Pat,Rec).
trustFull(hca,Rec,hospital) :- isRecord(Rec).
trustFull(hospital,Rec,mIS) :- isRecord(Rec).
trustFull(hospital,Rec,X) :- isClinician(X), isRecord(Rec).
```

Below we introduce the constraint to verify whether only the clinicians of the patient can have patient information.

```
:- trust(Pat,Rec,Cli,N), owns(Pat,Rec), isClinician(Cli),
   not isClinicianOf(Cli,Pat).
```

The DLV system reports an inconsistency since all Clinicians are authorized to have the personal information of any patient. Ideally we would authorize only the clinician of the patient to have patient data.

Example 5. The trust relationship among actor in Figure 6 and in Figure 7 is formalized in Table 7 and is described below:

1. Patient trusts completely HCA and he trusts directly his Clinician,
2. HCA trusts completely Hospital,
3. Hospital trusts completely Medical Information System, and
4. Medical Information System trusts completely Clinicians.

We can check whether only the clinicians of the patient can have patient personal information according to Example 4. The DLV system report an inconsistency: in the current design every Clinician is implicitly authorized to have patient personal information. To resolve this problem, we have to change the trust model using the following trust relation between the Medical Information System and the Clinician.

```
trust(mIS,Rec,Cli,1) :- isClinicianOf(Cli,Pat),owns(Pat,Rec).
```

In other words, the *Medical Information System* allows an actor to access directly the records of a patient if the actor is the physician of the patient.

We can now analyze the complete trust and functional model. In particular, we check whether the delegater trusts the delegatee. The refined result is that patient's consent must be sought for any other agent such as clinician's colleagues to be able to access at patient medical information, and the patient must be notified of every access. So the clinician has to request a consulting to colleagues through the hospital and the patient must give the permission to access the data.

It is also possible to make additional queries aimed at verifying a number of security principles such as least-privilege, or need-to-know policies as done by Liu et al. [20] in their security requirements model formalized in Alloy.

6   Conclusions

The main contribution of this paper is the introduction of a formal model and a methodology for analyzing trust during early requirement engineering. To this end, we have proposed an enhancement of Tropos that is based on the clear separation of functional dependencies, trust and delegation relationships. This distinction makes it possible to capture organization-oriented security and trust requirements without being caught into the technical details about how these will be realized through digital certificates or access control mechanisms. The modeling process we envision has the advantage of making clear why and where trust management and delegation mechanisms are necessary, and which trust relationships or requirements they address.

The framework we proposed supports the automatic verification of security requirements and trust relationships against functional dependencies specified in a formal modeling language. The model can be easily modified to account for degrees of trust. Levels of trust can be captured by using a qualitative theory for goal analysis. See [14] for details.

Plans for future work include adding time to trust models and analyzing these new features with the Formal Tropos T-Tool [11].

References

1. S. Abiteboul, R. Hull, and V. Vianu. *Foundations of Databases.* Addison-Wesley, 1995.
2. R. Anderson. A security policy model for clinical information systems. In *Proc. of the 15th IEEE Symp. on Security and Privacy.* IEEE Comp. Society Press, 1996.
3. R. Anderson. *Security Engineering: A Guide to Building Dependable Distributed Systems.* Wiley Computer Publishing, 2001.
4. P. Bresciani, F. Giunchiglia, J. Mylopoulos, and A. Perini. TROPOS: An Agent-Oriented Software Development Methodology. *JAAMAS*, (To appear).
5. J. Castro, M. Kolp, and J. Mylopoulos. Towards Requirements-Driven Information Systems Engineering: The Tropos Project. *Inform. Sys.*, 27(6):365–389, 2002.

6. L. Chung and B. Nixon. Dealing with non-functional requirements: Three experimental studies of a process-oriented approach. In *Proc. of ICSE'95*, 1995.

7. R. Crook, D. Ince, L. Lin, and B. Nuseibeh. Security requirements engineering: When anti-requirements hit the fan. In *Proc. of RE'02*. IEEE Computer Society, 2002.

8. A. Dardenne, A. V. Lamsweerde, and S. Fickas. Goal-directed requirements acquisition. *Science of Computer Programming*, 1991.

9. T. Dell'Armi, W. Faber, G. Ielpa, N. Leone, and G. Pfeifer. Aggregate functions in disjunctive logic programming: Semantics, complexity, and implementation in dlv. In *Proc. of IJCAI'03*. Morgan Kaufmann Publishers, 2003.

10. P. T. Devanbu and S. G. Stubblebine. Software engineering for security: a roadmap. In *ICSE - Future of SE Track*, pages 227–239, 2000.

11. A. Fuxman, L. Liu, M. Pistore, M. Roveri, and J. Mylopoulos. Specifying and analyzing early requirements: Some experimental results. In *Proc. of ICRE'03*, page 105. IEEE Computer Society, 2003.

12. A. Fuxman, M. Pistore, J. Mylopoulos, and P. Traverso. Model checking early requirements specifications in tropos. In *Proc. of RE'01*, pages 174–181, Toronto, August 2001. IEEE Computer Society.

13. P. Giorgini, F. Massacci, and J. Mylopoulos. Requirement Engineering meets Security: A Case Study on Modelling Secure Electronic Transactions by VISA and Mastercard. In *Proc. of ER'03*, Chicago, Illinois, 13-16 October 2003.

14. P. Giorgini, E. Nicchiarelli, J. Mylopoulous, and R. Sebastiani. Formal reasoning techniques for goal models. *J. of Data Semantics*, 1, 2003.

15. S. Guttorm. Eliciting security requirements by misuse cases. In *Proceedings of TOOLS Pacific 2000*, 2000.

16. Jan Jürjens. Towards Secure Systems Development with UMLsec. In *Proc. of FASE'01*, 2001.

17. N. Li, B. N. Grosof, and J. Feigenbaum. Delegation logic: A logic-based approach to distributed authorization. *ACM TISSEC 03*, 6(1):128–171, 2003.

18. N. Li, W. H. Winsborough, and J. C. Mitchell. Beyond proof-of-compliance: Safety and availability analysis in trust management. In *Proc. of Symposium on Security and Privacy*, 2003.

19. L. Liu, E. Yu, and J. Mylopoulos. Analyzing security requirements as relationships among strategic actors. In *Proc. of SREIS'02*, North Carolina, 2002. Raleigh.

20. L. Liu, E. Yu, and J. Mylopoulos. Security and privacy requirements analysis within a social setting. In *Proc. of RE'03*, pages 151–161, 2003.

21. T. Lodderstedt, D. Basin, and J. Doser. SecureUML: A UML-Based Modeling Language for Model-Driven Security. In J.-M. Jezequel, H. Hussmann, and S. Cook, editors, *Proc. of UML'02*, volume 2460, pages 426–441. Springer, 2002.

22. J. McDermott and C. Fox. Using abuse care models for security requirements analysis. In *Proc. of ACSAC'99*, December 1999.

23. H. Mouratidis, P. Giorgini, and G. Manson. Modelling secure multiagent systems. In *Proc. of AAMAS'03*, pages 859–866. ACM Press, 2003.

24. I. Sommerville. *Software Engineering*. Addison-Wesley, 2001.

25. T. Tryfonas, E. Kiountouzis, and A. Poulymenakou. Embedding security practices in contemporary information systems development approaches. *Information Management and Computer Security*, 9:183–197, 2001.

26. E. Yu and L. Cysneiros. Designing for privacy and other competing requirements. In *Proc. of SREIS'02*, North Carolina, 2002. Raleigh.

Towards Dynamic Security Perimeters for Virtual Collaborative Networks

Ivan Djordjevic[1] and Theo Dimitrakos[2]

[1] Department of Electronic Engineering, Queen Mary, University of London, UK, E1 4NS
ivan.djordjevic@elec.qmul.ac.uk
[2] Central Laboratory of the Research Councils, Rutherford Appleton Lab., OX11 0QX, UK
t.dimitrakos@rl.ac.uk

Abstract. Rapid technological advancements capitalising on the convergence of information (middleware) and communication (network) technologies now enable open application-to-application communication and bring about the prospect of ad hoc integration of systems across organisational boundaries to support collaborations that may last for a single transaction or evolve dynamically over a longer period. Architectures for managing networks of collaborating peers in such environments face new security and trust management challenges. In this paper we will introduce the basic elements of such an architecture emphasising trust establishment, secure collaboration, distributed monitoring and performance assessment issues.

1 Introduction

The Internet provides a ubiquitous, standards-based substrate for global communications of all kinds. Rapid advances are now being made in agreeing protocols and machine-processable message/document formats that will soon enable open application-application communication and bring about the prospect of *ad hoc* integration of systems across organisational boundaries to support collaborations that may last for a single transaction or evolve dynamically over many years. Effectively, we will witness on-demand creation of *dynamically-evolving, scalable Virtual Organisations (VO)* spanning national and enterprise borders, where the participating entities pool resources, capabilities and information to achieve common objectives.

As a motivating example consider the scenario from Figure1. As a part of the scientific project, researcher Alice needs to perform on-line material analysis using specialised services provided by different Application Service Providers (ASP1 and ASP2). Such services may include analysis tools (hosted at another institution SH1), pre-existing data sets (held by a remote data archive SH2), additional computation power outsourced to a supercomputing centre acting as ASP1. The goal is, as the analysis proceeds, to create overlaying security perimeters, protecting different virtual collaborations that may exist at a time (as a firewall would do in a fixed topology), while ensuring the security of each member as defined by its local administrator.

Alice belongs to team of researchers assigned to a local administrator at the University. The main activities of the material analysis are executed by end-to-end

C.D. Jensen et al. (Eds.): iTrust 2004, LNCS 2995, pp. 191–205, 2004.

services CSI1 provided by ASP1, and CS2 provided by ASP2. We assume that CSI1 is using subservices executed in house at ASP1 who is responsible for administering CSI1 and its subservices, whereas ASP2 is effectively outsourcing some of the subservices needed for executing CSI2 to different service hosts SH1 and SH2. Each administrator wants to protect its local "private" resources from the general "public" which may include hostile agents. At the same time seamless interaction between Alice and the end-to-end services, as well as CSI2 and its outsourced subservices, is highly desirable in order to facilitate collaboration objectives, i.e., material analysis.

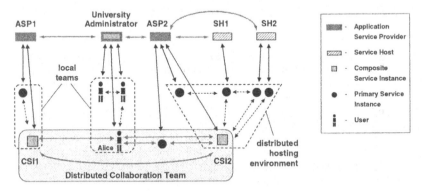

Fig. 1. A motivating scenario

This scenario highlights several issues related to secure collaboration in dynamic virtual organisations:

- Collaboration of resources that are controlled by different institutions. Each institution will have their own policies on access control and conditions of use.
- Resources may be called upon to participate in the task without previous knowledge of the other participants. Trust between resources has to be established in real time on a peer-to-peer basis.
- Resources need to be protected from their collaborators and the whole collaboration team has to be protected from outsiders including other entities residing with the participating institutions.
- The same resource may interact in different collaborations. A separation between those interactions has to be achieved.
- Different security conditions may be applied for different parts of the resource, including restrictions on data.
- Collaborating resources may play different roles in their organisation and various collaborations, and different (potentially conflicting) security policies may apply.
- There is no central administrative point. Security has to be achieved via devolved policy management combined with distributed enforcement at a peer level.
- Complex trust relationships may hold between collaborating resources (users or services) and their managers: Trust of a resource may evolve over time based on the direct observations of its collaborators, witnessing whether it is performing as expected, given its role. Also, changes of the trust level in a manager may reflect on the trust level in the resources it manages, and vice versa.

A suitable architecture must be able to provide a security and trust management infrastructure that meets these requirements. In this paper we introduce the basic elements of such architecture and gradually explain how it aims to address the above requirements, emphasising on trust establishment, secure collaboration, distributed monitoring and performance assessment issues.

The community management model was first proposed in [10] and developed further in [6] for multi-domain security management in virtual organisations. It exploits a variation of the distributed firewall concept [1]. Policy is defined at the system-management level and distributed to the end-entities (client hosts) by the means of the certificates and firewall rules, where it is enforced by each entity participating in the Virtual Collaboration. The security perimeter can be easily extended to safely include remote hosts and networks, therefore eliminating any topological obstacles. Some of the functionalities and performance were tested through simulation, and results are reported in [9]. In this paper we introduce further enhancements and more complete description of the system. Section 2 gives the overview of the improved architecture, and section 3 describes trust management model based on monitoring and performance assessment of the entities in the system.

2   Overview of the Proposed Architecture

The architecture presented here provides mechanisms where Closed Collaboration Teams (CCT) can be dynamically altered in terms of membership and policy constraints. The interaction model of the proposed architecture integrates a layered peer-to-peer model (between collaborating resources as well as between the managers administering resources), with a centralised community management model (between members and their local managers) and a master/slave model (between security managers and enforcement agents). It supports on-demand creation and management of dynamic virtual collaborations in the form of secure groups of peers (users, services, resources, etc.) that cut across geographical and enterprise boundaries. The proposed architecture has been developed with two main goals in mind:
-    Enabling communication within dynamically created collaboration teams, that is: secure, scalable, accountable, robust and independent of network topology.
-    Enforcing security perimeters, which adapt to the highly dynamic evolution of a collaboration group (in terms of membership and security policy).
These goals are addressed through the following means:
-    Certificates to manage CCT membership and privileges.
-    Role based security policies describing permissions, prohibitions and obligations within CCTs, set by, and negotiated between, the community mangers.
-    Multi-layered end-entity security enforcement mechanism to protect individual members within a collaboration group and the collaboration group as a whole.
-    Monitoring and assessing evidence the performance of peers in executing a collaborative task across heterogeneous administrative and security domains.
Within this architecture, trust in the network entities and the system itself is supported in the following ways:
-    Establishment and propagation of trust via digital certificates.
-    Protecting the collaborating entities and maintaining trust in the operation of the system by securing entity interactions with dynamic, distributed security perimeters that extend the functionality of a distributed firewall to the service and application layers.

- Monitoring operation and assessing evidence about the performance of an entity in enacting a task in a given context.

2.1 Community Management Model

The community management model distinguishes several types of roles that participate in the formation of CCT environment.

Local Security Managers (LSM) are responsible for population of clients. At client's initial setup, LSM defines its security policy through means of certificates and policy rules, and controls it as long as client remains active. During this period, clients can request to create a new CCT or to join to a number of existing CCTs that are managed by their own or any other manager. This is done by the manager in charge of the CCT, through creation of CCT-specific certificate for the appropriate client.

CCT Managers maintain a number of CCTs, from the group creation until its termination (which is normally until the last member leaves). They manage group memberships, maintain the level of CCT security by defining authorization privileges and assigning them to CCT members through certificates, and update the group membership and policy. From the perspective of client, LSM and CCT manager can be the same entity, only performing different role in each context.

Clients (or peers) are networked entities and can be (human) agents, applications, or service instances. Functionality for supporting CCT and policy enforcement is localised to each host. Upon initial setup provided by its LSM, client is free to participate in a number of CCTs, during which period it contacts the corresponding CCT Manager(s).

Once admitted in the group, CCT members interacts, without manager's involvement, by presenting a group certificate embedded in the messages they interchange[1]. Messages with certificate not matching the required group certificate are either deleted or ignored without further processing. The creation of inter-organization CCTs is supported through interactions between LSMs and CCT Managers, which may be viewed as CCT members at a level above the level of the teams they manage.

Figure2 illustrates the examples of *local CCT* (where all the members belong to the domain of the same LSM; e.g. Loc1 and Loc2) and *virtual CCT* (where the members reside in different organizational domains, initially affiliated to different LSMs; e.g. Vir1 and client Y). Having this in mind, the notion of local CCT could be treated as a 'special case', where member may contact CCT Manager directly since the CCT Manager and LSM are the same entity for that particular client (client Y within CCT Loc1). Different types of interactions in the CCT environment (given in Figure2) are:

- *member-to-member (me2me)*: direct p2p communication between the CCT members (e.g. file transfers, white boarding, procedure calls, process invocation). This is supported with a group certificate, issued by a CCT manager in charge.
- *member-to-manager (me2ma)*: regarding the interactions related to CCT management, e.g. manager's updates of group policy, and for the clients' negotiation with the CCT Manager for creating/joining a new group.

---

[1] For this, SPKI certificates could be used, to support use of groups for identifying set of users within a name space [23]

- *manager-to-manager (ma2ma)*: direct peer-to-peer communication between LSMs and CCT Managers. For example, this would include negotiating the introduction of a new CCT member, negotiating policy updates, propagating performance assessment or intrusion detection information, etc.

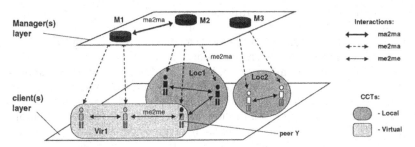

Fig. 2. Types of interactions and groups within the CCT environment

2.2   Security Management and Enforcement Model

Group management within the CCT environment is supported through the use of public key certificates (for authentication), attribute certificates (for authorization) and encryption (for data confidentiality) [20]. Policy deployment model of the CCT architecture combines default security settings with a role-based access control approach. Policy is defined at the LSM / CCT manager level based on the anticipated role of the client in the organization / group, and distributed to the end-entities (client hosts), where it is enforced . The security perimeter can be easily extended to safely include remote hosts and networks, therefore eliminating any topological obstacles. There are two essentially different classes of policies:

- *Local Policies*, which are owned and maintained by the LSMs and apply to the clients associated with its organizational structure. Those policies are defined at the creation of the organizational structure, and are accordingly modified.
- *CCT Policies*, which are defined at the CCT creation and are maintained by the CCT manager. Depending on the scope of the group, those policies may be negotiated between the CCT manager and client's LSM, which can impose the constraints on the CCT policy suggested by the CCT manager.

Some policy deployment information is distributed to the client at the initial setup (registration). It comprises default firewall rules for the client host (for securing the lower level of the communication protocol stack), authentication certificate (that establishes the identity of a client within the architecture) and the access privileges (based on a defined role of a client within the organization). CCT policy is a shorter-term, more dynamic and addresses smaller population comparing to a local policy. It is defined based on the client's role in the group, and delivered at the joining time by means of the attribute certificate. It provides more sophisticated method in terms of access control, authorizing the members (only) to certain action within the group.

The actual policy deployment is always performed by the LSM. A (remote) CCT manager can interact with members only via their LSM(s). CCT policies and policy updates are communicated by the CCT manager to the LSM which has the responsibility for their deployment among its clients. Once delivered, it is enforced at the enforcement agents at the client's host.

Trust Establishment. Authentication of the entities within the CCT environment is supported through the use of PKI certificates (PKC) [15]. The certificate structure of each organization participating in the CCT environment can be seen as a single-level PKI, where the LSM is an issuer of local PKCs to clients. At initial registration, client and the LSM perform mutual authentication via PKC issued by some of the commercial CAs (Certification Authority). Upon this, the LSM creates a local public-key certificate, to be used by a client for all the authentication-related purposes within the CCT environment. Through use of a 'local' PKC the LSM keeps control of who is registered with the organization and for how long (e.g. via the validity period of the PKC). Local PKC is used at client's negotiation with the administrator for creation or joining a group, or mutual authentication of the CCT members prior to the establishment of p2p session within the group. The 'commercial' PKC are used within the CCT environment for the authentication of the manager nodes, and as a 'root' certificate upon which the trust and legitimacy of the local certificates is built on.

Group management and member's privileges within the particular CCT are regulated through "authorization certificates". Through usage of attribute certificates (AC) the issuing authority can specify a set of credentials authorizing the holder of the certificate to claim certain privileges [12]. Within the context of the CCT architecture, AC issuer is CCT manager, which defines the group policy and sets the credentials granted to each group member. Credentials are an abstraction of the privileges, and each group member is granted the credentials that relate to its anticipated role in the group, upon entering the group. Credentials are used to inform security policy enforcement as described in section *Distributed Security Enforcement*. In a similar way, the LSM defines the organizational policy and delivers it to a client at the initial setup (local policy, as defined before). The privileges specified here do not express the possible relationships within the organization (since all peer-to-peer communication is carried out via CCTs); rather, they can be used for the LSM to put a constraint on the CCT policy that applies to the client, and prohibit certain actions. This can be also done by the LSM while endorsing a client's membership to a CCT.

Normally, AC does not contain the holder's public key, but it may contain the reference to the PKC and / or CA which can verify the holder's PKC. In such a way, PKC and AC (which are presented separately) can be easily correlated for the verification. This also allows the flexibility in the policy definition, since the PKC (and client's duration in the environment) will normally last for a longer time than the AC (and the membership to a group).

The separation of concerns between credentials, roles and policy statements improves the scalability of the architecture and the flexibility of enforcement:

- Roles, being more generic than member IDs, reduce the overhead of managing and enforcing security policies.
- Modification of policies associated with a role does not necessitate issuing new and revoking old attribute certificates (AC) for the whole CCT.
- Although, changes to the role of a member in the CCT may necessitate issuing of new AC by the CCT manager, no changes need to be made in the CCT policy.

-   The enforcement mechanism at entity does not need to maintain information about the enforcement of the complete set of policies that may apply to a large network. Instead it is concerned only with the policies relevant to the CCTs it participates in, and from those only the subset of rules needs to be retrieved and enforced during the CCT interactions.

When member leaves a CCT (or its certificate has been revoked), this information needs to be passed to the rest of the CCT in order to maintain the level of security. In the current approach, this is performed directly by the CCT manager (either periodically or on as-needed basis).

Secure communication. Communication is secured through message encryption. Symmetric keys are used for the interactions where large amount of data is transferred (since introducing less processing overhead) or where the number of entities sharing them or the duration of their usage is not significant. In addition, every of the signalling messages is digitally signed with a sender's private key (from the key pair where public key is a basis for the PKC, naturally providing the basis for non-repudiation and accounting. This is illustrated via an example given in Figure3.

Alice wants to join a CCT. The whole process is initiated by the client (Alice) through the join request message to its LSM (M_1). Alice authenticates herself at the LSM via PKC, previously assigned by the same entity at registration.

If the authentication and the request are approved, the LSM contacts the appropriate CCT manager authenticating itself via PKC issued by the commercial CA (M_2). If this has been performed satisfactorily, CCT manager creates a symmetric key and delivers it to the LSM, encrypted with the LSM's public key (M_3). The message also contains the PKC of the CCT manager, enabling the LSM to authenticate the CCT manager. This ends the phase of the authentication: public keys are temporarily stored to check the signature until the joining process is completed, and the symmetric encryption key is kept by both of the parties in order to support any subsequent communication related to this CCT. This key is periodically being updated by either of the parties, and (in this example) it is needed until Alice leaves the CCT. Now, the LSM forwards the Alice's request to the CCT manager (M_4). If the CCT manager accepts the request[2], it defines the Alice's privileges as a CCT member (via attributes within the AC, and compiles the CCT policy rules and the list of current CCT members. This data is delivered to the LSM (M_5), encrypted with the inter-manager key. Upon the receipt, the LSM decrypts and examines the CCT-related data, and if the terms are accepted forwards it to Alice (M_6) (now encrypted with Alice's public key)[3].

This concludes the process of the joining – Alice is now member of the CCT and can start peer-to-peer communication with the rest of the group (e.g. Bob). Before the peer-to-peer session can commence, group members authenticate themselves by presenting their PKI certificates, in order to establish initial trust at each other (M_7 & M_8). At this stage, entities may (optionally) contact each other's LSMs for the purpose of the certificate verification (not shown in the diagram). If this process is performed satisfactorily by both parties, Bob will create the symmetric key (to be

---

[2] The acceptance of the request depends on the policies of LSM and CCT Manager, and other concerns such as trust between the entities involved in this process.

[3] Rejection would lead to re-negotiation, with revised AC being presented by a CCT manager.

used between him and Alice for the purpose of this session), and delivers it securely, encrypted with Alice's public key ($\mathbf{M_8}$). This key is used to exchange the appropriate attribute certificates ($\mathbf{M_{9/10}}$)[4], as well as for the encryption of subsequently transferred data ($\mathbf{M_{11/12}}$).

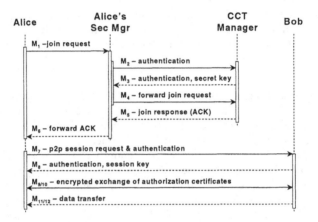

Fig. 3. Inclusion of new member in CCT and subsequent me2me communication

As more than two entities may participate in the same interaction session within a group, the protocol also supports more complex multicast interactions, using '*N root/leaf pairwise keys*' algorithm for key distribution [25]: the initiator of the session (*root*) generates a list of the participants (*leaves*) and sends it with the requests to each of them. The leaves respond with the acceptance/rejection message, upon which the root creates the record of the public keys of the members who accepted the session, and exchanges the encryption key only with them. This approach contributes the scalability since the most time consuming operation, public-key encryption, is minimized.

Distributed Security Enforcement. The separation between policy specification and enforcement is one of the key features of our scheme that brings the flexibility and scalability of policy deployment, consistent with the proposed interaction model.

CCT policies are defined by the CCT manager, but enforced by policy enforcement agents residing at each individual host (Figure4). Enforcement agents are controlled and (re)configured by the corresponding LSMs using a master/slave interaction model. Neither the client nor the CCT manager can access and reconfigure these enforcement agents. This controls personalised CCT member access through the security perimeter of the corresponding CCT member based on the AC it is provided with, creating the shell at the level of the executed application or service. The additional protection is supported at the network level, through performing packet

---

[4] The AC carries the information about the privileges of a CCT member, and in part reflects both the policy of that CCT, as well as the member's 'profile' (over the set of the CCTs it is involved in). Encryption of the AC assures that this information is not publicly disclosed.

filtering and monitoring of incoming traffic[5], which is common for the hosting environment that may serve several clients. Security perimeters for each individual member contribute to the formation of a distributed security where enforcement is managed by LSM of each member and coordinated by the CCT manager of the group around which the distributed perimeter is established.

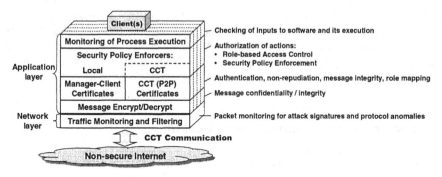

Fig. 4. Instance of multi-layered architecture for distributed security enforcement, localized at each CCT member

With every incoming peer-to-peer interaction, attributes from the AC indicate the sender's role and the associated policies dictate which of its requests and actions (e.g. in the sense of Remote Procedure Calls) are authorized. Similarly, the policies associated to the sender's role dictate if its requests or intended actions (e.g. in the sense of Remote Procedure Calls) should be blocked or delayed by its end-point firewall instance. For every interaction, per-message security checks are performed at a distributed security perimeter instance:

- For an outgoing message from the CCT member, the intended action is checked against the set of member's privileges within the CCT and, if compliance is confirmed, it is wrapped with the appropriate certificate and sent via the firewall.
- For an incoming message, after packet stream is examined, the message is verified against the appropriate certificate. As explained earlier, attributes within the AC are related to sender's role, and the intended action is clarified at the policy enforcers, in terms of sender's credentials, prior to executing the specific request. Finally, the message is passed through the application-level monitoring, and onto the application layer.

If at any point non-compliance with the security policy is detected, communication is blocked and the appropriate action taken (generating the alarm, logging the event, etc.). Notably, blockage of unauthorized actions may happen at either endpoint depending on the CCT and local policies that may apply.

CCT policies and policy updates are communicated by CCT manager to the corresponding LSMs which have the responsibility for their deployment among their local clients that participate in that CCT. Deployment is initiated by compiling the CCT policy statements and distributing to the corresponding members the resulting end-point enforcement rules that apply to them. Prior the deployment or update, the

---

[5] For a simpe implementation of an analogous mechanism in the Linux OS kernel, see [17].

LSM inspects policy suggested by a CCT Manager. Clearly, devolution of policy control may lead to the appearance of conflicts between policies: At present we have made a simplifying assumption that in the case of a conflict between the local and CCT policy, local policy prevails and will always override the CCT policy. In future versions of the architecture we expect to introduce a dedicated distributed mechanism addressing the resolution of conflicts between CCT and local security policies.

The independent research presented in [16] is similar to this aspect of our work. It proposes Virtual Private Services that should provide separation of policy management and enforcement, mainly focusing on the issues related to the mechanisms for distributed access control enforcement. Also, there are technologies [22] promising to facilitate implementations of functionalities providing evidence-based and role-based security on web services based commodity platforms.

3   Performance Monitoring and Assessment

An additional level of security enforcement is that of performance assessment including the monitoring of task execution at the application level (noted in Figure4). A simple demonstration based on the monitoring of software execution and inputs to the software have already been documented [21], although not in a distributed scheme. Need for the more comprehensive assessment scheme that can be used for a variety of purposes (SLA performance, electronic contracts, security) has been clarified in [7]. For the purpose of the CCT architecture, we propose a distributed implementation of a multi-layer scheme of "monitors", which collect evidence/data by all clients in the group. These events of interest are communicated to the relevant entities where the analysis is performed.

In such a scheme the evidence is associated to the observation of events, which is reasonable for virtual organisations built on top of dynamic service environments[6]. In such environments, a CCT Monitor act a as an intermediary facilitating event collection: it collects events generated as a result of CCT interactions and either they forward them to a CCT management capability (responsible to assessing performance) or they analyse them and generate a derived event for the attention of the CCT management. The derived event may depend on the occurrence of a number of potentially interdependent events within a CCT.

The following roles need to be established in order to support performance monitoring during the enactment of interactions within a CCT.

-   *Monitor Sensor* enables monitoring of the activities of parties, and recording the relevant events. It can also signal a suspected non-performance to the Arbitrator (regarding performance assessment, see below) if it detects such an event.
-   *Monitor Correlation Agent* enables the correlation of individual events that may be observed in different local parts of a CCT (that correspond to the subset of CCT members associated with same LSM).
-   *Monitor Notification Service* implements the notification mechanism for sending warning messages to indicate detection of a possible non-compliance event.

---

[6] Such environments, distributed over WAN, typically use asynchronous communication of events often taking place on a "push" basis: "consumers" subscribe to events and "producers" are obliged to notify them. In such situations, the occurrence of an event may be uncertain.

We distinguish three levels of monitoring:

1. Monitoring at each member, about the events relating to the inbound/outbound communication of a CCT member and the individual actions a member performs.
2. Monitoring within a local part of CCT, which may involve correlation of observations within that locality.
3. Monitoring across the different localities of a CCT which focuses on interactions between members across the local parts of the CCT and may involve correlation of observations made in each locality.

Depending on the configuration of a local part of CCT, we distinguish three different options for monitoring (Figure5), which can also be combined into hybrid schemes:

Centralised monitor capability at each CCT locality is subscribed to significant events relating to the performance of a collaborative task, evaluating them against the normative behaviour descriptions. In **me2me** communication, its functionality is restricted to observing the events, monitoring network traffic and occasionally intercepting messages. Should events created within a CCT locality need to be communicated outside the team, Monitor takes the role of the intermediary in such communication and invokes the Monitor Notification Service as appropriate.

Devolved monitor is an abstraction of a collective realisation of a monitoring capability. Each CCT member comes with its own "atomic" monitoring capability, contributing to the formation of a collective opinion about the event's occurrence. Devolved monitoring appears to be a natural choice for CCTs formed in the absence of uniform and sophisticated underlying infrastructure management services.

Locally Coordinated Monitor combines the behaviour of devolved monitoring with a centralised coordinator (residing at the CCT manager) who weights the evidence provided by each local member vs. trust in member's monitoring capability. Each member contributes evidence as a part of its **me2ma** communication (potentially distinguished and encoded in a special **me2ma** certificate). If evidence about interdependent events needs to be correlated in order to account for an observation, Monitor Correlation Agent needs to be realised and invoked.

Devolved monitors are also suitable for maintaining provenance information related to the member that can be used by the member in case of dispute. Centralised and locally coordinated monitors focus on higher-level overview within the local part of the CCT for the purposes of group management. Each monitoring option captures Monitor behaviours that are operationally different (when viewed from within a CCT) but observationally similar (when viewed from the outside of a CCT). In addition, both monitors & sensors operate in master-slave mode, controlled by the LSMs.

The Monitor capability of a (virtual) CCT effectively amounts to a network of *local CCT Monitors*, each of which is responsible for monitoring of the activities of parties, and recording/ notifying about the relevant events within its local part of a CCT. Each local CCT monitor participating in a *virtual CCT monitor* is subscribed to significant events, and when these occur evaluates them against the local policies for these events by invoking a local Monitor Correlation Agent, if necessary. Significant events of interest for the CCT management (which may be the result of a correlation of local events) are communicated through the local Monitor Notification Service. A further correlation of these events and evaluation against CCT policies may then take place at the (virtual) CCT Monitor capability associated with the CCT management.

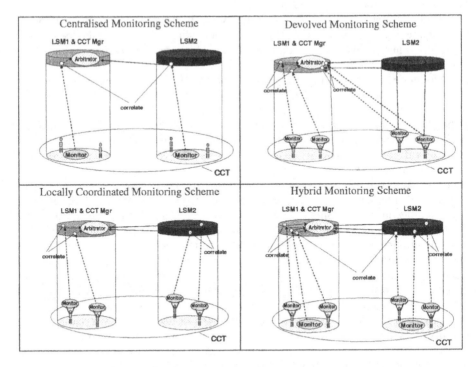

Fig. 5. Overview of different monitoring options and their combination in a hybrid scheme

Performance assessment for interactions within a CCT local is facilitated by an *Arbitrator* capability associated with the CCT Manager, capable of arbitrating about the performance of a CCT member or LSM (based on evidence provided by a CCT Monitor) and making a judgement about the extent of deviation or non-performance[7]. Although confidence parameters may be associated with an event, we do not assume any complex reasoning / decision making by a monitor. Effectively, monitors report the events (or results of a correlation of events), even when they themselves can only get second hand evidence. The CCT Arbitrator does the reasoning and makes the decisions, taking into consideration its confidence in the competence of the contributing local monitors. The monitors can supply degrees of confidence with each reported event, to form a basis for the Arbitrator's reasoning and decision-making.

CCT Arbitrator enables measuring deviation from expected or prescribed behaviour, which in turn can be used for assessing the performance of an entity (Member or LSM) in performing a task. Together with information collected about past performance or reputation in performing similar tasks in different CCT contexts a CCT manager can form opinions about:

---

[7] For example, neural networks could be used to detect deviation from typical behaviour.

- Whether the current interaction is a possible attack, based on the significance of a deviation (e.g. detection of an intruder) or correlation of different behaviours that fit the pattern of a distributed or coordinated attack by a group of intruders [2].
- Performance of a CCT member or a number of them in enacting a contract (e.g. SLA or multiparty contract modelling a collaboration agreement) [7].
- Competence of a member in performing a specific task.
- Competence of a local Monitor (Sensor) in making reliable observation.
- Competence of a Monitor Correlation Agent in correlating a collection of interdependent observations.
- Competence of a LSM in controlling the enforcement of the agreed CCT policies.
- Competence of a member in enforcing the prescribed CCT policies.

In the case of security violation or non-compliance by a CCT member, and depending on the extent and type of deviation or non-compliance, the CCT Arbitrator will initiate either a mediation process, managed by a *Mediator*, or the enforcement of any sanctions applicable, to be instructed by the CCT Manager and carried out by the corresponding LSM through the Enforcement Agents residing at that member.

In addition, the evolving history of the past performance assessments in similar contexts may provide the basis for building a reputation of the network entities potentially associated with a CCT. Such information can also contribute to the derivation of confidence about an entity's anticipated performance in a CCT, or guide the discovery and engagement of suitable entities in a CCT.

4   Conclusions and Further Work

Security, trust and compliance to the collaborative business agreements are the main prerequisites for successful functioning and operation of Virtual Organizations (VO).

In this paper, we have presented an integrated architecture for dynamic and trusted management of the secure and distributed collaborations, where evidence-based trust may impact role-based security and relationships in the system. Within our architecture, trust in the network entities and the system itself is supported in the following ways:

- Establishment of trust via digital certificates.
- Maintaining the trust by securing the interaction s in the system with dynamic distributed perimeters.
- Evaluating and building the trust through performance assessment of the entities involved.

We are currently evaluating a number of approaches [11], [13], [14], [18] in order to identify suitable trust metrics that would: 1) allow an entity to quantify the trustworthiness of another entity about a specific task; 2) support the effective integration of reputation systems into the CCT architecture model. Other aspects of future work include the introduction of a suitable language for specifying and negotiating policies, mechanisms for resolving conflicts between policy statements, and the potential of automatic generation of "executable" commands for the enforcement agents from the suitable policy statements. In that context, a number of existing solutions is being considered [2], [4], [5], [19].

Related work includes the Globus Project's Community Authorization Service (CAS) [26] enhancement of Grid Security Infrastructure (GSI), which provides an intermediate layer for establishment of trust relationships between specific clients and services, and is responsible for managing policies that govern access to (parts of) a community's resource. Both CAS and the CCT architecture incorporate a community management model, separate policy specification from enforcement, and use potentially short-lived (attribute) certificates. However, unlike CAS, our architecture avoids delegation of user rights: when entering a CCT, clients are granted access rights associated with the role they assigned to. Also, CAS focuses on authentication and distributed enforcement of authorisations, whereas our architecture integrates dynamic network management, communication security and distributed enforcement of access policies. Finally, our architecture can capture complex organisational structures as hierarchies of "local" groups that represent intra-enterprise security administrative domains, and multi-institutional collaborations as "virtual" inter-enterprise communities that cross multiple domains. This capability is not built into CAS and it is not straightforward to implement.

Parts of the presented architecture have been tested through simulation, and results are reported in [9]. Current plans include implementing a variant of the architecture for securing the groups of service instances that may need be created and integrate in order to collaboratively execute a composite application in a Grid-based Application Service Provision scenario, in the context of the European project GRASP [8], [24].

Acknowledgements. The work reported in this paper has been funded in part by EPSRC; the UK Council for the Central Laboratory of the Research Councils (CCLRC); Information Society Technologies grants IST-2001-35464 (Grid-based Application Service Provision) and IST-2001-34910 (iTrust: Working Group on Trust Management in Dynamic Open Systems) of the Framework Programme 5 of the European Commission.

References

[1]   Bellovin S.M. *Distributed Firewalls*; login:, Magazine of USENIX, Nov.1999,pp.37-39.
[2]   Bradshaw J., et al: *Representation and reasoning about DAML-based policy and domain services in KAoS*. Proc of 2nd Int Joint Conference on Autonomous Agents and Multi Agent Systems (AAMAS2003), Melbourne, Australia, 14-18 July 2003.
[3]   Braynov S.: *On Future Avenues for Distributed Attacks*. Proc of 2nd European Conference on Information Warfare and Security (ECIW'03), July 2003. pp. 51-60
[4]   Chadwick D.W., Otenko A.: *RBAC Policies in XML for X.509 Based Privilege Management*. Proc. IFIP SEC 2002, Kluwer Academic Publishers 2002.
[5]   Damianou N., Dulay N., Lupu E., Sloman M.: *The Ponder Policy Specification Language*. Proc. Policy 2001: Workshop on Policies for Distributed Systems and Networks, Bristol, UK, 29-31 Jan. 2001, Springer-Verlag LNCS 1995, pp. 18-39.
[6]   Dimitrakos T., Djordjevic I., Matthews B., Bicarregui J., Phillips C. *Policy Driven Access Control over Distributed Firewall Architecture*. Proc of Policy2002, IEEE Computer Society 2002, ISBN 0-7695-1611-4, pp. 228-231.

[7]   Dimitrakos T., Djordjevic I., Milosevic Z., Jøsang A., Phillips C.: *Contract Performance Assessment for Secure and Dynamic Virtual Collaborations*, Proc. of EDOC'03, 7th IEEE Int Enterprise Distributed Object Computing Conference, 2003.

[8]   Dimitrakos T., Randal Mac D., Yuan F., Gaeta M., Laria G., Ritrovato P., Serhan B., Wesner S., Wulf K.: *An Emerging Architecture Enabling Grid-based Application Service Provision*. Proc of the 7th IEEE Int Enterprise Distributed Object Computing Conference (EDOC03), September 16-19 2003, Brisbane, Australia IEEE Press 2003

[9]   Djordjevic I., Phillips C.: Architecture for Secure Work of Dynamic Distributed Groups, Proc of 1st IEEE Consumer Communication and Networking Conference (CCNC'04), Las Vegas, Nevada, USA, 5-8 January 2004.

[10]   Djordjevic I., Phillips C.: *Certificate-Based Distributed Firewalls for Secure E-Commerce Transactions*. Journal of the Institution of British Telecommunications Engineers (IBTE), Vol. 2, part 3, 2001, pp. 14-19.

[11]   Dragovic B., Hand S., Harris T.L., Kotsovinos E., Twigg A. Managing Trust and Reputation in the XenoServer Open Platform. In Trust Management, 1st Int Conference, iTrust 2003, Heraklion, Crete, Greece, LNCS 2692 Springer 2003, pp 59-74.

[12]   Farrel S., Housley R.: *An Internet Attribute Certificate Profile for Authorization*, RFC 3281, Network Working Group, IETF, April 2002.

[13]   Gray E., Seigneur J-M, Chen Y., Jensen C.D. Trust Propagation in Small Worlds. In Trust Management, 1st Int Conference, iTrust 2003, Heraklion, Crete, Greece, May 28-30, 2003, Proc LNCS 2692 Springer 2003, pp 239-254

[14]   Golbeck J., Parsia B., and Hendler J.: *Trust networks on the semantic web*. Proc of Cooperative Intelligent Agents 2003, Helsinki, Finland, August 2003.

[15]   Housley R., Polk W., Ford W., Solo D.: *Internet X.509 Public Key Infrastructure Certificate and Certificate Revocation List (CRL) Profile*, RFC 3280, Network Working Group, IETF, April 2002.

[16]   Ioannidis S., Bellovin S.M., Ioannidis J., Keromytis A.D., Smith J.M.: *Design and Implementation of Virtual Private Services*. Proc of 12th IEEE Int Workshop on Enabling Technologies: Infrastructure for Collaborative Enterprises. 9-11 June 2003. Linz, Austria. IEEE CS pp. 269-275

[17]   Jin H., Xian F., Han Z., Li S.: *A Distributed Dynamic micro-Firewall Architecture with Mobile Agents and KeyNote Trust Management System*. Proc of 4th Int. Conference on Information and Communications Security, LNCS 2513, 2002. pp. 13-24

[18]   Jøsang A.: *A Logic for Uncertain Probabilities*. International Journal of Uncertainty, Fuzziness and Knowledge-Based Systems, 9(3):279–311, June 2001.

[19]   Lalana Kagal et al., *Towards Authorization, Confidentiality and Privacy for Semantic Web Services*, Proc of AAAI 2004 Spring Symposium on Semantic Web Services.

[20]   Menezes A., Oorschot P.van, Vanstone S.: *Handbook of Applied Cryptography*. CRC Press, 1996. ISBN: 0-8493-8523-7,

[21]   Munson J.C., Wimer S.: *Watcher: The Missing Piece of Security Puzzle*. proc of 17th Annual Conference on Computer Security Applications (ACSAC2001), pp. 230-239

[22]   Security in Microsoft.NET Framework; Analysis by Foundstone, Inc. & CORE Security Technologies, 2000; http://www.foundstone.com/pdf/dotnet-security-framework.pdf

[23]   Maywah A.J.: "An Implementation of a Secure Web Client Using SPKI/SDSI Certificates", MSc Thesis, Dept of Elec. Engineering and Comp. Science, MIT. 2000.

[24]   GRASP Homepage, http://www.eu-grasp.com

[25]   Wallner D., Harder E., Agee R.: "Key Management for Multicast: Issues and Architectures", RFC 2627, Network Working Group, IETF, June 1999.

[26]   Globus CAS. http://www.globus.org/security/CAS/

Human Experiments in Trust Dynamics

Catholijn M. Jonker[1], Joost J.P. Schalken[1,*],
Jan Theeuwes[2], and Jan Treur[1,3]

[1]Vrije Universiteit Amsterdam, Department of Artificial Intelligence
De Boelelaan 1081a, 1081 HV Amsterdam, The Netherlands
http://www.cs.vu.nl/~{jonker, joosts, treur}
{jonker, joosts, treur}@cs.vu.nl

[2]Vrije Universiteit Amsterdam, Department of Cognitive Psychology
De Boelelaan 1111 , 1081 HV Amsterdam, The Netherlands
http://www.psy.vu.nl/~Theeuwes,   J.Theeuwes@psy.vu.nl

[3]Universiteit Utrecht, Department of Philosophy
Heidelberglaan 8, 3584 CS Utrecht, The Netherlands.

Abstract. In the literature, the validity of theories or models for trust is usually based on intuition and common sense. Theories and models are not often verified experimentally. The research reported here contributes results of experiments on the dynamics of trust over time depending on positive or negative experiences. In previous research a number of dynamic properties for such trust dynamics were identified, but not verified empirically. As a continuation of this work, now these properties have been verified in an experimental setting. The outcomes of the experiment (involving a substantial number of 238 subjects) are discussed and related to the previously formulated dynamic properties.

1 Introduction

Trust is omnipresent in all our interactions with other people; e.g., [1], [2], [4], [11]. Without trust, the every day social life which we take for granted is simply not possible [11], cited in [7]. Our society, in which each individual plays its own niche role in complex network of social interactions, would grind to a halt due to a lack of cooperation. A difficulty with the concept trust, is that it is impossible to observe it, or to directly relate it to other simple observable facts. This may be one of the reasons why not many sociologists addressed the concept until recently [12].

1.1 Characterising Trust by Entailed Behaviour

Elofson describes trust as "the reliance upon the characteristics of on object, or the occurrence of an event, or the behavior of a person in order to achieve a desired but uncertain objective in a risky situation." [5]. Luhmann gives a similar definition of

---

* Currently at Vrije Universiteit Amsterdam, Department of Information Management and Software Engineering, De Boelelaan 1081a, 1081 HV Amsterdam, The Netherlands. URL: http://www.cs.vu.nl/~joosts. Email: jjp.schalken@few.vu.nl.

C.D. Jensen et al. (Eds.): iTrust 2004, LNCS 2995, pp. 206–220, 2004.

trust: "Trust is a reliance in turbulent conditions on some number of certainties and on other individuals' actions, that affect one's own welfare, that despite conditions largely unknown can be counted on to act in a predictable and presumably benevolent fashion" [11]. Trust can also be defined as "the degree of confidence that you feel when you think about a relationship" [13] as cited in [5]. Or as "an interpersonal or interorganizational state that reflects the extend to which the parties can predict one another's behavior, can depend on one another when it counts; and have faith that the other will continue to act in a responsive manner despite an uncertain future." [16].

The above characterisations of trust look forward in the sense that once a state of trust is there in an agent, they explain how this is used by the agent to make decisions on behaviour. The backward perspective in the sense of the question how a trust state was reached, i.e., how trust is gained or lost over time is left out of consideration in these characterisations.

1.2   Dynamics of Trust Based on Experiences

Trust is not a static mental state, but instead a dynamic one, as trust can change over time. This makes the question of what generates, maintains, substitutes, or collapses trusting relations [6] important. One of the central hypothesis in the research reported here is that trust is based on observed events in the real world. Lewis and Weigert state the same when they state that trust is formed by "observations that indicate that members of a system act according to and are secure in the expected futures constituted by the presence of each other for their symbolic representations." [9]. Elofson identifies the same origins of trust in "Trust is the outcome of observations leading to the belief that the actions of another may be relied upon" [5].

Events that are observed in the real world can only be interpreted within the context in which they take place. This context defines whether an event helps in achieving ones goals or not and also helps understanding the situation in which the other was placed (e.g., sometimes you cannot really blame someone for not helping you.). Wels and Van Loon point at a similar issue when they say "Every event is created by a different ensemble of interactions; all sense making is relative to this level specifity. Hence, the meaning attached to the events to the concepts vary not only in relation to different actors, but also to different contexts." [15].

In [8], a formal framework to model dynamics of trust is given. In the framework some of the events in the world are considered trust-influencing experiences. Such experiences are either positive or negative, in other words may increase your trust in something or someone, or decrease it. According to this framework the trust that is acquired by an actor depends on two variables, the initial trust and the trust dynamics. The model for trust dynamics specify how an agent adjusts its trust in someone or something based on experiences.

1.3   Trust Dynamics Experiments

In a number of recent articles on intelligent agents and (formal) trust models the validity of certain models is only "proven" with an argumentation that appeals to common sense. The extent to which the models are correct (either in a descriptive or in a normative sense) is not measured. The only way to assess the correctness of a trust model, which claims to describe cognitive processes related to trust, is to perform experiments with human test-subjects. Or as Smet, Wels and Van Loon put it: 'We need, however, to stop making speculative claims based on grand, but rather unsubstantiated, theorising if we are to make any proper sense out of trust and co-operation.' [14].

In this research the focus is on the question of how to adjust trust based on experiences and to verify that experiences really do influence trust in other persons, organisations or objects. In this paper a description is given of the experiment that has been conducted to determine whether and in what form trust is really influenced by experiences as has been suggested in literature (see for example [9; 5; 8]), and to determine if some regularities occur in the extend and direction to which trust is influenced by experiences.

In this paper, Section 2 describes the design of the experiment. In Section 3 the outcomes of the preliminary validation tests in the experiment are presented. Section 4 presents the outcomes of the final experiments. In Section 5 the outcomes are compared to dynamic properties of trust as have been identified in previous work. Section 6 concludes the paper.

2   Design of the Experiment

Possible angles to examine the dynamics of trust are to focus on the factors that influence how initial trust is established or to focus on how trust is influenced by events. In the research reported in this paper the focus is on how events influence trust.

2.1   Factors Affecting a Trust State

Numerous factors influence the impact an event has on someone's trust. These factors can be divided into two categories: factors that influence how an event is evaluated and factors that influence the relative weight an experience has on someone's trust, in relation to all the other experiences that person had and his or her initial trust value. An example of a factor that could influence how an event is evaluated is kinship: generally people will feel much more left in the lurch if a family member does not co-operate than if a stranger is uncooperative. An example of a factor that could influence the relative weight of an experience is the amount of time passed since the event took place: people might place more trust in a photocopier that failed to work two years ago than they would in a photocopier that malfunctioned just two hours ago.

The difference between the evaluation of an event and the relative weight is that the evaluation of an event is dependent on the context in which the event took place, whereas the relative weight may depend on the total collection of experiences over time of that person. Usually the evaluation of an event remains unchanged after the event has occurred, whereas the relative weight of an experience will usually change over time as the person has acquired more experiences. However, it may be possible for an evaluation of an event to change if a person acquires more information about the context in which the event took place. The focus of this research is on the factors that influence the relative weight an experience has.

Time is one of the important factors that influences the relative weight of an experience. The amount of influence an event has decreases over time, as is demonstrated by Derrida in the specific context of giving gifts [3], cited in [15]. In [8] it is suggested that the temporal order in which the events occurred, could influence the impact an event has on the trust state. Following this, in this study the temporal order of events has been used as the factor that influences the relative weight of an experience.

2.2 Overview of the Experiment

In the experiment, subjects have been presented with sequences of short stories (written in Dutch) that each describe an event that occurred with an organisation or an object. Within a single sequence all stories deal with the same object or organisation. After each story the subject is asked to state (on a five-points Lickert scale) how much trust he or she has in the object or organisation. The subject is instructed to base her trust in the object or organisation on all stories that have been presented. The difference in the trust values the subject assigns to an object or organisation shows how the trust in that organisation or object has been affected by the experiences. By varying the order of the events, these differences in trust values allow the measurement of how experiences and the order in which the experiences occur, influence a person's trust in an organisation or object.

The questions have been presented to the subjects over the Internet. Distributing the questionnaire over the Internet has two distinctive advantages: first of all the subjects can complete the questionnaire when it suits them and therefore the response rate of potential subjects has been relatively high (the estimated response rate was 35%), even though almost no financial incentive to participate in the experiment has been offered. A potential drawback of distributing the questionnaires over the Internet is that there is little control over the environment in which the subject fills in its questionnaire.

For their participation in the experiment the subjects were offered a lollipop and the chance to win a single reward of € 20. In total 238 people participated in the experiments, which brings the estimated response rate to 35% (78 personal invitations have been sent by e-mail to relatives, friends and participants of the pre-tests of the experiment, 250 flyers have been handed out on campus and an open invitation to participate in the experiment has been posted on the Usenet newsgroup of the department of Mathematics and Computer Science, which has an estimated reach of 350 persons).

As the experiment tries to determine the effect of experiences with an object or organisation on the amount of trust a person has in that object or organisation, an operationalisation of the concept amount of trust is necessary. In this experiment we will use a five-point Lickert rating scale to allow subjects to state the amount of trust they have in the object or organisation. The five-point trust rating scale contains the following levels: "veel vertrouwen" (much trust, 5) "redelijk vertrouwen" (a reasonable amount of trust, 4) "neutral" (neutral, 3) "weinig vertrouwen" (little trust, 2) "heel weinig vertrouwen" (very little trust, 1).

In the test the effect of experiences with an organisation or an object on the trust in that organisation or object is measured. The effect of the experiences on trust is measured by exposing the subject to multiple events with a certain organisation or object and measuring the trust in the object or organisation between every event using the trust rating scale described above.

It is time-consuming and expensive to let the subjects have real interactions with objects and organisations, as this would require subjects to undergo the experiment in a lab in which the interactions can be simulated. This is a main reason why in this experiment instead of undergoing real interactions with objects and organisations the subject have been presented with stories that describe certain experiences.

2.3 The Scenarios

For this experiment two scenarios have been written: in one scenario the subjects deal with a photocopier and in the other scenario the subjects interact with a travel agency. Each scenario consists of an introduction and ten distinctive stories, five of which are positive (written to induce trust) and five of which are negative (written to induce distrust).

The topic of the scenarios (a photocopier and a travel agency) have been chosen so that not many people have strong emotional feelings about the subject (as one could have with the Dutch railroad corporation or the tax authority) which could influence the results of the experiment. The stories have been written in a neutral tone, to prevent to explicitly direct the subject to the 'desired' response. On top of that stories do not cross-reference each other, as the stories had to be presented in a randomised order.

Photocopier scenario. The first scenario contains an introduction and ten stories, which describe experiences a user can have with a photocopier that uses a debit card. It is assumed that the subjects have had prior experiences with photocopiers that use debit cards (this assumption holds for almost all students). After each event the subject can indicate his or her trust in the photocopier. In the following table the introduction and the some of the stories can be found (both in Dutch and translated into English):

Story no.	Content of story
	Introduction
	Je moet morgen een voordracht geven over een paper die je geschreven hebt. Hiervoor heb je sheets nodig, en voor elk van de toehoorders een hand-out en een kopie van je paper.
-	Tomorrow you have to give a presentation about a paper you wrote. For this presentation you need transparencies and for each member of the audience a hand-out and a copy of your paper.

	Positive experiences
1	Je kopieert de kaft van het paper apart, omdat dit op speciaal papier gekopieerd moet worden. Om te kijken of de kopieermachine het gekleurde karton, dat je voor de kaft wil gebruiken, aankan maak je eerst één proefkopie. Na een geslaagde proefkopie begin je met kopiëren.
	You copy the cover of the paper separately, because it needs to be copied on special paper. To see if the photocopier can handle the colored carton, which you want to use as a cover, you first make a single test copy. After a successful test copy you start copying.

	Negative experiences
1	De kopieermachine werkt met een kaartsysteem. Na het maken van een aantal kopieën is je oude kaart op, daarom ga je naar de receptie om een kopieerkaart te kopen. Vervolgens weigert de machine te kopiëren, omdat volgens de machine de nieuwe kaart leeg is.
	The photocopier works with a debit card-system. Having made a number of copies, your old card runs out of debit, so you go to the reception to purchase a new debit card. Thereupon the machine refuses to copy, claiming the new card is empty.

Travel agency scenario. The second scenario contains an introduction and ten stories, which describe experiences a user can have with a travel agency. After each event the subject can indicate his or her trust in the travel agency.

2.4 Balancing the Experiment

In our study the subject received two series of each 10 stories. The first sequence of stories deals with an object, a photocopier, and the second sequence deals with an organisation, a travel agency. In each sequence half the stories were positive (designed to induce trust) and half the stories were negative (designed to induce distrust).

In the study half the subjects first received the negative stories for the copier or the travel agency and after that the positive stories for the copier or the travel agency and half the subjects first received the positive stories. This made it possible to study both the increase and decrease in trust. Within a sequence of positive or negative stories the order of the stories has been determined randomly, in order to prevent side effects from the order of the stories.

To prevent carry-over effects of the first part of the test to the second part of the test, half the subjects that received in the first part of the test a sequence with first negative stories and after that positive stories will receive in the second part of the test a sequence with first negative stories and after that positive stories and the other half of the subjects will receive in the second part of the test a sequence with first positive stories and after that negative stories. This way four different paths through the test are created, which is illustrated in the following table.

3   Analysis of the Results: Preliminary Validation Tests

In this section the outcome of the two preliminary validation tests (to test the experience stories) and the final experiment are briefly discussed and the data is analysed to draw some preliminary conclusions. To determine whether the stories that describe interactions with the photocopier and the travel agency have the desired positive or negative effect on the trust in that photocopier and the travel agency, a preliminary test has been executed.

Table 1. Sequences in which the stories are presented to the subject

experiment groups	stories about photocopier	stories about travel agency
1	first five positive stories, followed by five negative stories	first five positive stories, followed by five negative stories
2	first five negative stories, followed by five positive stories	first five negative stories, followed by five positive stories
3	first five positive stories, followed by five negative stories	first five negative stories, followed by five positive stories
4	first five negative stories, followed by five positive stories	first five positive stories, followed by five negative stories

In the preliminary test 80 subjects were presented with a form on which a single description of an experience with the photocopier and a single description of an experience with the travel agency were recorded. After reading each story, the subjects were asked to answer whether they would have more trust, the same amount of trust or less trust in the photocopier or travel agency after the described event.

In the preliminary test each story has been presented eight times. Unwanted carry-over effects from the story about the photocopier onto the responses on the story about the travel agency where prevented, because 50% of the stories about the travel agency were preceded by a positive story about the photocopier and 50% of the stories about the travel agency were preceded by a negative story about the photocopier.

In Tables 2 and 3 the effectiveness of the stories about the photocopier can be found. In these tables one can see that all negative stories about the photocopier have the desired effect (in all cases the trust either decreases or remains the same). The effect of the positive stories is not as good as that of the negative stories, but when comparing the groups of positive stories and negative stories, the effect is still visible and significant, as Cramer's V = 0.720, (cf. [10], pp. 14-15) which means that a signification correlation exists between the category of the stories and its outcome. Therefore all stories depicted in the tables have been used in the further experiments.

In Tables 4 and 5 the effectiveness of the stories about the travel agency can be found.

Table 2. Answers on photocopier story: per story

Answer on photocopier story * Story number on photocopier Crosstabulation												
Count												
		Story category on photocopier										Total
		positive stories					negative stories					
		1	2	3	4	5	1	2	3	4	5	
Answer on photocopier story	more trust	6	2	3	2	3						16
	less trust				1	1	7	6	4	6	5	30
	no change	2	6	5	5	4	1	2	4	2	3	34
Total		8	8	8	8	8	8	8	8	8	8	80

Table 3. Answers on photocopier story: overall

Answer on photocopier story * Story category on photocopier Crosstabulation				
Count				
		Story number on photocopier		Total
		positive stories	negative stories	
Answer on photocopier story	more trust	16		16
	less trust	2	28	30
	no change	22	12	34
Total		40	40	80

In Table 4 one can see that all stories, except for positive story 2 and negative story 1, have the desired effect on the trust in the travel agency. Comparing the effects of the group of positive and negative stories about the travel agency (see), it is clear that there is a difference between the effects of the positive and negative stories. This difference is significant, as Cramer's V = 0,735 (cf. [10], pp. 14-15).

We can conclude based on the above crosstables that although the effects of the stories are not perfect (in which case positive stories would only increase trust and negative stories would only decrease trust), the overall effect of the stories is significant and therefore the stories can be used for the experiment.

4 Analysis of the Results: Final Experiment

In total 294 subjects started with the final experiment. This means that 294 people opened the first web-page of the questionnaire of the final experiment. From these 294 subjects 238 subjects (81%) completed the full questionnaire. The other 19% of

Table 4. Answers on travel agency stories: per story

Answer on travel agency story * Story number on travel agency Crosstabulation												
Count												
		Story number on travel agency										Total
		positive stories					negative stories					
		1	2	3	4	5	1	2	3	4	5	
Answer on travel agency story	more trust	6	2	5	6	5						24
	less trust	1	1			1	2	5	7	5	8	30
	no change	1	5	3	2	2	6	3	1		3	26
Total		8	8	8	8	8	8	8	8	8	8	80

Table 5. Answers on travel agency stories: overall

Answer on travel agency story * Story category on travel agency Crosstabulation				
Count				
		Story category on travel agency		
		positive stories	negative stories	
Answer on travel agency story	more trust	24		24
	less trust	3	27	30
	no change	13	13	26
Total		40	40	80

the subjects were either not able to complete the questionnaire because of technical problems, decided to stop during the experiment or did not respond to a question within a given time limit of 15 minutes between each question. Only the data obtained from subjects that fully completed the questionnaire has been used for analysis.

After the subject has been presented with both pre-tests, the main part of the test begins. In the main test the effect of experiences with an organisation or an object on the trust in that organisation or object is measured. The effect of the experiences on trust is measured by describing various experiences in small stories and instructing the subject to state his or her trust in the object or organisation after having went through such an experience. Trust in a certain object or organisation is stated using the five-points trust rating scale described in Section 2. Each scenario consisted of an introduction and ten distinctive stories, five of which were positive (written to induce trust) and five of which were negative (written to induce distrust). For more details, see Section 2. In this following section the results of the main part of experiment are presented.

In the Figures 1 to 4 below the dynamics of trust, for both the photocopier and the travel agency are plotted. In the plots the median of the trust values are displayed. We can immediately see that trust increases when the subject had a positive experience and that trust decreases as negative experiences are received. Moreover, as we can see, there is a clear difference between the between the plots that start with negative experiences and the plots that start with positive experiences.

To determine the significance of the difference, a 2-way between subjects ANOVA test was performed on the means of the positive and negative experiences within a single scenario. The ANOVA test takes both the experience (positive or negative) and the order in which experiences are presented (positive-first or negative-first) into account. From the results we can see that both factors have an effect on trust in the object or organization at a significance level beyond 0,001. Furthermore we can conclude that there is no significant interaction between experience (positive or negative) and the order in which experiences are presented.

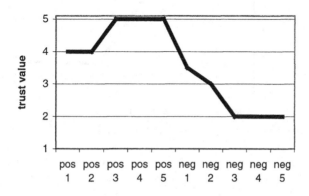

Fig. 1. Dynamics of trust in Photocopier: positive experiences first

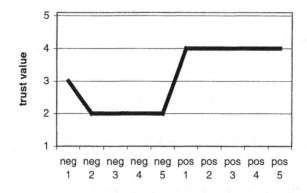

Fig. 2. Dynamics of trust in Photocopier: negative experiences first

Having examined and established the order effect of experiences for mean trust scores, now the duration of the effect is established.

For the stories about the photocopier, the negative effect, of first receiving negative stories, on the trust score after receiving positive experiences remains significant for the whole trail. The positive effect, of first receiving positive stories, on the trust score after positive experiences remains significant only for the first three turns, after which the difference becomes insignicant (at the 0.05 significance level).

For the stories about the travel agency, the negative effect, of first receiving negative stories, on the trust score after receiving positive experiences remains significant a single round. The positive effect, of first receiving positive stories, on the trust score after positive experiences remains significant only for the first turn, after which the difference becomes insignicant (at the 0.05 significance level).

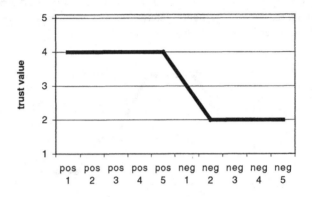

Fig. 3. Dynamics of trust in Travel Agency: positive experiences first

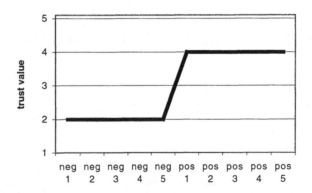

Fig. 4. Dynamics of trust in Travel Agency: negative experiences first

5   Relating the Outcomes to Previous Work

In [8] a number of (possible) dynamic properties of trust have been identified. In this section the outcomes of the experiments are compared to the most relevant of these dynamic properties.

Positive and Negative Trust Extension

After a positive experience an agent will trust more or the same amount, but never less. After a negative experience an agent will trust less or the same amount, but never more.

From the figures in Section 3, Tables 3 and 5 it can be seen that in a large majority of cases these two properties hold. In particular, negative trust extension always holds, both for the photocopier and the traveling agency. Positive trust extension holds in 95% of the cases for the photocopier and in 92.5 % of the cases for the travelling agency. Other evidence that by and large these properties hold can be found in the graphs in Section 4. In none of the graphs depicting the median values a transition can be found that violates one of the two properties. Of course these results heavily depend on the chosen stories as being positive or negative. For example, if a story was classified as positive, whereas it only is felt as a slightly positive experience, it would be reasonable to assume that a very high level of trust can decrease to a slighly less high (but still positive) trust level by this experience.

Other properties in [8] address the flexibility of trust: can negative trust be made positive (again) by offering the appropriate types of experiences, and vice versa? From our analysis in [8] the following more or less opposite properties would be possible

Degree of Trust Dropping or Trust Gaining N

After N negative events the trust will be negative.
After N positive events the trust will be positive.

Negative or Positive Trust Fixation of Degree N

After N negative events the agent will never trust anymore and its trust will remain the least possible. After N positive events the agent will forever trust (even when faced with negative events) and its trust will remain maximal.

These trust fixation properties are more or less the opposite of the previous ones. In [8] we could not indicate which of them would be more realistic. On the basis of the experiments, now it is suggested that trust fixation does not occur, at least in contexts as investigated. In the graphs depicted in Section 4, negative or positive trust fixation of degree N does not occur for N < 6. For higher N it was not tested in the experiments.

From the graphs in Section 3 it can be seen that for the photocopier, 3 negative experiences in a row are sufficient to get a negative trust (no matter how positive trust was), and for the travelling agency 2 negative experiences are sufficient. So, N = 3, resp. N = 2 apply in these cases, i.e., for the photocopier the property 'degree of trust dropping 3' holds, and for the traveling agency 'degree of trust dropping 2' holds. For the positive side, in both cases 2 positive experiences are sufficient to get trust positive again, so the property 'degree of trust gaining 2' holds for both cases.

An effect that does occur, however, in the photocopier context, is that after a series of negative experiences (see Figure 2), the level of trust does not become as high as in the case of no negative experiences (see Figure 1). More refined properties than the ones above can be formulated to account for this relative form of trust fixation. Notice that in the traveling agency context this effect does not occur.

6 Discussion

In papers on trust models the validity of models is usually based on intuition and common sense only. The extent to which models are correct is rarely verified experimentally, which is considered a lack in the literature on trust; cf. [14]. The research reported here contributes results of experiments on the dynamics of trust over time depending on positive or negative experiences. In [8] a number of dynamic properties for trust dynamics were identified, indeed mainly on the basis of intuition and common sense. As a continuation of this work, now these properties have been verified in an experimental setting. Even if sometimes these properties may seem clear or self-evident at first sight, without any empirical verification they remain speculative.

By the above experimental results it can be shown that positive experiences can be identified that (usually) have an increasing or at least nondecreasing effect on trust, and negative experiences that have a decreasing or at least non-increasing effect. Here it appears easier to destroy trust than to build trust: the designed negative experiences show a stronger negative effect on trust than the positive effect shown by the designed positive experiences (see Tables 2 to 5).

Moreover, it is shown that trust can be flexible in the following sense: trust that has become positive can be made negative if a number of subsequent negative experiences occur, and trust that has become negative can become positive if a number of subsequent positive experiences occur. This may give an indication for handling trust in open system applications. If it is noticed that an agent has encountered a number of negative experiences, then it can be arranged that this agent should have a number of positive experiences first, for example, by paying extra attention to this agent and offer special services.

A number of issues can be investigated in more depth. First of all, it may be investigated in how far the same patterns can be found in other contexts. There may be contexts where, in contrast to the contexts used in our experiments, trust fixation does occur. For example, after a number of serious negative experiences with your partner in a relationship, trust may have gone forever, and not be (re)gained by positive experiences.

A related issue is to investigate further the notions of positive and negative experiences. What types of experiences qualify as such? One may be tempted to consider a positive (resp. negative) experience by definition as an experience that usually increases (resp. decreases) trust. However, a more independent definition would be more valuable. For example, the positive experiences are experiences leading to satisfaction of a certain type and level, the negative ones are experiences leading to frustration of a certain type and level? This also implies that a more fine-grained scale between positive and negative may be relevant. A more fine-grained scale would also enable to classify the experience stories based on the results in Tables 2 to 5 (which show that the stories differ in their impact on trust).

Another issue is the notion of trust used by the subjects. In our experiments a kind of folk-psychological trust notion was assumed in each of the subjects. A more fundamental approach would not use the word 'trust' in the experiments, but would define trust by the decisions (e.g., in relation to specific goals or tasks of the agent) that are made based on certain trust levels, and ask the subjects about these decisions, instead of their level of trust. However, in such an approach other factors (other than trust) affecting such decisions may have to be taken into account as well.

An important further question is in how far subjects are equal in they way in which they show trust dynamics. Our hypothesis is that substantial individual differences between subjects may exist, for example in initial trust attitudes (e.g., positive or negative initial bias), in trust-steadyness (how sensitive trust is w.r.t. new experiences), or in (non-initial) positive or negative biases in trust dynamics. The number of subjects in our study was not low (238), but to obtain statistics for individual differences, a reasonable number per type of subject is needed. Further experimental work is planned to address this issue.

Acknowledgements. The authors are grateful to the anonymous reviewers putting forward a number of further suggestions that have been used to improve the text.

References

1. Barber, B., The Logic and Limits of Trust. New-Jersey: Rutgers University Press, 1983.
2. Castelfranchi, C. and Falcone, R., Principles of trust for MAS: cognitive anatomy, social importance, and quantification. In: Proceedings of the International Conference on Multi Agent Systems 1998 (ICMAS'98). IEEE Press, 1998.
3. Derrida, J., Given time. Counterfeit money. Chicago: Chicago University Press, 1992.
4. Deutsch, M., Trust, trustworthiness, and the F scale. In: Journal of Abnormal and Social Psychology, vol.: 61, no. 1, 1960, pp. 138-140.
5. Elofson, G., Developing trust with intelligent agents: An exploratory study. In: Proceedings of the First International Workshop on Trust, 1998, pp. 9-19.
6. Gambetta, D., Foreword. In: (Gambetta, D.) Trust: Making and breaking of cooperative relations. Oxford: Basil Blackwell, 1988.
7. Good, D., Individuals, Interpersonal relations, Trust. In: (Gambetta, D.) Trust: Making and breaking of cooperative relations. Oxford: Basil Blackwell, 1988.
8. Jonker, C. M., and Treur, J., Formal analysis of models for the dynamics of trust based on experiences. In: F. J. Garijo, M. Boman (eds.), Multi-Agent System Engineering, Proceedings of the 9th European Workshop on Modelling Autonomous Agents in a Multi-Agent World, MAAMAW'99. Lecture Notes in AI, vol. 1647, Springer Verlag, Berlin, 1999, pp. 221-232.
9. Lewis, D. and Weigert, A., Social atomism, holism and trust. In: Sociological Quarterly, 1985, pp. 445-471.
10. Liebetrau, A.M. (1983), Measures of Association, In (John L. Sullivan and Richard G. Niemi, eds.): Sage University Paper series on Quantitative Applications in the Social Sciences, vol 32. Beverly Hills and London: Sage Publications, Inc.
11. Luhmann, N., Trust and Power. New York: John-Wiley, 1979.
12. Luhmann, N., Familiarity, confidence, trust: problems and alternatives. In: (Gambetta, D.) Trust: Making and breaking of cooperative relations. Oxford: Basil Blackwell, 1988.
13. Rempel, J. K., Holmes, J. G. and Zanna, M. P., Trust in close relationships. In: Journal of Personality and Socal Psychology, vol.: 49, 1985, pp. 95-112.
14. Smets, P., Wels, H. and Van Loon, J., Trust and co-operation in theory and everyday life. In: Smets, P., Wels, H. and Van Loon, J. (eds.), Trust & Co-operation, Symbolic exchange and moral economies in an ages of cultural differentiation. Amsterdam, The Netherlands: Het Spinhuis, 1999.

15. Wels, H. and Van Loon, J., Making sense of trust and co-operation: theoretical perspectives. In: Smets, P., Wels, H. and Van Loon, J. (eds.), Trust & Co-operation, Symbolic exchange and moral economies in an ages of cultural differentiation. Amsterdam, The Netherlands: Het Spinhuis, 1999.
16. Zalman, G. and Moorman, C., The importance of personal trust in the use of research. In: Journal of Advertising Research, October-November, 1998, pp 16-24.

Using Trust in Recommender Systems: An Experimental Analysis

Paolo Massa[1] and Bobby Bhattacharjee[2]

[1] International Graduate School in Information and Communication Technologies
University of Trento, 38050 Povo (TN), Italy,
massa@itc.it
[2] Department of Computer Science, University of Maryland, College Park, Maryland,
bobby@cs.umd.edu

Abstract. Recommender systems (RS) have been used for suggesting items (movies, books, songs, etc.) that users might like. RSs compute a user similarity between users and use it as a weight for the users' ratings. However they have many weaknesses, such as sparseness, cold start and vulnerability to attacks. We assert that these weaknesses can be alleviated using a Trust-aware system that takes into account the "web of trust" provided by every user.

Specifically, we analyze data from the popular Internet web site *epinions.com*. The dataset consists of 49290 users who expressed reviews (with rating) on items and explicitly specified their web of trust, i.e. users whose reviews they have consistently found to be valuable.

We show that any two users have usually few items rated in common. For this reason, the classic RS technique is often ineffective and is not able to compute a user similarity weight for many of the users. Instead exploiting the webs of trust, it is possible to propagate trust and infer an additional weight for other users. We show how this quantity can be computed against a larger number of users.

1 Introduction

Recommender Systems (RS) [8] are widely used online (e.g. in *amazon.com*) to suggest items that users may find "interesting". These recommendations are generated using two main techniques: content-based, and collaborative filtering. Content-based systems require manual intervention, and do not scale to large item bases. Collaborative filtering (CF) [2] systems do not depend on the semantics of items under consideration; instead, they automate the recommendation process based solely on user opinions.

While CF algorithms are promising for implementing large scale recommender systems, they have their share of problems. The problems with pure CF systems can be classified in three domains: problems affecting new user start up, sparsity of useful information for existing users, and relatively easy attacks on system correctness by malicious insiders. We describe these attacks in detail in Section 1.2. In this paper, we propose an extension to pure CF systems, and assert that our extension addresses all of the problems with currently implemented

C.D. Jensen et al. (Eds.): iTrust 2004, LNCS 2995, pp. 221–235, 2004.

collaborative filtering algorithms. Specifically, we argue that these problems can effectively be solved by incorporating a notion of *trust* between users into the base CF system. To this end, we present an analysis of a large scale deployed recommender system (*epinions.com*): our work clearly identifies the problems with the base CF system, and we describe how trust-based extensions would solve these problems for this data set, and for similar systems.

The contributions of this paper are three-fold:

- We articulate specific problems with collaborative filtering systems currently deployed, and present a new solution that addresses all of these problems.
- We present a thorough analysis of a large, existing RS data set, and show that the problems we identified do exist in reality. (Note that we do not specifically show the existence of malicious insiders, but it is clear that such an attack is possible on the base system).
- We present preliminary results that show that our trust-based solution does alleviate or eliminate the problems that we identify in the base system.

The rest of the paper is structured as follows: first, we introduce Recommender Systems (Section 1.1), their weaknesses (Section 1.2) and how trust-awareness can alleviate them (Section 1.3). Section 2 presents experiments on *epinions.com* that support our thesis while Section 3 concludes discussing new research lines based on the provided evidence.

1.1   Recommender Systems

Recommender Systems (RS) [8] suggest to users items they might like. Two main algorithmic techniques have been used to compute recommendations: Content-Based and Collaborative Filtering. The Content-Based approach tries to suggest to the user items similar to her previous selections. To achieve this, content-based RSs need a representation in terms of features of the items. Such a representation can be created automatically for machine-parsable items (such as news or papers) but must be manually inserted by human editors for items that are not yet machine-parsable (such as movies and songs). This activity is expensive, time-consuming, error-prone and highly subjective. Moreover, for some items such as jokes, it is almost impossible to define the right set of describing features and to "objectively" classify them.

Collaborative Filtering (CF) [2], on the other hand, collects opinions from users in the form of ratings to items. When asked for a recommendation, the system identifies similar users and suggests the items these users have liked in the past. The interesting point is that the algorithm doesn't need a representation of the items in term of features (i.e. genre and actors for movies) but it is based only on the judgments of the user community. Because of this, CF can be applied to virtually any kind of item: papers, news, web sites, movies, songs, books, jokes, locations of holidays, stocks. Since CF techniques don't require any human intervention for tagging content, they promise to scale well to large item bases. In the rest of this paper we concentrate on RSs based on CF.

The traditional input to a CF algorithm is a matrix that has a row for every user and a column for each of the items. The entry at each element of the matrix is the user's rating of that item. Figure 1 shows such a matrix.

Table 1. The users × items matrix of ratings is the classic input of CF.

	Matrix Reloaded	Lord of the Rings 2	Titanic	La vita è bella
Alice	2	5		5
Bob	5		1	3
Carol		5		
Dean	2	5	5	4

When asked for a recommendation by an user (recommendee), a standard CF algorithm performs 3 steps.

- It compares the recommendee against every other user in the community computing a user similarity coefficient.

  Different techniques have been proposed for this task. Pearson correlation coefficient is the best performing and most used [3]. Proposed alternatives are Constrained Pearson correlation coefficient, Spearman correlation coefficient and cosine similarity [3]. The Pearson correlation coefficient $w_{a,u}$ (Equation 1) represents the similarity of user a with user u with regard to their ratings on items and is defined as:

$$w_{a,u} = \frac{\sum_{i=1}^{m}(r_{a,i} - \overline{r}_a)(r_{u,i} - \overline{r}_u)}{\sqrt{\sum_{i=1}^{m}(r_{a,i} - \overline{r}_a)^2 \sum_{i=1}^{m}(r_{u,i} - \overline{r}_u)^2}} \qquad (1)$$

  where m is the number of items rated by both a and u, $r_{a,i}$ is the rating given by user a to item i and $\overline{r}_a$ is the mean of ratings of a. The coefficient is in $[-1,1]$. It is important to underline that the coefficient can be computed only if there are items rated by both the users.

- It predicts the recommendee's rating for every item she has not yet rated.

  The predicted rating (Equation 2) that user a might give to item i is the mean rating of a plus the weighted sum of deviation from mean rating for every user where the weight is the user similarity with user a.

$$p_{a,i} = \overline{r}_a + \sum_{u=1}^{n} w_{a,u}(r_{u,i} - \overline{r}_u) \qquad (2)$$

  It is possible to consider only the k most similar users or all the users. The user similarity of a with every user is used as a weight for the opinions of that user. Intuitively if user A is very similar to user B, the opinions of user A are given importance when creating a recommendation for user B.

- It suggests to the user the items with highest predicted ratings.

1.2   Weaknesses of Recommender Systems

RSs are a very useful tool for dealing with information overload since they can suggest to an user the few items worth consuming out of a huge item set. We have seen that Collaborative Filtering can be applied in every domain and with no additional efforts required for human editors to tag content or classify items.

Despite the potential, we believe RSs have still failed in unveiling their disruptive power because of a number of weaknesses we present in the rest of the Section.

Data Sparseness. A realistic CF matrix would contains millions of users and millions of items. In practice users only rate a few of the entire set of items and this results in a very sparse matrix.

The "sparseness" of a CF matrix is the percentage of empty cells. *Eachmovie* and *Movielens*[1], two of the public datasets typically used in research, are respectively 97.6% and 95.8% sparse. We will see in Section 2 that the *epinions.com* dataset has even higher sparseness. Sparseness is also a huge problem for freshly created RSs that, when start operating, have no ratings at all.

Consequence of sparseness is that, on average, two users, picked uniformly at random, have low overlap. For this reason, the Pearson coefficient is noisy and unreliable. In practice, it is often the case that there is no intersection at all between users and hence the similarity is not computable at all.

Singular Value Decomposition has been proposed as a technique for dimensionality reduction and consequent reduction of sparseness [9]. However, on extremely sparse datasets, it has shown no improvements over standard techniques.

Cold start. A second weakness is the so called "cold start problem" [5]. This is related to the situation when a user enters the system and has expressed no ratings. CF cannot compute a recommendation under such cases. We define "cold start users" as the users who have expressed less than 5 ratings. With these users, RSs present the biggest problems and are usually unable to make good quality recommendations. However, these are the users who need good quality recommendations as an incentive to continue using the system.

Attacks on Recommender Systems. Another concern is related to the existence of users that want to maliciously influence the system: if the process of creating recommendations is known and if the ratings of every user are publicly available (as it is in *epinions.com*, for instance), a very simple but effective attack is the following. Let suppose the malicious principal wants the system to recommend to user *target* the item *spambook*. She can simply create a new user *fakeuser*, rate in the same way all the items rated by user *target* and also rate with the highest possible rating *spambook*. In this way, when looking for users similar to *target*, the system will assign to *fakeuser* a user similarity of 1 and will weight her rating on *spambook* the most and will probably end up recommending *spambook* to user *target*. The malicious users can even create a whole bunch of fake users

---

[1] For publicly available datasets, see www.grouplens.org

reinforcing each others. In general it is also possible to trash the dataset quality by automatically creating many users with pseudo-random rating profiles. We believe that this kind of attacks were not a problem for current commercial RSs because they are centralized and creating a user and rating items it is a time-expensive activity. This is true unless the attacker can create a bot doing this but there is no economic incentive for now in doing this, even if we see this can become a sort of very effective "hidden" commercial spam. We are not aware of research lines taking into account this as a problem for RSs. We think it will become a huge concern as soon as RSs start becoming more decentralized systems [6], in the sense that users profile will not be stored in the hard disks of one central RS server but will be spread across the sites of community members and publicly available in well defined semantic formats.

RSs are hard to understand and control. The last weakness is reported in some papers [4,10] that say how users often see RSs as a black box and are not aware of their working model. In fact, with current RSs it is very hard (or impossible) for the user to control the recommendation process so that if the RS starts giving bad quality recommendations, usually the user just stops using it [11].

1.3   Solution to Weaknesses: Trust-Awareness

We believe that taking into consideration trust relationships between principals in the system will alleviate the problems that beset RSs.

In the rest of the Section, we define our trust model and give anecdotal evidence that trust-awareness can solve the previously stated weaknesses. Section 2 will confirm the claims based on an empirical analysis of *epinions.com* dataset.

A trust statement is an explicit assertion of the fact a user trusts another users. User *A* can only create trust statements specifying the users she trusts. In the context of Trust-aware Recommender Systems, a trust statement made by user *A* towards user *B* means that user *A* consistently finds the reviews and ratings of user *B* valuable.

A trust (or social) network is constructed by aggregating every trust statement. A trust network is a graph in which nodes are users and directed edges are trust statements.

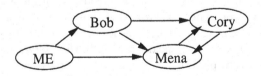

Fig. 1. A Trust network. Arrows are trust statements.

Trust metrics [1] can be used to propagate trust over the social network. Intuitively, if *A* trusts *B* and *B* trusts *C*, it is possible to infer something about how much A might trust C. Trust metrics can be used exactly for inferring trust in unknown users depending on the social network. In this paper we analyze how trust can be used to extract useful information for making recommendations and overcome the previously cited RSs weaknesses for a real community. We leave as a future work the proposition of a trust metric able to actually predict trust values in unknown users.

We have seen in Section 1.2 that because of the high sparseness of the CF matrix, it is rare that two users have rated some items in common (we present evidence of this in Section 2). However, the Pearson correlation coefficient can be computed only on overlapping items. Thus, for any given user, the number of other users with whom it is possible to compute similarity is low. Instead, propagating trust over the social network allows to reach a larger portion of the user base. In this way it is possible to compute an alternative weight related to how much we should take other users into account when computing a recommendation.

Cold start users, who are the most critical users for standard CF, can benefit highly from trust propagation as long as they provide at least one trusted friend in the community. This can be an effective mechanism to rapidly integrate new users, especially if compared with standard CF where users are usually required to rate at least 10 items before to receive a recommendation.

Further the attack we outlined in Section 1.2 is not effective as long as the fake users are not trusted by any real user.

Unlike traditional RS, that are often seen by users as black boxes [4,10], we think that the concept of social network is easier to grasp. Human Computer Interaction studies [10] are needed to investigate the best ways to visualize the social network and how this could help the user in understanding the recommendation model and in controlling it.

It is important to note that trust metrics predict personalized values of trust in unknown users. For this reason, the inferred trust in user A can be different for user B and user C and depends on their different webs of trust. This is different from what many current online systems do. For example, PageRank [7] (used by *google.com*) computes a global value for every web page that is the same for every searcher, *ebay.com* computes a unique global value for every buyer and seller as well, as does *slashdot.org* for its contributors.

Lastly, even if trust-awareness can be introduced inside a single centralized server, centralized approaches of data collection in general are subject to the following huge disadvantages. Expressing information (what you like, who you like) in a centralized RS server means that only that server will be able to use it. This results in users profiles being scattered in portions on many different, not cooperating servers and every single server suffers even more of sparseness. Moreover, this means the user cannot move from one RS to another without losing her profile (and, with it, the possibility to receive good recommendations). We also believe it does not make sense to introduce concerns about trust and then leave the computation of recommendations out of possible user control. We think Trust-aware Recommender Systems [6] demand a decentralized environment where every user publishes their information (trust and ratings) in some Semantic Web format and then every machine has the possibility of aggregating this information and computing recommendations on behalf of her user.

In this Section, we have argued that Trust-awareness alleviates problems with standard RSs. In the rest of the paper, we present results from a large deployed system that support our claims. We begin with an overview of our data set.

2 Experiments on Epinions.com

In this Section we present experimental results on *epinions.com* that show that our trust-based solution does alleviate the problems that we stated in Section 1.2. We begin by explaining how the dataset was collected. We then present some statistics of the community such as number of expressed reviews and friends and ratings distribution across items. We then analyze the differences in computability for the two quantities that can be used as weights for every user: Pearson coefficient and Trust. We show how the second is computable on many more users than the first and how this is especially true for "cold start users".

Epinions.com is a web site where users can review items (such as cars, books, movies, music, software, ...) and also assign numeric rating in the range from 1 (min) to 5 (max). Users can also express their *Web of Trust*, i.e. "reviewers whose reviews and ratings they have consistently found to be valuable"[2] and their *Block list*, i.e. a list of authors whose reviews they find consistently offensive, inaccurate, or in general not valuable. While the *Web of Trust* of every user is public and everyone can see it with a browser, the *Block list* is kept private by *epinions.com*. Since *epinions.com* does not provide a complete list of users or items, we obtained the dataset by crawling the *epinions.com* web site during November 2003. We conducted a depth-first search starting from some users who were classified as Advisors in the category Movies, Books and Online Stores & Services and repeatedly following all the users in their web of trust. For every user we also fetched all the reviews the user made. The information collected for every user is shown in Figure 2.

Of course, because of the way we obtained the dataset, we did not fetch all the users; in fact we downloaded all the users that were reachable walking the web of trust of starting users. If there were users not trusted by some of the reached users they were not added to our dataset. The same argument applies for items. In the collected dataset there are only the items that were rated at least once by one of the reached users.

2.1 Statistics on the Community

Our dataset consists of 49290 users who rated a total of 139738 different items at least once. The total number of reviews is 664824. The sparseness of the collected dataset is hence 99.99135%. This sparseness is very high if compared to

---

[2] From the Web of Trust FAQ (http://www.epinions.com/help/faq/?show=faq_wot)

Table 2. The table shows an example of the information we collected for every user.

Username	an-epinions-user				
URL	http://www.epinions.com/user-an-epinions-user				
Web of trust	trusted user URL	added on date			
	/user-my-friend1	Nov 18 '03			
	/user-my-friend2	Nov 17 '03			
	...	...			
Written re-views	item name	item URL	class	rating	date
	Dragonheart	/mvie_mu-1071583	Videos & DVDs	5	Sep 30 '02
	Caribbean Pot	/Caribbean_Pot	Restaurants	3	Aug 19 '03
	...	...	...	...	...

the 2 public datasets *Eachmovie* and *Movielens* (respectively, 97.6% and 95.8%) commonly used in research. We believe one of the reasons is that *Eachmovie* and *Movielens* have a smaller item base (1628 and 3900 movies, respectively). Moreover, rating an item on *epinions.com* is a time-expensive activity since the user must write a review of at least 20 words. Instead the two research systems presented the user many movies in the same web page and allowed her to rate all of them simultaneously with few clicks.

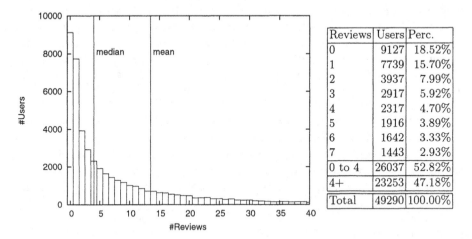

Fig. 2. Numbers of users who created *x* reviews. The vertical lines are the mean (13.49) and the median (4). Note the high percentage of "cold start users" (users who have less than 5 reviews).

We would like to stress the fact that *epinions.com* is a very well known site with a big and active community and nevertheless it has such a sparse matrix of ratings. The problem of sparseness is even bigger for Recommender Systems that have just started operating or those that don't have a large community base. Moreover it is important to remember that the items that are in our dataset received at least one rating (that's because of how we collected the data); if we were to consider all the ratable items on *epinions.com* the theoretical sparseness would have been even much higher.

Figure 2 shows the number of users who created a certain number of reviews. The mean number of created reviews is 13.49 with a standard deviation of 34.16. The median is 4. In particular, 9127 users created 0 reviews while the maximum number of reviews created by one user is 1023. It is important to have a look at what we have called "cold start users", users who expressed less than 5 reviews. They are 26037 and represent 52.82% of the population.

Figure 3 shows the number of users who have expressed a certain number of friends (we call friends of *User A* the users that are in the web of trust of *User A*). The mean number of friends is 9.88 with a standard deviation of 32.85. The median is 1. In particular, 15330 users (31.30%) expressed 0 friends, i.e. have their web of trust empty, and one user added 1760 users to her web of trust.

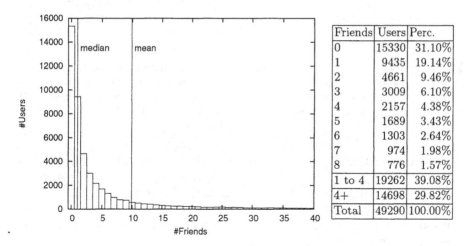

Friends	Users	Perc.
0	15330	31.10%
1	9435	19.14%
2	4661	9.46%
3	3009	6.10%
4	2157	4.38%
5	1689	3.43%
6	1303	2.64%
7	974	1.98%
8	776	1.57%
1 to 4	19262	39.08%
4+	14698	29.82%
Total	49290	100.00%

Fig. 3. Numbers of users who expressed x friends. The vertical lines are the mean (9.88) and the median (1).

Though not directly related to our results, it is interesting to note the distribution of ratings. In our dataset, 45% of the ratings are 5 (best), 29% are 4, 11% are 3, 8% are 2 and 7% are 1 (worst). The mean rating is hence 3.99.

In order to compute the user similarity between 2 users, a very important quantity is the distribution of reviews over items. It makes a big difference for the overlapping of 2 random users if the ratings generally concentrate on few items rated by almost everyone or if they are uniformly distributed over the item base. Figure 4 shows the distribution of ratings over items. Note that the vast majority of items (precisely 78465 corresponding to 56.15% of the item base) received only one review and this makes them totally useless for computing user similarity between users, infact their columns in the matrix only contains one rating value and so, along these columns, there doesn't exist 2 users that overlap and can be compared. Only 11657 items (corresponding to 8.34%) have 10 or more reviews.

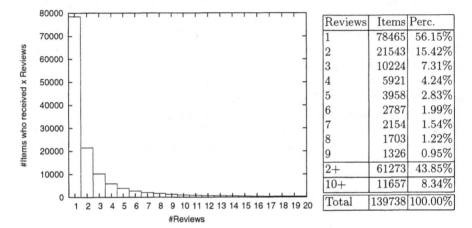

Reviews	Items	Perc.
1	78465	56.15%
2	21543	15.42%
3	10224	7.31%
4	5921	4.24%
5	3958	2.83%
6	2787	1.99%
7	2154	1.54%
8	1703	1.22%
9	1326	0.95%
2+	61273	43.85%
10+	11657	8.34%
Total	139738	100.00%

Fig. 4. Number of reviews received by Items. Note that 78465 items (56.15%) received only 1 review and are totally useless for computing user similarity. Since we fetched only the items when present in a user's review, in our dataset there are no items with 0 reviews, while instead on *epinions.com* they are the greatest part.

We have seen that the sparseness in the users × items matrix of ratings is very high (99.99135%) and that the greatest part of items received few reviews. In Section 2.2, we will show how this results in low overlapping among user ratings and hence in reduced computability of Pearson coefficient. In Section 2.3, we will show how trust propagation suffers less from the sparseness and allows to infer "trust" in a larger number of users.

2.2   Computability of User Similarity

When predicting the rating of user A on an item, RSs (based on Collaborative Filtering) first compute a similarity coefficient of user A against all the other users. This coefficient is then used to weight the ratings given by other users.

As argued in Section 1.3, we could also use direct or propagated trust as a weight for the opinions of other users.

We show here how user similarity between 2 users is a quantity that can be usually computed against a very small portion of the user base and usually can be computed only based on a small number of overlapping items producing a noisy and unreliable value. Instead the number of users reachable through some trust chain is generally very high. Along a chain of trust is possible to propagate and infer trust using a trust metric.

This difference in the number of users in which it is possible to compute similarity and trust is even exacerbated for cold start users, i.e., users who expressed few ratings and friends. These users are usually the largest portion of users and also the ones that will benefit the most from good quality recommendations.

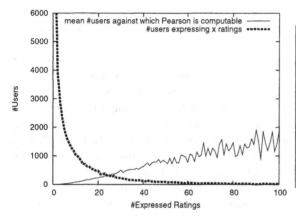

User base	Nr. Users	Frac. of Total	Mean Nr. Comparable Users
All	49290	100.00%	160.73
Cold	26037	52.82%	2.74
10-	33504	67.97%	11.27
20-	40597	82.36%	33.53
50+	2661	5.40%	1447.88
100+	882	1.79%	2162.52

Fig. 5. The thick line plots the number of users who have expressed a specific number of ratings. For each of these users, the thin line plots how many *comparable* users exist in the system on average. (By comparable we mean that the 2 users have rated at least 2 items in common). The table groups results for class of users depending on number of expressed ratings.

In Figure 5 we plot the number of comparable users averaged over all the users who created a certain number of reviews. We define 2 users comparable if they have rated at least 2 items in common. On every comparable user it is possible to compute the Pearson correlation coefficient and to use it as a weight for that user. Unsurprisingly, the users who created many reviews have a higher number of users against which Pearson is computable. However the plot shows that even for that users the coverage over user base is very limited: for example, the 54 users who created 60 reviews have a mean number of users against which Pearson is computable of 772.44 that is only the 1.57% of the entire user base.

Figure 5 shows only a portion of the total graph in fact the y axis can go up to 49290 users and the x axis up to 1023 items. In an ideal system, it would be possible to compare one user against any other user; in this case the mean number of users would have been 49289 independently of the number of written reviews.. Instead, Figure 5 makes evident how on *epinions.com* dataset, the technique is far from ideal.

Let us now concentrate on "cold start users" who, by the way, are the majority of users in the system. For them (as shown in the 2nd row of the table in Figure 5) Pearson is computable on average only against 2.74 users over 49290!

And also only 1413 of the 26037 cold start users have at least 10 users against which Pearson is computable. It is worth noting that, even for the most overlapping user, Pearson correlation coefficient is computable only against 9773 user that is 19.83% of the entire population.

This plot is a stray evidence of how Pearson correlation coefficient is often incomputable and hence ineffective.

2.3   Computability of Trust

In this Section, we provide evidence about the potential use of trust in alleviating the RSs problems.

We have suggested that, for a given user (the recommendee), it is possible to compute trust in every other user and then use this computed quantity as a weight for those users. Trust (either direct or propagated) can potentially also be even combined with user similarity. In this paper, we simply provide evidence of the fact that it is possible to infer a trust value on a big portion of the user base. For this reason, we compute for every user the minimum number of steps needed to reach every other user. In this way, for every recommendee, we end up with some class of equivalence on trust: all the users reachable in one step (direct friends), the users reachable in 2 steps (friends of friends), etc. We are of course aware that it makes a big difference if a user at distance 2 from the recommendee is trusted by only one of her friends of by all of her friends, but the goal of this paper is not to propose a suitable trust metric for the domain but just to show that propagating trust is feasible and has the potential to solve RSs weaknesses. Note that on our dataset, sophisticated inference is difficult because the collected *epinions.com* trust data is binary, i.e. users either completely trust others (or not).

Figure 6 shows the mean number of users at a certain distance. The different lines represent different subsets of users (all users, users who created less than 5 and more than 100 reviews). Some users cannot reach all the other users through any trust chain. Such users are not considered when computing the mean number of users at a certain distance. Table of Figure 6 shows for different class of users the number of users who are connected to everyone in the system. Considering that 15330 users provided 0 friends and of course cannot reach all the other users through some trust chain, over the remaining users (33960) almost everyone (32417) is connected to every user in the network. Of the 1543 users who cannot reach every other user, 1224 are users who provided just one friend in their web of trust.

The mean distance over all users is 4.56 (see table of Figure 6). One user has a mean distance of 9.67 (maximum) and another one (who has 1760 users in her web of trust) has a mean distance of 2.89 (minimum). These data show that the trust network is very connected and in part this depends also on the way we collected the dataset.

Figure 6 shows that, for users who wrote more than 100 reviews, other users are generally closer in the trust network (and hence a trust metric could infer trust more easily). For cold start users, other users are in general less close but

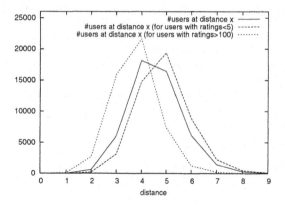

Userbase	#Users reaching all	Mean mean dist	Mean max dist
All users	32417	4.56	10.40
ratings<5	13106	4.87	10.71
ratings<10	18540	4.79	10.63
ratings<20	24397	4.71	10.54
ratings>50	2570	3.90	9.75
ratings>100	860	3.78	9.62
friends=1	8211	5.11	10.96

Fig. 6. The Figure shows the mean number of users at distance x for different class of users. The table shows, for different class of users, the users who are connected to every other user (in absolute value and in percentage), the mean of the mean distances and the mean of the max distances.

anyway many of them are reachable so that it is possible to predict a trust value for them. It is important to note how even for users with just one friend (last row of table of Figure 6), trust can be very effective. In fact, the mean distance averaged only over them is 5.11 (compared with 4.56 over all users). We believe that just adding one friend is a very easy and quick way to bootstrap the system. In this way, the system can be able to make good recommendations soon also to new users (who are generally also "cold start users" since they have provided few ratings as well).

We now summarize the results of the previous figures in Table 3 which provides the final argument. In fact it shows how, for a given user, the standard CF technique (Pearson correlation coefficient) on average allows to compute user similarity only on a small portion of the user base, precisely 160.73 over 49290 (less than 1%!). On the other hand, by propagating trust it could be possible to infer trust in the other users and use this value as an alternative weight when creating a recommendation. For the average user, in one trust step it is possible to cover 9.88 users (direct friends), in 2 steps 399.89 users (friends of friends), in 3 steps 4386.32 users and in 4 steps 16333.94 users. In computing these values we considered also the users who were not able to reach all the other users, for example the users who provided 0 friends.

The previous difference in coverage of the user base with the two techniques is even exacerbated in the case of "cold start users", users who expressed less than 5 ratings. The mean number of users against which Pearson is computable for this class of users is only 2.74 (0.0056% of the users). Instead propagating trust it is possible to reach 94.54 users in just 2 steps and 9120.78 in 4 steps.

In this Section we have analyzed how on a dataset of real users (*epinions.com*), using a trust metric in order to assign a trust weight to unknown users can potentially be much more effective than computing user similarity as

Table 3. Mean number of comparable users with different methods: Trust and Pearson correlation coefficient. For trust, we indicate the mean number of users reachable through some trust chain in at most x steps. For Pearson, we indicate the mean number of users against which Pearson coefficient is computable (i.e. overlap of at least 2 items). Both are computed over every user (even the ones with 0 ratings or 0 friends).

Mean number of Comparable users for all user					Mean number of Comparable users for cold start users				
propagating Trust (up to different distances)				using Pearson	propagating Trust (up to different distances)				using Pearson
1	2	3	4		1	2	3	4	
9.88	400	4386	16334	161	2.14	**94.54**	1675	9121	**2.74**

traditional RSs do. In the next Section, we summarize the contributions and discuss which research lines the provided evidence opens up.

3   Contribution and Future Work

This paper presents evidence that Recommender Systems [8] that incorporate trust can be more effective than systems based on classic techniques, such as Collaborative Filtering (CF). In particular, CF involves the computation of a user similarity measure (for example, Pearson Correlation Coefficient [2]). We have shown how this quantity, on average, is computable only against a very small portion of the user base and is, in most cases, a noisy and unreliable value because computed on the few items rated in commons by two users. Instead, trust-aware techniques can produce a trust score for a very high number of other users; the trust score of a user estimates the relevance of that users' preferences.

We have argued how even for "cold start users", i.e. users who provided few ratings and usually are the majority, trust propagation could be very effective (especially when compared with Pearson correlation coefficient that is almost always incomputable). The reported evidence opens the way to a number of research paths we briefly explore in the rest of the Section.

Trust metrics. Of course not all the users at the same distance should be trusted the same. A trust metric [1], given a trust network, infers trust in unknown users. Studying different trust metrics is certainly important in a time when more and more data about real social networks are starting to become available in electronic format. Trust propagation is a compelling research line especially when applied to social networks who have weighted trust relationships (ex: A trusts B 0.7 and C 0.1). In this sense it would be very interesting to analyze also the web of distrust of *epinions.com* users. A special attention should deserve research about possible attacks from malicious users. We have a project and a Wiki for studying these issues[3].

---

[3] The Wiki (a writable web site) is at http://moloko.itc.it/trustmetricswiki/moin.cgi

Comparison of Trust and User Similarity. The next steps will be to analyze what the relationships between Trust and User Similarity are: e.g., how often and how much are they consistent? In which cases a trust metric suggests a user that happens to be very dissimilar or vice versa does not find a very similar user? A user reviews more items in common with her friends than with a random user? Based on this comparison, successful ways to combine User Similarity and Trust in order to decide a weight for the users' ratings can be proposed.

Recommendations computation. The final goal is to produce recommendations using Trust-aware Recommender Systems and to compare these recommendations with traditional systems. We will analyze the performances of systems that use only trust (inferred with different trust metrics), only user similarity and combinations of the two.

User acceptance. Human Computer Interaction studies [10] are needed to investigate the best ways to visualize the social network and how this could help the user in understanding the recommendation model and to control it.

References

1. Jennifer Golbeck, James Hendler, and Bijan Parsia. Trust networks on the Semantic Web. In *Proceedings of Cooperative Intelligent Agents*, 2003.
2. D. Goldberg, D. Nichols, B.M. Oki, and D. Terry. Using collaborative filtering to weave an information tapestry. *Communications of the ACM*, 35(12):61–70, 1992.
3. J. Herlocker, J. Konstan J., A. Borchers, and J. Riedl. An Algorithmic Framework for Performing Collaborative Filtering. In *Proceedings of the 1999 Conference on Research and Development in Information Retrieval*, 1999.
4. J.L. Herlocker, J.A. Konstan, and J. Riedl. Explaining Collaborative Filtering Recommendations. In *Proc. of CSCW 2000.*, 2000.
5. D. Maltz and K. Ehrlich. Pointing the Way: Active Collaborative Filtering. In *Proc. of CHI-95*, pages 202–209, Denver, CO, 1995.
6. Paolo Massa. Trust-aware Decentralized Recommender Systems. Phd Proposal, 2003, University of Trento, http://sra.itc.it/people/massa/massa03trustaware.pdf.
7. Lawrence Page, Sergey Brin, Rajeev Motwani, and Terry Winograd. The pagerank citation ranking: Bringing order to the web. Technical report, Stanford Digital Library Technologies Project, 1998.
8. P. Resnick and H.R. Varian. Recommender systems. *Communications of the ACM*, 40(3):56–58, 1997.
9. B. Sarwar, G. Karypis, J. Konstan, and J. Riedl. Application of dimensionality reduction in recommender systems–a case study. in ACM WebKDD Workshop, 2000.
10. K. Swearingen and R. Sinha. Beyond algorithms: An HCI perspective on recommender systems. in ACM SIGIR 2001 Workshop on Recommender Systems, New Orleans, Lousiana, 2001.
11. Jeffrey Zaslow. If TiVo Thinks You Are Gay, Here's How to Set It Straight. The Wall Street Journal, 26 November 2002.

Modeling Controls for Dynamic Value Exchanges in Virtual Organizations

Yao-Hua Tan[1], Walter Thoen[1], and Jaap Gordijn[2]

[1] Free University, Dept. of Economics and Business Administration, The Netherlands. ytan@feweb.vu.nl
[2] Free University, Dept. of Computer Science, The Netherlands. gordijn@cs.vu.nl

Abstract. The e^3-*value* modeling tool was developed for the design of a value proposition for virtual organizations. However, it is less suitable for designing the control structure of the virtual organization. We show how e^3-*value* can be extended using legal concepts such as ownership, possession, usufruct and license. We also introduce value object transfer diagrams that show the transfers of value objects graphically and that can be used for elicitation of the required control mechanisms in order for the virtual organization to function properly and with a level of risk that is acceptable to all parties in the virtual organization.

1 Introduction

Virtual organizations are an important new governance structure for many transactions. A virtual organization can be defined as 'an organization network, which is structured and managed in such a way that it operates vis à vis customers and other external stakeholders as an identifiable and complete organization' [11].

The design of a virtual organization is far from trivial. It is a balancing act between potentially conflicting interests and concerns of participating enterprises. Many approaches suggest that a suitable starting point for designing a virtual organization is the value proposition(s) of such an organization (see e.g. [17] and [3]). Such a proposition contains at least two important elements: (1) a description of the participating actors, the value adding activities they perform and the objects of economic value they exchange with each other and with their customers, and (2) a description of contracts including inter-organizational controls. Since participants in a virtual enterprise do not trust each other on forehand with respect to the objects of economic value they exchange, contracts and supporting controls are used to enable secured participation in a virtual enterprise.

The proposition of a virtual enterprise can be described in many ways, e.g. by natural language as it is often done in practice. In this paper however, we propose a more formal, conceptual modeling, based way to lay down this proposition. Mylopoulos (1992) defines conceptual modeling as 'the activity of formally defining aspects of the physical and social world around us for the purpose of understanding and communication'. Natural language has a few serious drawbacks,

C.D. Jensen et al. (Eds.): iTrust 2004, LNCS 2995, pp. 236–250, 2004.

compared to formal modeling, such as noise (irrelevant information), silence (omission of important information), over specification, contradictions, ambiguity, forward references, and wishful thinking (Mayer 1985). Consequently, we advocate to conceptualize the value proposition thoroughly to create a shared understanding of the proposition at stake. Specifically in the case of virtual enterprises, with involvement of different types of stakeholders representing different interests and concerns of companies the risk of mis-understanding is high. Additionally, (semi-) formal conceptual models allow for proper analysis and provide a starting point for the design of inter-organizational information systems that support the virtual enterprise.

In this paper we present an approach for designing a virtual organization both from a value proposition and trust/control perspective. We first discuss design and life-cycle models of virtual organizations (Sec. 2). These models show that contractual elements in terms of value objects to be exchanged and inter-organization controls are an important tool for structuring virtual organizations. Then we introduce in Sec. 3 the e^3-value methodology for conceptualizing a virtual enterprise's value proposition [6,7]. As we will see in Sec. 4, the e^3-value methodology is suitable for representing a value proposition but lacks functions for representing trust and associated control issues. To this end, we introduce a new description technique, called a value object transfer diagram, to analyze the vulnerabilities of the members (See Sec. 5). Finally, in Sec. 6, we present our conclusions.

2   Modeling Tools for Designing Virtual Organizations

Let us first look a design approach for virtual organizations in general, before we look at the modeling tools in detail. In [3] Carson et al. present a framework for designing institutions. In this framework the virtual organization is called an Institutional Arrangement (IA) and is distinguished from the Institutional Environment (IE). Carson et al. describe their framework as follows:

'The framework begins with a consideration of the desired outputs and the activity sets required to bring about these outcomes. Then we design contractual, ownership, and social elements of IAs that support these joint profit-maximizing activity sets according to our remediable efficiency tests. We proceed in a staged manner, moving from contractual to ownership to social (relational and reputational) elements of the IA.'

The Carson et al. framework is shown in Figure 2. In literature on virtual organizations the assumption is made that a virtual organization rapidly restructures itself if circumstances change. However, it is not obvious when the virtual organization should restructure or when it should remain as is. For example, if restructuring the virtual organization would cause an existing member to be much worse of, then this member would obviously object to the restructuring. Carson et al. use 'the remediable efficiency criterion' to evaluate a possible restructuring. The remediable efficiency criterion as defined as:

An IA (and the activity set that it allows) is remediably efficient if it max-imizes the joint profit created in an Marketing Value System (MVS) subject to the IA's feasibility given (1) the IE and characteristics of the proposed activity set and (2) switchover costs associated with transitioning into and out of the IA. ([3], page 118)

Hence, only in case joint profit-enhancing actions require reallocation to align efficiency with own-firm profits a new IA comes into consideration. The virtual organization will have to be restructured every time the members have identi-fied this kind of joint profit-enhancing actions. If we assume that this happens frequently, then it is important the elements that make up the structure of the virtual organization are flexible enough.

The assumption that Carson et al. make is that contractual arrangements are the least complex and that social norms are the most complex elements of the structure. Their argument is that 'when feasible, contracting poses the least complex IA design problem because it uses fine-grained support from the IE judiciary, i.e. the system of courts of law, and the IE polity, i.e. the form of political organization, to bind parties to joint profit making (JPM) activity sets" and 'social elements of IAs are ... more complex to develop because they depend minimally on the IE polity and judiciary and almost entirely on norms in the IE and IA to support JPM activity sets'.

Social norms are indeed hard to design as Carson et al. claim. For example, we agree that trust, which is an important concept in the social norms described by Carson et al., is difficult to build or 'design'. However, if (strong) social norms that can support the virtual organization already exist, then it might be easier to rely on these social norms rather than to design new contractual elements. Whether contractual elements can replace social norms is actually a debated topic. For instance, Sitkin and Roth state that 'legalistic remedies have been described as weak, impersonal substitutes for trust' [13]. More dramatically stated, it might be impossible to set up a virtual organizational at all if there is insufficient trust or lack of social norms. Social norms are a much stronger foundation for a virtual organization than contractual norms. In our opinion contractual elements should, therefore, only be used in case no suitable social norms exist. In other words, the contractual elements used to structure the virtual organization should be appropriate to the existing social norms.

3   The e^3-value Methodology

The Carson et al. framework stresses that it should be clear to all members what joint profit the institution is going to achieve and what individual profits each member is going to make. In other words, it is important that the members reach a good and mutual understanding of what the value proposition to the customer is and what value each members contributes to the overall value proposition, what risks and vulnerabilities exist, and how the virtual organization deals with the risks in terms of the control structure of the virtual organization.

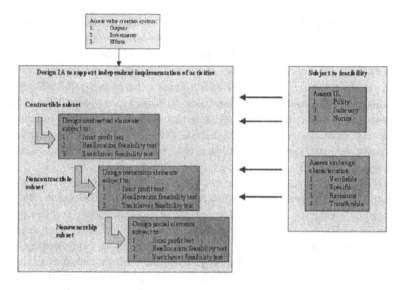

Fig. 1. Design Framework for Institutional Arrangements.

The e^3-value theory [6,7] provides a (graphical) conceptual modeling tool for designing and analyzing the value proposition and value exchanges between the members of the virtual organization and between the virtual organization and its customers.

The theory is specifically developed for exploring networked organizations as virtual enterprises are. These organizations tend to be complex in a sense that they consist of many enterprises that offer a joint product or service. Therefore, they are hard to understand at first sight, so it is worthwhile to conceptualize such organizations. Consequently, the e^3-value theory has specific modeling constructs to conceptualize *who* offers *what* of economic value to *whom* and expects *what* in return. This contrasts to relatively straightforward examples of e-business such as a single web-shop; the essentials here can be expressed by natural language or forms of structured English that prescribe how to outline a value proposition.

The purpose of the e^3-value theory is to provide a *shared* understanding of a virtual enterprise's proposition by thoroughly conceptualizing it. A shared understanding is important because, in practice, the development of a virtual organization's proposition involves a number of persons, all speaking 'different' languages resulting in different interpretations of the proposition. A virtual enterprise consists of other (virtual) enterprises, which in turn are represented by different stakeholders (e.g. CxO's, marketing stakeholders, ICT people and persons dealing with trust issues). The conceptualization constructs (see below) force to ask specific questions to enterprises involved and to steer the discussion to arrive at a shared understanding of the proposition at stake.

Additionally, with tool support it is possible to check whether a proposition is well-formed. An example of such a check is the 'socket'-rule: an enterprise only offers an object of value if and only if s/he obtains another object of economic value in return. Also, it is possible (with tool support) to assess whether a value proposition seems to be profitable for all enterprises involved. In short, we ask enterprises to assign economic value to objects they obtain and deliver, make assumptions on their quantity, and use these numbers to calculate the net cash flow for each enterprise involved (see [7] for more information). At http://www.cs.vu.nl/~gordijn/tools.htm, the reader can download such a tool with these capabilities.

Finally, an e^3-value model can be used as a starting point for further analysis and design. In this paper, we use a virtual enterprise's value model for design and assessment of trust- facilitating controls. Other examples are the design of inter-organizational business processes and supporting information systems.

Figure 2 shows an easy to understand e^3-value model representing that a supplier offers some object of value to a customer and obtains a fee in return. We keep this value web deliberately simple, to explain our formalization. The grey legend on top of Figure 2 is not part of the e^3-value modeling, but is just included to explain the various elements that make up the value model. We now briefly introduce the elements of the e^3-value modeling technique (based upon [7]). In the coming sections we discuss the concepts, such as actor, value object and value exchange in more details.

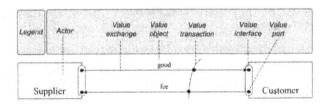

Fig. 2. A supplier and a customer exchanging objects of value. (Note: The grey area and superimposed text are only for explanatory purposes and are not part of the e^3-value modeling technique itself)

Actor. An actor is perceived by its environment as an independent economic (and often also legal) entity.

Value Object. Actors exchange value objects, which are services, products, money or even consumer experiences. The important point here is that a value object is of value for one or more actors.

Value Port. An actor uses a value port to show its environment that it wants to provide or request value objects. The concept of port enables us to abstract away form the internal business processes, and to focus only on how external actors can be 'plugged' in.

Value Interface. A value interface models what an actor offers to *and* requests from the environment. Value objects are exchanged via ports, which in turn are part of a value interface. A value interface assumes atomicity: either *all* ports exchange objects of value or none at all. How this is accomplished is not expressed by e^3-*value* models but a matter of robust process design. This atomicity should in many cases be observed by inter-organizational controls that e.g. can start escalation procedures as soon as atomicity is violated.

Value Exchange. A value exchange is used to connect two value ports with each other. It represents one or more potential trades of value objects between value ports. As such, it is a prototype for actual trades between actors. It shows which actors are willing to exchange value objects with each other.

Value Transaction. A value interface prescribes the value exchanges that should occur, seen from the perspective of an actor the value interface is connected to, because all ports in a value interface should exchange objects, or none at all. Sometimes, it is convenient to have a concept that aggregates all value exchanges, which define the value exchanges that must occur as consequence of how value exchanges are connected, via value interfaces to actors. We call this concept a value transaction. In its simplest form, a transaction is between two actors. However, a transaction can also be between more than two actors. We call such a transaction a *multi-party* transaction.

The e^3-*value* methodology does not tell what specific value exchanges and transactions should be included in the model. Rather, the designer has to go through an elicitation process to find the value exchanges and transactions. It is usually not very hard to list the core value exchanges. For instance, in a sales transaction between a buyer and a seller the core (primary) activities, deliver and pay, will spring to mind immediately and these result in primary value exchanges such as *good* and a *fee*. However, other (secondary) activities such as 'arrange insurance', 'obtain import license' and 'inspect goods' do not immediately spring to mind, but they might be necessary or at least desirable for the successful completion of the primary value transaction.

Secondary activities can be broadly classified in two groups. One group of activities is required to complete the transaction. We call those the 'doing tasks' (see also [1,2]). The other group are activities that are required to monitor the transaction, which we call 'control tasks' (see also [1,2]). The activity 'obtain import license' is an example of a 'doing' task as this activity is required (by some governments) to complete the transaction. The activities 'arrange insurance' and 'inspect goods' are control tasks as these activities are not required to complete the transaction. These activities can be included in the model of the transaction in order to assure that the transaction completes to everyone's satisfaction. In other words, the control tasks are included to alleviate problems that could result from the actions of the members or that could be the result of outside forces (such as the weather, political decisions or technical failures).

The problems that the members foresee with respect to the actions of the members are usually a trust issue. For example, a member is not sure that another member is capable of delivering the required value (e.g. the quality might be an issue) or that the other member might not be willing to delivery the right value under all circumstances (e.g. when there is room for opportunism). Mayer et al. define trust as 'The willingness of a party to be vulnerable to the actions of another party based on the expectation that the other party will perform a particular action important to the trustor, irrespective of the ability to monitor or control that other party' [10]. Hence, in case a member is not willing to be vulnerable to the actions (or a particular action) of another members then we have a trust issue. It is an accepted principle in the literature that a lack of trust can be compensated by the introduction of control mechanisms (see for instance [4,8,13,14,15,16]). In this paper we focus on the design of the control tasks and we use value object transfer diagrams to scan the value exchanges for vulnerabilities.

4   Value Modeling from a Control Perspective

In the previous sections we discussed the importance of contractual control elements for the design of virtual organization. Modeling the trust and control aspects of the contract using (graphical) modeling tools based on the e^3-*value* theory, before or during the drafting of the contract, can improve that quality of contract and can facilitate the negotiation process between the members of the virtual organization. In this section we introduce the general concepts that can be used from a *control* perspective to model business transactions.

We have attempted to stay as close as possible to the definitions in the e^3-*value* ontology [6,7]. However, we have evaluated the e^3-*value* definitions from control modeling perspective. As a result, we introduce several extensions. We will use the following general concepts: actor, role, value object and value object transfer.

Actor. We define the concept of actor in the same way as in the e^3-*value* theory: 'An actor is perceived by his/her environment as an economically independent (and often also legal) entity.' Enterprises and end-consumers are examples of actors. A profit and loss responsible business unit, which can be seen as economically independent is an actor, although such a unit is not a legal entity.

Value Activity and Role. While designing controls, it is convenient to model business transactions without knowing which individual agent is going to participate in that transaction yet. To that end, the e^3-*value* theory proposes *value activity*. This is defined as an activity, which is beneficial for at least one actor. The latter is important, because we want to assign activities to performing actors, and so at least one actor should be interested in the execution of such an activity.

Instead of *value activity* we use the concept of *role* from the research on interorganizational trust building from Bons[1]: 'A *role* is a model of a meaningful cluster of external activities, recognized by the business world'. With external activities Bons refers to those actions that can be observed by other actors. Typical roles in the business world are buyer, seller, bank, freight forwarder, insurer etc. An actor is said to perform a role, implying that in the business transaction the actor will perform the actions that the role comprises. In our ontology an actor is always associated with a role. A role, however, can be used without any actor being associated with it.

Value Object. In the e^3-*value* ontology a value object is defined as follows: 'A value object is a service, a product, or even an experience, which is of economic value for at least one of the actors'. We extend this definition because we want to explicitly include rights, and in particular intellectual property rights, such as copyrights, patents and trademarks, in the definition. Intellectual property rights have always played an important role in many business transactions. Moreover, with the capability to distribute or deliver certain products by means of digital networks we believe that recognizing intellectual property rights and related legal constructs, such as licenses, in value modeling and trust modeling this is becoming even more important. In e^3-*value* ontology a value object has a *name* as the only property. We add *type* as property in our ontology. The Type property can have the following values: product, service, right and experience. We also extend the ontology by adding as properties some legal constructs that are usually associated with a value object. These legal constructs are: *Ownership*, *Possession*, *Usufruct* and *License*. The following three constructs are used for value objects of type products, and are defined as follows (Webster online):

Ownership: the state, relation, or fact of being an owner (see http://www.webster.com/cgi-bin/dictionary?book=Dictionary).

Possession: a) the act of having or taking into control b) control or occupancy of property without regard to ownership

Usufruct: the legal right of using and enjoying the fruits or profits of something belonging to another

An example of the distinction between these three concepts is that you can be the owner of a house, the tenant can have possession of the house, and a third party can have the usufruct of the house by being entitled to the rent.

These three legal constructs are a property of the value object concept in our model. The value of these properties is always a reference to an actor or a role. In other words, what is important in our ontology is which actor or role has ownership, possession or usufruct of a value object.

For value objects of the type Right we use the constructs Ownership and Usufruct in the same way as for products. In addition we use the construct License in respect to rights. We define a license as follows (based on Webster): "*License*: a permission granted by a competent authority to engage in an activity otherwise unlawful."

Services and experiences cannot be owned or possessed or licensed. A service or an experience can be based on rights owned or licensed. For example, a certain service can be so unique that it can be patented and hence can only be offered by the patent owner. However, we will not say that the actor owns the service in case he owns the patent. The same holds for experiences. Of course, this changes nothing about the fact that a value can be assigned to a service and experience. The value of the service or experience can be exchanged for another value object.

Value Object Transfer. The legal constructs associated with value objects are important for modeling control structures, because business transactions are usually about the exchange of value objects between actors. The legal constructs allow us to be more precise about what we mean with 'the exchange of value objects' as we can now distinguish between a transfer of ownership, a transfer of possession, a transfer of usufruct and a transfer of a license.

An exchange of a value object can of course be any combination of these transfers. The simplest exchange is the exchange in which all transfers occur together. In international trade the transfer of ownership and the transfer of possession, however, are often separated. Typically in the Letter of Credit control procedure, the seller of a value object can first transfer possession to a freight forwarder and retain the ownership and then later, e.g. after receiving payment, transfer the ownership to the buyer. After becoming the owner the buyer can request a transfer of possession from the freight forwarder. The Bill of Lading, which is issued by the forwarder when he receives the goods from the seller, is a control document in the letter of credit procedure that is used to prove that the seller has transferred the possession of the goods to the forwarder.

Many interesting situations exist in which a product is sold in combination with a license. Typical examples are CDs and DVDs. CDs and DVDs are physical products combined with a license to play music or watch a movie. However, it is important to distinguish the license from the product. The same physical DVD is combined with a *license for personal use* when a consumer buys it in a store and is combined with a *rental license* when sold to a video rental shop (usually in return for a much higher fee in the latter case). In Figure 4 the e^3-*value* model of a DV rental scenario is shown.

Note, however, that by renting a DVD from the shop the consumer gets a license for personal use from the copyright owner not from the shop! When an actor without the special rental license lends a DVD to another actor (i.e. only the possession of the physical object is transferred), then no license for personal use is granted by the copyright owner. When the new possessor would watch the DVD, then he would violate the copyright! In the next session we introduce value object transfer diagrams that allow us to model these details in a more precise manner.

5   Value Object Transfer Diagram

We use a Value Object Transfer Diagram to visualize the value object transfers. The diagram consists of roles, transfers and tokens. The colored tokens represent the concepts ownership, possession, usufruct, license and value. The transfers represent the transfer of one or more concepts.

An important distinction is that e^3-*value* models are static models whereas the value object transfer models are dynamic. The e^3-*value* model shows the value exchanges between the roles without modeling the actual flow of value through the model. The value object transfer diagram uses the concept State

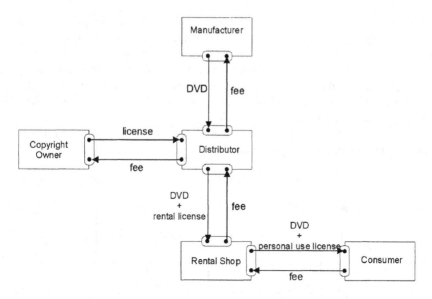

Fig. 3. An e^3-*value* model of the DVD rental scenario

for capturing the dynamics. A state is defined as any distribution of the tokens over the roles.

The idea is that the diagrams are used to graphically show the transfers of value objects that take place in a business transaction whilst leaving the sequencing open for further planning. Note that the difference between for instance a 'pre-payment' scenario and a 'post-payment' scenario is the sequencing of the transfers, and not the transfers that make up the business transaction. The sequencing is left for a later stage because the scenarios are quite different from trust perspective. For example, in a typical post-payment scenario goods are delivered before any money is received in return. If there are no controls in place then the party delivering the goods needs to have sufficient trust in the other party paying eventually in order for the parties to be able to agree on this scenario. Whether the trust levels are sufficient or not, is a question that needs to be answered at a later stage of our approach. At that stage there might be a negotiation between the parties and controls might have to be added in order to reach a satisfactory agreement. The intention of the diagrams presented here is to make the parties aware of the trust issue related to this particular value exchange.

Note that this is also an important distinction from process modeling tools, such as Petri Nets, state-transition diagrams or workflow management systems. In the process modeling tools the sequencing of actions is very important. This makes such models very useful for specifying the execution of transactions, but not for the trust design that is the subject of this paper.

Figure 5 shows a Value Object Transfer Diagram for the simple international trade example described above. Initially, all tokens, i.e. value object concepts, are with role 1, i.e. the seller. Then transaction t1 fires and the possession is transferred to role 2, i.e. the freight forwarder. Then transaction t2 fires and the ownership and usufruct are transferred to role 3, i.e. the buyer. And finally transaction t3 fires and the possession is transferred to role 3, i.e. the buyer. Note that in international trade the transition t2 usually takes the form of sending the Bill of Lading to the buyer and that transition t3 requires the buyer to show the bill of lading to the freight forwarder.

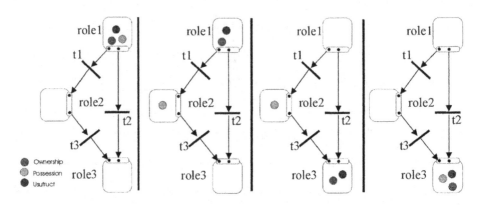

Fig. 4. Value Object Transfer Diagram.

The value object transfer diagram as shown in Figure 5 is a mix of elements from the e^3-*value* models and of Colored Petri Nets. To make this mix possible of these two representation tools we will not assume the Petri Net property that it must an a-cyclic graph, i.e. that there should be no loops. We will later explain why we need these cycles, and also how it can be easily repaired in order to get a proper Petri Net. The most important reasons that we allow for cycles is that a value object can be transferred back and forth between two or more roles. The value object transfer diagrams can be converted into The value interface and value ports are taken from the e^3-*value* models and the colored tokens and transitions and arcs are taken from colored petri nets.

Also note that Figure 5 is obviously not a complete transaction. For example, the payment, i.e. the transfer of ownership of a monetary value object, from the buyer to the seller is not included in this figure. The freight forwarder has to be paid by either the seller or the buyer for his service too. The service provided by the freight forwarder is also a value object according to our definition. As it is unintuitive to talk about the ownership or possession of a service or an experience, we will simply refer to a 'transfer of value' in relation to value objects of the type service and experience.

The issue of ownership is not fully covered by existing international conventions and can thus differ in the various national laws [18]. For instance for the transfer of ownership many national laws make a distinction between register goods, such as houses and cars and non-register goods. The legal requirements related to these distinctions might differ among the national laws though. In the Value Object Transfer diagram we will not take any specific legal requirements into account regarding a transfer of ownership, we simply assume that a transfer of ownership occurs or does not occur and if it occurs it is always successful.

Note again that the Value Object Transfer Diagram is quite different from the e^3-value models. The purpose of the Value Object Transfer Diagram is to model how the value objects flows from one actor/role to another actor/role during the execution of a transaction. The purpose of the e^3-value models is to model what value objects actors offer in exchange for other value objects. Moreover, the e^3-value models assume that the exchange of value objects is atomic at the level of the value interface. According to Gordijn, 'This ensures that if an actor offers something of value to someone else, s/he always gets in return what s/he wants. How this is ensured is a matter of a robust business process design, legal agreements, or sometimes use of technology, but this is not of interest for the value model'([5], page 53). Designing control mechanisms to ensure atomicity is exactly what the research described in this paper aims to accomplish. Hence, in order to support the design of robust business processes with the appropriate control structure, after the business opportunity has been clearly established using e^3-value models in the first phase of the life-cycle, we have to assume that the exchange of value objects is not atomic at the level of the value interface.

In Figure 5 a part of the DVD rental example is shown in a value object transfer diagram. The figure represents the part of the scenario in which the consumer rents a DVD from the rental shop and later returns the DVD, i.e. the value transfers for the manufacturer and distributor are not shown.

The figure shows three states 1) the begin state before the DVD is rented, 2) the intermediate state in which the consumer has rented the DVD and 3) the final state in which the consumer has returned the DVD.

There are six value object transfers. In the first transfer t1, the rental shop transfers the possession of the DVD to the consumer in return for which the consumer transfers the ownership, possession and usufruct of some money to the rental shop (transfer t2). At the same time the copyright owner transfers a person use license to the consumer (transfer t3). We are now in the intermediate state where the consumer has the possession of the DVD and a personal use license to watch it. Note that the copyright owner has not received anything in return for transferring the license. This is because the copyright owner has received a fee beforehand from the distributor, which is not shown in the diagram.

When the consumer returns the DVD, i.e. the consumer transfers the possession of the DVD back to the rental shop (transfer t5) and at the same time the consumer returns the license to the copyright owner (transfer t4). Note that we would have a trust problem if the consumer would get nothing in return for transfer t4 and transfer t5 and the scenario would terminate after transfer 5. If

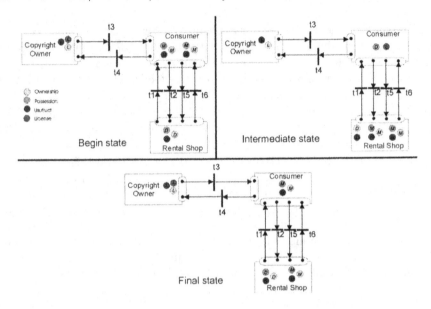

Fig. 5. Value Object Transfer diagram for DVD example.

there was no incentive for the consumer to execute transfers t4 and t5, then why would he do so? This is where the control structure becomes important.

There are several possible control mechanisms that we could introduce to provide an incentive for the consumer to return the DVD. First of all, the rental shop, copyright owner and consumer should have a contract governing the entire exchange. The contract should state that the consumer is obliged to return the possession of the DVD and the license at some point. The institutional environment is of course important as the IE might have to enforce this contract. However, the strength of the incentive for the consumer to return the DVD depends on how the IE would enforce the contract. If the IE would just make the consumer return the DVD without a penalty, then the consumer could easily decide to wait for this to happen. Therefore, an additional control mechanism to ensure a prompt return of the DVD would be a penalty clause in the contract, which stipulates a (monetary) penalty for a late return.

In Figure 5, however, we have opted for another control mechanism; namely a deposit. We assume that in transfer t2 the amount of money paid by the consumer covers two things: 1) the fee for renting the video and 2) a deposit (note that in Figure 5 there are two monetary value objects). Therefore, there is a final transfer t6 in which the rental shop transfers the deposit back to the consumer after the transfers t4 and t5 have occurred.

The value object transfer diagrams can support the designer to find the transfers that might require control mechanisms and to model the relevant value transfer aspects for the design of appropriate control mechanisms. The DVD rental example, which at first appears to be very simple, turns out to be quite complex if we model the actual value object transfers and control mechanisms.

As we mentioned above the value object transfer diagrams are not always a-cyclic. In particular, in the above figure many of the arcs constitute loops between actors. This is not in accordance with the basic definition of Petri nets that it should be a-cyclic graphs. However, the value object transfer diagrams can be easily converted into colored Petri nets. The role places will have to be separated in several places in the colored petri net, ensuring that a token can never be in the same place more than once. For example, transfer t3 and t4 constitute a cycle. But if we would represent the actor Copyright Owner twice, then we could remove this cycle by first having transfer t3 from Copy Right to Consumer and then subsequently transfer t4 from Consumer to the second instance of Copy Right Owner. A similar approach also works for the other cycles. This also shows that an explicit representation of the actual process flow would become much more complicated, and less insightful for modeling the value exchanges and corresponding control mechanisms. The morale here is, as with most representation formalisms, that the correctness of a representation formalism critically depends on the modeling objective. Modeling value exchanges apparently requires a slightly different perspective than pure process modeling.

Here we extended e^3-value with a kind of Petri nets to represent the dynamic transfer of the legal constructs. Other formalisms are also widely used to model legal aspects. For example, there is a long tradition of deontic logic to model legal notions (see e.g. [9]). However, most of these formalisms focus mainly on the representation of static legal aspects, whereas we focused on the dynamic aspects of the transfer of legal constructs. In [12] a deontic logic is discussed based on dynamic logic. In future research we plan to investigate the relation between our value object transfer diagrams and this deontic this logic.

6   Conclusions

In this paper we have discussed the importance of designing the control structures of virtual organizations and the importance of having the right modeling tools for this task. The e^3-value theory provides a (graphical) modeling tool for elicitation of the value proposition of the virtual organization and the value exchange between the members of the virtual organization. We have shown that the e^3-value theory, however, does not allow us to design the control structure of the virtual organization which in our opinion can be equally important to a proper value proposition. The e^3-value theory is intended to model a virtual enterprise's proposition from a business value perspective only. Consequently the theory is not detailed enough about the actual transfer of value objects. To overcome these constraints on the e^3-value theory we introduced models that enable a more detailed analysis of the value object transfers. We used important legal constructs such as ownership, possession, usufruct and license to achieve this. We also introduced the idea of value object transfer diagrams to model the transfers graphically.

References

1. R.W.H. Bons. *Designing Trustworthy Trade Procedures for Open Electronic Commerce*. PhD thesis, EURIDIS and Department of Business Administration, Erasmus University, Rotterdam, NL, 1997.
2. R.W.H. Bons, R.M. Lee, and R.W. Wagenaar. Designing trustworthy interorganizational trade procedures for open electronic commerce. In *Global Business in Practice, Tenth International Bled Electronic Commerce Conference, Bled, Slovenia*, 1997.
3. S.J. Carson, T.M. Devinney, G.R. Dowling, and G. John. Understanding institutional designs within marketing value systems. *Journal of Marketing*, 63:115–130, 1999.
4. T.K. Das and B.S.Teng. Between trust and control: developing confidence in partner cooperation in alliances. *Journal of Decision Support Systems*, 23(3):491–512, 1998.
5. J. Gordijn. *Value-based Requirements Engineering - Exploring Innovative e-Commerce Ideas*. PhD thesis, Vrije Universiteit, Amsterdam, NL, 2002. Also available from http://www.cs.vu.nl/~gordijn/.
6. J. Gordijn and J. M. Akkermans. Designing and evaluating e-Business models. *IEEE Intelligent Systems - Intelligent e-Business*, 16(4):11–17, 2001.
7. J. Gordijn and J.M. Akkermans. Value-based requirements engineering: Exploring innovative e-commerce ideas. *Requirements Engineering Journal*, 8(2):114–134, 2003.
8. S.D. Jap and S. Ganesan. Control mechanisms and the relationship life-cycle. *Journal of Marketing Research*, 1998.
9. A. Jones and M. Sergot. Deontic logic in the representation of law: Towards a methodology. *Artificial Intelligence and Law*, 1(1), 1992.
10. R.C. Mayer, J.H. Davis, and F.D. Schoorman. An integrative model of organizational trust. *Academy of Management Review*, 20(3):709–734, 1995.
11. M. Mazzeschi. What is a virtual enterprise? In *presentation ESoCE*, 2000.
12. J-J.Ch. Meyer, R.J. Wieringa, and F.P.M. Dignum. The role of deontic logic in the specification of information systems. In J. Chomicki and G. Saake, editors, *Logics for Databases and Information Systems*, pages 74–81, Boston/Dordrecht, 1998. Kluwer.
13. S.B. Sitkin and N.L. Roth. Explaining the limited effectiveness of legalistic 'remedies' for trust/distrust. *Organization Science*, (4):367–392, 1993.
14. Y.H. Tan and W. Thoen. Toward a generic model of trust for electronic commerce. *International Journal of Electronic Commerce*, 5(2):61–74, 2000.
15. Y.H. Tan and W. Thoen. Formal aspects of a generic model of trust for electronic commerce. *Journal of Decision Support Systems*, 33:233–246, 2002.
16. Y.H. Tan and W. Thoen. Electronic contract drafting based on risk and trust assessment. *International Journal of Electronic Commerce*, to appear, 2003.
17. Virtual Vertical Enterprise (VIVE). *VIVE Final Report*. ESPRIT 26854.
18. A. von Ziegler, J.H. Ronoe, C. Debattista, and O.B. Plegat-Kerrault. *Transfer of Ownership in International Trade*. CC publication 546, ICC publishers, Paris.

Analyzing Correlation between Trust and User Similarity in Online Communities

Cai-Nicolas Ziegler and Georg Lausen

Institut für Informatik, Universität Freiburg,
Georges-Köhler Allee, Gebäude 51,
79110 Freiburg i.Br., Germany

{cziegler,lausen}@informatik.uni-freiburg.de

Abstract. Past evidence has shown that generic approaches to recommender systems based upon collaborative filtering tend to poorly scale. Moreover, their fitness for scenarios supposing distributed data storage and decentralized control, like the Semantic Web, becomes largely limited for various reasons. We believe that computational trust models bear several favorable properties for social filtering, opening new opportunities by either replacing or supplementing current techniques. However, in order to provide meaningful results for recommender system applications, we expect notions of trust to clearly reflect user similarity. In this work, we therefore provide empirical results obtained from one real, operational community and verify latter hypothesis for the domain of book recommendations.

1 Introduction

Computational trust models [15,21,17] are becoming invaluable goods for today's networked worlds where uncertainty and anonymity prevail. According to Marsh [14], trust can render agents less vulnerable to others and may enhance collaboration significantly.

Recently, approaches incorporating trust models into recommender systems are gaining momentum [20,11,8], synthesizing recommendations based upon opinions from trusted peers. Most notably, *decentralized* recommender systems cannot rely upon generic collaborative filtering methods only, scaling poorly. These systems require novel approaches that allow some prefiltering and neighborhood formation, like, for instance, trust.

Trust therefore becomes supplementary or even surroagate filtering mechanism. However, in order to provide *meaningful* results, one should suppose trust to reflect user similarity to some extent. Clearly, recommendations only make sense when obtained from like-minded people having similar taste.

Hence, Abdul-Rahman and Hailes [2] claim that given some predefined domain and context, e.g., communities of people reading books, its members commence creating ties of friendship and trust primarily with persons resembling their own profile of interest. Reasons for latter phenomenon are manifold and

C.D. Jensen et al. (Eds.): iTrust 2004, LNCS 2995, pp. 251–265, 2004.

mostly sociologically motivated, like people's need for some sort of social affiliation. For instance, Pescovitz [24] describes endeavors to identify trust networks for crime prevention and security. Hereby, its advocates operate "on the assumption that birds of a feather tend to flock together [...]". However, though belief in correlation of trust and user similarity has been widely adopted and presupposed, thus constituting the foundations for trust-based recommender and rating systems, to our best knowledge, no endeavors have been made until now to provide "real-world" empirical evidence. We claim that latter correlation not only represents some desired, but even an *essential* and vital feature for reasonable application of trust to those systems. Profound empirical analysis therefore becomes indispensable, constituting our major contribution.

Hence, we want to investigate and analyze presence or absence of latter correlation, relying upon data mined from an online community focusing on books. Studies involve several hundreds of members telling which books they like and which other community members they trust, hence substantiating our results extensively. Our motivation mainly derives from incorporating trust models into *decentralized* recommender systems, exploiting trust not only for selecting small neighborhoods upon which to perform collaborative filtering, but also for intelligent prefiltering of relevant, similar peers.

In section 2, we briefly outline existing approaches dealing with the incorporation of trust into reputation systems and online recommenders. Section 3 presents experiments we performed in order to investigate correlation between trust and similarity. Hereby, large parts of latter section are devoted to the conception and makeup of our novel approach to profile similarity computation, designed in order to render our experiments feasible. Suggestions for exploitation of correlation between trust and similarity are offered in section 4, while section 5 mentions open questions and possible future work.

2   Recommender Systems and Trust

Online recommender systems [26] intend to provide people with recommendations of products they might appreciate, taking into account their past ratings profile and history of purchase or interest. Hereby, distinctions between three types of filtering systems are made [7], namely collaborative, content-based and economic. While content-based filtering, also dubbed item-to-item correlation [29], takes into account properties attributed to the nature of products themselves, collaborative filtering relies upon building "neighborhoods of like-minded customers" [28] whose rating history may then serve to generate new recommendations. Economic filtering has seen little practical application until now and exerts marginal impact only.

Recent studies [31] have shown that people tend to prefer receiving recommendations from people they *know* and *trust*, i.e., friends and family-members, rather than from online recommender systems. Some researchers have therefore commenced to focus on computational trust models as appropriate means to supplement or replace current collaborative filtering approaches. Kautz et al. [9]

mine social network structures in order to render fruitful information exchange and collaboration feasible. Olsson [23] proposes an architecture combining trust, collaborative filtering and content-based filtering in one single framework, giving only vague information and insight. Another agent-based approach has been presented by Montaner et al. [20], who introduce so-called "opinion-based" filtering. Hereby, Montaner claims that trust should be *derived* from user similarity, implying that friends are exactly those people that resemble our very nature. However, Montaner's model only extends to the agent world and does not reflect evidence acquired from real-world social studies concerning the formation of trust. Similar agent-based systems have been devised by Kinateder [11,10] and Chen [5].

Apart from research in agent systems, online communities have also discovered opportunities through trust network leverage. For instance, Epinions (*http://www.epinions.com*) provides information filtering facilities based upon personalized "webs of trust" [8]. Guha tells that latter filtering approach has been greatly approved and appreciated by Epinion's members. However, justifications and causal analysis underpinning these findings, like indications of correlation between trust and interest similarity, have not been subject to Guha's work. All Consuming (*http://allconsuming.net*) represents another community combining ratings and trust networks. Unlike Epinions, All Consuming only poorly exploits synergies between social filtering and trust.

3   Analyzing Correlation between Trust and Similarity

Recent studies [31] have provided evidence that users tend to rely upon recommendations from friends and family members, i.e., people they trust, more than upon those from online systems. However, Sinha's experiments only included nineteen people, rendering his results fairly applicable. Furthermore, those studies did not investigate the *reasons* which made people stick to their friends' opinions rather than automated collaborative filtering. We believe that given an application domain, such as, for instance, the book-reading domain, people's trusted peers are considerably more similar to their sources of trust than arbitrary peers. More formally, let A denote the set of all community members and $\mathrm{trust}(x)$ the set of all users trusted by x:

$$\forall x \in A : \frac{\sum_{y \in \mathrm{trust}(x)} \mathrm{sim}(x,y)}{|\,\mathrm{trust}(x)|} \gg \frac{\sum_{z \in A \setminus \mathrm{trust}(x)} \mathrm{sim}(x,z)}{|A \setminus \mathrm{trust}(x)|} \tag{1}$$

For instance, given that agent x is interested in Sci-Fi and AI, chances that y, trusted by x, also likes these two topics are much higher than for peer z not explicitly trusted by x. Various social processes are involved, such as participation in those social groups that best reflect our own interests and desires. Some recommendation and reputation systems based upon trust have already been proposed [8,23], exploiting latter expected correlation between trust and interest similarity, but none have provided clear evidence that trust *does* correlate to profile similarity.

3.1 Model and Data Acquisition

Our study intends to close latter gap by analyzing rife user information collected from the All Consuming book-reading community. Hereby, we have opted for All Consuming for mainly two reasons. First, all information published on its site may be accessed without violation of copyright and without any other legal limitations. Second, All Consuming provides both, personal webs of trust that link users to peers they trust, as well as data about the books people have completed and are currently reading.

Information Model. Before delving into the details and makeup of application data our tools have been mining and collecting, we depict our underlying information infrastructure.

(a) **Set of agents** $A = \{a_1, a_2, \ldots, a_n\}$. Set A contains all agents part of the book-reading community.

(b) **Set of books** $B = \{b_1, b_2, \ldots, b_m\}$. All published books are comprised in set B, i.e., all those books that possess an International Standard Book Number. Latter ISBN consequently serves as the globally unique identifier for all $b_i \in B$.

(c) **Set of partial trust functions** $T = \{t_1, t_2, \ldots, t_n\}$. Every agent $a_i \in A$ has one partial trust function $t_i : A \to [0,1]^{\perp}$ that assigns continuous trust values to its peers. Functions $t_i \in A$ are partial since agents generally only rate small subsets of the overall community, hence rendering t_i sparse:

$$t_i(a_j) = \begin{cases} p, \text{ if } \mathrm{trust}(a_i, a_j) = p \\ \perp, \text{ if no trust rating for } a_j \text{ from } a_i \end{cases} \tag{2}$$

We define high values for $t_i(a_j)$ to denote high trust from a_i in a_j, and low values near zero to express low trust, respectively.

(d) **Set of partial book rating functions** $R = \{r_1, r_2, \ldots, r_n\}$. In addition to functions $t_i \in T$, every $a_i \in A$ has one partial function $r_i : B \to [-1, +1]^{\perp}$ that expresses his liking or dislike of books $b_j \in B$. No person can read and rate every book published, so functions $r_i \in B$ are necessarily partial.

$$r_i(b_j) = \begin{cases} p, \text{ if } \mathrm{rates}(a_i, b_j) = p \\ \perp, \text{ if no book rating for } b_j \text{ from } a_i \end{cases} \tag{3}$$

Intuitively, high positive values for $r_i(b_j)$ denote that a_i highly appreciates b_j, while low negative values near -1 express utter dislike, respectively.

(e) **Taxonomy C over set $D = \{d_1, d_2, \ldots, d_l\}$ of book categories.** Book category descriptors $d_k \in D$ represent topics and categories that books $b_j \in B$ may fall into. Hereby, topics can express broad or narrow categories.

Taxonomy C arranges all $d_k \in D$ in an acyclic graph by imposing partial subset order $\subseteq$ on D, similar to class hierarchies known from object-oriented languages. Hereby, *inner* topics $d_k \in D$ with respect to C are all topics having subtopics, i.e., an outdegree greater zero. On the other hand, *leaf* topics are topics with zero outdegree, i.e., most specific categories. Furthermore, taxonomy C has exactly one top element $\top$, which represents the most general topic and has zero indegree.

(f) **Book descriptor assignment function** $f : B \rightarrow 2^D$. Function f assigns a set $D_i \subset D$ of book topics to every book $b_i \in B$. Note that books may possess *several* descriptors, for classification into one single category generally entails loss of precision. Furthermore, all $d \in D_i$ are expected to represent *leaf* nodes with respect to taxonomy C.

The following section will now relate our formal environment model to an actual scenario, hereby making use of variable and function bindings introduced above.

Data Acquisition. All Consuming represents one of the few communities that allow members to express which other agents they trust as well as which items, in our case books, they appreciate. Hereby, users may import their list of trusted persons from other applications like FOAF [6]. Likewise, All Consuming also offers to automatically compile information about books its members have read from their personal weblog. Members may furthermore explicitly assert trust statements and indicate books they own, have read, like most, and so forth.

Trust assertions from user a_i to a_j in All Consuming are *boolean*, either denoting *full* trust, i.e., a_i explicitly states trust in a_j, or *no* trust, if a_i does not. Hence, our real-world scenario is less precise than our model, where we have defined $t_i : A \rightarrow [0,1]^\perp$ instead of $t_i : A \rightarrow \{0,1\}$. Moreover, book mentions in All Consuming seldom reflect "real" ratings, like dislike or liking. They rather indicate that agent a_i has *read* or *purchased* book b_j. These statements therefore count among *implicit* ratings, which nevertheless provide valuable information. Clearly, people tend to only buy and read books they expect to appreciate. In fact, numerous recommender systems are purely based upon implicit ratings [22] since user incentive to provide explicit ratings generally tends to be low [3]. Compared to our model presented in section 3.1, book rating information r_i for user a_i obtained from All Consuming is therefore more imprecise, mapping books b_j to values 0 or 1 instead of $[-1,+1]$. Hereby, we define $r_i(b_j) = 1$ to denote that a_i actually *has* mentioned b_j, and $r_i(b_j) = 0$ that a_i has not.

Our tools have mined data from about 2,074 weblogs contributing to the All Consuming information base, and 527 users issuing 4.93 trust statements on average. These users have mentioned 6,592 different books altogether. In order to obtain category descriptors $f(b_i)$ for all discovered books b_i, we have written several web extraction tools which have mined latter classification information from the Amazon online bookshop (*http://www.amazon.com*). For each book,

Amazon provides an average of about 4 classification topics. These topics represent leaf nodes relating to the huge Amazon book taxonomy, comprising $13,394$ categories after duplicate removal and data cleansing. We have extracted the taxonomy from the Amazon Associates pages via screen scraping tools written particularly for this purpose. Note that the Amazon book taxonomy induces a *tree* structure on our set of categories D, hence making each node d_k have at most one parent d_m. We adopt this model for our approach to user similarity computation and hence suppose taxonomy C to define a tree.

3.2   User Similarity Computation

In order to analyze correlation between trust and user similarity, we need mathematical models indicating how to *compute* latter similarity. Hereby, the book domain bears some notable differences to most other domains like videos, computer games, and DVDs. First, every published book is uniquely identified by its ISBN, which makes it easy to ensure interoperability and gather supplementary information from various other sources, e.g., mentioned category descriptors from Amazon for any given ISBN. Second, the set of published books is vast and much larger than for videos or DVDs. Consequently, profile overlap, i.e., the amount of books two given users $a_i, a_j \in A$ have both rated, is generally small. Common techniques used in collaborative filtering, such as computing Pearson's correlation coefficient [30,25], are therefore bound to fail within our context. Even more advanced techniques, like Sarwar's singular value decomposition [28], cannot reduce dimensionality satisfactorily for our book domain.

Profile Generation. We propose another, more reasonable approach which does not represent users by their respective *book*-rating vectors of dimensionality $|B|$, but by vectors of interest scores assigned to *topics* taken from the book categories taxonomy C. Our method is inspired by Middleton's work on the application of ontologies for content-based filtering [19,18] but goes much further.

Since $|C|$ is equal to the number of categories, user profile vectors shrink to size $|D|$, which tends to be significantly lower than $|B|$. Moreover, making use of profile vectors representing interest in *topics* rather than book *instances*, we can exploit the hierarchical structure of taxonomy C in order to generate overlap and make similarity computation more meaningful: for every leaf category $d_{j_k} \in f(b_j)$ of books b_j agent a_i has mentioned and thus implicitly rated, we also infer an interest score for all super-topics of topic d_{j_k} in user a_i's profile vector. However, interest score assigned for super-topics decreases with increasing distance from leaf d_{j_k}. We furthermore normalize profile vectors with respect to the amount of score assigned, according overall fix score s. Hence, suppose that $v_i = (v_{i_1}, v_{i_2}, \dots, v_{i_{|D|}})^T$ represents the profile vector for user a_i, where v_{i_k} gives the score for topic $d_k \in D$. Then we require the following equation to hold:

$$\forall a_i \in A : \sum_{k=1}^{|D|} v_{i_k} = s \qquad (4)$$

We now formally define the profile generation algorithm for user a_i as follows: suppose that $B_i = \{b_j \in B \,|\, r_i(b_j) = 1\}$ constitutes the set of all books user a_i has mentioned and thus implicitly rated. Due to normalization, the score for each book $b_j \in B_i$ amounts to $s \,/\, |B_i|$, which is proportional to the number of distinct books a_i has mentioned. Consequently, for each topic descriptor $d_{j_k} \in f(b_j)$ categorizing book b_j, we obtain topic score $\mathrm{sc}(d_{j_k}) = s \,/\, (|B_i| \cdot |f(b_j)|)$. Topic score for b_j is hence distributed evenly among its topic descriptors.

Now suppose that $(p_0, p_1, \ldots, p_q)$ gives the path from top element $p_0 = \top$ to leaf node $p_q = d_{j_k}$ within our tree-structured taxonomy C for any given $d_{j_k} \in f(b_j)$. Hence, topic descriptor d_{j_k} has q super-topics. Score normalization and inference of fractional interest for super-topics imply that descriptor topic score $\mathrm{sc}(d_{j_k})$ may *not* become *fully* assigned to d_{j_k}, but in part to all its ancestors $p_{q-1}, \ldots p_0$, likewise. We therefore introduce another score function $\mathrm{sco}(p_m)$ that represents the eventual assignment of score to topics p_m along the taxonomy path leading from $p_q = d_{j_k}$ to p_0:

$$\sum_{m=0}^{q} \mathrm{sco}(p_m) = \mathrm{sc}(d_{j_k}) \tag{5}$$

Furthermore, we require that the interest score $\mathrm{sco}(p_m)$ accorded to p_m, which is super-topic to p_{m+1}, depends on the number of siblings $\mathrm{sib}(p_{m+1})$ of p_{m+1}. The less siblings p_{m+1} possesses, the more interest score is accorded to its super-topic p_m:

$$\forall m \in \{0, 1, \ldots, q-1\} : \mathrm{sco}(p_m) = \frac{\mathrm{sco}(p_{m+1})}{\mathrm{sib}(p_{m+1}) + 1} \tag{6}$$

We hereby assume that sub-topics have *equal shares* in their super-topic within taxonomy C. Clearly, this assumption may imply certain issues, e.g., when certain sub-taxonomies are much denser than others [27]. However, reasonable solutions to mitigate latter effect would require explicit annotation of the taxonomy telling semantic distances from sub-topics to super-topics, which is not the case for the Amazon book taxonomy and most other taxonomies.

Equations 5 and 6 describe conditions which have to hold for the computation of leaf node p_q's profile score $\mathrm{sco}(p_q)$ and the computation of scores for its taxonomy ancestors p_k, where $k \in \{0, 1, \ldots, q-1\}$. We hence derive the following recursive definition for $\mathrm{sco}(p_q)$:

$$\mathrm{sco}(p_q) := \frac{\mathrm{sc}(d_{j_k})}{g_q}, \tag{7}$$

where

$$g_0 := 1, \; g_1 := 1 + \frac{1}{\mathrm{sib}(p_q) + 1},$$

and $\forall n \in \{2, \ldots, q\}$

$$g_n := g_{n-1} + (g_{n-1} - g_{n-2}) \cdot \frac{1}{\mathrm{sib}(p_{q-n+1}) + 1}$$

Having computed sco(p_q), we may now apply Equation 5 to compute all other scores sco(p_k). These scores are then used to update profile vector v_i of user a_i, adding scores for the respective topics in v_i. The procedure is repeated for every book mention $b_j \in B_i$ and every descriptor $d_{j_k} \in f(b_j)$.

Example 1 (Topic score assignment). Suppose the taxonomy given in Figure 1 which represents a tiny fragment from the original Amazon book taxonomy. Let user a_i have mentioned 4 books, namely *Matrix Analysis, Fermat's Enigma, Snow Crash,* and *Neuromancer.* For *Matrix Analysis,* 5 topic descriptors are given, one of them pointing to leaf topic *Algebra* within our small taxonomy.

Suppose that $s = 1000$ defines the overall accorded profile score. Then the score accorded to descriptor *Algebra* amounts to $s / (4 \cdot 5) = 50$. Ancestors of leaf *Algebra* are *Pure, Mathematics, Science,* and top element *Books.* Score 50 hence must be distributed among these topics according to Equation 5 and 6. Application of Equation 7 gives score 29.087 for topic *Algebra.* Likewise, applying Equation 6, we get 14.543 for topic *Pure,* 4.848 for *Mathematics,* 1.212 for *Science,* and 0.303 for top element *Books.* These values are then used to update the profile vector v_i of user a_i. Note that after elimination of numerical errors inferred by rounding, summation of latter scores yields exactly score 50.

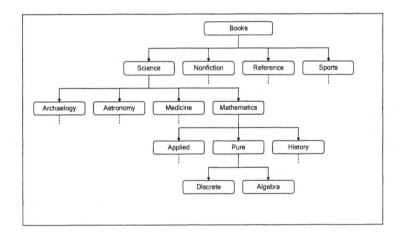

Fig. 1. Small fragment from the Amazon book taxonomy

Profile Similarity Computation. The presented approach computes flat profile vectors $v_i \in [0, s[^{|D|}$ for agents a_i, assigning score values between 0 and maximum score s to every topic d from the set of book categories D. However, one still needs to match these profile vectors against each other in order to come up with one single similarity metric value. Sarwar et al. [28] count nearest-neighbor techniques like Pearson's correlation coefficient [30,25] and cosine similarity, widely known from information retrieval, among the most popular approaches used for measuring profile proximity. We opt for Pearson correlation instead of cosine similarity since Pearson's correlation coefficient also allows for detecting *negative* correlation. For two given profile vectors $v_i, v_j \in [0, s[^{|D|}$, Pearson correlation is defined as below:

$$\mathrm{PCorr}(a_i, a_j) = \frac{\sum_{k=0}^{|D|} (v_{i_k} - \overline{v_i}) \cdot (v_{j_k} - \overline{v_j})}{\sqrt{\sum_{k=0}^{|D|} (v_{i_k} - \overline{v_i})^2 \cdot \sum_{k=0}^{|D|} (v_{j_k} - \overline{v_j})^2}} \tag{8}$$

Hereby, $\overline{v_i}$ and $\overline{v_j}$ give mean values for vectors v_i and v_j. In our case, because of profile score normalization, both values are identical, i.e., $\overline{v_i} = \overline{v_j} = s / |D|$. Values for $\mathrm{PCorr}(a_i, a_j)$ range from -1 to $+1$, where negative values indicate negative correlation, and positive values positive correlation, respectively. Clearly, people who have read many books in common also have high similarity. For generic approaches to collaborative filtering, the opposite direction also holds, i.e., people who have *not* read many books in common have *low* similarity. Our approach, on the other hand, may compute high similarity values even for pairs of agents that have little or even no books in common. Clearly, quality hereby highly depends on the taxonomy's design and level of nesting. According to our scheme, the more score two profiles v_i and v_j have accumulated in same branches, the higher their computed similarity:

Example 2. (Positive correlation) Suppose a_i has read only one single book b_m, bearing exactly one topic descriptor that classifies b_m into *Algebra*. Agent a_j has read another book b_n assigned to one of the leaf nodes[1] of *History*. Then $\mathrm{PCorr}(a_i, a_j)$ will still be reasonably high, for both profiles have significant overlap in categories *Mathematics* and *Science*.

On the other hand, negative correlation occurs when users have completely diverging interests. For instance, in our information base mined from All Consuming, we had one user reading books mainly from the genres of Sci-Fi, Fantasy, and AI. Latter person was rather negatively correlated to another one reading books about American history, politics, and conspiracy theories.

3.3 Experiment Setup and Analysis

We now proceed to describe the two experiments we have performed in order to analyze possible correlation between user similarity and trust. In both cases, experiments are run on data obtained from All Consuming, as has been described in section 3.1. Considering the slightly different composition of information the two experiments were based upon, we expected the first to define some upper bound for correlation analysis, and the second one some lower bound. Results obtained confirmed our assumption.

---

[1] Leaf nodes of *History* are not shown in Figure 1.

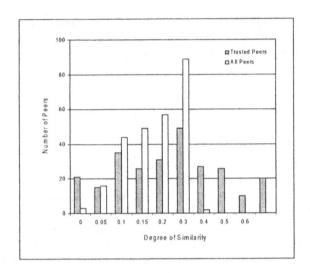

Fig. 2. Results obtained from our upper-bound analysis

Upper-bound Analysis. Before running our first experiment, we applied data cleansing and duplicate removal to the All Consuming's active user base of 527 members. First, we pruned all users a_i having less than three books mentioned, removing them from user base A and defining $t_j(a_i) = 0$ for all other users $a_j \in A$. Next, we deleted all users a_i from our test base which did not issue any trust assertions. Interestingly, some users created *several* accounts. We discovered latter "duplicates" through searching account names for similarity patterns and via tracking identical or highly similar profiles in terms of books mentions. Eventually, we removed self-references, i.e., users trusting themselves.

Through data cleansing, 266 users were removed from our initial test set, leaving 261 users for our experiment to run upon. We denote the reduced set of users by A' and corresponding trust functions by $t'_i(a_j)$. For our first experiment, we proceeded as follows: for every single user $a_i \in A'$, we generated its profile vector and computed similarity with each profile of all *trusted* peers $a_j \in \{a \in A' \mid t'_i(a) = 1\}$. Then we took the average of these proximity measures and recorded latter value in some table. Next, we computed similarity of a_i's profile with the profiles of *all* agents, except a_i itself, from dataset A'. Again, we took the average of these proximity measures and stored the resulting value.

In 173 cases, users were more similar to their trusted peers than to the entirety of A'. The opposite held for only 88 users. On average, users had similarity score 0.247 with their trusted peers, while only 0.163 with *all* users of A'. In other words, users were more than 50% more similar to trusted agents than arbitrary peers. Histogram representations showing the distribution of similarity values for both cases of our first experiment are given in Figure 2.

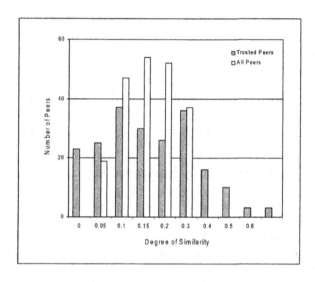

Fig. 3. Histogram representation of our lower-bound analysis

Lower-bound Analysis. The first experiment conducted underpins that peers tend to trust agents being significantly more similar than usual. However, we have to consider that All Consuming bears one feature that *proposes* friends to new users a_i. Hereby, All Consuming chooses users which have at least one book in common with a_i. Hence, we had to suppose that our first experiment was biased and too optimistic with respect to correlation between trust and similarity. Consequently, we pruned user set A' even further, eliminating trust statements whenever trusting user and trusted user had at least one book in common. We call latter user base A'', now reduced to 210 trusting users, and indicate its respective trust functions by $t_i''(a_i)$. Clearly, our approach to eliminate All Consuming's intrusion into the natural process of trust formation entailed the removal of many "real" trust relationships between agents a_i and a_j. These relationships had been established because of a_i actually knowing and trusting a_j, and not because All Consuming proposed a_j as an appropriate match to a_i. Proceeding for experiment two in exactly the same fashion as for its predecessor, we then expected results to be biased towards the other direction, i.e., unduly lowering correlation between trust and user similarity. Bear in mind that in A'', users have not one single book in common with their trusted peers.

Results obtained from the second experiment confirmed our expectations, being less indicative for an existing correlation between trust and user similarity. Nevertheless, similarity of users with trusted peers still significantly exceeded average similarity. In 112 cases, users were more similar to their trusted fellows than arbitrary peers. The opposite held for 98 users. Similarity between trusting users and trusted agents amounted to 0.164, while average similarity between any two arbitrary users only made 0.134. Hence, even for our lower-bound experiment, users were still about 23% more similar to their trusted fellows than arbitrary agents.

We may conclude our experimental analysis noticing that without exact knowledge of how much noise All Consuming's friend recommender adds to our obtained results, we expect "true" correlation between trust and similarity to reside somewhere within our computed upper and lower bound. At any rate, sufficient evidence has been provided exposing that similarity may substantially increase when considering trusted peers opposed to arbitrary ones.

4   Exploiting Correlation between Trust and Similarity

Knowledge about positive correlation between trust and interest similarity may be exploited for diverse applications. In particular, we envision trust to play an important role for *decentralized* recommender systems. These filtering systems suppose distributed data and control and currently face various problems inherent to their very nature:

(a) **Credibility and attack-resistance.** The Semantic Web and other open systems lack dedicated mechanisms and facilities to verify user identity. Hence, these systems tend to encourage insincerity and fraudulent behavior. Moreover, penalization and banishment are hard to accomplish and facile to short-circuit. Collaborative filtering becomes particularly suceptive to attack, for malicious users simply have to create profiles replicating the victim's in order to obtain high similarity. Then they can lure the victim into buying items the purchase of which may provide some utility for the attacker.

(b) **Product-user matrix sparseness.** Communities often limit the number of ratable products, therefore avoiding product-user matrices from becoming overly sparse. Besides, Ringo [30] and other systems require users to rate items from *small product subsets* to generate user profiles with sufficient overlap. However, decentralized recommender system cannot suppose reduced item sets. Bear in mind that controlling product set contents and having users rate certain goods presupposes some central authority.

(c) **Computational complexity and scalability.** Centralized systems are able to control and limit the number of members. Depending on the community's size, large-scale server clusters ensure proper operativeness and scalability. In general, recommender systems imply heavy computations. For instance, collaborative filtering systems compute Pearson correlation for users a_i offline rather than on-the-fly. Recall that coefficients $\text{PCorr}(a_i, a_j)$ have to be computed for every other agent $a_j \in A$. Clearly, this approach does not work for large decentralized systems. Sensible prefiltering mechanisms which still ensure reasonable recall are needed.

Clearly, trust succeeds to address the credibility problem. Every agent builds its own neighborhood of trusted peers, relying upon direct trust statements and those from trusted peers, likewise. For deriving trust, numerous metrics have been proposed during the last decade, among those [16], [1], [4], and [13]. However, we believe that local group trust metrics like Levien's Advogato [12] and Appleseed [33] best fit neighborhood formation in decentralized systems [32]. Unfortunately, trust cannot handle product-user matrix sparseness, nor substantially reduce dimensionality. Supplementary approaches are needed, e.g., taxonomy-based filtering techniques similar to the one proposed.

Increased computational complexity and loss of scalability are mitigated and may even be eliminated when supposing positive correlation between trust and user similarity. Note that our complexity issue itself does not require latter correlation: limiting collaborative filtering to selected peers part of agent a_i's trust neighborhood only entails complexity reduction, too. However, when supposing that trust does *not* reflect similarity, serious tradeoffs are implied, for scalability comes at the expense of recall. Mind that trust neighborhood A_{a_i} of agent a_i only represents one tiny fraction of the overall system A. Moreover, latter fraction not necessarily contains similar peers. Instead, trusted agents are on average no more similar than arbitrary ones. Recall, i.e., the proportion of agents a_j with $sim(a_i, a_j) \geq t$ found by the filtering process, degrades proportionally to $|A|/|A_t|$. On the other hand, when assuming that trust *does* correlate with similarity, respective degradation does not take place equally fast, thus ensuring reasonable recall.

Guha's approach [8] relies upon trust networks as only filtering mechanism, clearly exploiting latter correlation. Positive user feedback seems to justify his design decision. Nevertheless, we believe that trust should rather *supplement* than replace existing filtering techniques. For instance, ex-post application of collaborative filtering to computed trust neighborhoods A_{a_i} might boost precision significantly.

5   Discussion and Outlook

We have articulated our hypothesis that correlation between trust and user similarity exists when the community's trust network is tightly bound to some particular application. Empirical evidence has been provided based upon data obtained from the All Consuming book-readers' community. To our best knowledge, suchlike experiments have not been performed before, since communities incorporating explicit trust models are still very sparse.

We believe that our results will have substantial impact for ongoing research in recommender systems, where discovering user similarity plays an important role. Decentralized approaches will especially benefit from trust network leverage. Hereby, the outstanding feature of trust networks refers to sensible prefiltering of like-minded peers and credibility of recommendations. Arbitrary social networks, on the other hand, only allow for computation complexity reduction.

Though backing our experiments with information involving several hundreds of people, studies for distinct interest domains are required. We would also like to run our analysis on communities larger than All Consuming.

References

1. ABDUL-RAHMAN, A., AND HAILES, S. A distributed trust model. In *New Security Paradigms Workshop* (Cumbria, UK, September 1997), pp. 48–60.

2. ABDUL-RAHMAN, A., AND HAILES, S. Supporting trust in virtual communities. In *Proceedings of the 33rd Hawaii International Conference on System Sciences* (Maui, HW, USA, January 2000).

3. AVERY, C., AND ZECKHAUSER, R. Recommender systems for evaluating computer messages. *Communications of the ACM 40*, 3 (March 1997), 88–89.

4. BETH, T., BORCHERDING, M., AND KLEIN, B. Valuation of trust in open networks. In *Proceedings of the 1994 European Symposium on Research in Computer Security* (1994), pp. 3–18.

5. CHEN, M., AND SINGH, J. P. Computing and using reputations for internet ratings. In *Proceedings of the 3rd ACM Conference on Electronic Commerce* (Tampa, FL, USA, 2001), ACM Press, pp. 154–162.

6. GOLBECK, J., PARSIA, B., AND HENDLER, J. Trust networks on the semantic web. In *Proceedings of Cooperative Intelligent Agents* (Helsinki, Finland, August 2003).

7. GOLDBERG, D., NICHOLS, D., OKI, B., AND TERRY, D. Using collaborative filtering to weave an information tapestry. *Communications of the ACM 35*, 12 (1992), 61–70.

8. GUHA, R. Open rating systems. Tech. rep., Stanford Knowledge Systems Laboratory, Stanford, CA, USA, 2003.

9. KAUTZ, H., SELMAN, B., AND SHAH, M. Referral web: Combining social networks and collaborative filtering. *Communications of the ACM 40*, 3 (March 1997), 63–65.

10. KINATEDER, M., AND PEARSON, S. A privacy-enhanced peer-to-peer reputation system. In *Proceedings of the 4th International Conference on Electronic Commerce and Web Technologies* (Prague, Czech Republic, September 2003), vol. 2378 of *LNCS*, Springer-Verlag.

11. KINATEDER, M., AND ROTHERMEL, K. Architecture and algorithms for a distributed reputation system. In *Proceedings of the First International Conference on Trust Management* (April 2003), P. Nixon and S. Terzis, Eds., vol. 2692 of *LNCS*, Springer-Verlag, pp. 1–16.

12. LEVIEN, R. *Attack Resistant Trust Metrics*. PhD thesis, UC Berkeley, Berkeley, CA, USA, 2003.

13. LEVIEN, R., AND AIKEN, A. Attack-resistant trust metrics for public key certification. In *Proceedings of the 7th USENIX Security Symposium* (San Antonio, Texas, USA, January 1998).

14. MARSH, S. *Formalising Trust as a Computational Concept*. PhD thesis, Department of Mathematics and Computer Science, University of Stirling, Stirling, UK, 1994.

15. MARSH, S. Optimism and pessimism in trust. In *Proceedings of the Ibero-American Conference on Artificial Intelligence* (Caracas, Venezuela, 1994), J. Ramirez, Ed., McGraw-Hill Publishing.

16. MAURER, U. Modelling a public key infrastructure. In *Proceedings of the 1996 European Symposium on Research in Computer Security* (1996), E. Bertino, Ed., vol. 1146 of *Lecture Notes in Computer Science*, Springer-Verlag, pp. 325–350.

17. MCKNIGHT, H., AND CHERVANY, N. The meaning of trust. Tech. Rep. MISRC 96-04, Management Informations Systems Research Center, University of Minnesota, MN, USA, 1996.

18. MIDDLETON, S., ALANI, H., SHADBOLT, N., AND DE ROURE, D. Exploiting synergy between ontologies and recommender systems. In *Proceedings of the WWW2002 International Workshop on the Semantic Web* (Maui, HW, USA, May 2002), vol. 55 of *CEUR Workshop Proceedings*.

19. MIDDLETON, S., DE ROURE, D., AND SHADBOLT, N. Capturing knowledge of user preferences: Ontologies in recommender systems. In *Proceedings of the First International Conference on Knowledge Capture* (Victoria, British Columbia, Canada, October 2001).

20. MONTANER, M., LÓPEZ, B., AND DE LA ROSA, J. Opinion-based filtering through trust. In *Proceedings of the Sixth International Workshop on Cooperative Information Agents* (Madrid, Spain, September 2002), S. Ossowski and O. Shehory, Eds., vol. 2446 of *LNAI*, Springer-Verlag, pp. 164–178.

21. MUI, L., MOHTASHEMI, M., AND HALBERSTADT, A. A computational model of trust and reputation. In *Proceedings of the 35th Hawaii International Conference on System Sciences* (Big Island, HI, USA, January 2002), pp. 188–196.

22. NICHOLS, D. Implicit rating and filtering. In *Proceedings of the fifth DELOS Workshop on Filtering and Collaborative Filtering* (Budapest, Hungary, 1998), ERCIM, pp. 31–36.

23. OLSSON, T. Decentralized social filtering based on trust. In *Working Notes of the AAAI-98 Recommender Systems Workshop* (Madison, WI, USA, 1998).

24. PESCOVITZ, D. The best new technologies of 2003. *Business 2.0*, 11 (November 2003). Time Inc. Publishing.

25. RESNICK, P., IACOVOU, N., SUCHAK, M., BERGSTORM, P., AND RIEDL, J. GroupLens: An open architecture for collaborative filtering of netnews. In *Proceedings of ACM 1994 Conference on Computer Supported Cooperative Work* (Chapel Hill, NC, USA, 1994), ACM, pp. 175–186.

26. RESNICK, P., AND VARIAN, H. Recommender systems. *Communications of the ACM 40*, 3 (1997), 56–58.

27. RESNIK, P. Using information content to evaluate semantic similarity in a taxonomy. In *Proceedings of the 14th International Joint Conference on Artificial Intelligence* (Montreal, Canada, 1995), pp. 448–453.

28. SARWAR, B., KARYPIS, G., KONSTAN, J., AND RIEDL, J. Application of dimensionality reduction in recommender systems - a case study. In *ACM WebKDD Workshop* (Boston, MA, USA, August 2000).

29. SCHAFER, B., KONSTAN, J., AND RIEDL, J. Recommender systems in e-commerce. In *Proceedings of the 1st ACM Conference on Electronic Commerce* (Denver, CO, USA, 1999), ACM Press, pp. 158–166.

30. SHARDANAND, U., AND MAES, P. Social information filtering: Algorithms for automating "word of mouth". In *Proceedings of the ACM CHI'95 Conference on Human Factors in Computing Systems* (1995), vol. 1, pp. 210–217.

31. SINHA, R., AND SWEARINGEN, K. Comparing recommendations made by online systems and friends. In *Proceedings of the DELOS-NSF Workshop on Personalization and Recommender Systems in Digital Libraries* (Dublin, Ireland, June 2001).

32. ZIEGLER, C.-N. Semantic web recommender systems. In *Proceedings of the Joint ICDE/EDBT Ph.D. Workshop 2004* (Heraklion, Greece, March 2004).

33. ZIEGLER, C.-N., AND LAUSEN, G. Spreading activation models for trust propagation. In *Proceedings of the IEEE International Conference on e-Technology, e-Commerce, and e-Service* (Taipei, Taiwan, March 2004), IEEE Computer Society Press.

Trust Development and Management in Virtual Communities

Tanko Ishaya and Darren P. Mundy

Centre for Internet Computing, University of Hull,
Scarborough Campus, Filey Road, Scarborough, UK
{t.ishaya, d.p.mundy}@hull.ac.uk

Abstract. The web is increasingly used as a platform and an enabler for the existence of virtual communities. However, there is evidence that the growth and adoption of these communities is being held back by many barriers- including that of trust development and management. This paper discusses the potential benefits and barriers to the introduction of trust development and management in virtual communities. Based on the analysis of the barriers and benefits of trust development and management, mechanisms for supporting its development and management is proposed and presented. Ideas for further research are presented and discussed. The paper is based on ongoing research and is part of a research bid towards the introduction of a trust development and management framework to support the creation of trusted virtual communities.

1 Introduction

Trust is a term with many meanings and perceptions. For example, [16] defines trust as *"the willingness of a party to be vulnerable to the actions of another party based on expectations that the other party will perform a particular action important to the trustor irrespective of the ability to monitor or control that party"*. The same trust is defined as *"the firm belief in the competence of an entity to act dependably, securely and reliably within a specified context" (assuming dependability covers reliability and timeliness)"* [8]. These different perceptions make it extremely difficult to navigate through the literature on trust. There are also many theories on trust, some of which diverge from each other only in their identification of the grounds on which it is based. However, most diverging theories cluster either within the rational[1] or the social[2] perspective. The distinctions and correlation between the two perspectives has been established in [12], [13]. Based on which, a complementary perspective has been defined in which trust is conceptualised as complementary between individual's expectations and willingness [13].

One very important feature of trust is that it is something that people use everyday and most people are relatively good at making decisions with some form of trust in-

---

[1] Based on calculations that weigh the cost and benefits of certain courses of action between members [14]

[2] Based on moral duty which entails suspension of self-interest in favour of a collective orientation [16]

C.D. Jensen et al. (Eds.): iTrust 2004, LNCS 2995, pp. 266–276, 2004.
© Springer-Verlag Berlin Heidelberg 2004

volved [19]. In the physical world, trust is developed and managed based on our experience of others, information we have received about them and how they appear to us. The trusting decisions we make are based on the situation we find ourselves in, and how we want to apply it. Since trust is an experiential phenomenon, it grows or shrinks depending on time and experience [13], [15]. In many cases, people use general trusting judgement based on similar experiences or situations in the past to make decision. Then, the decision made may lead to further relationships where trust is developed over time. Generally, there are at least two different layers of trust, which are an initial judgement and a more complex experiential trust [20].

In a virtual community this would mean the belief that a user will carry out actions responsibly in the context of the rules of the virtual community. Trust development covers how the user will obtain trust and perhaps increase their trust level within the community. Trust management determines how trust will be assigned, modified and revoked. All this makes trust a very subjective phenomenon. The number of people we can relate to within a physical community is limited by distance and physical constraints. In the virtual world, the number of people on-line or in a virtual community only limits the number of people that one can potentially relate to. In the physical domain there are established frameworks, legal, ethical and others that provide protection and assurance upon which trust is built. In the virtual domain guidelines and boundaries become much more difficult to define and trust becomes increasingly more difficult to determine. Here, security measures become a crucial trust development factor.

Despite intensive developments in the area of virtual communities and the wide variety of software tools available from many different vendors, there is increasing evidence that the lack of trust with respect to online communities constitutes a psychological trait to participants of online communities [13], [14]. One of the causes of this psychological trait is that it is not possible to identify trusted virtual environments. Similarly, the extent in which miscreants, for example paedophiles, use untrusted virtual communities like chat rooms are matters of concern to society. Research is therefore required to help better promote an appropriate use of virtual communities by providing recommendations for building trust relationships within them.

The purpose of this paper is to present, analyse and discuss potential benefits and barriers to the introduction of trust development and management in virtual communities, with the aim of proposing mechanisms for building and managing such a trusted virtual community. In the next section, the main benefits that could be gained from the development of trusted virtual communities are presented. Section 3, describes some of the barriers identified as a result of an initial investigation carried out. Section 4, describes the proposed set of mechanisms for trust development and management. Section 5 concludes the paper with further research.

2 Potential Benefits from the Development of Trusted Virtual Communities

A lot of benefits from the development of trusted virtual communities have been identified in e.g. [5] [6] [13]. Based on this vast available literature on trust and virtual communities, benefits from the introduction of trusted virtual communities can be broken down into three categories society, organisational and personal benefits. Each of these categories is briefly described and presented below.

2.1   Society Benefits

Social scientist Fukuyama in his book "Trust: The Social Virtues and the Creation of Prosperity" suggests that there are two cultures of trust low and high, which businesses exist in. Businesses existing in low trust cultures are almost exclusively family owned whereas in high trust cultures an organisational structure has been developed where trust is placed in professional managers [6]. Fukuyama contends that low trust communities e.g. South America, North Korea, China result in less vital economies than high trust communities for example within Japan, USA and Europe. Whilst the view that *"trust is the major determinant of economic performance and the social virtue par excellence"* [24] may not be completely accurate it is fair to say that trust does generate social capital for example in relationships, agreements, decisions and transactions. This would seem to suggest that trusted virtual communities will provide both social and economic benefits.

It is important to realise however that personal traits towards trust development and management differ considerably between individuals. Kramer in his paper on "Trust and Distrust in Organisations" [24] identifies six bases of trust within organisations these are dispositional, history-based, third party conduits, category based, role-based and rule-based. Papers by Creed & Miles [5], Lewicki & Bunker [17], Sheppard &Tuckinsky & Mayer et al [18] are identified in Kramer's paper as considerable research focused in this area. Therefore a trusted virtual community may have multiple definitions and will not just be characterised by the existence of a secure technological infrastructure. A trusted virtual community will be realised through the existence of multiple infrastructural elements including security, trust development mechanisms, trust management mechanisms, legal frameworks and psychological conditioning. A good example of a trusted virtual community is eBay where trust relationships exist based on the historical actions of members (forming reputations) and rules are evident which members should adhere to. Those members not conforming to the rules may end up disregarded by the community and deemed untrustworthy.

2.2   Organisational and Group Benefits

Within organisations Kramer identifies three benefits of trust these are economic prosperity (through reduced costs of transaction), organisational social structures and infrastructure support [24]. Reduced transaction costs come as a direct result of costs associated with building trust and making associated decisions. For example, if a company receives a bid from a company that they have never worked with before they are likely to check out the company's background, check other organisations dealings with the company, check for solvency etc. Trusted virtual communities between organisational parties have the potential to support economic judgement and the decision making process thereby lowering transaction costs and increasing prosperity. For example, there may be certain rules on membership of the virtual community e.g. you may have to prove the organisation is economically sound.

Trust also helps in the generation of organisational social structures which leads to willingness to share information, ideas e.g. as in [5], [12], [13]. In a trusted virtual community individuals may be more willing to provide information, reveal personal experiences, and become involved in group discourse. For example, in a trusted virtual community set-up purely for specific disease sufferers, members may be more willing to talk about the effects the disease is having on their lives and how they have coped with the effects.

Finally, Fukuyama's high trust cultures are evident in the final benefit of trust in organisations that of trust in authority figures. This leads to a streamlined decision process, again leading to reduced transaction costs. In a virtual community this may mean the trust in a recognised individual or party to authorise membership of the community.

2.3   Personal

Looking at trusted virtual communities from a personal perspective, perhaps the greatest benefit will be in terms of enhanced safety and security for the more vulnerable members of our society. Bruce Schneier, a world renowned Information Security expert suggests that all security involves trade-offs and trade-offs are subjective [21]. At present poor trade-offs in personal security are being made within chat rooms by younger members of the community, leaving them open to abuse from miscreants in society. The paper "Online grooming and UK law" [2] written recently by Childnet International directed to the UK Home Office details cases like: *"Patrick Green, a thirty three year old export clerk, made contact with a twelve year old girl in a teen-age chat room"* [2]. After convincing the girl he was in love with her, he made a series of indecent assaults. The paper also points to a survey carried out in USA where it found 1 in 5 youths (from ages 10-17) online receive unwanted approaches by members of society. Trusted virtual communities are just one of the mechanisms that could help to alleviate the problem, others include education, changes to the legal system and improved virtual community management and monitoring procedures.

A further personal benefit of trusted virtual communities could be the removal or reduction of risk in financial transaction. This benefit can be directly inferred from the economic prosperity benefits that organisations could receive through trusted communities.

3   Potential Barriers to Trust Development and Management

A number of MSc Internet Computing dissertation projects were undertaken in the filed of trust, at the University of Hull, in order to establish the importance of trust in virtual communities, and to identify potential barriers to trust development and management. Questionnaires were administered for the collection of data.

Based on analysis of the results, the authors have identified five areas containing potential barriers to trust development and management in virtual communities. The areas identified are: sociological, psychological, technological, legal and economic. A summary of each of the categories containing barriers is presented below.

3.1 Sociological Barriers

We have identified earlier in the paper that culture plays a part in trust development and management. Cultural barriers therefore may exist towards trust in electronic environments, for example attitudes towards electronic signatures amongst different age ranges within society. Criminology (the study of criminal behaviour) may also provide us with insights into how trusted virtual communities could be used in criminal activity. For example, on eBay a member could build up their reputation over time then make one high value transaction, which they do not fulfil.

3.2 Psychological Barriers

Trust is not just about having a trusted infrastructure in place. How do we build up stakeholders trust in the virtual community? Psychological barriers may prevent stakeholders trusting the virtual community and its members, therefore negating any benefits. As we have seen time and time again in other projects the views and psychological reactions of stakeholders are crucial to the success of a project [1], [23]. Taking the disease chat room stated previously members may be unlikely to communicate if they cannot trust that other members really do have the same condition.

3.3 Technological Barriers

The main technological barriers are those surrounding the security aspects, keeping unwanted members out whilst securing the privacy of messages within the community. We need to examine how we determine people are actually members of the community (authentication), what access privileges they have (authorisation), how to keep messages private within the community (privacy and encryption), how to monitor usage (audit), how to register members and how to revoke their status should they become unwanted (registration and revocation). We also need to determine security policies governing the development of trusted virtual communities, e.g. how do we define what a trusted virtual community is? What infrastructure needs to be in place? etc... We also need to examine stakeholder's responses to technology. It has been found in prior literature that technological aspects can undermine trust and usage [2],[6] i.e. use of surveillance technology.

3.4 Legal Barriers

It is important that trusted virtual community implementations are backed up by solid legal infrastructure for example, so that electronic transactions cannot be reputed by any non-fulfilling party, messages can be traced back for libellous statements and privacy within recognised trusted virtual communities must be assured. Legislation exists at present but may in some situations be too complex to provide legal protection; for example, an electronic signature provides message authentication, integrity and non-reputability. However, in the UK and most of Europe's legal systems, for an electronic signature to be considered admissible in court as evidence, it must be be a

so called advanced electronic signature. *"An "advanced electronic signature" means an electronic signature –*
(a) which is uniquely linked to the signatory,
(b) which is capable of identifying the signatory,
(c) which is created using means that the signatory can maintain under his sole control, and
(d) which is linked to the data to which it relates in such a manner that any subsequent change of the data is detectable;" [9]

This suggests that an admissible electronic signature must have been created using a secure signature creation device such as a personal smart card and be backed up by a qualified certificate created by a recognised secure Certification Authority (CA). People generating trusted virtual communities should also be aware of other legal acts such acts covering privacy and the use of encryption. A legal framework is required for the generation of trusted virtual communities needs to be published, where data transmitted can be held admissible in court.

3.5 Economic Barriers

Trusted virtual communities may face very large economic barriers. The level of trust placed in a community may depend on the infrastructure in place and the structures designed to support it. Infrastructure has an associated economic cost and it is reasonable to assume that a more complex infrastructure may be more expensive to implement and maintain. For example, moderated chat rooms can swiftly grow to a level at which they become not maintainable or very expensive to maintain. Economic barriers also exist in the development of a secure infrastructure to facilitate the development of trust. For example, if all members of the community are expected to go through some form of authentication process (i.e. to ensure they are who they say they are) and authorisation process (i.e. to ensure they have authority to access the virtual community), this could attract significant costs.

4   Potential Mechanisms for Supporting the Provision of Trust

It is easy to lose sight of the fact that conventional security technologies, even perfectly implemented do not constitute trust development and management [2]. All the new protocols, ciphers, patches etc currently available for securing the web seem to translate to securing the network, web servers and clients. Since trust is conceptualised as expectations and willingness [13], it needs to be managed in several layers- including network connection as well as social aspects of human interaction. It is based on this that mechanisms proposed in this paper require considerations involving all aspects of human interaction that uses a virtual communication medium. This is simply because, the medium for virtual communication systems does not make themselves untrusted entities. It was generally observed that levels of uncertainty and vulnerability are high within virtual communities, since there are no standardized procedures or guaranteed controls over individual behaviour. In this situation, trust and commitment are the only common mechanisms for team cooperation. Although trust is needed both in face-to-face and computer-mediated communication, it is a prerequisite for success when a collaborative task involves the risk of individualistic or deceitful behaviour by others. Evidence from [13], shows that people are reluctant to use computer-mediated systems for collaboration, because lack of face-to-face contact reduces trust and commitment. This was further proved in Rocco's investigation in 1998, where trust proved to be possible only in face-to-face communication or in an initial face-to-face meeting for virtual communities. Proposed mechanisms for trust development involves - Socio-technical stakeholder participation, Identification of elements of trust, Identification of the processes of building and maintaining virtual trust, Guidelines towards the development of a security infrastructure to support differing levels of trusted virtual communities and finally the creation of trust development and management frameworks.

4.1 Socio-technical Stakeholder Participation

Since, the web is now a social phenomenon that will affect people who do not even use it, a socio-technical study [25] is required into stakeholder perceptions towards the introduction of trusted virtual communities. We need to investigate stakeholder's views on trusted virtual communities and allow communities to define their own views. Informed citizens must consider, analyse, and present the impact of automating trust decisions online.

4.2 Identification of the Elements of Trust

Studies should be undertaken to define the elements of trust. An example of the elements of trust generated for consideration are presented in Table 4.1.

Table 4.1. Elements of Trust

Elements	Related Questions
Identity	What are their names, age, sex, origin etc
Presence	Who is around?, Are they present? Etc..
Location	Where are they? Are they in different parts of the globe?
Skills	What are their skills?
Experience	How much experience have they got/ do they need?
Culture	What are their beliefs? What are their cultural differences? Are there cultural effects?
Expectations	What are the individual and group expectations?
Values/Attitudes	What are their values and attitudes?
Language	Are there language differences? Are their language concepts different?
Commitment	How committed are they?
Willingness	How willing are they to share information?
Communication	How open and effective are the communication media?

4.3 Defining Trust Building and Maintenance Process

Each virtual community member should define processes for trust building and maintenance process. Research from [13] for example has examined and defined a five-stage process of building trust presented in Table 4.2. These processes overlap and are reinforced, but there is a level of shift over time. The initial expectation of trust is based on the transference of members - both in face-to-face and virtual communities- followed by the intentionality process driven by personalisation. Over time, information gleaned from virtual interactions will evoke the predictability and capability processes. For most of the virtual community's life, all these processes are likely to operate in concert in developing trust. Although, [13] has taken a pragmatic assumption that building trust is a linear progression. Yet, at the same time, because of the fact that trust may break down and have to re-start, the linear progression of trust may be inhibited. Thus, in each of the linear stages of building trust, there should be a mechanism for its maintenance.

Table 4.2. Trust Building Processes

Trust Process	Factors for Building Trust in virtual teams
Calculative	Involvement of professional networks Define and agree on team rules Assigning power to execute punishment Disclosure of potential gains and losses Multi-modal communication
Competence	Disclosure and resolution on status, power, expertise of members Multi-modal communication Level of shared experiences Reputation information
Predictive	Reputation information Social information exchange Frequent task-based interaction
Intentionality	Amount of social dialogue Length of relationship Identification of shared team goals
Transference	Basic communication Individual propensity Having information about individuals

4.4 Development of Secure Infrastructure to Support Trusted Virtual Communities

We must develop guidelines for the construction of secure infrastructure, which will help to support the development of trusted virtual communities. We need to look in further detail at the level of security required to provide a secure environment for members of trusted virtual communities and if indeed security in any form is actually required in differing environments. Security factors which must be assessed in the creation of trusted virtual communities are presented in Table 4.3.

Table 4.3. Security Factors

Security Factor	Types of questions which need to be addressed
Authentication	- What level of authentication do we need for members of the trusted virtual community? - Who is going to be responsible for managing the authentication process?
Authorisation	- How can we ensure that unauthorised parites cannot access the trusted virtual community? - Who is going to manage authorisation?
Integrity	- How can our trusted virtual communtiy members be sure that messages from other members have not been altered? - How can we prevent messages within the virtual community from being modified?
Privacy	- Do messages within the trusted virtual community need to be encrypted? - For whom do messages need to be encrypted i.e. should all members be able to read all messages? - Who is going to manage encryption/decryption key distribution?
Audit and Enforcement	- Do we need to monitor activities within the trusted virtual community? - What should the procedures be and how can we enforce them?

4.5 Development of Trust Development and Management Frameworks

Development of trust management frameworks and tools should not be merely seen as a cryptographer's problem in ensuring a trust within virtual communities. While, the authors recommend for proper implementation of security infrastructure, other issues such a policies, legal and financial issues should be integrated to any framework or tool for trust development and management.

5   Conclusions and Future Work

Developing and managing trust online is not a straightforward task. The absence of face-to-face contact makes the sources of trust in virtual communities fundamentally different. This paper has discussed the potential benefits and barriers to the introduction of trust development and management in virtual communities. Mechanisms for building and managing such a trusted virtual community has been proposed and presented. Mechanisms presented in the paper are at a high level and conceptual, further research will be carried out in order to formalize, test and implement the model.

The authors have submitted grant applications to the UK Engineering and Physical Sciences Research Council (EPSRC) and UK Economic and Social Research Council (ESRC) to generate financial support towards the development of a trust development and management framework.

References

[1] Bergey et al. Why Reengineering Projects Fail. Technical Report. Carnegie Mellon University. CMU/SEI-99-TR-010 ESC-TR-99-010. 1999

[2] Childnet International. Online Grooming and UK Law. See http://www.childnet-int.org/downloads/online%20grooming.pdf (December 2003)

[3] Cialdini, R.The triple tumor structure of organizational behavior. In Codes of Conduct Messick, D.M. and Tenbrunsel, A.E. (eds). New York, Russel Sage Foundation. 1996

[4] Corritore, C., Wiedenbeck, S. and Kracher, B. 2001, The elements of online trust, *Proceedings Conference on Human Factors and Computing Systems,* Washington, 2001: 504-505, Available: http://portal.acm.org/tosem/

[5] Creed, W.D. and Miles, R.E. Trust in Organizations: a conceptual framework linking organizational forms, managerial philosophies, and the opportunity of costs of controls. In Trust in Organizations, Kramer,R.M and Tyler, T.R. (eds), Thousand Oaks, CA, Sage, 1996, pp16-38

[6] Fukuyama, F. The Virtual Handshake: E-Commerce and the Challenge of Trust. Merrill Lynch Forum White Paper, 2001 see http://www.ml.com/woml/forum/ecommerce1.htm (December 2003)

[7] Glass, R. Software Runaways. Pearson Education POD; 1st edition, ISBN: 013673443X, 1998

[8] Grandison, T and Sloman, M,*"A Survey of Trust in Internet Applications"*,IEEE Communications Surveys and Tutorials, Fourth Quarter 2000, http://www.comsoc.org/pubs/surveys/

[9] Her Majesty's Stationery Office. The Electronic Signatures Regulations 2002. Statutory Instrument 2002, No.318, Crown Copyright

[10] Hitchings, J (1995). Deficiencies of the traditional approach to information security and the requirements for a new methodology. Computers and Security, 14, p377-389

[11] Hoffman, D., L., Thomas, P., N. and Peralta, M. 1999, Building Consumer Trust Online, *Communications of ACM* [Electronic], vol. 42, no. 4, pp. 80-85, Available: http://portal.acm.org/tosem/

[12] Ishaya, T and Macaulay, L (2003) Establishing E-Commerce Customer-Supplier Trust. In Proceedings of IEEE 3rd International Interdissciplinary Conference on Electronic Commerce (ECOM-03), October 16-18 2003, Gdansk, Poland.

[13] Ishaya, T., and Macaulay, L. (1999) "The role of trust in virtual teams ". Electronic Journal of Organizational Virtualness 1(1): 140-157, ISSN:1422-9331.

[14] Jarvenpaa, S.R., Knoll, K., and Leidner, D.E.(1998) Is anybody Out There? Antecedents of Trust in Global Virtal Teams. *Journal of Management Information Systems,* Vol. 14 No.4 (*spring* 1998), 29-64.

[15] Jones, S., Wilikens, M., Morris, P. and Masera M. 2000, Trust Requirement in E-Business, *Communications of ACM* [Electronic], vol. 43, no. 12, pp. 81-87, Available: http://portal.acm.org/tosem/

[16] Lane, C., and Bachmann, R. (eds). Tust within and between organisations. Oxford University Press (1998).

[17] Lewicki, R., and Bunker, B. (1996) Developing and Maintaining trust in work relation-ships. *Trust in Organisations,* Kramer, R and Tyler, T (Eds) Sage publications, Thousand Oaks, Calif., (1996), 114-139.

[18] Mayer, R.C., Davis, J.H., and Schoorman, F.D. An integrative model of organisational trust. *Academy of Management Review, 20,3*(1995) 709-734.

[19] McKnight, H., Choudhury, V. and Kacmar, C. 2002, The Impact of initial consumer trust on intentions to transact with web site: a trust building model, *Strategic Information System* [Electronic], Special Issue "Trust in the Digital Economy" Volume 11 Issues 3-4, Available: www.sciencedirect.com

[20] Papadopoulou, P., Andreou, A., Kanellis, P. and Martakos, D. 2001, Trust and relation-ship building in electronic commerce, *Internet Research* [Electronic], vol. 11, issue 4, pp. 322-332, Available: http://proquest.umi.com

[21] Schneier, B. Beyond Fear: Thinking Sensibly About Security in an Uncertain World, Springer-Verlag New York Inc.; ISBN: 0387026207, 2003

[22] Shneiderman, B. 2002, Designing Trust Into Online Experiences, *Communications of ACM* [Electronic], vol. 43, no. 12, pp. 57-59, Available: http://portal.acm.org/tosem/

[23] UK Cabinet Office. Review of Major Government IT Projects. Successful IT: Modern-ising Government in Action.

[24] Kramer, R. Trust and Distrust in Organisations: Emerging Perspectives, Enduring Ques-tions, Annual Reviewof Psychology, 1999

[25] Viller, S. and Sommerville, I. Social analysis in the requirements engineering process: from ethnography to method. IEEE Conference on Requirements Engineering, 1999, 6-13

Managing Internet-Mediated Community Trust Relations

Michael Grimsley[1], Anthony Meehan[2], and Anna Tan[3]

[1] Centre for Regional, Economic and Social Research, Sheffield Hallam University,
Pond Street, Sheffield, UK, S1 1WB
m.f.grimsley@shu.ac.uk
[2] Security and Requirements Group, Computing Department, The Open University,
Walton Hall, Milton Keynes, UK, MK7 6AA
a.s.meehan@open.ac.uk
[3] London Borough of Camden, Town Hall Extension
Argyle Street, London WC1H 8NG, UK
anna.tan@camden.gov.uk

Abstract. This paper advances a framework for analysing and managing community trust relations. The framework is based upon an analysis of the evidence for different forms of trust in community relations and of the experiential dimensions of community relations that promote trust levels. It features a community trust cycle, a trust compact and an experience management matrix which collectively support managers in addressing the relational dynamics of community trust relations. We show that this framework can be used to analyse relations that are mediated by ICT and that the framework supports the identification of opportunities to better promote ICT-mediated trust development and promulgation.

1 Introduction

We are interested in providing information and communication technologies (ICT) to mediate the trust-based relationship between communities and participative organisations and institutions. Specifically, we are engaged in a research programme to identify principles and develop frameworks that designers and managers of ICT can use that facilitate community processes and the achievement of community objectives through the medium of trust.

We view trust as making possible the achievement of community objectives that would not be attainable in its absence [1], [2]. Lin and Warren observe that trust enables people to form more extensive cooperative networks, and to benefit from the more extensive cooperation [3], [4]. Community-based trust relations are an expression (possibly the principal expression) of a community's capacity to cooperate to achieve a better quality of life than would otherwise be available if its members acted merely as individuals.

C.D. Jensen et al. (Eds.): iTrust 2004, LNCS 2995, pp. 277–290, 2004.

Within a community individuals relate to a wide range of institutions: families, voluntary organisations, cultural and community associations, institutions providing public services and democratic and legislative fora. Relations with and between these institutions all operate on the basis of some level of mutual trust. Institutions tend to have a consultative and/or representative function, through which members express views and seek to exert influence. They also feature some kind of support or service function which, at its most general, is the medium through which benefits of participation are realised (emotional support, health care, community housing, social and/or cultural identity).

Trust allows all parties in a relationship to avoid the transaction costs involved in enforcing and regulating cooperation through detailed contracts, establishing monitoring and regulating bodies, managing litigation and maintaining a legal framework that is concerned with specifying conditions for cooperation and responding to breaches of agreement [5].

Further, it is clear that regulatory behaviours have associated opportunity costs. The diminution of regulatory effort facilitated by trust allows the realisation of opportunities, otherwise denied, to engage in new and more diverse community relations. If, in turn, these new relations are, or come to be, conducted on the basis of trust, then there is the prospect of something of a 'virtuous spiral' of trust promulgation in the community.

This view of trust suggests that one strategy for promoting trust-based community participation and is to identify the elements of positive trust relations that exist between members of a community and its participative institutions and thence seek ways to enhance access to these relations and, indeed, extending this opportunity to those who are otherwise socially excluded. This is one part of a vision for e-Democracy which recognises that ICT can mediate relations between community members and participative agencies.

The remainder of this paper elaborates a framework for managing community trust relations and illustrates its use in the context of a case study. In section 2 we review the evidence for the relation between levels of community trust and peoples experience of community institutions (and public services in particular). In section 3 we use this analysis to develop a framework for managing trust relations. Section 4 uses the framework to reflect upon a prominent experiment in ICT-mediated community participation undertaken in the London Borough of Camden. Section 5 makes some concluding remarks and describes future work.

2   Experiential Trust in Communities

In this section we outline the relational basis of trust within communities. We distinguish between two forms of trust (horizontal and vertical) and describe the connection between people's experience of relations with community institutions and levels of both these forms of trust.

In addition, we have identified three experiential factors of relations between community members and service providers that appear to underpin expressed levels of trust. The first of these was how well informed people felt in relation to these community services. The second was the extent to which they felt an enhanced sense of control in their personal lives as a result of the relationship. The third was the extent to which people felt they were able to influence provision of services in the community.

In the remainder of this section we summarise previous work which provides evidence for different forms of trust and for the experiential dimensions of trust in turn. The results in this section arise from two large-scale community surveys. The South Yorkshire Social Capital Survey (SYSCS) [6] was designed and supervised by a local consortium of governmental and non-governmental agencies. Households were randomly sampled and one adult per sampled household was interviewed. Responses from 4220 individuals were obtained. The Housing and Regeneration in Coalfield Communities (HARCC) Survey [7] was commissioned by the Housing Corporation and the South Yorkshire Coalfields Health Action Zone. This postal survey, in which more than one person per household was sampled, obtained 1341 responses. The surveys were independent of each other. (For a fuller account, see [8].)

2.1   Horizontal and Vertical Trust

Community-based trust has two distinct components corresponding to so-called horizontal and vertical trust [9]. Horizontal trust arises from relations between family, friends, neighbours, etc. Vertical trust arises from relations with local councils and providers of public services (we examined relations with schools, health facilities, transport, environment, police, civic planning, local amenities, and others). These two forms of trust appear correlated ($r \approx 0.2$; $p \approx 0.01$). Having established sound evidence of two distinct, but correlated, dimensions of community trust, all of our subsequent analyses treat these trust components independently.

2.2   Experiential Dimensions of Trust

There appear to be at least three experiential dimensions arising from relations between members of a community and community institutions or agencies. We characterise these components as *information*, *control* and *influence*.

Information. The information component represents the extent to which experience of any relationship contributes to a person's sense of being well informed. There is a strong, positive, relationship between how well informed individuals feel and the levels of both vertical and horizontal trust expressed.

Control. The control component captures the extent to which the quality of any relationship contributes to a person's sense of control in their personal life. This is characterised by an awareness of there being 'more means to achieve any one goal or aspiration', which we have called the 'opportunity space'. There is a strong, positive, relationship between perceptions of personal control and the level of vertical trust expressed. The relation to horizontal trust is weaker, but still significant.

Influence. The influence component reflects the extent to which a person feels able to influence decision-making via the relation. Fig. 3(a-b) illustrates the relation between perceptions of personal influence and levels of trust. There is a strong, positive, relationship between perceptions of personal control and the level of vertical trust expressed. The relation to horizontal trust is weaker, but also significant.

3   Framework for Analysing and Managing Internet-Mediated Community Trust Relations

We have seen that, from the point of view of community relations, two forms of trust are (partially) determined by three experiential variates. The identification of these variates, and their role in promoting trust, suggests that they should each be addressed in planning and managing relations between community members and community institutions. The framework we present aims to support that objective.

The framework has three elements. The first is a *Community Trust Cycle* which illustrates the trust-based relation between community members and community institutions. The second is a *Community Trust Compact* which is used to negotiate shared understanding of the trust relationship. The third is the *Experience Management Matrix*, which supports each party in determining its participative strategy.

3.1 Community Trust Cycle

The Community Trust Cycle (Fig. 1) provides a framework for understanding the generation and propagation of trust arising from relations within a community [8], [10]. Horizontal trust is generated and expressed in relations with peers in the community. Vertical trust is generated and expressed in relations with community institutions. Levels of trust are promoted by a sense of being able to influence the policies and practice of the community and its institutions. Experience of the support and/or service function of these institutions and amenities also reinforces trust. In this case, two experiential factors are at work, the quality and quantity of information available and the extent to which the support/service relation facilitates a sense of enhanced control or autonomy in the community.

ICT has a number of distinctive roles in mediating the trust relations in this cycle. It can contribute to the connectivity of community, e.g., at the level of family, friends, neighbourhoods, community organisations; it can facilitate contributions to the formation of policy and, of course, to the election of officers/representatives; it can disseminate information about the role of community institutions and can mediate peoples interactions with those agencies.

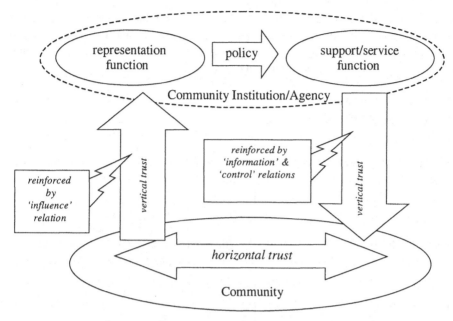

Fig. 1. Community Trust Cycle

3.2   Community Trust Compact

The Community Trust Compact is an agreement between the parties to a trust-based relation that establishes the basis of participation (a compact is a voluntary, as opposed to enforceable, agreement). In some cases it may be formally negotiated and agreed, but in others it may be informal or even assumed. The compact we propose is structured to reflect Simons's systems to facilitate empowerment in a relationship [11]. A similar approach has been used by Duane and Finnegan to develop a management framework for managing employee empowerment and control in an intranet [12]. In the contexts considered by Simons, and later by Duane and Finnegan, one party has both power and authority over another. Accordingly, we have sought to adapt the scheme to better reflect the fact that the trust-based relationships we seek to support are between parties who share a more subtle and complex distribution of power and authority (e.g., consider the power and authority distribution between and elected council and its electorate, or between a parent and child and a community crèche).

In Fig. 2, we identify the systems which we believe should pertain. The intended outcome of the negotiations over this compact is a shared understanding between the parties as to what services are provided, the values underpinning this provision, the range of entitlements that are available and how these depend upon responsible and trustworthy use of them.

Agreeing and managing the elements of this compact is a significant undertaking, not least in respect of the effectiveness of communication that is needed if trust is not to be undermined during the early stages of a relationship. Parties should seek to nurture the trust relationship, perhaps starting with modest objectives and building towards a capacity to manage significant engagements [13].

Trust Control System (after Simons, 1995)	Activity
Establish Community Values	Consult, discuss, and seek to agree, values that underpin the relationship. Describe high-level behaviours that express these values.
Standardise Entitlement	Agree definition of entitlement. It may be useful to distinguish between equity in a relation (parties have the same opportunities but outcomes/experiences may differ) and equality in a relation (parties experience the same outcome).
Determine Bounded Freedoms	Agree boundaries that denote changed levels of experience of the relationship (often expressed as changed entitlement in the context of service provision).
Define Incentives and Penalties	Identify and agree behaviours that are necessary to make transitions across entitlement boundaries (e.g. enhanced/diminished access or rights).
Monitor Performance	*Jointly* monitor and review adherence to values and behaviours as described above and enact changes to bounded freedoms.

Fig. 2. Activity framework for managing trust-based relations.

3.3 Experience Management Matrix

The Experience Management Matrix is based upon the inter-relation of the three experiential factors we have identified as contributing to trust, information, control and influence. The intuition behind the instrument is that the experiential factors we have identified apply to both parties in a trust-based relationship. Thus, for each party, there is scope for shaping the overall trust relationship by managing the communication of information, the distribution of control and the deployment of influence in respect of the other party. This gives rise to nine separate dynamics in the trust relation, each of which features a range or scale of behaviours that will shape the experience of the other party (Fig. 3)

Project Activity	Target Experience in Community Group/Agency		
	Sense of being well-informed	Sense of personal control	Sense of being able to influence
Information Strategy	How should information be structured and organised to promote well-informedness? Address the volume, quality, and scope (breadth) of information, and the effectiveness with which it is communicated.	What information is needed and how can it be organised to promote a sense of personal control? Address the information needed to make clear the scope for alternative courses of action/opportunity.	What information is needed to facilitate the formation of informed views and how to convey them appropriately and effectively? What information is needed to provide evidence that community views have been considered and/or acted upon?
Distribution of Control	With whom should the initiative lie in the elicitation/provision of information? For each information element of the information strategy (see row 1, above) determine whether it should be reactivly or proactivly communicated.	In persuit of the shared objective of the trust-relationship, how might responsibility for the subtasks and objectives be distributed between the parties? Demonstrate flexible practice (distribution of tasks) in respect of the distinctive needs of each individual, group or agency in the community.	With whom should the initiative lie in the elicitation of views on current and future policy? Establish a consultative dialogue. Adapt (standard) provision in light of expressed needs.
Deployment of Influence	What balanced and (preferably) independent evidence is available to legitimate current policy and practice?	How might perceptions of needs be changed so that any diminution of the space of alternative courses of action/opportunity is not experienced as a diminution of a sense of control?	What negotiation strategies will be perceived as trustworthy? Adopt coordinative (recognises others priorities) or even integrative (trades off own low priorities if they meet other party's high priorities) negotiation styles.

Fig. 3. Experience Management Matrix - nine dynamics arise from the 'product' of the three experiential factors promoting trust in a two-party relationship. The approach each party takes to the development and management these strategies (triggered by the questions featured in the cells of the matrix) will determine the experience of the other party or parties in the relation in such in such a way as to promote or undermine trust.

To illustrate the use of the matrix, we provide some examples of how these dynamics may be elaborated. First, consider the problem of determining an information strategy that will engender a sense of being well informed in the second party (row 1, column 1 of the matrix in Fig. 3). Complex organisations need complex structures to organise the information they need to convey to widely differing parties. Key issues include determining an appropriate volume of information to be provided (more is not always better), the quality and depth of the information (e.g. accuracy/clarity/ accessibility), and the scope of the information (e.g. does it cover the most common/basic requirements, does it extend to special/unusual requirements, does it refer to alternative, possibly competing, sources of support/service).

Second, consider how the control available to one party can be deployed to induce a sense of being well informed in the other party (row 2, column 1 of the matrix in Fig. 3). In relation to provision of information, the experiential scale has two poles: the first represents a purely reactive strategy for information provision (information is provided only when asked for), the alternate pole is proactive information provision.

Finally, consider how the deployment of influence may promote a sense of being well informed (row 3, column 1 of the matrix in Fig. 3). The experiential dimension in this case ranges from absence or denial of access to information which has been used to inform policy through to the elicitation of evidence, and provision of a clear rationale, for current policy. (The positive effect of this strategy is enhanced if the evidence is seen to be independent.)

4   Applying the Framework

In this section, we shall give an illustration of how the framework may be applied. The framework can be used in the *de novo* development of a project. However, as in this example, it can be used in a 'sense-making' context: here we analyse the evolution of a project designed to enhance access to public advice services in North London.

4.1   CamdenNet and CASweb

CamdenNet (www.camdennet.org.uk) provides community groups in the London Borough of Camden with an online computer presence. CamdenNet allows individual community groups to:

- promote functions and services
- publicise events and announce news
- hold online discussions
- conduct surveys and polls
- allow people to download forms, reports, leaflets, etc

Community sites are self-administered by authorised administrators who configure the site, manage content and control access.

CamdenNet is an initiative by the London Borough of Camden as part of their strategy to support the work of local community organisations. Currently, there are twenty-nine groups using the services. Their fields of interest are diverse, including ethnic minority cultural associations, Lesbian & Gay associations, elderly groups, regeneration initiatives, self-help, residents & tenants associations, young peoples' organisations, parents groups, conservation groups.

Conceptually, CASweb has its origins in CamdenNet but is a distinct project, due for launch in March 2004. CASweb is an initiative from five Local Authorities (Boroughs) of the London Central Partnership (Camden, Islington, Kensington & Chelsea, Westminster and City of London), supported by the Office of The Deputy Prime Minister. The aim of the CASweb project is to improve the quality and accessibility of public advice services available to residents of the boroughs. The strategy is based upon use of internet technology to enhance public access to advice services, facilitate sharing of successful practice between agencies. There is also an aspiration on the part of the funding bodies to realise efficiencies in advice service provision.

As with CamdenNet, CASweb will provide community advice agencies with an online computer presence. CASweb provides the same basic tools and capacities as CamdenNet (see above). However, more interestingly, the architecture of CASweb has significant enhancements which are specifically designed to promote inter-agency awareness and communication and cooperation. The most prominent enhancements are a communication model which features extensive opportunities for dialogue and discussion between agencies together with a document and knowledge sharing layer. Viewed by its developers as an Advice Service Portal, CASweb features include promoting awareness of:

- most active discussion fora
- newest discussion fora
- most widely referenced 'sharable' documents
- most recently posted 'sharable' documents
- randomly selected news stories from across participants' sites
- randomly selected events from across participants' sites
- a randomly selected 'featured site'
- active member and user surveys & polls
- directory of CASweb registered services

Advice agencies apply to the council for access to the CASweb service. The project staff supports agencies in designing their site, largely through the provision of technical training in the use of a range of software tools that the project has developed. Agency sites are self-administered – each agency registers one or more administrators who have authority to manage site content and control access.

4.2 Sense-Making – Applying the Trust Management Framework

The concept and forms of trust, as social capital, which we have explored above, applies extensively in understanding these projects and, in particular, when interpreting the evolution of the CamdenNet architecture to that of CASweb. This becomes more evident when we consider this evolution through the 'lens' of the framework we introduced in section 3. We shall apply each element of the framework, in turn.

Cycle of trust propagation. The cycle of trust propagation (Fig. 1) provides a means by which we identify the relevant community and institutions and the trust relations and forms of trust which arise therefrom. In the case in point at least three viewpoints can be taken. The first concerns the trust relation between the borough councils of the partnership and the community groups and their managers and administrators who support their individual sites. The second concerns the relation between those who are individual participants in the community group (in many cases, users of their information services) and the community groups/agencies as community institutions. The composition of these two viewpoints yields a third trust relation, which represents the relation between community group participants and the borough councils (this is the relation that is mediated through the auspices of community group/agency). There is insufficient space in this paper to consider all of these relational perspectives here – for purposes of illustration we consider only the first.

In both cases, the community layer is populated not by individuals in the community but by individual community groups (CamdenNet) or individual advice agencies (CASweb). In each case, these groups are very diverse. They vary in many degrees e.g. of specialisation, professionalisation, funding basis, etc. Further, the groups and agencies vary in the nature and quality of their relations between each other; not least because the social, legal, political and economic environment they operate in produce both cooperative incentives and competitive tensions [13]. The promotion of trust, and specifically horizontal trust, between these community groups/agencies will be a significant enabler for sharing of successful practice.

The Borough Councils of Camden and of the London Central Partnership constitute the institution element of the model, respectively. The relationship between community groups/advice agencies and borough councils can be complex. For example, many advice agencies will seek to preserve an identity that is independent of their local council (not least because they may advise individuals in relation to council services). Hence, the introduction of infrastructual support, in the form of CASweb, by the five councils of the partnership, is not without its derivative tensions.

Vertical trust derives from the community groups' experience of the Camden-Net/CASweb 'service'. The project workers address the issues of promoting a sense of being well-informed and sense of enhanced control through the provision of training a support of site administrators and of granting those administrators a high level of autonomy in managing their respective sites.

Trust Compact. CamdenNet and CASweb may be compared using the Trust Compact (The results are presented in Fig. 4).

Trust System	CamdenNet/CASweb
Establish Community Values	Values in CamdenNet were implicit – summarised by the criteria used for registration represented as 'public interest, not-for-profit'. In CASweb the desire to promote trust-based cooperation between agencies has led to additional values related to the themes of contributing and sharing.
Standardise Entitlement	Equality: participating agencies enjoy the same provision without any (initial) distinction as to their 'constitutional character' (e.g. whether they are statutory/voluntary or professional/non-professional). Equity: agencies are treated in the same way. However, CASweb supports 'kite-marking' which differentiate service providers on the basis of assessments by independent third parties, such as professional associations or funding agencies.
Determine Bounded Freedoms	Largely undefined in either project. In both cases there is an implicit boundary signalled by the existence of an informal procedure for managing complaints against agencies. The additional values of CASweb imply there may be other boundaries, e.g., absence of sharing behaviour.
Define Incentives and Penalties	Also largely undefined in both cases. The values (above) imply an appreciation of the value of participation and sharing but there is currently no explicit articulation of this incentive. The existence of penalties is indicated indirectly through reference to a complaint procedure.
Monitor Performance	Procedures for monitoring are undefined. The existence of a complaint procedure which may be initiated by a member of the public or by another group/agency implies that responsibility for monitoring lies with community members.

Fig. 4. Trust Compact used to compare projects.

Experience Management Matrix. Finally, we shall apply the Experience Management Matrix in making the comparison. The result of this is presented in Fig. 5.

Project Activity	Sense of being well-informed	Target Experience in Group/Agency	
		Sense of control	Sense of influence
Information Strategy	Well-developed promotional and technical materials provided for participants of both projects.	Comprehensive information and training is available to support agencies in designing and managing their web presence.	Participating agencies are actively encouraged to contribute ideas for additional CamdenNet/CASweb functions.
Distribution of Control	Highly proactive disemination strategy. Active networking amongst community groups and advice workers by project officers.	Both projects are characterised by participants having a high degree of control in the functioning of their service from the outset. This is achieved through training of agency-based administrators. The additional facilities of CASweb represent a significant enhancement the space of possible actions or opportunities, *one of the defining characteristics of an increased sense of control.*	Ongoing consultative dialogue with agencies, especially when site are being developed initially. Highly adaptable provision in light of initially expressed and then developing needs. CASweb has included functions suggested by participants thus providing evidence of influence to those participants.
Deployment of Influence	CamdenNet and CASweb have recently sought involvement of independent researchers who will provide balanced and independent evaluation of current and evolving policy.	Perceptions of needs are influenced through the provision of additional tools for participants. Influence may be represented as by the expression *the medium is the message.*	CamdenNet and CASweb team seeks to be highly responsive to expressed needs of participating agencies.

Fig. 5. Experience Management Matrix comparison of the CamdenNet and CASweb projects

The framework has served to clarify the trust-relations at work in both projects. Applying the Community Trust Cycle introduced an important distinction to be made when identifying 'the community'. On this occasion, we have avoid the possible confusion between a community of groups/agencies with the community of individual users of those bodies (these relations should be analysed separately).

The components of the Trust Compact indicate that, for both projects, there may be something to be gained from making more explicit many of the values, boundaries, incentives, etc. that are currently implicit. Indeed, the communication that is necessary between all parties involved in such a task will, when managed appropriately, promote trust levels and cooperation.

The completion of the Experience Management Matrix indicates that the thrust of the CASweb development has been two-pronged: enhancing a sense of control in the participating agencies by increasing the space of possible actions they can take, with a clear emphasis on actions that constitute cooperation with other agencies, thus promoting horizontal trust; enhance a sense of influence by responding to expressed needs. These are important developments but the absence of comparable developments in relation to the other experiential dynamics points to a future agenda.

5 Conclusion and Future Work

On the basis of earlier research which identified different forms of trust within a community, and of the experiential dimensions of community relations that appeared to promote trust levels, we have advanced a framework for analysing and managing community trust relations. The framework features a community trust cycle, a trust compact and an experience management matrix which collectively support managers in addressing the relational dynamics of community trust relations. We have shown that this framework can be used to analyse relations that are mediated by ICT and that the framework supports the identification of opportunities to promote trust development and promulgation.

Future work will focus upon evaluating the medium and long-term effectiveness of the CASweb service (launched in March 2004) in terms of promoting trust-based expressions of cooperative behaviour between participating agencies.

References

1. Coleman, J.: Foundations of Social Theory. Harvard University Press, Cambridge, MA. 1990.
2. Fukuyama, F.: The Social Virtues and the Creation of Prosperity, London, Free Press, 1995
3. Lin, N.: Social Capital: a Theory of Social Structure and Action. Cambridge: Cambridge University Press, 2001

4. Warren, M.E.: Social Capital and Corruption. In: Dario Castiglione: Social Capital: Inter-disciplinary Perspectives. EURESCO conference on Social Capital, Exeter, UK, 15-20 September 2001.
5. Smith, C.: Trust in Social Relations: Building Confidence and Missing the Target, 2nd Workshop on Trust Within and Between Organisations, Amsterdam, October 2003, European Institute for Advanced Studies in Management (EIASM), 2003.
6. Green. G., Grimsley, M., Suokas A., et al: Social Capital, Health and Economy in South Yorkshire Coalfield Communities. Centre for Regional Economic and Social Research, Sheffield Hallam University, Oct 2000.
7. Green, G., Grimsley, M., Stafford, B.: Capital Accounting for Neighbourhood Sustainability, Centre for Regional Economic and Social Research, Sheffield Hallam University 2001.
8. Grimsley, M, Meehan, A, Green, G, Stafford, B,: Social Capital and Community Trust and e-Government Services. In P. Nixon and S. Terzis (eds.): First International Conference on Trust Management, Hiraklion, Crete, Greece, May 2003. Lecture Notes in Computer Science (LNCS 2692) Springer-Verlag, Berlin Heidelberg 2003, pp165-178
9. Braithwaite, V., Levi, M. (eds): Trust and Governance. New York: Russell Sage Foundation, 1998
10. Grimsley, M, Meehan, A, Green, G, Stafford, B,: Enhancing social capital and community trust through the design of technologically mediated access to government and public services, 2nd Workshop on Trust Within and Between Organisations, Amsterdam, October 2003, European Institute for Advanced Studies in Management (EIASM), 2003.
11. Simons, R.: Levers of Control. Harvard Business School Press, Boston MA. 1995.
12. Duane, A. and Finnegan, P.: Managing empowerment and control in an intranet environment. Information Systems Journal 13 (2), 133-158.
13. Vangen, S. and Huxman, C.: Nurturing Collaborative Relations. Journal of Applied Behavioural Science. Vol. 39 No. 1, March 2003, 5-31

Reasoning About Trust:
A Formal Logical Framework

Robert Demolombe

ONERA Toulouse
Toulouse, France
Robert.Demolombe@cert.fr

Abstract. There is no consensus about the definition of the concept of
trust. In this paper formal definitions of different kinds of trust are given
in the framework of modal logic. This framework also allows to define a
logic for deriving consequences from a set of assumptions about trust.
Trust is defined as a mental attitude of an agent with respect to some
property held by another agent. These properties are systematically analysed and we propose 6 epistemic properties, 4 deontic properties and 1
dynamic property.
In the second part of the paper more flexible notions of trust are introduced: qualitative graded trust, trust defined in terms of topics and
conditional trust.

1 Introduction

The concept of trust is quite complex, it can be interpreted in many different
ways and there is no consensus about its definition [10,12,14,13,15,7,11,6]. That
is the reason why we believe it is interesting to propose clear definitions that
can be accepted, or rejected, but whose meaning is not a matter of discussion.
That is the main purpose of this paper, and that is why the formal definitions
are presented in formal logic.

In fact, we see three different kinds of problems related to trust. The first
one is to define the facts that support trust. Trust can be supported by series of
observations, or by reputation, or by an analysis of the situation. For example,
one may trust a supplier about his capacity to deliver goods in time because he
observed that in the past goods have been delivered in time, or because many
people say that there are delivered in time, or because he knows the details of
the supplier's organisation and he can conclude that there are good reasons to
believe that they are delivered in time.

The second problem is to find the appropriate rules to derive consequences
of a set of assumptions about trust, where the assumptions may be supported
by the kinds of techniques we have mentioned just before.

The third problem is to use information about trust to take decisions. For
example, if a manager has to assign a task to an employee he may select the
employees in function of his trust about their capacities. We can say that in

C.D. Jensen et al. (Eds.): iTrust 2004, LNCS 2995, pp. 291–303, 2004.
© Springer-Verlag Berlin Heidelberg 2004

general trust is used to complete our lack of information. It is better to have uncertain information derived from trust than to have nothing.

In this paper, in addition to a formal analysis of the definition of trust, we concentrate on reasoning about trust. That is we ignore the first and the third problems. Notice that the three problems can be investigated independently.

The starting point of our analysis is that trust is a mental attitude of an agent with respect to another agent [1]. Here we take agent in a very broad sense. An agent may a human agent or an artificial agent like a robot, or a sensor, or a program.

This attitude is a sort of belief about some property of an agent. Here we distinguish what we call belief, strong belief and knowledge. We say that an agent believes that some proposition holds if he has some justification for this belief and he believes that his justification may be wrong. For example, I believe that John is not at the University because his car is not at the parking. I know that sometimes John comes using a bicycle, therefore I may be wrong, but this justification is better than complete ignorance and it is enough to support my belief.

We say that an agent strongly believes that some proposition holds if he has some justification for his belief and he believes that this justification is true, though in reality it may be false. For example, I strongly believe that John is at the University because his car is at the parking and I believe he his the only driver of his car.

Finally, we say that an agent knows that some proposition holds if he has some justification for his knowledge and this justification is a true justification. For example, I know that John is at the University because I see him.

In the context of trust no information can be taken as a true information in the sense of knowledge. Then, if we say that some agent a trusts b with respect to some property that means that a strongly believes that b satisfies this property.

Now we can make more specific which kind of property may be trusted. In a previous work [4] we have only considered epistemic properties, like sincerity and credibility (see also [3]). Here we have also considered deontic properties like honesty, and dynamic properties like capacity.

In the section 2 of this paper we analyse epistemic properties, and in the section 3 we analyse deontic and dynamic properties. Finally, in the section 4 more flexible definitions are proposed. They include qualitative graded trust, synthetic trust about topics and conditional trust.

2   Trust about Epistemic Properties

To define epistemic properties we consider to what extend one of the following facts implies another one. These facts are denoted by:

---

[1] Here we take inspiration from a talk given by Andrew J.I. Jones in an informal workshop organised at the University of Lisbon in September 1997. One of his intuitive ideas is that "agent a trusts agent b if a believes that b will act in accordance with a norm which a believes b accepts". More details can be found in [9].

p: it is the case that p.

$B_a p$: the agent a believes that p is the case.

$I_{a,b}p$ the agent a has informed the agent b that p is the case.

Then, the epistemic properties are defined as follows.

Sincerity. The agent b is sincere with regard to a for p iff if b informs a about p then b believes p. This property is formally represented by:

$$I_{b,a}p \rightarrow B_b p$$

Cooperativity. The agent b is cooperative with regard to a for p iff if b believes p then b informs a about p. That intuitively means that b does not hide p to a. This property is formally represented by:

$$B_b p \rightarrow I_{b,a}p$$

Credibility. The agent b is credible (or competent) about p iff if b believes p then p is the case. This property is formally represented by:

$$B_b p \rightarrow p$$

Vigilance. The agent b is vigilant about p iff if p is the case then b believes p. For example, in an airport the fact that an air traffic controller is vigilant about the fact that some aircraft has landed means that if the aircraft has landed the controller believes that it has landed. This property is formally represented by:

$$p \rightarrow B_b p$$

Validity. The agent b is valid with regard to a for p iff if b informs a about p then p is the case. For example, if the agent b is a sensor used to detect that a door is open, b is valid about the fact that the door is open means that if b sends the information that the door is open, then it is the case that the door is open. This property is formally represented by:

$$I_{b,a}p \rightarrow p$$

Completeness. The agent b is complete with regard to a for p iff if p is the case then b informs a about p. In the example of the sensor that means that if the door is open then the sensor sends the information that the door is open. This property is formally represented by:

$$p \rightarrow I_{b,a}p$$

Notice that all these definitions are defined in terms of implications. It may be tempting to define them in terms of conjunctions. For example, one could consider a definition of credibility of the form $(B_b p) \wedge p$. However, it is clear that the fact that b is **not** credible means that b believes p and p is not the case, which is represented by $(B_b p) \wedge \neg p$ which is logically equivalent to the negation of $B_b p \rightarrow p$, and it is not equivalent to the negation of $(B_b p) \wedge p$. The same argument can be used to convince ourselves that the other definitions must also be defined with an implication.

It can also be noticed that all these properties are pairwise independent. For example, an agent may be sincere and not cooperative, and he may be as well cooperative and not sincere. However, three, or more, properties may be related. For example, validity is a consequence of sincerity and credibility, and completeness is a consequence of vigilance and cooperativity (see section 2.3).

2.1   Formal Definitions of Trust

Now we can define trust about these properties. We adopt the following notation:

$K_a p$: the agent a strongly believes that p is the case.

For the formal definitions we consider a modal propositional language with the modal operators we have presented above (see [2]).

We say, for example, that the agent a trusts b for his sincerity about p iff a strongly believes that b is sincere about p.

Trust is a mental attitude that is expressed in terms of strong beliefs because if the agent a does not believe that his justifications are true justifications, then that means that a may have some doubts about b's sincerity, and in that case we cannot say that a really trusts b.

Trust of the agent a with regard to b about p for the property $prop$ is denoted by $Tprop_{a,b}p$. Then, trust for sincerity, cooperativity, credibility, vigilance, validity and completeness are respectively denoted by: $Tsinc_{a,b}(p)$, $Tcoop_{a,b}(p)$, $Tcred_{a,b}(p)$, $Tvigi_{a,b}(p)$, $Tval_{a,b}(p)$ and $Tcomp_{a,b}(p)$. Their formal definitions are:

$$Tsinc_{a,b}(p) \overset{\text{def}}{=} K_a(I_{b,a}p \to B_b p)$$

$$Tcoop_{a,b}(p) \overset{\text{def}}{=} K_a(B_b p \to I_{b,a}p)$$

$$Tcred_{a,b}(p) \overset{\text{def}}{=} K_a(B_b p \to p)$$

$$Tvigi_{a,b}(p) \overset{\text{def}}{=} K_a(p \to B_b p)$$

$$Tval_{a,b}(p) \overset{\text{def}}{=} K_a(I_{b,a}p \to p)$$

$$Tcomp_{a,b}(p) \overset{\text{def}}{=} K_a(p \to I_{b,a}p)$$

The formal definitions of the epistemic properties can be criticised because they are based on the material implication. That leads to a well known paradox. For example, for the definition of sincerity we can infer that b is sincere with regard to a for p in the situation where b has not informed a about p (i.e. when we have $\neg I_{b,a}p$). In other terms, an agent who says nothing is sincere.

The intuitive definition of sincerity should be that in every circumstances where b informs a about p then b believes p. This raises the well known issue of the formal representation of entailment which has no satisfactory solution.

To avoid too complex definitions we have accepted material implication, but since in the definition of trust the material implication is in the scope of the modal operator K_a the consequences are less dramatic. Nevertheless, if a strongly believes that it is not the case that b has informed a about p (i.e. $K_a(\neg I_{b,a}p)$) then we can infer that a trusts b about b's sincerity. In the section 4, for the formalisation of graded trust we have used a conditional connective that avoids these problems.

2.2 Axiomatics

In addition to the axiom schemas and inference rules of propositional logic we have the following axiom schemas and inference rules.

The modal operator B_a obeys the system (KD) (see [2]). Then, in addition to the necessitation rule we have:

$$(K1)\ \ B_a(p \to q) \to (B_ap \to B_aq)$$

$$(D1)\ \ \neg(B_ap \wedge B_a\neg p)$$

The modal operator K_a obeys the system (KD) plus the axiom schema (KT).

$$(K2)\ \ K_a(p \to q) \to (K_ap \to K_aq)$$

$$(D2)\ \ \neg(K_ap \wedge K_a\neg p)$$

$$(KT)\ \ K_a(K_ap \to p)$$

The schema (KT) intuitively means that a believes that what he believes is true. That is, a has no doubt about the truth of p. This schema characterises the notion of strong belief.

The modal operator $I_{a,b}p$ is not a normal operator it is a classical operator according to Chellas's classification [2]. For this operator we only have the rule of substitutivity of equivalent formulas.

$$(RE1)\ \ \frac{\vdash p \leftrightarrow q}{\vdash I_{a,b}p \leftrightarrow I_{a,b}q}$$

These modal operators are not independent. In particular strong beliefs are a special kind of beliefs. Then, we have:

$$(KB)\ \ K_ap \to B_ap$$

Also it is assumed that communication between the agents works perfectly well in the sense that each agent knows which message has been sent or has not been sent. Then we have:

$$(OBS1) \quad I_{b,a}p \to K_a(I_{b,a}p)$$

$$(OBS2) \quad \neg I_{b,a}p \to K_a(\neg I_{b,a}p)$$

2.3   Logical Properties

As mentioned before trust about validity and about completeness are not independent of trust about other properties. We have:

$Tsinc_{a,b}(p) \wedge Tcred_{a,b}(p) \to Tval_{a,b}(p)$

$Tvigi_{a,b}(p) \wedge Tcoop_{a,b}(p) \to Tcomp_{a,b}(p)$

It is also interesting to see what can be infered from the performance of the communication action $I_{b,a}p$ depending on what the agent a trusts. We have:

$Tsinc_{a,b}(p) \to (I_{b,a}p \to K_a(B_bp))$

$Tval_{a,b}(p) \to (I_{b,a}p \to K_ap)$

$Tcoop_{a,b}(p) \to (\neg I_{b,a}p \to K_a(\neg B_bp))$

$Tcomp_{a,b}(p) \to (\neg I_{b,a}p \to K_a(\neg p))$

These properties show that we can infer information from the fact that b has not informed a about p in a similar way as we can infer information from the fact that b has informed a about p.

If we analyse the properties that relates trust for compound formulas of the form $p \wedge q$, $p \vee q$ or $\neg p$, in function of trust for p and q we see that these properties are very weak.

For the conjunction we have the following property if $prop = cred$ or $prop = vigi$ [2]:

$Tprop_{a,b}(p) \wedge Tprop_{a,b}(q) \to Tprop_{a,b}(p \wedge q)$

If for the modality $I_{b,a}$ we accept the axiom schema of monotonicity (M) $I_{b,a}(p \wedge q) \to I_{b,a}(p) \wedge I_{b,a}(q)$ the property holds for $prop = val$ and $prop = sinc$, and if we accept for this modality the axiom schema of closure (C) $I_{b,a}(p) \wedge I_{b,a}(q) \to I_{b,a}(p \wedge q)$ the property holds for $prop = comp$ and $prop = coop$. Acceptation of (M) and (C) comes to accept that saying p and q independently has the same consequences as saying $p \wedge q$.

Notice that the following implication never holds [3].

$Tprop_{a,b}(p \wedge q) \to Tprop_{a,b}(p) \wedge Tprop_{a,b}(q)$

---

[2] We omit the proofs since they are very simple exercises.

[3] This is a bit surprising. For example, if a trusts b for his credibility for $p \wedge q$ (i.e. $K_a(B_b(p \wedge q) \to (p \wedge q)))$ we might expect that a trusts b for his credibility for p (i.e. $K_a(B_bp \to p)$). The reason why this property does not hold is that even if the set of worlds where we have $B_b(p \wedge q)$ is included in the set of worlds where we have $p \wedge q$, we cannot infer that the set of worlds where we have B_bp is included in the set of worlds where we have p.

For the disjunction we have no property. That is $Tprop_{a,b}(p \vee q)$ does not imply $Tprop_{a,b}(p)$, and $Tprop_{a,b}(p)$ does not imply $Tprop_{a,b}(p \vee q)$.

For the negation the only property that holds is:

$Tvigi_{a,b}(p) \rightarrow Tcred_{a,b}(\neg p)$

If we accept the axiom schema $\neg B_a(p) \rightarrow B_a(\neg p)$ the property $Tcred_{a,b}(p)$ $\rightarrow Tvigi_{a,b}(\neg p)$ holds. However, this axiom schema can be accepted only for the agents who have complete beliefs. If they have incomplete beliefs it leads to contradictions [4].

It is tempting to think that trust should be transitive. In fact, and this shows the benefit of formal definitions for reasoning about trust, this is not the case.

For example, if we assume that a trusts b about b's sincerity with regard to a for p, and b trusts c about c's sincerity with regard to b for p, should we infer that a trusts c for c's sincerity with regard to a for p? The answer is "no".

Indeed, in formal terms the question is: does $K_a(I_{b,a}p \rightarrow B_b p)$ and $K_b(I_{c,b}p \rightarrow B_c p)$ implies $K_a(I_{c,a}p \rightarrow B_c p)$? It is easy to define a counter example. Intuitively we can understand that from $K_a I_{c,a}p$ we can infer nothing using a's trust about b and b's trust about c.

However, if b says to a that c is sincere with regard to him (a) for p, and if a trusts that b is valid for what b said, then it can be infered that a trusts that c is sincere with regard to a for p.

The formal proof below shows that from the hypothesis (H1) and (H2) we can infer $Tsinc_{a,c}p$.

(H1) $Tval_{a,b}(I_{c,a}p \rightarrow B_c p)$

(H2) $I_{b,a}(I_{c,a}p \rightarrow B_c p)$

(1) $K_a(I_{b,a}(I_{c,a}p \rightarrow B_c p)) \rightarrow (I_{c,a}p \rightarrow B_c p)$ (H1), (Definitions)

(2) $I_{b,a}(I_{c,a}p \rightarrow B_c p)$ (H2)

(3) $I_{b,a}(I_{c,a}p \rightarrow B_c p) \rightarrow K_a I_{b,a}(I_{c,a}p \rightarrow B_c p)$ (OBS1)

(4) $K_a I_{b,a}(I_{c,a}p \rightarrow B_c p)$ (2), (3), (MP)

(5) $K_a(I_{c,a}p \rightarrow B_c p)$ (1), (4), (K)

(6) $Tsinc_{a,c}(p)$ (5), (Definitions)

3   Trust about Deontic and Dynamic Properties

To define deontic properties we analyse the possible links between the actions performed by the agents on one hand, and the obligations to perform actions on the other hand. The intuitive goal of this analysis is to define the deontic properties of the agents with regard to their fulfillment of a given regulation. We adopt the following notations:

$E_a p$: the agent a brings it about that p.

Op: it is obligatory that p.

As usual permission is defined in function of obligation. We have $Pp \overset{\text{def}}{=} \neg O\neg p$, and Pp is read: it is permitted that p.

---

[4] For example, if the agent a only believes $p \vee q$ we can infer $\neg B_a p$ and $\neg B_a q$, and then $B_a(\neg(p \vee q))$ which contradicts $B_a(p \vee q)$.

We first analyse the links between the fact that a brings it about that p and the fact that it is obligatory that a brings it about that p [5].

Obedience. The agent a is obedient for bringing it about that p iff if it is obligatory that a brings it about that p then a brings it about that p. In short terms, a does what is should do. This property is formally represented by:

$$OE_a p \rightarrow E_a p$$

Laziness. The agent a is lazy for p iff if a brings it about that p then it is obligatory that a brings it about that p. We call this property "laziness" because, by contraposition, if it is not obligatory that a brings it about that p then a does not brings it about that p. In other terms a only does what he is obliged to do. This property is formally represented by:

$$E_a p \rightarrow OE_a p$$

Notice that this definition is logically equivalent to $P\neg E_a p \rightarrow \neg E_a p$.

Now we analyse the links between the facts represented by $E_a p$ and $PE_a p$.

Active. The agent a is active for p iff if it is permitted that a brings it about that p then a brings it about that p. Intuitively that means that a performs an action as soon as it is permitted to perform this action. This property is formally represented by:

$$PE_a p \rightarrow E_a p$$

Honesty. The agent a is honest for p iff if a brings it about that p then it is permitted that a brings it about that p. Then, an honest agent only does what it is permitted to do. This property is formally represented by:

$$E_a p \rightarrow PE_a p$$

Trust about obedience, laziness, active and honesty are respectively denoted by: $Tobed_{a,b}(p)$, $Tlazi_{a,b}(p)$, $Tacti_{a,b}(p)$ and $Thone_{a,b}(p)$. We have the formal definitions:

$$Tobed_{a,b}(p) \overset{\text{def}}{=} K_a(OE_a p \rightarrow E_a p)$$

$$Tlazi_{a,b}(p) \overset{\text{def}}{=} K_a(E_a p \rightarrow OE_a p)$$

$$Tacti_{a,b}(p) \overset{\text{def}}{=} K_a(PE_a p \rightarrow E_a p)$$

$$Thone_{a,b}(p) \overset{\text{def}}{=} K_a(E_a p \rightarrow PE_a p)$$

The axiomatics for reasoning about these properties is defined as follows.

---

[5] Since we are interested by individual properties we have not considered the links between the facts represented by p and Op.

For the operator O we have adopted the simplest logic which is the standard deontic logic (more sophisticated deontic logics can be found in [1]). This logic is formalised by a (KD) system. Then, we have:

$$(K3) \quad O(p \to q) \to (Op \to Oq)$$

$$(D3) \quad \neg(Op \land O\neg p)$$

The E_a operator is a classical operator. It is assumed that this operator is a success operator. Then, we have the inference rule and axiom schema:

$$(RE2) \quad \frac{\vdash p \leftrightarrow q}{\vdash E_a p \leftrightarrow E_a q}$$

$$(T) \quad E_a p \to p$$

To analyse dynamic properties we have introduced the modal operator H_a (see [8]).The sentence $H_a p$ can be read: the agent a attempts to brings it about that p. We consider below the links between the facts represented by p and $H_a p$.

Ability. The agent is able to bring it about that p iff if a is in the context c that makes possible to bring it about that p [6] and a attempts to bring it about that p, then p is obtained. This property is formally represented by:

$$c \to (H_a p \to p)$$

Of course, in this definition p denotes a propositional constant, not a propositional variable like in the axiom schema (T).

The property formally represented by $p \to H_a p$ means that if p is the case then the agent a attempts to bring it about that p. This corresponds to no property which has an intuitive meaning.

Trust about ability is denoted by $Tabil_{a,b}(p,c)$ and it is defined by:

$$Tabil_{a,b}(p,c) \stackrel{\text{def}}{=} K_a(c \to (H_a p \to p))$$

The modal operator H_a is a classical operator that obeys the inference rule:

$$(RE3) \quad \frac{\vdash p \leftrightarrow q}{\vdash H_a p \leftrightarrow H_a q}$$

4   More Flexible Definitions of Trust

4.1   Graded Trust

In section 2 the definitions of trust have the general form: $K_a(\phi_b \to \psi_b)$. For example, for sincerity we have $K_a(I_{b,a}p \to B_b p)$. The intended meaning is that a strongly believes that in all the circumstances where we have ϕ_b we also have

---

[6] We would like to thank the anonymous referee who pointed out the necessity for an agent to be in a given context to be able to exercise his ability.

ψ_b. That is, the set of worlds (compatible with what a strongly believes) where we have ϕ_b is included in the set of worlds where we have ψ_b. In most of the real situations our trust is less rigid and we strongly believe that the first set is "more or less" included in the second set.

To formalise this notion of "more or less" included we have introduced the connective $\Rightarrow_i$ which is indexed by the "level of inclusion" i. The formula $\phi \Rightarrow_i \psi$ intuitively means that ϕ entails ψ at the level i.

The semantics of this connective is defined in a similar way as the conditional connective defined in [2]. For a given world w of a given model M we have:

$M, W \models \phi \Rightarrow_i \psi$ iff $f_i(w, |\phi|_M) = |\psi|_M$

where $|\phi|_M$ denotes the set of worlds w' such that $M, w' \models \phi$ [7].

In a model a function f_i has to be defined for each level i. A very particular case might be to define f_i like a probability, that is to have: $f_i(w, |\phi|_M) = |\psi|_M$ iff $\frac{card|\phi \wedge \psi|_M}{card|\phi|_M} = i$, where $card|\phi|_M$ denotes the cardinality of the set $|\phi|_M$. However, in many applications such quantitative levels have no intuitive meaning and we propose to have only qualitative levels for which is defined a partial order relation denoted by $i < j$.

For the different kinds of properties $prop$ we denote the level of trust by $Tprop^i_{a,b}(p)$ and we have definitions of the form:

$$Tprop^i_{a,b}(p) \overset{\text{def}}{=} K_a(\phi_b \Rightarrow_i \psi_b)$$

For example, in the case of sincerity we have: $Tsinc^i_{a,b}(p) \overset{\text{def}}{=} K_a(I_{b,a}p \Rightarrow_i B_b p)$.

We think that a possible method to assign an intuitive meaning to each level is to assign some particular agent to each level and to use these agents as references for each level.

For example, if the agent r is used as a reference for the level i with regard to some proposition p, it is possible to assign the level i to another agent b if a trusts b in the same way (at the same level) as a trusts r. More formally, if r is the reference for the level i we should have $Tprop^i_{a,b}(p)$ iff $Tprop^i_{a,r}(p)$.

The consequences of graded trust are graded beliefs. We adopt the notation: $B^i_a p$: the agent a believes at the level i that p is the case.

If we have $K_a(\phi \to \psi)$ from $K_a\phi$ we can infer $K_a\psi$, but if we have $K_a(\phi \Rightarrow_i \psi)$ from $K_a\phi$ we can only infer the weaker consequence $B^i_a\psi$. Then, we have the following axiom schema:

$$(K_i) \quad K_a(\phi \Rightarrow_i \psi) \to (K_a\phi \to B^i_a\psi)$$

---

[7] In the definition of conditionals in [2] we have in the satisfiability condition $f_i(w, |\phi|_M) \subseteq |\psi|_M$. A consequence of this definition is that we have $\models \psi \to \psi'$ $\Rightarrow \models (\phi \Rightarrow_i \psi) \to (\phi \Rightarrow_i \psi')$ (see the rule RCK in [2]) and we do not want this property for the connective $\Rightarrow_i$. Indeed, in $\phi \Rightarrow_i \psi$ the connective $\Rightarrow_i$ expresses to what extend the fact that a world is in $|\phi|_M$ entails the fact that this world is in $|\psi|_M$. If we accept the definition given in [2] from $\phi \Rightarrow_i \psi$ we can infer $\phi \Rightarrow_i \psi \vee \phi$, and in general the "strength" of the entailment in $\phi \Rightarrow_i \psi$ is not the same as its strength in $\phi \Rightarrow_i \psi \vee \phi$.

The links between graded beliefs and strong beliefs are defined by the following schemas:

If $j \leq i$, $B_a^i \phi \rightarrow B_a^j \phi$.

For every i, $K_a \phi \rightarrow B_a^i \phi$.

4.2   Trust with Respect to Topics

In general trust is not specific to a proposition p. Rather an agent trusts another agent for all the propositions related to a given topic. For instance, the agent a may trust b with respect to his validity for all the propositions that are about the topic "nuclear".

In [5] Demolombe and Jones have defined the property:

$A(t, \text{"}p\text{"})$: the sentence named by "p" is about the topic t,

and they have defined a logic for reasoning about sentences of the form $A(t, \text{"}p\text{"})$. This logic is weaker than a classical logic. The only inference rule is:

$$if \; Var(p) = Var(q), \quad \frac{\vdash p \leftrightarrow q}{\vdash A(t, \text{"}p\text{"}) \leftrightarrow A(t, \text{"}q\text{"})}$$

where $Var(p)$ denotes the set of propositional variables in p.

We denote by $Tprop_{a,b}(t)$ the fact that a trusts b with respect to $prop$ for the topic t and we have the formal definition:

$$Tprop_{a,b}(t) \stackrel{\text{def}}{=} \forall \text{"}p\text{"}(A(t, \text{"}p\text{"}) \rightarrow Tprop_{a,b}(p))$$

Moreover, it is quite natural to define a structure over the set of topics with the notion of specificity. We denote by $t' \; isa \; t$ the fact that the topic t' is more specific than t. For example, the topic "nuclear weapon" is more specific than the topic "nuclear". According to this structure we adopt the axiom schema:

$$t' \; isa \; t \rightarrow (A(t', \text{"}p\text{"}) \rightarrow A(t, \text{"}p\text{"}))$$

4.3   Conditional Trust

There are many situations where an agent trusts another agent only in some particular circumstances. For instance, let us suppose that the agent b is the sensor that detects that the door is open. An agent a may trust b with regard to his completeness for the fact that the door is open (represented by p) only if the electric power is on (represented by q).

This kind of trust is formally represented by $K_a(q \rightarrow (p \rightarrow I_{a,b}p))$.

In general, the fact that a trusts b for p in the circumstances represented by q is denoted by $Tprop_{a,b}(p|q)$ and we have the formal definition:

$$Tprop_{a,b}(p|q) \stackrel{\text{def}}{=} K_a(q \rightarrow prop(p))$$

where $prop(p)$ is any property about p of the kind that we have seen in the section 2 or 3.

It is worth noting that conditional trust would not be correctly represented by: $q \rightarrow K_a(prop(p))$, because what the agent a trusts depends on what he strongly believes (i.e. $K_a q$) and not on the fact that really holds (i.e. q).

We have the intuitive property:

$$Tprop_{a,b}(p|q) \rightarrow (K_a q \rightarrow Tprop_{a,b}(p))$$

5   Conclusion

We have defined trust as a mental attitude of an agent with respect to another agent which has been called strong belief. We have shown that this property may be an epistemic, a deontic or a dynamic property.

These properties have been systematically analysed in the framework of modal logic. The technic was to consider facts represented by p, $B_a p$ and $I_{b,a} p$, for epistemic properties, facts represented by $E_a p$, $OE_a p$ and $PE_a p$, for deontic properties, and facts represented by $H_a p$ and p for dynamic properties. An axiomatic characterisation has been given for the modal operators involved in these definitions.

This analysis has allowed to "rediscover" some intuitive properties and to exhibit some of them that are non trivial.

At the beginning trust is defined for a specific fact p and we only consider two situations: an agent trusts, or does not trust, another agent. In the second part of the paper have been introduced more flexible definitions that are closer to the definitions used in practical applications. Graded trust allows to represent several qualitative levels of trust. Trust about topics allows to define more generic trust. Finally, conditional trust allows to relativize trust to some particular circumstances. These extensions of the notion of trust could be easily combined to define, for example, graded trust defined in terms of topics.

References

1. J. Carmo and A.J.I. Jones. Deontic Logic and Contrary-to Duties. In D. Gabbay, editor, *Handbook of Philosophical Logic (Rev. Edition)*. Reidel, to appear.
2. B. F. Chellas. *Modal Logic: An introduction*. Cambridge University Press, 1988.
3. R. Demolombe. Validity Queries and Completeness Queries. In *Proc. of 9th International Symposium on Methodologies for Intelligent Systems*, 1996.
4. R. Demolombe. To trust information sources: a proposal for a modal logical framework. In C. Castelfranchi and Y-H. Tan, editors, *Trust and Deception in Virtual Societies*. Kluwer Academic Publisher, 2001.
5. R. Demolombe and A.J.I. Jones. On sentences of the kind "sentence "p" is about topic "t": some steps toward a formal-logical analysis. In H-J. Ohlbach and U. Reyle, editor, *Logic, Language and Reasoning. Essays in Honor of Dov Gabbay*. Kluwer Academic Press, 1999.
6. G. Elofson. Developping trust with intelligent agents: an explanatory study. In C. Castelfranchi and Y-H. Tan, editors, *Trust and Deception in Virtual Societies*. Kluwer Academic Publisher, 2001.

7. R. Falcone and C. Castelfranchi. Social trust: a cognitive approach. In C. Castelfranchi and Y-H. Tan, editors, *Trust and Deception in Virtual Societies*. Kluwer Academic Publisher, 2001.

8. A.J.I. Jones. A logical framework. In J. Pitt, editor, *The Open Agent Society*. John Wiley and Sons.

9. A.J.I. Jones. *Communication and meaning: An essay in applied modal logic.* Synthese Library. Reidel, 1983.

10. A.J.I. Jones. On the concept of trust. *Decision Support Systems*, 33, 2002.

11. A.J.I. Jones and B.S. Firozabadi. On the characterisation of a trusting agent. Aspects of a formal approach. In C. Castelfranchi and Y-H. Tan, editors, *Trust and Deception in Virtual Societies*. Kluwer Academic Publisher, 2001.

12. F.J. Lerch and M.J. Prietula. How do we trust machine advice. In *Third International Conference on Human-Computer Interaction*, 1989.

13. S. March. Trust in distributed Artificial Intelligence. *Lectures Notes in Computer Science*, 830, 1994.

14. P.Oerbaek. Can you Trust your data. *Lectures Notes in Computer Science*, 915, 1995.

15. K. Thompson. Reflections on Trusting Trust. *Communications of ACM*, 27(18), 1984.

Trust Mediation in Knowledge Management and Sharing

Cristiano Castelfranchi

Institute for Cognitive Sciences and Technologies – CNR
T³-*Trust Theory & Technology Group*
c.castelfranchi@istc.cnr.it

Abstract[1]. The aim of this paper is to provide a theory of the role trust plays in knowledge sharing processes, by exploiting a cognitive model of the goals and beliefs of an agent involved in the decision of *passing* and/or *accepting* knowledge[2], and a related model of the symmetrical or asymmetrical trust relationships within a group (Trust-Nets). This theory is based on the claim that trust is a fundamental mediator in knowledge sharing, so as most authors studying Knowledge Management assert. Anyway they do not analyse the relationship between trust and knowledge circulation theoretically, what is the objective of our work. Considering knowledge sharing as a decisional act founded on two different socio-cognitive actions: to *pass* knowledge and to *accept* knowledge, we build a cognitive model of agent's mind when passing or accepting it, that is a list of his/her goals and beliefs in accordance with which s/he decides if sharing knowledge or not; several of them are trust ingredients. Thus, trust - as mental attitude (a specific set of beliefs and expectations) - comes into play in knowledge sharing process. However, in our analysis trust is not only a subjective disposition (towards others) but it is also an act (the act of trusting somebody) and a social (more or less stable) relationship. This is why we also analyse trust relations not in mental terms but in structural-relational terms, as a net of "channels" for knowledge circulation.[3]

---

[1] This research has been carried out within the PAR research project of University of Siena and the TICCA project (Trento ITC) as for the trust net and knowledge management, and within the European *Alfebiite* project as for the basic model of trust. I would like to acknowledge Rosella Postorino's contribution: during her thesis (I was the supervisor of), she was both collecting data in a real business organization (I thank dott. Thomas Schael for supervising her in this activity) and discussing and working with me about knowledge management theories and trust. Many thanks also to Rino Falcone and Maria Miceli for discussions and comments.

[2] For an extended theory of this – also based on an empirical investigation - see Castelfranchi & Postorino "Trust Relationships and Knowledge Sharing in Organizations" (in preparation).

[3] The two reference models we take into consideration in our work are: the socio-cognitive model of trust developed for socio-psychological, organisational and computational studies by Castelfranchi and Falcone, and Knowledge Management studies.

C.D. Jensen et al. (Eds.): iTrust 2004, LNCS 2995, pp. 304–318, 2004.
© Springer-Verlag Berlin Heidelberg 2004

1 The Knowledge Management Perspective and the Issue of Trust

Knowledge Management is a discipline which considers knowledge as the most important organization's resource and as a strategy whose objective is to collect, manage and put knowledge in action, so that it circulates and develops continuously. Managing and diffusing an enterprise's knowledge capital determines the innovation of products, processes, organisational models and answers to the customers improving its competitive position. This kind of knowledge concerns creativity, problem solving, disposition to dialogue, uncertainty management and sensitiveness towards cultural context in which the organisation operates.

We assume as references in this domain two of the most relevant contributions to organisational knowledge studies; those provided by Nonaka & Takeuchi (1995) and Davenport and Prusak (1998).

Nonaka & Takeuchi affirm that knowledge creation core is the conversion of tacit knowledge in explicit one and vice versa. The knowledge distinction in tacit and explicit dates back to Polanyi (1967) who defined tacit knowledge as personal, peculiar of a context and therefore hard to be codified comparing it to explicit knowledge that is only the ice-berg peak of the whole knowledge corpus and can be on the contrary codified and transferred through a formal and systematised language. The two "epistemological" (Nonaka & Takeuchi, 1996) knowledge dimensions are complementary. Knowledge can be created and diffused just through their continuous interaction, that is *Knowledge Spiral*. Knowledge creation process is also the creation of *Ba* (Nonaka, Konno & Toyama, 2001), the specific time and space where interactions and interpersonal relationships from which knowledge cannot be separated take place: it is the platform where knowledge concentrates.

The four modalities of knowledge conversion are:

1. *socialization*: conversion of tacit knowledge in tacit one through the building of an interaction field where organisation members can exchange experiences and share mental models. It is the modality of *originating ba*, where members meet face-to-face and share emotions and feelings like *care* including also commitment, love and *trust*;
2. *externalisation*: conversion of tacit knowledge in explicit one through dialogue, using metaphors and analogies. It is the modality of *dialoguing ba* and of peer-to-peer interaction;
3. *combination*: the elaboration of knowledge through knowledge networks enabling collaboration also thanks to information technology (*systematising ba*);
4. *internalisation*: the conversion of explicit knowledge in tacit one through the process of learning by doing "on the site": in a shared time and space where focused training with colleagues and senior members helps to underline specific mental patterns (*exercising ba*).

In "high care" organisations members tend to bestow knowledge: they form a social network supporting the individual who is not afraid to ask help in performing his/her task because all members share "care" value and are accessible at every level. Members are indulgent towards errors (*idem*), because sharing the value of learning and developing new knowledge, important not for power gaining but for the satisfaction of a common goal: problem solving and task performing, that is the base of strict cooperation (Castelfranchi, 1998). In this view the relevance of trust in knowledge creation process is evident, even though not analytically explicated. In fact every such step of this 'knowledge conversion' requires trust. Sharing knowledge (both in 'externalisation' and in 'combination') is a specific action, due either to personal purposes (for personal advantages) or to shared objectives and values (cooperation for common goals), or to role duties, or finally to habits and routines. In all these different motivational sets some form of either implicit confidence (in routines and habits, or in role playing) or of explicit trust evaluations (of the others and of the context) is always needed. Analogously, in 'socialisation' a trust atmosphere (see §4.) is both the result and the condition of the process; while 'internalisation' presupposes trust in the senior member one is adopting as a model, and in the established practices.

Davenport and Prusak (1998) consider knowledge as a changeable mix of structured experiences, values, information about the context and intuitions coming from experience, providing a model where new information and experiences are incorporated. It finds itself in individuals' heads and is embedded in organisation's documents, routines, processes, practices and norms. It is different from information but derives from it so as information differs from data but is formed by them. The authors stress the importance of trust in Knowledge Management sustaining that it supports the "knowledge market". This market is based on reciprocity, reputation and altruism working effectively only thanks to trust, that must be *visible* (members must see that passing their knowledge people receive real acknowledgement: they must experience reciprocity directly); *ubiquitous* (because if even one part of internal knowledge market is not trustworthy, the whole market becomes asymmetric and less efficient) and must *come from the top* (if top managers are not perceived as trustworthy from members but exploiting others' knowledge for personal incomes a distrust atmosphere will spread in the organisation, while if their image is positive this will influence also the whole organisation's perceived trustworthiness). Trust must be promoted through frequent face-to-face meetings.

Knowledge management is characterised by three processes: **generation, codification** and **transfer of knowledge**, that can often be inhibited by friction factors: first of all the lack of trust, whose remedy is the establishment of relationships and personal contacts among people sharing the same culture and language.

Other authors writing about Knowledge Management emphasise the importance of trust. Sveiby (1996) considers trust the crux of knowledge sharing and suggest to invest in human resources, encouraging meetings among members working at the same projects, promoting dialogue and pleasant environments where good relationships without fear can grow. Gundry (2000) affirms that trust is necessary for communication, knowledge exchange and information sharing typical of cooperative team work. He underlines the circular relation between knowledge sharing and trust: if trust helps information exchange, people tend also to trust persons who share knowledge more than others.

Notice that all these authors make clear statements about the crucial role of trust and correctly focus on the issue, but they are rather generic and vague. Not having a well defined model of trust they cannot account for how and why precisely trust mediates and "is the crux" of knowledge sharing and management.

A definitely richer contribution to our theme is provided by Jones and George (1998). They distinguish trust in conditional and unconditional, considering the latter as the ideal condition for knowledge sharing in an organisation. They argue that an agent starts a trust interaction with another behaving as if s/he trusts him/her: it's a "by default" and blind trust, the first step of a potential interaction that helps a future trust relationship establishment[4] more than starting with diffidence; the "null degree" trust is *conditional trust*: it induces agents to interact until they behave correctly, promoting future interactions until they develop positive feelings and opinions about others' trustworthiness; the highest form of trust is *unconditional trust* based on values sharing: the more agents interact the more they understand to share the same values, so they do not trust "by default" as before, but because they experienced directly other's trustworthiness and his/her adoption of their same values. This kind of trust encourages cooperation not only because it supports colleagues in following a common goal as conditional trust does, but also because it lets them feel at ease in asking help or knowledge: if all members share the value of cooperativeness, then nobody should feel inadequate or threatened for his/her position of "dependence". Moreover, the belief of sharing the same values incites the agent to sacrifice his/her personal interest and to trust unconditionally colleagues who become even friends. In the end, since tacit knowledge is embedded in social interactions and transferred by them and since social interactions are supported by unconditional trust, then tacit knowledge sharing is possible until members trust each other unconditionally.

This distinction is very interesting, even though the meaning of 'unconditional trust' is not so clear: is it trust without evidences justifying it or is trust without control or is trust without counterpart? Anyway, it is sure that *values sharing* – but only when values are *prosocial* - facilitates trust relationships: other's behaviour is more predicable, because the agent can attribute to colleagues the same values s/he adopts. In the end, even though Jones sand George do not explicate it theoretically, it is deducible that unconditional trust is less expensive than conditional one, which needs information, accepts less risk and is always subject to control. We will discuss this issue later.

2 What Trust Is: A Socio-cognitive Model

The Socio-Cognitive model of trust (for a more complete presentation see Castelfranchi and Falcone 1998;2000;2002; Castelfrabchi & Tan, 2001; Falcone and Castelfranchi, 2001) is based on a portrait of the mental state of trust in cognitive terms (beliefs, goals). This is not a complete account of the psychological dimensions of trust: it represent the most explicit (reason-based) and conscious form. The model does not account for the more implicit forms of trust (for example trust by default, not based upon explicit evaluations, beliefs, derived from previous experience or other sources) or for the affective dimensions of trust, based not on explicit evaluations but on emotional responses and an intuitive, unconscious appraisal.

The word *trust* means different things, but they are systematically related with each other. In particular, three crucial concepts have been recognised and distinguished not only in natural language but in the scientific literature. Trust is at the same time:

- a mere *mental attitude* (prediction and evaluation) towards an other agent, a simple *disposition*;

---

[4] Because trust creates trust (Falcone & Castelfranchi, 2001). This default attitude has been proved for ex. by Axelrod to be a good precondition for promoting cooperation even among self-interested agents.

- a *decision* to rely upon the other, i.e. an *intention* to delegate and trust, which makes the trustor "vulnerable"{6};
- a *behaviour*, i.e the intentional *act* of trusting, and the consequent *relation* between the trustor and the trustee.

In each of the above concepts, different sets of cognitive ingredients are involved in the trustier's mind. The model is based on the BDI (Belief-desire-intention) approach for modeling mind, that is inspired to the Bratman's philosophical theory. First of all, in the trust model only an agent endowed with both goals and beliefs can "trust" another agent. Let us consider the trust of an agent X towards another agent Y about the (Y's) behaviour/action α relevant for the result (goal) g when:

X *is the (relying) agent, who feels trust; it is a cognitive agent endowed with* internal explicit goals and beliefs (the *trustier*);

Y is the agent or entity which is trusted (the *trustee*);

X trusts Y about g/α and for g/α.

In the model Y is not necessarily a cognitive agent (for instance, an agent can -or cannot- trust a chair as for as to sustain his weight when he is seated on it). On the contrary, X must always be a cognitive agent: so, in the case of artificial agents we should be able to simulate these internal explicit goals and beliefs. For all the three notions of trust above defined (*trust disposition, decision to trust*, and *trusting behaviour*) we claim that someone trusts some another one only relatively to some goal (here goal is intended as the general, basic teleonomic notion, any motivational representation in the agent: desires, motives, will, needs, objectives, duties, utopias, are kinds of goals). An unconcerned agent does not really "trust": he just has opinions and forecasts. One trusts another only relatively to a *positive expectation*, i.e. for something s/he wants to achieve, that s/he desires. If x does not have any concern and goal, she cannot really decide, nor care about something (welfare): she cannot subjectively «trust» somebody. Second, trust itself *consists of* beliefs.

2.1 A Cognitive Anatomy of Trust

Since Y's action is useful to X (trust disposition), and X has decided to rely on it (decision to trust), this means that X might delegate (act of trusting) some action/goal in his own plan to Y. This is the strict relation between trust disposition, decision to trust, and delegation.

The model includes two main basic beliefs (*evaluations*) (we are considering the trustee as a cognitive agent too):

_ *Competence Belief*: a *sufficient evaluation* of Y's abilities is necessary, X should believe that Y is useful for this goal of its, that Y can produce/provide the expected result, that Y can play such a role in X's plan/action.

– *Willingness Belief*: X should think that Y not only is able and can do that action/task, but Y actually will do what X needs (under given circumstances). This belief makes the trustee's behaviour predictable.

Another important basic belief for trust is:

_ *Dependence Belief*: X believes -to trust Y and delegate to it- that either X needs it, X depends on it (*strong dependence*), or at least that it is better to X to rely rather than do not rely on it (*weak dependence*). In other terms, when X trusts someone, X is in *a strategic situation*: X believes that there is interference and that his rewards, the results of his projects, depend on the actions of another agent Y.

Obviously, the willingness belief hides a set of other beliefs on the trustee's reasons and motives for helping. In particular, X believes that Y has some motives for helping it (for adopting its goal), and that these motives will probably prevail -in case of conflict- on other motives, negative for it. Notice that motives inducing to adoption are of several different kinds: from friendship to altruism, from morality to fear of sanctions, from exchange to common goal (cooperation), and so on (figure 2). This is why, for example, it is important to have common culture, shared values, the same acknowledged authorities between trustier and trustee.

2.2 Internal vs. Environmental Trust

Another important characteristic of the socio-cognitive model of trust is the distinction between trust 'in' someone or something that has to act and produce a given performance thanks to its *internal characteristics*, and the global trust in the global event or process and its result which is also affected by *external factors* like opportunities and interferences. Trust in Y (for example, 'social trust' in strict sense) seems to consists in the two first prototypical beliefs/evaluations identified as the basis for reliance: *ability/competence* (that with cognitive agents includes knowledge and self-confidence*)*, and *disposition* (that with cognitive agents is based on willingness, persistence, engagement, etc.). Evaluation about external opportunities is not really an evaluation about Y (at most the belief about its ability to recognize, exploit and create opportunities is part of our trust 'in' Y). We should also add an evaluation about the probability and consistence of obstacles, adversities, and interferences. Trust can be said to consist of or better to (either implicitly or explicitly) imply the *subjective probability* of the successful performance of a given behaviour α, and it is on the basis of this subjective perception/evaluation of risk and opportunity that the agent decides to rely or not Y. However, the probability index is based on, derives from those beliefs and evaluations. In other terms the global, final probability of the realization of the goal g, i.e. of the successful performance of α, should be decomposed into the probability of Y performing the action well (*internal attribution*) and the probability of having the appropriate conditions (*external attribution*) for the performance and for its success, and of not having interferences and adversities (*external attribution*). This decomposition is important because:
- the trustier's decision might be different with the same global probability or risk, depending on its composition (for example for personality factors);
- trust composition (internal Vs external) produces completely different intervention strategies: to manipulate the external variables (circumstances, infrastructures) is completely different than manipulating internal parameters.

2.3   Degrees of Trust

The idea that trust is gradual quantity is common (in common sense, in social sciences, in AI). However, since no real definition and cognitive characterization of trust is given, the quantification of trust is quite *ad hoc* and arbitrary, and the introduction of this notion or predicate is semantically empty. On the contrary, we claim that there is a strong coherence between the cognitive definition of trust, its mental ingredients, and, on the one side, its value, and on the other side, its social functions and its affective aspects. More precisely the latter are based on the former.

In our model we ground the degree of trust of *x* in *y*, in the cognitive components of *x*'s mental state of trust. More precisely, *the degree of trust is a function of the subjective certainty of the relevant beliefs*. We use the degree of trust to formalise a rational basis for the decision of relying and betting on *y*. We also claim that the "quantitative" aspect of another basic ingredient is relevant: *the value or importance or utility of the goal g*. In sum,

> *the quantitative dimensions of trust are based on the quantitative dimensions of its cognitive constituents.*

For us trust is not an arbitrary index with operational importance, without a real content, but it is based on the subjective certainty of the relevant beliefs which support each other and the decision to trust (Figure 1).

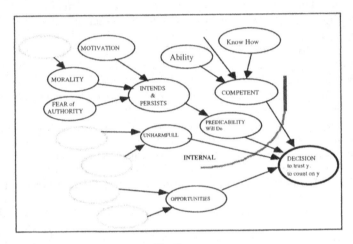

Fig. 1.

If we call $DoT_{XY\tau}$ the degree of trust of an agent *X* about *Y* on the task $\tau=(\alpha,g)$ we have: $DoT_{XY\tau} = DoC_X[Opp_Y(\alpha,g)] * DoC_X[Ability_Y(\alpha)] * DoC_X[WillDo_Y(\alpha,g)]$ where:

- $DoC_X[Opp_Y(\alpha,g)]$, is the degree of credibility of *X*'s beliefs about the *Y*'s opportunity of performing α to realize *g*;
- $DoC_X[Ability_Y(\alpha)]$, the degree of credibility of *X*'s beliefs about the *Y*'s ability/competence to perform α;
- $DoC_X[WillDo_Y(\alpha,g)]$, the degree of credibility of *X*'s beliefs about the *Y*'s actual performance;

$DoC_X[WillDo_Y(\alpha,g)] = DoC_X[Intend_Y(\alpha,g)] * DoC_X[Persist_Y(\alpha,g)]$ (given that *Y* is a *cognitive agent*)

In any circumstance, an agent *X* endowed with a given goal, has three main choices: i) to try to achieve the goal by itself; ii) to delegate the achievement of that goal to another agent *Y*; iii) to do nothing (relatively to this goal), renouncing.

Considered the simplified scenario in which only (i) and (ii) are the possible choices we have the Figure 2:

Where if $U(X)$ is the agent X's utility function, more specifically:

$U(X)_p{}^+$, the utility of the X's success performance; $U(X)_p{}^-$, the utility of the X's failure performance; $U(X)_d{}^+$, the utility of a successful delegation (the utility due to the success of the delegated action); $U(X)_d{}^-$, the utility of a failure delegation (the damage due to the failure of the delegated action).

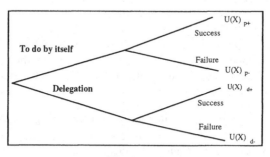

To do by itself

Success — $U(X)_{p+}$

Failure — $U(X)_{p-}$

Delegation

Success — $U(X)_{d+}$

Failure — $U(X)_{d-}$

Fig. 2.

In the above scenario, in order to delegate we must have:

$$DoT_{XY\tau} * U(X)_d{}^+ + (1 - DoT_{XY\tau}) U(X)_d{}^- > DoT_{XX\tau} * U(X)_p{}^+ + (1 - DoT_{XX\tau}) U(X)_p{}^-$$

where $DoT_{XX\tau}$ is the selftrust of X about τ.

More precisely, we have: $U(X)_p{}^+ = Value(g) + Cost\ [Performance(X)]$,

$U(X)_p{}^- = Cost\ [Performance(X)] +$ Additional Damage for failure; $U(X)_d{}^+ = Value(g) + Cost\ [Delegation(X\ Y)]$; $U(X)_d{}^- = Cost\ [Delegation(X\ Y)]+$ Additional Damage for failure

where is supposed that it is possible to attribute a quantitative value (importance) to the goals and where the costs of the actions (delegation and performance) is supposed to be negative. There is threshold for the decision to trust y (which entails a risk and a bet). We evaluate both the *external* attribution of trust, i.e. the environmental favoring conditions and opportunities for y's successful action, and the *internal* attribution of trustworthiness to y (trust *in* y). This trust *in* y has two facets: competence and willingness. Each of them is based on and analyzed in terms of other beliefs about y (for example y's motives or know how). The final decision about relying on y's action, will be taken on the basis of *the strength of those beliefs* about y and about the environment .

3   Mental Ingredients in Knowledge Sharing and the Role of Trust

In our perspective, *knowledge sharing* is both a state resulting from a process/activity and the process/activity in itself. This process entails on the subjective, cognitive site two fundamental decisions and actions:

1. to transfer, to pass a piece of knowledge (PassK);
2. to accept a given piece of knowledge (AccK).

In the former case, agent x decides whether passing or keeping knowledge; in the latter case, s/he decides whether accepting or rejecting it. (Castelfranchi, 2001)

Trust attribution supporting the decision to share knowledge is external and internal, as in the classic model of trust. Internal attribution is constituted by all agent x's beliefs about himself/herself and his/her own knowledge and about agent y. External attribution is constituted by all agent x's beliefs about the environment where interaction takes place, that is organisation intended as:

- a structure with rules, routines, procedures, represented by an authority A and defended by a controller C (that can coincide with A too) who has the right and the power to sanction positively or negatively workers' behaviour;
- the whole of members working in the same organisation, who are potential sources of information and of reputation about colleagues (so about x and y too);
- a set of sets of roles, infrastructures, and of practices, data and procedures, that should be appropriate for an efficacy and safe work.

Since in our perspective there are two crucial subjective and interpersonal moves for the knowledge sharing process, we examine them in terms subjective evaluations and expectations (that is: beliefs) about each others, about k, and about the organisational context. It will be clear that several of them are typical *trust beliefs* i.e. the beliefs that constitute trust as mental disposition.

3.1 Predictions about K-sharing

K-Sh is the result of two different socio-cognitive operations:

- passing or not-passing K (PassK);
- accepting or rejecting K (AccK).

Those moves determine the spreading of K in the social net (Castelfranchi, 2001) and their respective decisions are influenced by different factors, but both of them also depend on trust.

PassK is mainly influenced by centrifuge/outputting trust: the more X trusts Y the more s/he will be prone to pass her/his K to Y. More precisely, X should trust Y not generically, but *for specific features relevant for passing K to Y*:
1. X believes that Y is able to understand K, to understand the use of K;
2. X believes that *Y will appropriately use K* (for the Org purposes and advantage);
3. X trusts that Y will not make worse (and possibly improve) Y's *attitude towards X* (Y will reciprocate, or be grateful, or more friendly close, Y will increase trust towards X, etc.);
but also
4. X believes that Y trust him/her enough to <u>AccK</u> (belief about centripetal trust)
Plus other necessary beliefs:
5. X believes that Y needs K
6. The belief 1 – belief of competence – and also 2 often implies other two beliefs. If X doesn't experience Y's competence directly, it means that X relies on Y's *reputation*, that is X trusts other members of the organisation as sources of information about Y.
7. The belief 4 about Y's honesty (and so about his/her reciprocation too) implies that X believes that Y has an "Assumption of Normative Pertinence" and also a

Normative Goal (that is Y knows the rules and believes that they regard him/her too, so s/he has the goal to adopt and respect them)

8. X relies on the organisation in general, because s/he believes that if Y has been employed it means that s/he has got the necessary competencies to work in that organisation or the necessary formation to understand k.

9. X trusts that Y has not k so that s/he depends on X to get it

10. X believes that if Y shows not to have k, it's true (s/he doesn't deceive).

11. X trusts (or better: x believes, but s/he actually has no experience to which refer. so s/he hopes) that Kshar is an advantage, improving his/her work (this will be a reciprocation, even though not immediate)

12. *X trusts Organisation Authority*, that is s/he adopts the rules of the Organisation. so s/he trusts other members because s/he believes that they also adopt them and trust (have fear of) Authority and her capability to check and sanction.

13. X trusts of course the Controller too, that is his/her capability to check and evaluate who respects or disobey rules.

14. X believes that Y would like to be well-evaluated by X (that is Y's goal of good reputation).

15. X believes that Y has the goal to be trusted by X (that's why s/he will use correctly k, s/he will reciprocate...).

16. X is self-confident: he trusts his/her knowledge (or competence...).

17. *X trusts that k is adequate, important or necessary to (solve) a given situation or to be transferred to Y.* This is a question of self-confidence too, because X trusts his/her ability to evaluate how, when, how much and with whom sharing k.

18. Eventually X trusts the sources of information from which s/he received k.

19. *X trusts that s/he will not be replaced by another worker* (because of transferring his/her professional value, that is just k!) or at least to keep on being professionally acknowledged for his/her competencies, even though other people have them.

20. X trusts that s/he will receive a professional *acknowledgement* for his/her SharK, because s/he adopts the rule of K sharing.

AccK is mainly (but not only) influenced by centrifuge trust too but in another way; it depends *on how much X trusts Y as for being a competent and reliable source and as for being loyal and good-willing towards X* (not having reasons for deceiving X or for inducing X in error; how much Y is in competition with X, etc.)

1. X trusts that Y is well informed and competent

2. X trusts that Y is trustworthy, not deceiving: it means that Y believes that if X gives k then X believes that k is true.

3. X trusts that Y is *not hostile* with X, that means also that X believes that Y trust him/her enough to PassK (belief about *centripetal* trust)

These seem to be the three fundamental evaluations, the three specific aspects of X's trust in Y relevant for AccK. They influence X's trust in K passed by Y: K is a reliable K. Moreover an additional belief is necessary for AccK:

4. X believes that K is useful, is pertinent for some of his/her goal (not irrelevant).

As we can see, trust evaluations and expectations about the other agent, the organisation and its rules and structures, one-selves, and k are *a necessary ground* for the knowledge-sharing process and a crucial component of the mental attitudes that it requires in the organisational actors. This is why is not only reasonable to assume that trust is a precondition for knowledge sharing (and a result of it), but, more precisely, that it is a *mediator*, a *catalyst* of the process: it is a mental and interpersonal (cognitive, dispositional, and relational) precise condition for the two crucial steps in the organisational flow of knowledge. Thus, trust is also something that a policy of knowledge management must seriously take into account, build, and defend, by clearly knowing its nature and dynamics.

3.2 The Knowledge Sharing Circularity

It is interesting to notice that *in order to share "new" knowledge it is necessary to share previous knowledge*, or at least that x must believe to have some knowledge in common with the agent he passes knowledge to). First of all, this is necessary because some shared knowledge is presupposed for communicating and for understanding (for example a shared vocabulary and ontology, a shared encyclopedia, a shared context about work, roles, organisation, etc.). Second, because (as we will see in section 3.2) most of x's beliefs for PassK are in fact *common* and even *mutual* beliefs between x and y; x and y believe the same (and believe that the other believes so). For example, x and y must believe that k is useful for y's goal, that k is valid, etc. The knowledge sharing circularity (Figure 3 *a*) can be either an obstacle or an incentive. If x believes that y does not share a certain cultural or education background with him/her, then s/he can hesitate to pass knowledge to him/her or above all to accept k from him/her. Notwithstanding, if x perceives to share knowledge with y, she is more stimulated to transfer and accept other knowledge by him/her (it functions like that in the case of values sharing which is in a circular relationship with knowledge sharing). The relationship between trust and knowledge sharing is circular too (Figure 3 *b*): in order to trust y, x must either have information about y, helping him/her to evaluate y's trustworthiness or having knowledge in common with him/her that encourages the establishment of a trust relationship so as values sharing; on the other hand, in order to share knowledge, it is necessary **to have a trust relation** or atmosphere.

a   b

Fig. 3.

4   Trust as a Net and Its Prediction

Let us now analyse trust relationships not in mental terms (which represent the fine grain, the micro-level) but at a macro-level   in structural-relational terms, as "channels" for knowledge circulation (Busch et al., 2001). In fact, trust is not only a mental disposition founding decisions of reliance, delegation, collaboration; as we said at the beginning, it also is an action and an (establisheb or attempted) *social relation*. Trust relationships around an individual within a given community connecting her/him with other members creates a sort of trust-sociogram, that we call *TrustNet*. Let us characterise the main features and properties of such a network.

First of all, links in the net can be *unilateral* and *asymmetric*, or *bilateral*. They can be more or less strong/weak depending on the strength, intensity of trust (see § 2.3); links can be more or less permanent, stable, since this sociogram can either characterise a temporarily social situation: x has to rely upon somebody or choosing somebody for cooperation, or it can characterise a structure of acquaintance, of stable social "relations".

Let us first consider the TrustNet only from x's local and unilateral perspective: where x is the "source" of several trust attitudes/arrows towards others, i.e. *only centrifuge/outputting arrows.*

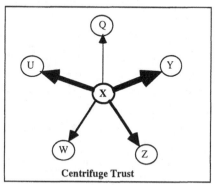

Centrifuge Trust

Fig. 4.

This kind of structure allows for some *predictions*.

The strength of x's trust in y is a predictor of x's choosing y for reliance, that is of x's counting upon y. However, this is not a perfect predictor, i.e. the differential amount of x's trust in y (compared with x's trust in z or w) does not completely determine x's choice. There are also other factors. How much is x dependent on y, z or w (Sichman et al. 1998)? How much does x need each of them? And which is the *cost* of relying upon y rather than upon z or w? In other words, not always the chosen partner is the most trusted. Although more risky certain relationships can be preferable, that is more convenient. In fact in our model describing the role of trust in decision (see Figure 2) an equation predicts whether x will rely upon y or not, on the basis of her/his degree of trust, but also of utility and *risk acceptance.*

Let's now come back to the general characterization of TrustNet for expanding our theory of links by adopting a less local and unilateral view. They can be:
1. Unilateral: X trusts Y but Y does not trust X.
2. Bi-directional: X trusts Y and Y trusts X.
   Bi-directional trust relationships can be distinguished in various kinds:
   – Bilateral: X trusts Y and Y trusts X in a completely independent way; each of them might even ignore if and how the other trusts her/him.
   – Reciprocal: X trusts Y also because (X believes that) Y trusts X.
   – Mutual (bi-reciprocal): X trusts Y also because (X believes that) Y trusts X, and *vice versa*, and both of them assume this.
3. Unbalanced: A link is unbalanced when the trust of X for Y is (perceived as) quite broader or stronger than Y's trust in X. It's balanced when their trust is of similar force.

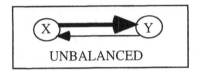

UNBALANCED

In case of Bilateral trust link (and especially for reciprocal and mutual one) we combined (add) the dimension of the two inverse arrows in a sort of broadness of a trust "channel" between X and Y.

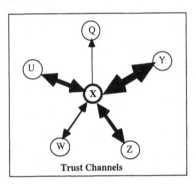

Trust Channels

Our claim is that:

> the TrustNet gives us a map of the important "channels" along which private or implicit knowledge becomes common and explicit, i.e. the channels along which knowledge is shared and circulates.(Falcone & Castelfranchi, 2002)

- First bronze prediction: the larger the channel the larger the flux of knowledge and its rapidity.
- Second bronze prediction: the more channels are bilateral and balanced the more uniformly shared knowledge is. This is also a measure of a trust "atmosphere" (see below).

A poor net (few links), subtle channels, unilateral attitudes proportionally reduces knowledge passing and accepting, thus the building of a *collective capital*.

"Trust Atmosphere". In this perspective it is possible to provide an operational notion and a model of the so called "Trust Atmosphere". We define it as:

> the diffuse perception (beliefs based on experience) within a group or organization G of the fact that "every body trusts everybody " or better that: the (great) majority of the members of G have multiple and mutual relations of trust.

Multiple means that each member (in average) has more than one centrifuge trust relation. We mean that there is not a trust atmosphere if simply each member has a specific and unique trust relations (although bilateral) in G: it is not enough that everybody trusts somebody. It is necessary to have that everybody trusts more than one agent in G, and is trusted by more than one agent. In other words, no one of the following structures would represent a real trust atmosphere.

Mutual means Bilateral + reciprocally known and reinforced by the trust of the other: i.e. each agent knows that the other trusts him and trusts the other <u>also</u> because of this.

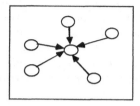 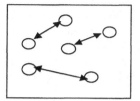 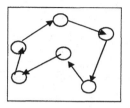

Obviously the notion of Trust Atmosphere is a **gradual notion**: it depends both on the percentage of agent in G that have reciprocal and multiple Trust relationships; on the degree of their trust; on the density, i.e. on the number of reciprocal trust arrows per node. The maximum will be when "everybody trusts very much everybody".

This disposition should be due to the **diffuse perception** of those relationships. i.e. the members of G share this representation of the G TrustNet, and share this representation because have occasions for observing trust acts among the others, towards oneself, and to listen to positive reputation spreading.

Moreover, something additional seems crucial for a climate or atmosphere of trust: the fact that trust relationships will mainly be of the "unconditional" kind or better that they are "trust by-default"[5] and implicit, affective forms of disposition. The last point is – till now – more difficult to be modeled (Castelfranchi, 2000).

5 Concluding Remarks

Trust has been identified in knowledge management literature as a crucial condition for the creation of an effective collective cognitive capital. However, no analytic model has been proposed about why and how this mediation works. We have proposed a cognitive model of trust, mainly in terms of beliefs (evaluations and expectations), to understand the precise mechanism of such a catalytic role of trust. We decomposed the knowledge sharing process in two basic decisions/actions of the participants: passing k and accepting k. We have carefully analysed the mental attitudes involved in those moves and thus in the knowledge sharing process. On such a basis, we have shown how trust ingredients are necessarily present and required while passing or accepting knowledge. After this micro-analysis of relevant cognitive presuppositions of knowledge management, we adopted a more coarse macro-level perspective, looking at trust not only as a psychological disposition but as a social relationship. We introduced the idea of a TrustNet with more or less strong and bilateral links, and on such a basis we introduced some prediction about knowldge circulation along the trust "channels".

On the basis of this analysis, we would like to conclude that: a) A *socio-cognitive view* of trust is necessary for modelling trust issues in organisations; b) while caring of making knowledge capital explicit and circulating, an organisation should care of what the *beliefs* of the actors about k, about the organisation values, authority, and infrastructure, about each-others are, and what they expect and feel on the basis of

---

5 'By-default' means that the rule of the agent is *"if you have no specific reasons for distrust and suspicion, be confident"* and not the other way around: *"if you have specific reasons for trust, be confident, otherwise be suspicious"*.

such beliefs. In knowledge management organisations should monitor and build the right expectations in their members. Knowledge management entails a cognitive, affective, and structural "trust management" in organisations. Knowledge sharing in fact is a phisiological (frequently non fully aware) process in any organisation and teamwork, it is supported by *a plurality of individual and social motives and values*, but in anycase presupposes somo for of trust among the agents and between the agent and the group/organisation.

References

Busch P.A., Richards, D., Dampney, C. *Mapping tacit knowledge flows within organisation X.* Department of Computing, Macquarie University, Sydney, Australia Email: {busch, richards, cdampney}@ics.mq.edu.au (2001)

Castelfranchi, C., (1998) Modelling Social Action for AI Agents. *Artificial Intelligence*, 103, 157-82.

Castelfranchi, C. (2000). Affective Appraisal vs Cognitive Evaluation in Social Emotions and Interactions. In A. Paiva (ed.) *Affective Interactions. Towards a New Generation of Computer Interfaces.* Heidelbergh, Springer, LNAI 1814, 76-106 .

Castelfranchi, C. (2001) Towards a Cognitive Memetics: Socio-Cognitive Mechanisms for Memes Selection and Spreading. *Journal of Memetics.- Evolutionary Models of Information Transmission,* 5. http://www.cpm.mmu.ac.uk/jom-emit/2001/vol5/castelfranchi_c.html

Castelfranchi C., Falcone R., (1998) Principles of trust for MAS: cognitive anatomy, social importance, and quantification, *Proceedings of the International Conference on Multi-Agent Systems (ICMAS'98)*, AAAI Press, pp.72-79.

Castelfranchi C., Falcone R., (2000), Trust and Control: A Dialectic Link, *Applied Artificial Intelligence Journal*, Special Issue on "Trust in Agents" Part1, Castelfranchi C., Falcone R., Firozabadi B., Tan Y. (Editors), Taylor and Francis 14 (8), 799-823.

Castelfranchi, C. Falcone R. (2002), Social trust Theory, in *"The Open Agent Society"* Jeremy Pitt (Ed.) John Wiley & Sons, Ltd .

Castelfranchi C. and Yao-Hua Tan (eds.) (2001) *Trust and Deception in Virtual Societies* , Kluwer Academic Publisher, Dordrecht,, ISBN 0-7923-6919-X

Davenport T. H. and Prusak, L.Working Knowledge: How Organizations Manage What They Know, Boston, MA: Harvard Business School Press, 1998

Falcone R., Castelfranchi C. (2002), The socio-cognitive dynamics of trust: does trust create trust? In *Trust in Cyber-societies: Integrating the Human and Artificial Perspectives* R. Falcone, M. Singh, and Y. Tan (Eds.), Springer Verlag)

Grundy, J, (2000) Trust in Virtual Teams. www.knowab.co.uk/wbwtrust.pdf

Jones, G. R., George, Jennifer M.. 1998. "The Experience and Evolution of Trust: Implications for Cooperation and Teamwork." *Academy of Management Review* 23 53 1-546

Nonaka,I. Konno, N. & Toyama,R. (2001) Emergence of "Ba". In Nonaka, I. & Nishiguchi, T. (eds.) Knowledge Emergence. Social, Technical, and Evolutionary Dimensions of Knowledge Creation. Oxford Univ. Press, N.Y.

Nonaka, I., Takeuchi, H., Umemoto, K., (1996) "A theory of organisational knowledge creation" International Journal of Technology Management 11(7/8) :833 – 845

Polanyi, M., (1967) The tacit dimension Routledge & Kegan Paul London U.K.

Sichman, J.S., Conte, R., Castelfranchi, C., Demazeau, Y. (1998) A Social Reasoning Mechanism Based On Dependence Networks. In M. Hunhs and M. Singh (Eds.) *Readings in Agents*. Morgan Kaufmann, S. Francisco, 416-21.

Sveiby, K.E. (1996) What is Knowledge Management? Internal Structure Intitiatives. Build Knowledge Sharing Culture. 3M, USA. www.sveiby.com.au/KnowledgeManagement.html

Enhanced Accountability for Electronic Processes

Adrian Baldwin

Trusted Systems Laboratory, Hewlett Packard Labs, Bristol, UK
{Adrian.Baldwin}@hp.com

Abstract. This paper proposes that accountability in electronic processes is enhanced by sharing certified event data between the participants. Enhancing transparency of processes allows those with the contextual information to understand the process and interactions to spot mistakes or fraud that others may miss. Enabling the sharing of this information makes accountability more interactive and allows for both a more intelligent and faster response to problems. This paper describes an evidence store that supports this level of interactivity thereby enabling interactive and intelligent accountability.

1 Introduction

The establishment and maintenance of trust between communicating and transacting parties on the internet is a fundamental requirement for successful e-business. Trust services [2] provide one approach based on trusted third parties running small specialist services engendering trust between interacting parties. Services range from those helping establish and maintain trust, through those helping communications and transactions to those ensuring parties are accountable for their actions. There are many examples of the first two types of trust service and this paper presents an interactive evidence store (or trusted audit system [3][6][20]) that leads to increased accountability between parties.

Accountability is promoted by transparency and therefore an evidence store should make the stored information accessible to all participants in a process. Participants in a process should then be encouraged to check the evidence trail (or have it integrated with their process systems). It is only a belief that the evidence trail will be checked by those who have knowledge of what occurred that makes it hard for participants to be dishonest. Making such checks interactive should not only enforce a level of intelligent accountability [16] but should also allow genuine mistakes quickly spotted, acknowledged and corrected.

The next section of this paper presents views on accountability and transparency and how they aid trust with section 3 discussing how an interactive evidence store helps meet these requirements and in doing so enhances accountability. The final sections of the paper are concerned with the technical questions as to how such an evidence store can be built. Firstly, the architecture of a prototype evidence store is presented as well as discussing how it can be trustably located within a standard IT infrastructure. Further sections deal with issues concerning ensuring that users can check the integrity of the evidence, ensuring the evidence is kept confidential and finally ways to help the user browse and understand the evidence.

C.D. Jensen et al. (Eds.): iTrust 2004, LNCS 2995, pp. 319–332, 2004.

2 Accountability and Transparency

Discussion of accountability and transparency has been in vogue in the press due to numerous accounting scandals. These two concepts are fundamentally linked together and linked to trust – it becomes easier to trust an entity you are interacting with when you have information about what has happened and you feel that they can be held accountable for their actions (or inactions). Discussions of accountability and transparency are often at a very high level (e.g. the audit of fortune 1000 companies) but the concepts remain critical at a localised level of individual transactions and business processes run between companies, consumers, and governments. Introducing a degree of accountability and transparency in processes at the level where entities interact also leads to a higher level of accountability within the whole organisation.

Accountability is the concerned with an entity taking responsibility for its actions in performing a particular task or against a particular plan. Hence, there a number of facets need to be considered when discussion accountability:

Plan – Ideally, there should be a clear statement about what each entity is being held accountable. This may be a well-defined plan; however, it could be a particular transaction with implicit conditions and constrains.

Identity – The entity or individual involved in an interaction needs to be clearly identifiable along with the role that they hold. There are many views on digital identities and how they can be secured [17] and the issue is not discussed further in this paper.

Evidence – As the task is performed there needs to be evidence of what has been done by whom and when so that it become clear that a process ran smoothly or if it failed why it failed.

Judgement – Part of the accountability process involves assessing the plan and evidence deciding what (if anything) went wrong and who to hold accountable for failures. Here we may loosely split judgement into two processes: firstly, evidence assessment where the pedigree of the evidence is weighed up and secondly, the judgement decision process looking across all relevant evidence.

Consequence – The result of a judgement process should be some form of consequence. There is no accountability unless there are potential consequences for a failure in performing an action. The consequences may also be implicit – it may be damage to reputation rather than an explicit fine. Ideally, the consequences should have two aims: correction that is set right the results of the failure and prevention that is to try to stop similar failures happening again.

Detection – Having evidence allowing a judgement to be made is not sufficient for accountability. There has to be a reasonable chance that failure will be detected. Without this, the judgement process and resultant consequences are ineffective, as they will often not be triggered.

Transparency is concerned with ensuring those interacting to perform a transaction or complete a task can see sufficient information to gain confidence that things are running smoothly. For participants to have confidence and trust the information they need to be confident that those sharing the information are accountable for this evidence and that this evidence is sufficient for holding each participant accountable for the success of the task.

In this manner, a transparent process very much aids accountability. Transparency provides information including the plan, events involved in meeting this plan, and the identities of performing the interactions. This information must be of a level understandable by the participants rather than in the form requiring an IT expert to piece together. Of course, for this information to be of value as evidence in an accountability framework it must be adequately secured and trustable.

The use of a secure and trustable evidence store keeping details of a transaction and the various interactions between users is an obvious aid for accountability. When errors and failures are detected, the participants can go to this trustable evidence store for a record of what has happened.

The Internet proved powerful initially because of the way it enhanced the ease of information sharing applying the same approach to an evidence store and encouraging the sharing of accountability information brings many benefits. Firstly, allowing all participants in a transaction easy access to a certified record allows them to check and validate their view either simplifying their claim or enabling them to realise their errors. More importantly, the store can be interactive and can be used during a long-lived interaction or process to find and correct errors so that there is less need for recourse to arbitration to correct the situation.

A major problem with many systems designed to aid accountability (such as audit services) is that it is hard to check the information and those empowered to check it (e.g. auditors) have little contextual information to confirm that an interaction was allowed and was correctly executed. Often checking the validity of a secure audit log will involve walking through all transaction checking they are all chained into a continuous set.

Encouraging those involved in a particular interaction to look at the related evidence in the store can help spot mistakes, errors and fraud that may otherwise remain uncovered. This is a principle widely adopted to reinforce security within the banking system – here we all receive bank statements and can check the correctness of the transactions and we are the only people who have the right contextual knowledge to check this information. Take another example of auditing accesses to medical records – an auditor may find an odd access to a record from a doctor in Cornwall during the summer but this may seem reasonable the patient was probably on holiday. The patent should notice invalid accesses – they know if the visited a doctor whilst on holiday.

The opening up of records does not reduce the likelihood that mistakes are made although it can encourage a higher degree of care. Mistakes happen but trust is often lost on the exposure of any resulting cover up or due to the inability to admit these mistakes.   Transparency and openness can require considerable energy and monitoring the data often falls to simplistic measures or can be very time consuming. Transparency itself does not engender trust it is only when linked with intelligent assessment of the evidence that true intelligent accountability [16] can start to be approached. Having such interaction and openness within a blame culture could be expensive as decisions can be slowed and risk taking reduced. Interactive accountability will be most effective where there is a culture of correction improvement rather than blame. Having processes open to interested parties rather than using arbitrary mechanisms could help bring about such change.

3   Interactive Accountability

The above discussion concerning accountability and transparency places an evidence store at the heart of an accountability system. Making this system interactive and available to participants in the interactions and processes helps ensure that events are regularly reviewed. This aids the detection process and helps ensure accountability processes are triggered. This section describes the basic properties required for an evidence store along with a discussion on how it interacts and aids the wider processes involved in accountability.

For these purposes, it is useful to think of a task being in the form of a number of interactions that could be defined in terms of a workflow, be hardcoded into an application or even be an ad-hoc set of interactions. Such sets of interactions could range from a user of an e-commerce site ordering things and gaining a certified view on deliveries; through a citizen submitting their tax form to the tax office gaining a view on various processing stages; to an integrated supply chain system operating between multiple companies. In these cases, the process is likely to be run on one entity but involving a number of participants. The interaction sets consist of a number of events (in a particular order). There will also be some expectation that particular events should be present within a particular order. Each user may be involved in a number of separate interactions.

The evidence store manages the evidence aspects of accountability hence it is expected to retaining information concerning some particular task or a small set of tasks. As the applications proceed, they send summaries of events into the evidence store. These summaries should characterise what happened at a level that is meaningful to the participants. The events should include the initial stages of a process including reference to any terms and conditions and contain information about what is agreed therefore representing the plan. The later stages in the process represent the actions in fulfilling the plan – although in reality, these elements may be far more intertwined.

Each event description should contain information about the type of interactions or process that it was generated from along with a transaction identifier grouping the events to a particular purpose, process or interaction set. Other information would include an event type, an identifier for the previous event in a sequence of events, a description of the event and two sets of attributes. The first is a set of roles and who was playing the role – for example submitter, purchaser seller and so on. The second is a set of data that will be event specific and useful in classifying and sorting events.

The evidence store thus gets event records that characterises some event that happens within an overall interaction. The evidence store needs to be concerned with preserving each event record, showing when it arrived (rather than when it claims to have been generated) the sequence of arrival and that the record has not been changed. To this extent, the event records are time-stamped (signed with time and sequence) on arrival recording although the independence of this process is essential. A harder issue for the evidence store is to demonstrate that the evidence set is complete and that events have not been removed.

The store acts as a repository for information sent by applications as such it is intended to contain a record of what it is given and not to judge the information. Having said this it is important that as evidence used in accountability is representative of events. The store is expected to perform some simple syntactic checks that the event data is well formed and the appropriate roles and data attributes are associated with particular event types.

Checking the source of events can help for example, if the event sent over a fully authenticated TLS link do certificates match an appropriate role within the event. In cases where processes are run on trusted platforms [18] or generated by processes running within secure hardware [4] further assurances of the correctness of the evidence can be given. Having certain pieces of evidence from such trusted systems can help ground trust in the other events that fit into a consistent sequence. Accountability is obviously enhanced by having well run and trustable systems generating event data – without these results may be open to question. Further grounding of the evidence trail can be achieved through allowing an interactive review – users can spot erroneous entries that do not fit their understanding of the process and errors either at the processes level or through rogue IT systems can be identified and corrected early.

The storing of evidence is of course only half the accountability story the other part is to enable detection and judgement processes leading to corrective actions. The act of assessing what happened and any resulting actions should be carried out with some intelligence and therefore should be a human guided process. The other aspect of judgement is the data collection and an assessment that it is trustable (aspects of capture were discussed above).

The evidence store needs to provide a lightweight evidence collection process for recovering data to review a particular set of interactions. Any participant in the process should be able and encouraged to review the event data and should have rights to query the evidence store. They also need assurances that the supplied record set has integrity – that is not only each event is as captured but also that the full set of records related to that user or a process has been returned. These aspects are discussed further in section 5.

The evidence system at the heart of the accountability system allows a user to make a query about records associated with a particular process instance, or a particular attributes or users and roles. Thus, there would be a query in the form:

$$\text{GetEvidence}(p_{ij}, \{<\text{role}_r=\text{user}_i>\}, \{\text{attrib}_a=\text{value}_v\})$$

Although the user may leave particular fields blank. For example, they could ask for all the records relating to a particular process or all records where they have a customer role.

The query will result in a set of events along with associated integrity information showing the data set represents all the evidence relevant to the query. When presented with raw event data the user may struggle to sort out what it means in terms of the interactions in which they are involved. Hence, the event records should be superimposed on models of the processes or interactions to aid the user through the event set and help them detect and check anomalies. This detection process is essential for accountability without a good mechanism for detecting failures entities are unlikely to be held to account at the same time anomalies may represent valid diversions from the process. Other more traditional detection mechanisms such as audit and recognising anomalous events should still be run. Having those involved in the process interact with the accountability system and detect problems helps achieve a higher level of accountability.

3.1   Example

The accountability model and prototype evidence store has been applied to medical workflow involving the patient referrals [8]. The example involves a number or roles within a GP's (primary care doctor) surgery and a hospital as well as a number of heterogeneous systems for writing and sending referrals from the GP to the hospital, for the review and classification of referral and for appointment setting. Currently the process is largely paper based but with the move to electronic patient records, there is a need to have an underlying accountability system replacing the paper trail.

The proposed accountability model does not stop at simply providing an alternative to the paper trail. It enables the participants in the process to review the events that occurred. For example, a GP or the patient could use it to check the referrals classification and that appointments are made. Errors at this level can be detected and rectified with such action also being recorded. Such information could be given by a more traditional workflow monitoring system that would itself aid accountability. It is important the participants can trust that the accountability data has integrity is complete and cannot be changed hence the evidence store could be an integral part of a process management system. Intelligent accountability is enabled through the ability to use the data as an authoritative record for dispute resolution processes.

3.2   Distributing Accountability

The above account discussed having an evidence store or audit system that would store information concerning a number of processes. It is clearly not feasible or desirable to have a central store for all information but a judgement process may need to examine a number or loosely related processes – here it is not reasonable to expect that they would use the same evidence store. For example, a hospital may have an evidence store for their processes; GPs may have similar, as would other hospitals. A patent wishing to query there treatment may wish to have a view of various processes involved in their treatment across multiple institutions.

From this point of view, it is important that for a particular process, a user knows where to look for an evidence store and this should be stated as part of the main process. Where processes are interrelated, they should refer to other evidence stores. Hence, it makes sense to link together the various event records where one process leads directly to a second process such links can be represented using a hyperlink like mechanism and placed with in the attribute set of the event representation.

Within each evidence store, there is an independent well-defined sequence for the events irrespective of the position specified in the event tuple structure. This is provided by the evidence store and can be used to order related or even unrelated events. As multiple evidence stores are used there is not well defined ordering between linked processes the sequence counters for each are independent.

Accurate global times could be used to provide orderings across multiple stores but the synchronisation process itself could be attacked. Independent clocks give some idea of ordering but within windows of the accuracy of each clock. Ties can be inserted by having protocols between services to have marked synchronisation points between the various evidence stores.

This lack of ordering may present some difficulties to a judgement process but with orderings defined within the bounds of clock, accuracies are considered easier to handle than the many technical issues associated with a running large central evidence store. As events need transmitting across IP networks, they travel different routes, are delayed at proxies and hence accurate ordering could still not be guaranteed.

4   Trusted Audit System

This previous sections described how an interactive evidence store can enhancing accountability in digital processes by ensuring that users involved in the processes can interact with the evidence trail. There are a number of issues about how such a scheme can be realised in a practical manner. The next section presents the architecture of a trusted audit system that meets the requirements of the evidence store.

Figure 1 shows the overall architecture of the system which should be though of as a trusted third party service. As with traditional audit service, events are received and added to the end of a log file. There is a notarization module that timestamps the event data hence providing integrity checks (as described in section 5). The ability for users to search and validate the event data is at the heart of the proposed accountability model and hence the event data is not only stored in a log file but it is indexed by the process identity and each role and attribute.

The store also manages the interactions with users allowing users to make queries based on a combination of the process instance identity, participants' roles or other attributes specified in an event schema. The system takes care to authenticate the user making a query then it checks their rights to see the event data against event store policies and only then is the event data returned. The event data is considered highly sensitive and therefore is kept encrypted in a way that is tightly linked to these authentication and authorisation operations as described in section 6.

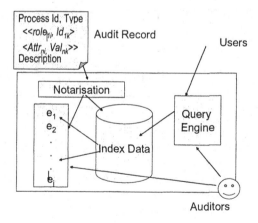

Fig. 1. The architecture of the evidence store

The evidence store needs to be thought of as an independent entity but from an operational perspective is best co-located with the systems generating the evidence. The store obviously needs backing up or replicating and this can be achieved by periodically moving data to a third party site. The integrity of the data is preserved by the notarisation structures but the process owner and participants would worry about the confidentiality of the event data. Both these problems are addressed by placing elements of the notarisation and data store within a virtual trust domain create using a hardware security appliance.

4.1   Hardware Security Appliances

The *hardware security appliance* (HSA) approach [4] offers a mechanism for running a service within its own trust domain that is physically located at the heart of conventional IT systems but protected from logical or physical interference from administrators. Other examples and models of securing applications using secure hardware are given in [21] [13] [22]. The HSA itself is a tamper resistant hardware device; for example, based on a *hardware security module* (HSM), which provides a safe environment for services to run. Such a device has active hardware protection [9] that will detect tampering resulting in the destruction of cryptographic material.

An HSM traditionally offers a cryptographic API such as PKCS#11 [19]; an HSA is a very similar – if not identical—physical device but with very different firmware allowing a service to be loaded, certified and configured. In doing so, the service binds together various critical security functions such as authentication, authorisation and audit along with cryptographic key usage into a simple service API. For example, an HSA based service has a trusted clock and can ensure that keys used in time stamping only use this clock – therefore time cannot be rolled back.

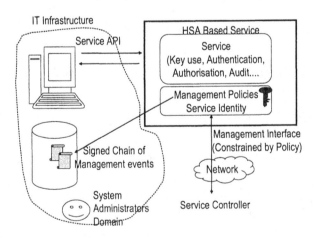

Fig. 2. A hardware security appliance creating a virtual trust domain

On a service being loaded into the HSA, it is configured with its own management policies and given its own identity, (e.g. a PKI based identity where the service provider issues a certificate for the service). As well as the service, offering its normal functional API it also defines how it can be managed and the initialisation binds it very strongly to a service controller. The service now operates within its own trust domain – physically enforced by the tamper resistance of the secure hardware and logically enforced through the limited service API and these initial management policies. The management policies define not only who controls the service but the extent of their control (even specifying no management control). These management functions can be carried out remotely using the PKI identities of the HSA based service and the service controller.

This has changed the secure hardware device from one offering a simple cryptographic interface to a service delivery model. Each of these services effectively runs within its own virtual trust domain that is managed and protected by the HSA device.

5   Demonstrable Integrity

The notarisation service can be thought of as a time-stamping service [1] that certifies each event by adding the time of receipt, a sequence number and then signing the whole structure. The integrity of the evidence trail is provided by the set of timestamps created on each piece of evidence. The ability to manipulate this service either by manipulating time, sequence or by gaining access to the private key would break trust in the evidence store. As such, this service is run within a virtual trust domain provided by an HSA. The HSA has a secure clock and sequence counter along with a service identity on seeing an event record it adds time, sequence, its identity and signs the structure. The secure hardware protects the clock and counter, as well as ensuring that this combination of operations (getting time, formatting the timestamp and signing) becomes atomic that is they cannot be separated.

A simple timestamp on its own does not provide the properties required of the evidence store. Users requesting a subset of the events via a query to the evidence store need to know that the data is part of the record and not just a time stamped event. Further and more importantly, they need to be able check that they have all records relevant to the query. Each of these requirements is achieved through interleaving the event records and then sealing them with the timestamp as described in detail in [3].

Two forms of chaining are used in notarisation – the first chains together the event records to preserve the concept of a log file. A chain of all events is not helpful to a user who only has a right to see small subsets of events without all events they cannot check the chain and hence cannot validate that events they are given are within the chain. As such, a summary chain is produced by blocking together hashes of the individual events so that any event can be found in this summary chain. This summary chain can itself be summarised until a chain of a reasonable size to publish can be created – as show in figure 3. This produces a structure similar to a hash tree often used for time stamping [15]. The evidence store returns the event and

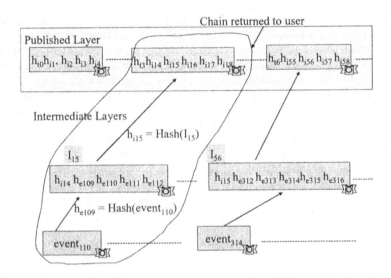

Fig. 3. Forming a summary of the evidence trail

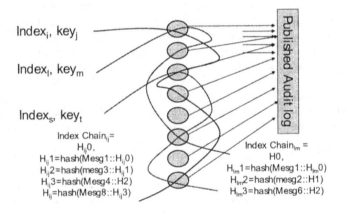

Fig. 4. The index chaining linking elements with common index values.

each intermediate node necessary to show that the event is traceable into the published summary log file. The production of each chain block is also encapsulated within the HSA based notarisation service to ensure that the integrity of the evidence trail cannot be modified.

The main property required by users will be to have confidence that they have been given all events related to their query or that if ones are missing it must be obvious. This is a hard problem for arbitrary queries but a solution based on index interleaving showing that the user has a continuous set of events relating to a single index is possible.

Each role and attribute field is considered as an index along with the process instance identifier. For each value that can be held in each index a chain is maintained by placing the hash of the previous record with the same index and value within the audit record before it is signed (see Figure 4). The evidence store ensures all events are indexed and so as part of the indexing process the hash of the previous records with the same index value pairs can be recovered. These are fed into the notarization system as part of the data for a timestamp and hence the resulting signed audit record is not only part of the main audit chain there are chains defining single index subsets of event records.

The index chaining ensures that there is a well-defined and verifiable sequence of records relating to the each value in an index. A start point is defined, as the first occurrence of a particular value and is included; here a start flag is placed instead of the hash of the previous record. This could allow collusion with the evidence store provider to drop previous data relating to an individual and to start a new trail. The user is well placed to spot that they are not seeing records for processes for which they were a part. Additionally, an auditor with access to all records can detect inconsistencies in the chaining. A user may also wish to see a well-defined (current) end-point to the trail – to do this they can place an event in the system containing the value and this should be the last event they see in the data returned.

The two chaining schemes interleave all the events within the evidence store and in doing so ensure that a user requesting a view on their data can trust the records returned. This is all based on the trust they feel they can place in the hardware protection of the notarisation service that certifies the records, as they are stored.

6   Confidentiality

The evidence store not only allows for the verification of evidence but also ensures the accountability data is available to the participants and not to other parties. The data must be stored for long periods and may be mirrored to multiple sites to ensure data survivability. Additionally the interactive nature of the evidence store implies that the data should be available online necessitating strong security solutions that are robust to attack. An interactive accountability framework may not be considered usable by participants unless they have a strong level of confidence that their data will be kept private.

The evidence store should be encrypted so that there is a degree of robustness from internal and external attack and so backup and mirroring solutions can easily be managed. Encrypting the accountability data leaves three major issues firstly, how to secure the indexes; secondly, how to manage the encryption keys; and thirdly, how to specify the access control in what is a dynamic and flexible system.

The current trusted audit prototype has two parts to the evidence store the indexing and log files containing the encrypted data. From a security perspective, it becomes important that a user (or administrator) cannot trivially extract information by correlating indexes from the different fields. To avoid this indexes are based on salted hashes of the data (and index name) rather than the raw data itself. A component service of the search runs within secure hardware and a user's search request will be passed to a service within this secure boundary. The request is authenticated, the right to search those indexes is checked and only when this succeeds it the salted hash released. Protecting the salted hash within the secure hardware makes systematic attacks on the data structures difficult although an observer viewing all requests could start to reconstruct a store and make certain correlations. Further index security could be gained by encrypting all nodes within an index tree (e.g. a b-tree) and ensuring that the index is only decrypted within the secure hardware – such solutions are considerably more complex.

The log file contains the data for each of the events received by the evidence store. An access management service is run within secure hardware to manage the encryption keys and link the use of these keys to the authentication and authorisation processes. The audit record containing all the interleaved timestamp data and the original event record is passed to this service along with the position in the file where it will be stored. The access management service then encrypts the data by generating a key based using the hash of a secret it maintains along with the position within the file. The encryption and later decryption happens within the secure hardware boundary so that the secret only exists within a set of secure hardware devices (and probably an escrow service for robustness).

The search returns the position of the encrypted data that is read and passed to the access management service in the secure hardware. This may link to the search session or independently authenticate the user. Once authenticated the decryption key is generated from the secret and storage position and the audit record is decrypted by the access management service but retained within the secure hardware. The authorisation check can now proceed and if this succeeds the audit event can be re-encrypted using a key suitable for the requesting user.

The authorisation check is based on an access control expression or policy (rather than a simple ACL [23]) that are provided to the access management service as it is created or by a controller nominated at start up. This means the policy is outside of the control of the normal administration staff. Where the secret is shared over several services, the policies are bound with the key as part of the sharing process.

The expression itself is a set of Boolean expression defined for the various event types. Each expression can refer to fields within the requester's identity including associated credentials along with fields within the event record. For example, the following expression would be used to control access to a medical record:

```
(match(event.GetRoleHolder("patient"),
                      Requestor.GetName()) or
    (match(event.GetRoleHolder("doctor"),
                      Requestor.GetName()) and
            RequestRequestor.HasCredential("doctor"))))
```

The expression specify that a person can get a record if their name matches that in the patent role in the record or if they have a doctor credential, and they are identified in the doctor role. Policies may well be more complex including specifications concerning auditor access rights and perhaps mandating intent to access is itself audited before continuing. This approach has been adopted, as it is believed to be simpler to specify and maintain generating explicit ACLs for each event.

7   Discussion

Many trust management projects such as [7] are somewhat limited in there scope Grandison and Sloman [10] point out that they are "mainly concerned with public key authorisations, authentication and access control but do not consider experiences of risk and trust analysis". In doing so they present tools for trust specifications and monitoring against this specification. Josang [14] also gives a wider definition for trust management as "the activity of collecting, codifying, analysing and presenting security relevant evidence with the purpose of making assessments and decisions regarding e-commerce transactions" and discusses the importance of evidence stating, "The evidence should include, in addition to belief and expectation of intent, proof of competence and correct behaviours".

In this paper, we have stressed the importance of having a transparent and interactive model of accountability to enhance trust. It is believed that trust management frameworks need to include such ideas including extensions to discuss the quality of evidence, the likelihood that evidence is checked and the need to have the user within the feedback loop.

8   Conclusion

This paper has presented an interactive accountability framework that engenders trust in electronic processes by allowing users to see an evidence trail and hence remain in control. A prototype has been described demonstrating that the evidence store upon which the interactive accountability is built is achievable. The evidence store has a particular concentration on trust in the privacy and integrity of the accountability data. This model allows a high degree of transparency and supports intelligent accountability in that those best placed to make judgements are included in the process.

References

[1]   Adams, C. and , P. Cain, D. Pinkas, R. Zuccherato – RFC 3161 Internet X.509 Public Key Infrastructure Time Stamp Protocol (TSP), http://www.ietf.org/rfc/rfc3161 (2001)

[2]   Baldwin, A., Shiu, S., Casassa Mont, M.: Trust Services: A Framework for Service based Solutions, In proceedings of the 26th IEEE COMPSAC, 2002

[3]   Baldwin, A. Shiu, S.:Enabling Shared Audit Data, In Proceedings of the 6th Information Security Conference Eds Boyd and Mao, Springer Verlag (2003)

[4]   Baldwin, A. and Shiu, S.,: Hardware Encapsulation of Security Services. In Compter Security: Proceedings of ESORICS 2003. Springer Verlag

[5]   Bayer, D., S.A. Haber and W.S. Stornetta. Improving the efficiency and reliability of digital time-stamping. In Sequences'91: Methods in Communication Security and Computer Science. pp329-334 Springer-Verlag 1992

[6]   Bellare, M., and Yee, B., Forward-Security in Private-Key Cryptography. Topics in Cryptology - CT-RSA 03, LNCS Vol. 2612Springer-Verlag, 2003

[7]   Blaze, M., Feigenbaum, J., Lacy J.: Decentralized Trust Management. In Proceedings of IEEE Conference on Security and Privacy 1996.

[8]   Ferreira, A., Shiu, S., Baldwin, A.: Towards Accountability for Electronic Patient Records The 16th IEEE Symposium on Computer-Based Medical Systems June 26-27, 2003,

[9]   Fips: Security Requirements for cryptographic modules. Fips 140-2 2001

[10]   Grandison, T., & Sloman, M.: *Trust management tools for internet applications* In Proceedings of 1st International conference on trust management. LNCS vol 2692 (2003)

[11]   Grimsley, M., Meeham, A., Green, G., and Staffor., B. Social capital, community trust and e-government services. Proceedings of 1st International conference on trust management. (2003)

[12]   Haber, S.A., W.S. Stornetta, How to timestamp a digital document. *Journal of Cryptography* 3(2):88-111 1991

[13]   Itoi, N. Secure Coprocessor Integration with Kerberos V5.USENIX Security (2000)

[14]   Josang, A., Tran, N.: Trust Management for E-Commerce. In Proceedings Virtual Banking 2000. http://195.13.121.137/virtualbanking2000/index.htm

[15]   Merkle, R. C., "Protocols for Public Key Cryptography", IEEE Symposium on Security and Privacy, pp 122-134, 1980

[16]   O'Neill O,: Question of Trust: BBC Reith Lectures 2002. Cambridge University Press 2002

[17]   Pato, J. Identity Management - Encyclopedia of Information Security, Kluwer, 2003. (TR HPL-2003-72)

[18]   Pearson S., B. Balacheff, L. Chen, D. Plaquin and G. Proudler. Trusted Computing Platforms: TCPA technology in comtext. HP Books, Prentice Hall (2002)

[19]   RSA Labs: PKCS#11 v2.11 Cryptographic Token Interface Standard. (2001)

[20]   Schneier, B., Kelsey, J., "Cryptographic Support for Secure Logs on Untrusted Machines," 7th USENIX Security Symposium Proceedings, USENIX Press, 1998.

[21]   Smith, S.W., E.R. Palmer and S. Weingart Using a High Performance Programmable Secure Coprocessor. In Proceedings of the 2nd International conference on financial cryptography. Lecture Notes in Computer Science. Springer-Verlag 1998.

[22]   Smith S.W. and D. Safford. Practical Private information retrieval with secure coprocessors. IBM Research T.J. Watson Research Centre (2000)

[23]   Ungureanu, V,. Vesuma, F. and Minsky N.H.,: A policy-based access control mechanism for the corporate Web In Proceedings of ACSAS'00 IEEE. (2000)

The Use of Formal Methods in the Analysis of Trust (Position Paper)

Michael Butler, Michael Leuschel, Stéphane Lo Presti, and Phillip Turner*

University of Southampton, SO17 1BJ, Southampton, United Kingdom
{mjb,mal,splp,pjt}@ecs.soton.ac.uk

Abstract. Security and trust are two properties of modern computing systems that are the focus of much recent interest. They play an increasingly significant role in the requirements for modern computing systems. Security has been studied thoroughly for many years, particularly the sub-domain of cryptography. The use of computing science formal methods has facilitated cryptanalysis of security protocols. At the moment, trust is intensively studied, but not well understood. Here we present our approach based on formal methods for modelling and validating the notion of trust in computing science.

1 Introduction

Recent years have seen a growing concern with security properties of computing systems. This concern is mainly caused by two reasons. First, there is an increasing number of faults in computing systems. This increase in turn ensues from two facts. The penetration of computing science in our professional and personal lives is still expanding, as new computing paradigms such as pervasive computing show. At the same time, programs become overly cluttered and computationally and semantically more complex. The second reason explaining security concerns is that the concept of security itself is widening. This is illustrated by recent problems like privacy breaches (e.g. spam) or violations of legal obligations (e.g. liability via software license).

Notions of trust are constituent in several cryptographic methods, representing the confidence in the association of a cryptographic key to the identity of a principal. Recent multidisciplinary studies on trust envisage the concept as a more general and richer notion than security. Many models of trust have been devised, each concentrating on disparate aspects, among which are recommendations and reputation, belief theory, or risk and uncertainty. It appears that the vast number of notions composing trust defies its systematic analysis.

Computing science formal methods [11] stem from mathematics and aim to help design, develop, analyse and validate software so that it is correct, error-free and robust. Formal models are built on well-known mathematical elements, like sets or functions, and can be analysed against accurate properties, such as consistency or completeness. Formal methods include Petri nets, abstract state machines, process calculi, temporal

---

* This work has been funded in part by the T-SAS (Trusted Software Agents and Services in Pervasive Information Environment) project of the UK Department of Trade and Industry's Next Wave Technologies and Markets Programme.

C.D. Jensen et al. (Eds.): iTrust 2004, LNCS 2995, pp. 333–339, 2004.

and belief logics, and languages such as Z [4], CSP [5] and Alloy [9]. The last decade has seen a trend to use formal methods in computing science, notably in the context of industrial software engineering, because they provide solid methods, produce clear models and have good tool support.

In this paper, we present in section 2 how the security field has used formal methods to solidly build some of its foundations on mathematically proven results. We show initial works in the application of formal methods in trust in section 3, arguing that trust is only at the beginning of its path to make the most of formal methods. Our structured approach based on UML [14] and B [13] formal methods is finally defined in section 4.

2   Formally Proving Security Properties

Security is one of the major problems that computer scientists have to confront nowadays. Security analysis of computing systems consists of creating models of how they operate, may be attacked, and should behave. Formal methods are helpful at modelling and validating existing computing systems with regard to security properties because they provide a structured approach and accurate notations.

In the context of security, the *system model* must not only abstract the programs implementing the system functionalities but also the communication protocols that are used. Formal approaches have been successfully applied to that latter task, for example with the Z notation or the B method [15]. Recently, the analysis [26] of layers of network protocols, involving the commonly used TLS/SSL protocols, have been a further beneficiary of the formal approach.

The model of the possible attacks to the system is called the *threat model* and defines the capabilities of the attacker. The Dolev-Yao threat model traditionally represents an attacker that can overhear, intercept, and synthesise any message and is only limited by the constraints of the cryptographic methods used. This omnipotence has been very difficult to model and most threat models simplify it, as, for example, the attacker in ubiquitous computing [22].

Next, the desired properties of the system need to be defined. Security encompasses six basic sub-properties: authentication, data integrity, confidentiality, non-repudiation, privacy, and availability. Specification of the chosen properties is in general dependent on the notation chosen for the system and threat models.

The last task is to verify that the security properties hold in the system model, complemented by the threat model if it exists. Many formal methods ease this step by applying powerful automated techniques, like test generation or model checking. General formal tools can be used, like the Coq theorem prover [3] that has been used for the verification of the confidentiality of the C-SET protocol [8], or specific ones devised, such as Casper [10] for compiling abstract descriptions to the CSP language, or SpyDer [23] to model-check security properties in the spy-calculus.

In summary, formal methods have benefited security analysis of computing systems by providing systematic methods and reusable tools in order to obtain mathematically proven results. The use of formal methods for security analysis is a very active domain, which evolves with progress from the formal methods and provides a testbed for them.

3   Formally Modelling Trust

Trust has recently attracted much focus, notably in the context of computing science and more specifically computer security. Marsh [24] gave an early (1992) formal model of trust, highlighting the combination of basic and general trust and agent capabilities into situational trust via ad hoc notations. Griffiths et al [21] made use of the Z formal notation to specify cooperative plans in multi-agent systems, annotating these plans with trust information. Many mathematical models have also been devised, for example in game theory (e.g. Birk's model [2]) or probability theory (e.g. Jøsang's Subjective Logic [1]).

More recently, Grandison [25] devised the SULTAN trust management system and his primitives were expressed in the manner of a logic programming language. SULTAN is similar to works on *trust policy languages*. Trust policy languages (which are inspired by security policies) specify what is permitted and prohibited regarding trust decisions, rather than expressing how. They were first devised in the context of Public Key Infrastructures, like IBM's Trust Policy Language or Fidelis [28]. Recent works exhibit more general policies, like those of the SECURE project [17] where domain theory is used to define trust policies able to specify spam filters.

Trust is a complex notion that is not well understood. Growing interest in modelling the notion of trust has given rise to a plethora of models and many aspects of trust are currently being studied. However, these models are difficult to compare directly because they are expressed in diverse ways, i.e. sociological or economic terms, and furthermore use specific notations, thus preventing an unambiguous interpretation. Identifying trust requirements is not always easy and, because they lead to a clearer model of a system and guide its analysis, formal specifications can ease that identification.

4   An Approach to the Modelling and Validation of Trust

The T-SAS (Trusted Software Agents and Services in Pervasive Information Environment) project [27] aims to identify critical trust issues in pervasive computing. In particular, it aims to develop tools and rigorous techniques for validating the trustworthiness of agent and Semantic Web/Grid technologies that support pervasive systems.

The identification of critical trust issues for pervasive environments is hampered by both the diverse literature on trust and lack of expertise by system designers and analysts at identifying issues of *trust*. As noted above, existing definitions of trust also tend to be either specific to particular problem domains, or contrarily, too general. This often leads to specifications impoverished of trust content suitable for analysis and formalisation. Finally, pervasive systems require that user-centric issues are at least as important as purely technical concerns.

To address these problems, whilst ensuring that scenarios studied are sufficiently realistic, the initial phase of this project has focused on the development of an analysis framework grounded in propitious (healthcare) scenarios and use-cases [16]. It is an iterative process of scenario validation by domain experts (e.g. clinicians), identification of trust issues with cross-scenario checking, and domain expert aided scenario maturation. As this process repeats, the scenarios become increasingly rich with trust related detail and the taxonomy of trust derived from the input scenarios stabilises. In our analyses, trust issues have fallen into eleven basic areas. Viz., Source versus Interpretation, Accuracy, Audit trails, Authorisation, Identification, Personal Responsibility, Reliability/Integrity, Availability, Reasoning, Usability and Harm. The relationship between trust categories was broadly in agreement with the literature.

Our current work focuses upon the formal specification stage of a software and hardware prototype. The prototype healthcare application operates on a PDA to support clinicians in a pervasive environment with medical image messaging services. This application is based on a use-case representing a clinician roaming in the pervasive environment of his hospital and using his PDA to display pictures on a neighbour device or to access the information of a patient in an adjoining bed. The PDA currently has image capture, wireless transmission and receipt and can provide telemetry for location determination. The prototype PDA and infrastructure provides furtive ground for dealing with real-time and practical issues whilst retaining many trust concerns.

Using a single method (whether formal or not) to develop complex software and/or hardware systems may limit the ability to adequately tackle complex problems in the large. Unfortunately, many issues of trust are interrelated and highly context dependent. Therefore, simplification of a system which results in loss of this context or corruption of trust interdependencies and interactions is dangerous.

Formal methods are often associated with applications with some critical aspect with severe consequences of fault. For example, safety-, economic-, or security-critical. We believe that users' trust in pervasive computing environments is prone to significant collapse and also that the consequences would be equally undesirable. In short, pervasive computing applications are trust-critical. Yet, the widespread adoption of formal techniques to deal with trust issues is not solely based on risk aversion – tools must be developed that will be used by software engineers, designers and system analysts. Also, formal specifications are not readily communicable to the non-specialist.

In addition to the ability to visually communicate and simplify complex designs, semi-formal techniques such as UML offer the developer additional benefits such as maintainability and re-usability. Despite several studies showing that formal development requires approximately the same overall effort as traditional approaches [12] whilst providing the detection and correction of specification errors early in the development life-cycle, uptake has again, remained slow.

Finally, given the currently limited understanding of trust, it seems sensible to adopt an approach that automatically detects inconsistencies and enables system designers to produce unambiguous and consistent specifications.

In order to successfully negotiate the problems of developers (expertise and thinking methods, visualization, re-usability, maintenance, communicability), we use UML case tools which provide a powerful visual notation which can itself be analysed, tested and validated automatically. The UML is an intuitive and powerful visual notation that decomposes a formal model of a system into various diagrams, such as class, collaboration or statechart diagrams. To automate validation of the models we need to use a method which allows formal proof. We chose the B language, which is an abstract machine notation that structures systems into hierarchy of modules. Each B module is made of components that are themselves refined at different levels of abstraction. Figure 1 portrays an overview of this approach.

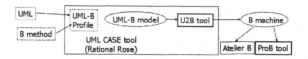

Fig. 1. Overview of approach

To annotate UML with B, we use a UML Profile, called UML-B [6], that defines a specific kind of UML model that has a particular semantics. Figure 1 illustrates a UML-B model. In UML-B, class and statechart diagrams are annotated with B code using an object-oriented dot style. A tool, called U2B [7], then automatically generates, whenever possible, an equivalent B specification from the UML-B model.

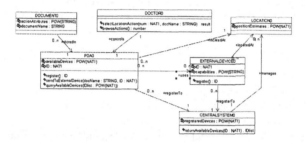

Fig. 2. UML-B screenshot

The final step is to validate our B models using a combination of automated test case generation (e.g. ProTest [19]) and model checking (e.g. ProB [18]). Figure 3 shows a screenshot of the ProB tool. The top left shows the B machine under examination, bottom left shows the current machine state and status of the invariants. Right of the figure shows the states visited during the model checking of the specification.

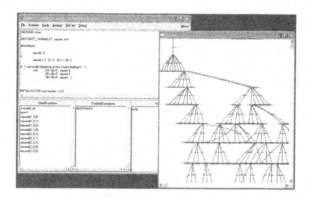

Fig. 3. ProB screenshot

In the context of our use-case, the basic components of trust will be expressed by means of invariants of the B machines. At this stage during our development, the invariants represent properties of the categories Accuracy, Authorisation, Identification and Reliability/Integrity that hold between the various elements of the system (e.g. PDA, Web Services, etc.). We are testing in these models, among other aspects, whether the PDA displays a picture on a wall-mounted screen in a trustworthy manner. Figure 2 shows an example class diagram relating a doctor, his PDA, a document (for viewing on an external device), an external device (display), and a centralised system for managing services based on the user's location, gained from WiFi 802.11 signal processing.

These tools will verify that our UML-B models are consistent, thus proving the trust properties that we have specified in the B invariants. If the properties do not hold, the test case or the counter-example provided by the model checker will enable us to analyse where the problem is and formulate a solution. We would then go into another round of modelling and validation. Finally, we note that this UML and B hybridisation has been favourably examined in an industrial setting, showing that not only are the features of the B-Method and UML complimentary, but that development with these tools was acceptable to commercial enterprise [20].

5 Conclusion

Formal methods for the specification of computer systems and their required properties have shown themselves a valuable tool for security analysis. Much work in the domain of trust devised more or less formal models, thus providing insight into the notion of trust but without formal proofs of the claimed results. The notion of trust remains elusive and has not yet achieved the same level of knowledge that security has.

The lack of formality in the followed approaches is sometimes the cause of misunderstanding and prevents the validation of the proposed models. We believe that validation is necessary to acquire a sufficient confidence in a model and formal methods can provide us with the tools to exhaustively check the proposed solutions. Here we suggest that the rigorous process of formal specification, with its associated techniques and tools for model checking and test case validation, will be as valuable to the study of trust as it has been to date for security.

Prior work in our project, based on several real-world scenarios and applications, produced a set of basic components of trust, which with tools for assisting formal specification and validation are being utilised to expedite formal analysis and test this suggestion. We believe that the practical application of formal methods can facilitate the development and evolution of the field of trust analysis in computing systems.

References

1. A. Jøsang. Trust-based decision making for electronic transactions. In *Proc. of the 4th Nordic Workshop on Secure IT Systems (NORDSEC'99)*, Sweden, November 1999.
2. Andreas Birk. Learning to Trust. In *Trust in Cyber-societies, Integrating the Human and Artificial Perspectives*, volume 2246 of *LNCS*. Springer, 2001.
3. B. Barras and al. The Coq proof assistant reference manual: Version 6.1. Technical Report INRIA RT-0203, May 1997.
4. C. Boyd. Security Architectures Using Formal Methods. *IEEE Journal on Selected Areas in Communications*, 11(5):694–701, June 1993.

5. C. Hoare. *Communicating Sequential Processes*. Prentice Hall, 1985.
6. C. Snook, M. Butler and I. Oliver. Towards a UML profile for UML-B. Technical Report DSSE-TR-2003-3, University of Southampton, UK, 2003.
7. Colin Snook and Michael Butler. Verifying Dynamic Properties of UML Models by Translation to the B Language and Toolkit. In *Proc of UML 200 Workshop Dynamic Behaviour in UML Models: Semantic Questions*, York, October 2000.
8. D. Bolignano. Towards the Formal Verification of Electronic Commerce Protocols. In *Proc. of the 10th Computer Security Foundations Workshop*. IEEE Computer Society Press, 1997.
9. D. Jackson. Alloy: a lightweight object modelling notation. *ACM Transactions on Software Engineering and Methodology (TOSEM)*, 11:256–290, 2002.
10. G. Lowe. Casper: A Compiler for the Analysis of Security Protocols. In *Proc. of the 10th IEEE Computer Security Foundations Workshop*, pages 53–84, USA, 1997.
11. J. Bowen. Formal Methods. http://www.afm.lsbu.ac.uk.
12. J. Draper, H. Treharne, B. Ormsby B. and T. Boyce. Evaluating the B-Method on an Avionics Example. *Data Systems in Aerospace Conf (DASIA'96)*, pages 89–97, 1996.
13. J-R Abrial. *The B-Book*. Cambridge University Press, 1996.
14. J. Rumbaugh, I. Jacobson and G. Booch. *The Unified Modelling Language Reference Manual*. Addison-Wesley, 1998.
15. M. Butler. On the Use of Data Refinement in the Development of Secure Communications Systems. *Formal Aspects of Computing*, 14(1):2–34, October 2002.
16. M. Butler and al. Towards a Trust Analysis Framework for Pervasive Computing Scenarios. In *Proc of the 6th Intl Workshop on Trust, Privacy, Deception, and Fraud in Agent Societies*, Australia, July 2003.
17. M. Carbone, M. Nielsen and V. Sassone. A Formal Model for Trust in Dynamic Networks. In *Proc. of the Intl Conf on Software Engineering and Formal Methods, SEFM 2003*, pages 54–61. IEEE Computer Society, 2003.
18. M. Leuschel and M. Butler. ProB: A Model-Checker for B. In *Proc of FM 2003: 12th Intl. FME Symposium*, pages 855–874, Italy, September 2003.
19. M. Satpathy, M. Leuschel and M. Butler. ProTest: An Automatic Test Environment for B Specifications. In *International Workshop on Model Based Testing*, 2004.
20. M. Satpathy, R. Harrison, C. Snook and M. Butler. A Comparative Study of Formal and Informal Specifications through an Industrial Case Study. IEEE/ IFIP Workshop on Formal Specification of Computer Based Systems, 2001.
21. N. Griffiths, M. Luck and M. d'Inverno. Annotating Cooperative Plans with Trusted Agents. In *Trust, Reputation, and Security: Theories and Practice*, LNAI 2631. Springer, 2002.
22. S. Creese, M. Goldsmith, B. Roscoe and I. Zakiuddin. The Attacker in Ubiquitous Computing Environments: Formalising the Threat Model. In *Proc. of the 1st Intl Workshop on Formal Aspects in Security and Trust*, pages 83–97, Italy, 2003.
23. S. Lenzini, S. Gnesi and D. Latella. SpyDer, a Security Model Checker. In *Proc. of the 1st Intl Workshop on Formal Aspects in Security and Trust*, pages 163–180, Pisa, Italy, 2003.
24. S. Marsh. Trust in Distributed Artificial Intelligence. In *Artificial Social Systems, (MAA-MAW'94*, LNCS 830, pages 94–112. Springer, 1994.
25. T. Grandison. *Trust Management for Internet Applications*. PhD thesis, University of London, UK, 2003.
26. The FORWARD project. Protocol Synthesis Feasibility Report, FORWARD Deliverable D2. http://www.nextwave.org.uk/downloads/forward_psfr.pdf.
27. University of Southampton and QinetiQ. T-SAS (Trusted Software Agents and Services in Pervasive Information Environment) project. http://www.trustedagents.co.uk.
28. W. Teh-Ming Yao. *Fidelis*: A Policy-Driven Trust Management Framework. In *Proc. 1st Intl Conf on Trust Management (iTrust 2003)*, Greece, May 2003.

Computing Recommendations to Trust

Piotr Cofta

E-Business & Security – Technology Platform, Nokia Group, Finland
piotr.cofta@nokia.com

Abstract. In a technology-intensive world humans are facing new problems stemming from the introduction of machine-intensive communication. The natural human ability to asses, accumulate and evaluate trust in other humans through direct interpersonal communications is significantly impaired when humans interact with systems alone. The development of applications that rely on trust, like electronic commerce, can be significantly affected by this fact unless humans can be better advised on trust.
This paper proposes a simple trust model used by the Intimate Trust Advisor (ITA), the conceptual device, to evaluate the recommendation to trust in the immediate technical environment. The model of trust discussed in this paper explores relationship between trust and complexity.

1 Introduction

As the world becomes more saturated with technology, direct face-to-face communication is being replaced by indirect communication means. The Internet and cryptography enable fast and secure information exchange, but reduce the natural human ability to evaluate and establish trust between communicating parties.

Trust is seen as the "lubricant of the social life" [1] and a critical factor affecting the introduction of several new technologies, e.g. mobile commerce. A lack of trust in technology itself may significantly hamper its future adoption.

This paper presents the model of trust that can be used to evaluate recommendations for trust-related decisions. This model can be used by the Intimate Trusted Advisor (ITA) [2]. The ITA is the conceptual device that provides the recommendation to its user regarding the trust in user's immediate technical environments. The model presented here is intentionally simple yet it is supposed to address some of the important aspects of the trust-building process.

The model assesses trust in technology-related entities. It works in two phases. First, entities are filtered whether they can be the subject of the proper trust relationship. The second phase generates the recommendation to trust by using the novel approach to interpret trust as the exchange process.

The authors are in the process to assess the validity of the model through a series of experiments.

C.D. Jensen et al. (Eds.): iTrust 2004, LNCS 2995, pp. 340–346, 2004.

2 Related Work

There is a significant amount of work dedicated to trust modelling. McKnight [3] provides the multi-stage interdisciplinary model of trust that can be used to evaluate trust. It is worth noting that this exhaustive model requires up to 16 input variables to provide the assessment of trust. Mui [4] provides an interesting computational model that base on the available history of relationships. Tan [5] study the simple model of transactional trust, linking trust with concepts like risk and gain. Even though no exact function is provided, the linkage between traditional domain of trust and economical indicators is noteworthy. Yan and Cofta [6] analyse domain-based trust models specific for mobile communication to explore transitional aspects of trust. Egger [7] study the model suitable for the electronic commerce, stressing the multi-stage approach to trust evaluation. English at al [8] analyses the trust models for entities within the global computing system.

Analysis of trust leads also to several trust-modelling languages that can be used to specify and calculate trust. Grandison [9] defined the specialised logic-based language SULTAN while Josang [10] constructed the trust-evaluation language on the basis of the logic of uncertain probabilities. Marsh [11] provides the analysis of the meaning of trust constructs that leads to the construction of the formal notation.

It is interesting that several works study dimensions of trust relationship, stressing internal contrasts between different aspects of trust. Castelfranchi [12] looks at the dialectics of trust and control, constructing the model to assess the degree of trust out of the contrast between those two concepts. Camp [13] study trust as the collision of paradigms in social sciences. Redwine [14] looks at the dynamics of trust to identify five dimensions of trust, each based on contrasting aspect.

The development of Internet gave way to several analysis of decision-support aids that base on trust relationship. For example, Urban [15] explores the ability to establish the web site that operates as the trusted shopping advisor. Muir [16] study trust between humans and machines to calibrate user's trust in decisions aids.

3 Trust and Complexity

There is a visible overflow of definitions of trust, due to its elusive and multi-dimensional nature. McKnight [17] states that trust has 17.0 definitions, comparing to the average of 4.7.

This paper bases its analysis on the complexity-based definition of trust, as formulated after Luhmann [18]. Similar formulation of the definition can be found in [19] while [20] provides the good comparison of Luhmann's approach to other foundations of the definition of trust.

Definition 1.

> *Trust is the subjective method to reduce the perceived complexity of future by assuming, on the basis of limited subjective knowledge, beneficial actions of independent actors.*

Luhmann's approach stems from contemplating the future as a multiplicity of possible paths. Some of those paths may lead to the desired development (e.g. reaching the goal), but the complexity generated by all the possibilities is beyond the comprehension of the human, thus possibly inhibiting any rational choice.

Trust is one of several means to deal with such complexity by reducing it to the manageable level. Trustor, expecting trustee to behave in the beneficial way, can subjectively eliminate the multitude of negative versions of the future (that may originate in the non-beneficial behaviour of the trustee), thus concentrating on remaining possibilities.

The definition brings up two interesting conclusions about the trust relationship. First, not all entities are entitled to the trust relationship, not because of lack of merits but because of lack of such necessity. There may be entities that have nothing to do with any of possible futures, being irrelevant to the path of event. Further, some entities are not independent actors, i.e. they are unable to act at their will, so that not trust is expected, but only confidence that such entities will follow their usual behaviour.

The second conclusion from this definition is that trust can be seen as a certain form of a transactional exchange where by trusting, the person (the trustor) exchanges the limited knowledge about the trustee for the benefit of the complexity of events being reduced.

4 Intimate Trust Advisor

The Intimate Trust Advisor (ITA) [2] is the conceptual personal device that evaluates the immediate technical environment of its user and communicates its recommendation regarding trust in such environment to its user. The ITA may use the remotely located supporting environment to evaluate the situation.

The reference architecture of ITA is provided on Fig.1. The assessment of trust is denoted as (a), the recommendation to trust as (b) while the user's decision to trust is identified as (c). The support that ITA may receive from the remote environment is identified as (d).

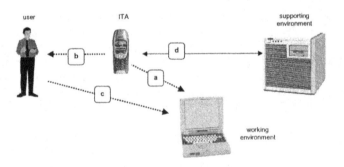

Fig. 1. ITA reference architecture

Even though the user is free to follow or to reject the recommendation provided by ITA, it is expected that ITA will be in many cases the only reasonable source of recommendation available to the user.

5 The Model

The model assumes that the person (the ITA user) at certain moment perceives the complexity of the future that may possibly lead to unfavourable outcome. The user understands that most of this complexity comes from other entities. The user asks ITA for advice regarding technology-related entities. Some of such entities may require the user to express his trust in them in order to proceed. The recommendation that ITA issues tells whether such trust should be expressed.

The model itself works in two steps. First, entities are filtered to identify those that are relevant to the current situation. The behaviour of relevant entities is analysed to determine whether the trust is needed. Finally, those entities that are both relevant and in the need for trust are analysed to determine the recommendation.

5.1 Filtering

Not all entities should be considered as candidates for the decision to trust as some of them may be simply out of scope of the current situation. The person is usually able to remove most of the entities from any considerations by classifying them as irrelevant. For example, the butterfly flapping its wings at the remote corner of tropical forest is believed not to interfere with a person crossing the street in Oxford (despite the concept of the 'butterfly effect'). Contrary, the driver in Oxford that is approaching the zebra crossing may interfere with the future.

Further, entities that are fully predictable do not need trust. The predictable entity may interfere with the course of events but its behaviour is known so that it can be taken into account. Predictable entities do not require trust, but only confidence in their predictability. As the authors have overheard once "You do not have to trust the train to follow tracks. It has little choice".

The authors argue that the technical device, complex enough, can be believed to act on its free will rather than in the predictable way, specifically if the user is not aware of all the principles that influence the behaviour of such device. For example, Chopra [21] acknowledges that people relate to machines as they are fellow human beings.

5.2 Decision to Trust

The decision to trust is usually defined through a complex interleaved list of properties as integrity or benevolence. This theoretical approach represents the stark contrast with the everyday practice of trusting someone who has been met on the first date or trusting the anecdotal second-hand car dealer.

The authors offer the model of the decision to trust that bases on complexity and is closely rooted in Luhmann's definition of trust, hoping that such model may better explain the phenomena of the ad-hoc trust in human behaviour.

The authors argue that it is the unmanageable complexity of the future that drives trust. What the would-be trustor is looking for is the reduction of complexity. The trustor is willing to trust the trustee in order to decrease his own (trustor's) burden. If not, then the trust is not needed as it does not solve any problem of the trustor.

The would-be trustor rationalises his decision to trust (or not to trust) on the basis of limited and incomplete knowledge about the trustee. Such knowledge may not give any rational foundation for trust, but it is used to make the decision, as this is the only knowledge available to the trustor.

The authors assume that the actual decision to trust represents the exchange between the available proof of trustworthy behaviour and the perceived promise of the reduction of complexity. In other words, the lack of proof can be compensated by the expected reduction in complexity and vice versa: the promise of minimal reduction can be compensated by the solid reputation.

The exchange model explains why the rationally untrustworthy people are trusted: they promise to reduce the complexity to the level that makes the offer attractive despite the lack of credits.

The exact relationship between those two variables is subject to further study, but as the starting point as well as for the purpose of ITA such relationship may be assumed to be as straightforward as the hyperbolic function t*r=const.

The authors further assume that the constant value that is present in this equation represents the inversion of the extent of the propensity to trust, the inherent willingness to trust. Therefore, the equation takes on the form:

$$t * r = 1 / p$$

where   t - extent of the proof of trustworthiness
r - net reduction in complexity
p - propensity to trust

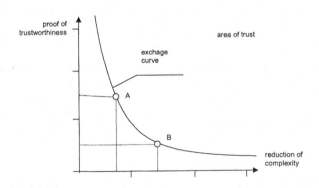

Fig. 2. The trust exchange curve

This consideration may lead to the following diagram, as shown on Fig. 2. All the points at and above the curve represents the combinations of proof and reduction that satisfy the need of the trustor. The borderline points A and B represent situations of little reduction, solid proof and of little proof but significant reduction, respectively.

5.3 Recommendation to Trust

Assuming that all the necessary values has been quantified, the recommendation to trust can be provided if the product of expected reduction in complexity and the perceived trustworthiness is located at or above the exchange curve defined by the user's propensity to trust. Such simple recommendation model can be extended to communicate the level of recommendation: whether ITA strongly 'believes' in the recommendation or merely suggests it, using e.g. the distance from the curve as the extend of recommendation.

6 Conclusions

This paper presents the simple, novel model of recommendations that bases on the definition of trust derived from Luhmann's works and stresses the relationship between the complexity and trust. The model describes how the recommendation to trust can be assessed in terms of reduction to complexity and extent of the proof of trustworthiness, and further related to the propensity to trust, resulting in the weighted recommendation. In addition, the filtering conditions of relevance and unpredictability are integrated into the model.

The model can be implemented in ITA, the Intimate Trust Advisor, the device that should help its user to make decisions regarding trust in the immediate technical environment. The model can be applied also to other situations and environments, e.g. to Internet commerce.

The model presented in this paper requires less input variables then other known ones. Values of those variables can be directly related to properties of the technical system that ITA is to evaluate or to the user of the device.

The proposed filtering function as well as the exchange function are simple to calculate and eventually lead to the single integrated indicator of the level of recommendations.

The authors plan a series of experiments to test the concept presented in this paper. Experiments will not involve the device itself, but they will concentrate on verifying whether the notion of 'trust as exchange' can be justified.

References

1. Fukuyama F: Trust: The Social Virtues and the Creation of Prosperity, Touchstone Books; ISBN: 0684825252; (June 1996)
2. Cofta P., Crane S.: Towards the Intimate Trust Advisor. Proc. of the First Int. Conf., iTrust, 2003, Lect. Notes in Comp. Sci. 2692, 2003.
3. McKnight, D. Harrison, Chervany Norman L.: What is Trust? A Conceptual Analysis and An Interdisciplinary Model. In Proceedings of the 2000 Americas Conference on Information Systems (AMCI2000). AIS, Long Beach, CA (August 2000).

4. Lik Mui, Mojdeh Mohtashemi, Ari Halberstadt: A Computational Model of Trust and Reputation. In Proc. Of the 35th Annual Hawaii International Conference on System sciences, 7-10 (Jan. 2002), Big Island, HI, USA.
5. Yao-Hua Tan, Walter Thoen: Formal Aspects of a Generic Model of Trust for Electronic Commerce. In: proc. of the 33rd Hawaii Int. Conf. on System Sciences 2000.
6. Zheng Yan, Piotr Cofta: Methodology to Bridge Different Domains of Trust in Mobile Communications. The First International Conference on Trust Management (iTrust2003), Crete, Greece, May 2003.
7. Egger F.N.: "Trust Me, I'm an Online Vendor": Towards a Model of Trust for E-commerce System Design. In: Szwillus G.& Turner T. (Eds.), CHI2000 Extended Abstracts: Conference on Human Factors in Computing Systems, The Hague, April 1-6, 2000: 101-102.; also in: http://www.ecommuse.com/research/publications/ chi2000.PDF
8. Colin English, Waleed Wagealla, Paddy Nixon, Sotirios Terzis: Trusting Collaboration in Global Computing System. In Proc. of the First Int. Conf., iTrust, 2003, Lect. Notes in Comp. Sci. 2692, 2003.
9. Tyrone Grandison, Morris Sloman: SULTAN - A Language for Trust Specification and Analysis. In http://www.hpovua.org/ PUBLICATIONS/ PROCEEDINGS/ 8_HPOVUAWS/Papers/Paper01.2-Grandison-Sultan.pdf
10. A. Jøsang: A Logic for Uncertain Probabilities. International Journal of Uncertainty, Fuzziness and Knowledge-Based Systems. 9(3), pp.279-311, June 2001.
11. Marsh S. P.: Formalising Trust as a Computational Concept. Doctoral dissertation, Univ. of Stirling, Scotland; also in http://www.iit.nrc.ca/~steve/Publications.html
12. Cristiano Castelfranchi, Rino Falcone: Trust and Control: A Dialectic Link. In: http://alfebiite.ee.ic.ac.uk/docs/papers/D3/4._TrustControl.pdf
13. L. Jean Camp, Helen Nissenbaum, Cathleen McGrath: Trust: A Collision of Paradigms. In Proc. of Financial Cryptography 2001. In http://itc.mit.edu /itel/docs/2001/trust_cnm.pdf
14. Samuel T. Redwine: Dissecting Trust and the Assurance-Violation Dynamics. In Proc. of the 36th Hawaii Int. Conf. on System Sciences (HICSS'03).
15. Urban G.L., Sultan F., Qualls W.: Design and Evaluation of a Trust Based Advisor on the Internet. In: http://ebusiness.mit.edu/research/papers/Urban.pdf.
16. Muir B. M.: Trust between humans and machines, and the design of decision aids. In: Int. J. Man-Machine Studies (1987). Vol.27, p. 527-539.
17. McKnight, D. Harrison, Chervany Norman L.: The meanings of Trust. In: http:// www.misrc.umn.edu/wpaper/wp96-04.htm
18. Niklas Luhmann: Trust and Power. 1979, John Willey & Sons.
19. Niklas Luhmann: Familiarity, Confidence, Trust: problems and Alternatives. In: Diego Gambetta (ed.) Trust: Making and Breaking Cooperative Relations. http://www.socilology.ox.ac.uk/papers/luhmann94-107.pdf.
20. Florian N. Egger: Consumer Trust in E-Commerce: From Psychology to Interaction Design. In J.E.J. prins (ed.) Trust in Electronic Commerce, Kluwer, 2002.
21. Kari Chopra, William A. Wallace: Trust in Electronic Environments. Proceedings of the 36th Hawaii International Conference on System Sciences (HICSS'03), 2003.

Picking Battles: The Impact of Trust Assumptions on the Elaboration of Security Requirements

Charles B. Haley[1], Robin C. Laney[1], Jonathan D. Moffett[2], and Bashar Nuseibeh[1]

[1] Department of Computing, The Open University,
Walton Hall, Milton Keynes, MK7 6AA, UK
{C.B.Haley, R.C.Laney, B.A.Nuseibeh}@open.ac.uk
[2] Department of Computer Science, University of York
Heslington, York, YO10 5DD, UK
jdm@cs.york.ac.uk

Abstract. This position paper describes work on *trust assumptions* in the context of security requirements. We show how trust assumptions can affect the scope of the analysis, derivation of security requirements, and in some cases how functionality is realized. An example shows how trust assumptions are used by a requirements engineer to help define and limit the scope of analysis and to document the decisions made during the process.

1   Introduction

Requirements engineering is about determining the *characteristics* of a *system-to-be*, and how well these characteristics fit with the desires of the *stakeholders*. A system-to-be includes all the diverse components needed to achieve its purpose, such as the computers, the people who will use, maintain, and depend on the system and the environment the system exists within. *Stakeholders* are those entities (e.g. people, companies) that have some reason to care about the system's characteristics. A description of these characteristics is the system's *requirements*.

Security requirements are an important component of a system's requirements. They arise because stakeholders assert that some objects, tangible (e.g. cash) or intangible (e.g. information), have direct or indirect value. Such objects are called *assets*, and the stakeholders naturally wish to protect their value. Assets can be harmed, or can be used to cause indirect harm, such as to reputation. Security requirements ensure that these undesirable outcomes cannot take place.

Security requirements often assume the existence of an *attacker*. The goal of an attacker is to cause *harm*. Leaving aside harm caused by accident, if one can show that no attackers exist, then security is irrelevant. An attacker wishes to cause harm by exploiting an asset in some undesirable way. The possibility of such an exploitation is called a *threat*. An *attack* exploits a *vulnerability* in the system to carry out a threat.

It is useful to reason about the attacker as if he or she were a type of stakeholder (e.g. [1; 9; 10]). The attacker would therefore have requirements; he or she wants a

C.D. Jensen et al. (Eds.): iTrust 2004, LNCS 2995, pp. 347–354, 2004.

system to have characteristics that create vulnerabilities. The requirements engineer wants the attacker's requirements to not be met. To accomplish this, one specifies sufficient *constraints* on the behavior of a system to ensure that vulnerabilities are kept to an acceptable minimum [11]. Security requirements specify these constraints.

A system-level analysis is required to obtain security requirements. Without knowledge of a system's components, the requirements engineer is limited to general statements about a system's security needs. Nothing can be said about how the needs are met. To determine security requirements, one must look deeper; we propose to use *problem frames* [8] to accomplish this. In a problem frames analysis, this means looking at and describing the behavior of *domains* within the context of the system.

While reasoning about security, a requirements engineer must make decisions about how much to trust the supplied indicative (observable) properties of domains that make up the system and evaluate the risks associated with being wrong. These decisions are *trust assumptions*, and they can have a fundamental impact on how the system is realized [13]. Trust assumptions can affect which domains must be analyzed, the risk that vulnerabilities exist, and the risk that a system design is stable. During analysis, trust assumptions permit the requirements engineer to pick battles, deciding which domains need further analysis and which do not.

This paper describes combining trust assumptions, problem frames, and threat descriptions in order to aid in derivation of security requirements. Section 2 provides background material on problem frames. Section 3 discusses security requirements. Section 4 describes the role of trust assumptions. Section 5 presents related work, and section 6 concludes.

2   Problem Frames

All problems involve the interaction of domains that exist in the world. The problem frames notation [8] is useful for diagramming the domains involved in a problem and the interconnections (phenomena) between them, and for analyzing their behavior. For example, assume that working with stakeholders produces a requirement "open door when the door-open button is pushed." Figure 1 illustrates satisfying the requirement with a basic automatic door system. The first domain is the door mechanism domain, capable of opening and shutting the door. The second is the domain requesting that the door be opened; including both the 'button' to be pushed and the human pushing the button. The third is the *machine*, the domain being designed to fulfill the requirement that the door open when the button is pushed. The dashed-line oval presents the requirement that the problem is to satisfy. The dashed arrow from the oval indicates which domain is to be constrained by the requirement.

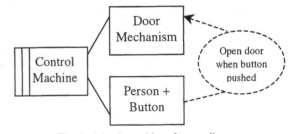

Fig. 1. A basic problem frames diagram

Every domain has *interfaces*, which are defined by the *phenomena* visible to other domains. Descriptions of phenomena of given (existing) domains are indicative; the phenomena and resulting behavior can be observed. Descriptions of phenomena of designed domains (domains to be built as part of the solution) are optative; one wishes to observe the phenomena in the future. To illustrate the idea of phenomena, consider the person+button domain in Figure 1. The domain might produce the event phenomena ButtonDown and ButtonUp when the button is respectively pushed and released. Alternatively, it might produce the single event OpenDoor, combining the two events into one.

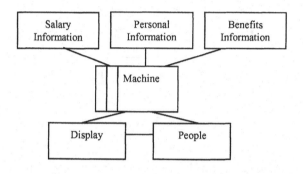

Fig. 2. Example Context Diagram

The two fundamental diagram types in a problem frames analysis are the *context diagram* and the *problem frame diagrams*. The context diagram shows all the domains in a system, and how they are interconnected. The problem frame diagrams each examine a *problem* in the system, showing how a given requirement (problem) is to be satisfied. In systems with only one requirement, the context diagram and the problem frame diagram are almost identical. For most systems, though, the domains in the problem frame diagrams are a projection of the context, showing only the domains or groups of domains of interest to the particular problem.

Figure 2 shows a context diagram for a system that will be used as an example throughout the remainder of this paper. The system is a subset of a Human Resources system. There are two functional requirements, of which we will consider the second.

- Salary, personal, and benefits information shall be able to be entered, changed, and deleted by HR staff. This information is referred to as *payroll information*.
- Users shall have access to kiosks located at convenient locations throughout the building and able to display an 'address list' subset of personal information consisting of any employee's name, office, and work telephone number.

The problem diagram for the second requirement (the 'address list' function) is shown in Figure 3. Phenomena are intentionally omitted. The security requirements will be added in the next section.

3   Security Requirements

Security requirements come into existence to prevent harm by attacks on assets [5; 11]. An asset is something in the context of the system, tangible or not, that is to be protected [7]. A threat is the potential for abuse of an asset that will cause harm in the context of the problem. A vulnerability is a weakness in the system that an attack exploits. Security requirements are constraints on functional requirements, intended to reduce the scope of vulnerabilities.

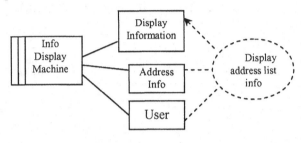

Fig. 3. Address list

The security community provides general categories for constraints, labeling them using the acronym CIA, and more recently more 'A's [12]:
- Confidentiality: ensure that an asset is visible only to those actors authorized to see it. This is larger than 'read access to a file', as it can include, for example, visibility of a data stream on a network.
- Integrity: ensure that the asset is not corrupted. As above, integrity is larger than 'write access to a file', including operations such as triggering transactions that should not occur.
- Availability: ensure that the asset is readily accessible to actors that need it. Availability is best explained by a counterexample, such as preventing a company from doing business by denying it access to something important.
- Authentication & accountability: ensure that the source of the asset, actor, or action is known. One example is the simple login. More complex examples include mutual authentication (e.g. exchanging cryptography keys) and non-repudiation.

By inverting the sense of these categories, one can construct descriptions of possible threats on assets. These *threat descriptions* are phrases of the form *performing action X on/to asset Y could cause harm Z* [5]. Referring to the example presented above, some possible threat descriptions are:
- Changing salary data could increase salary costs, lowering earnings.
- Exposing addresses (to headhunters) could cause loss of employees, raising costs.

To use the threat descriptions, the requirements engineer examines each problem frame diagram, looking to see if the asset mentioned in the threat is found in the problem. If the asset is found, then the requirements engineer must apply constraints on the problem to ensure that the asset is not vulnerable to being used in the way that the action in the threat description requires. These constraints are security requirements. The security requirements are satisfied by changing the problem in a way that changes the behavior of the domains.

Analysis of Figure 3 shows that there are vulnerabilities that allow the threats to be realized. Attackers can see the data on the network. Nothing prevents an attacker from accessing the system. In order to maintain confidentiality and integrity of the data, the network needs to be protected and employees need to be authenticated. A design decision is made to encrypt data on the network, and appropriate constraints and phenomena are added. Our next problem is employee authentication; we will solve this problem in the next section.

4   Trust Assumptions

A requirements engineer determines how a requirement is satisfied using the characteristics of the domains in the problem. A similar relationship exists between security requirements and trust assumptions; how security requirements are satisfied depends on the trust assumptions made by the requirements engineer.

We use the definition of trust proposed by Grandison & Sloman [4]: "[Trust] is the quantified belief by a trustor with respect to the competence, honesty, security and dependability of a trustee within a specified context". In our case, the *requirements engineer* trusts that some domain will participate 'competently and honestly' in the satisfaction of a security requirement in the context of the problem.

Adding trust assumptions serves two purposes. The first is to limit the scope of the analysis to the domains in the context. The second is to document how the requirements engineer chooses to trust other domains that are in the context for some other reason. To illustrate the former, assume a requirement stipulating that the computers operate for up to eight hours in the event of a power failure. The requirements engineer satisfies this requirement by adding backup generators to the system. In most cases, the engineer can trust the manufacturer of the generators to supply equipment without vulnerabilities that permit an attacker to take control of the generators. By making this trust assumption, the requirements engineer does not need to include the supply chain of the generators in the analysis.

Returning to our example, we see that trust assumptions must be added to the diagram to complete the picture. For example, the analysis does not explain why the encrypted networks and authentication are considered secure or how address information is to be protected. The IT organization convinces the requirements engineer that the encryption software and keys built into the system are secure, and that the keys control access to the address information. Choosing to accept the explanations, the engineer adds three trust assumptions (TA1 – TA3) to the problem frame diagram.

There are threats against the name and address information which indicate that confidentiality of the information must be maintained. To counter the threats, the requirements engineer proposes that the information be limited to people having authentication information and able to log in. The IT department refuses on cost grounds. The stakeholders refuse because of ease-of-use.

Further questioning reveals that the front door of the building is protected by a security guard; the guard restricts entrance to authorized personnel. The security manager agrees that the security guard can stand in for authentication. A trust assumption (TA4) is added, having the effect of changing the *people* domain to *employees* by restricting membership to people allowed in by the building security system. Figure 4 shows the resulting problem frames diagram.

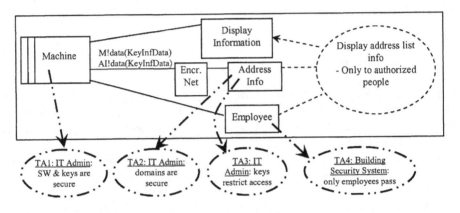

Fig. 4. Address list revisited

The example shows that trust assumptions restrict domain membership. For example, the building security system trust assumption restricts membership of the *people* domain to people acceptable to the door guard, effectively converting the domain to *employees*.

The *IT Admin: keys restrict access* trust assumption is a special case. The domain being limited is an 'others' domain representing people not permitted to see the data. This domain isn't in the context. Adding the domain and connecting the trust assumption would restrict the domain's membership to null. Rather than adding a null domain, the trust assumption is expressed in terms of its effect and attached to the domain that caused the trust assumption to come into existence.

5   Related Work

We are not aware of other work investigating the capture of a requirements engineer's trust assumptions about the domains that make up the solution to the problem.

Several groups are looking at the role of trust in security requirements engineering. In the *i** framework [14; 16], Yu, Lin, & Mylopoulos take an 'actor, intention, goal' approach where security and trust relationships within the model are modeled as "softgoals": goals that have no quantitative measure for satisfaction. The Tropos project [3] uses the *i** framework, adding wider lifecycle coverage. Gans et al [2] add distrust and "speech acts". Yu and Cysneiros have added privacy to the mix [15]. All of these models are concerned with analyzing trust relations between actors/agents in the running system. As such, an *i** model complements the approach presented here, and in fact can be used to determine the goals and requirements.

He and Antón [6] are concentrating on privacy, working on mechanisms to assist trusting of privacy policies, for example on web sites. They propose a context-based access model. The framework, like *i**, describes run-time properties, not the requirements engineer's assumptions about the domains forming the solution.

6 Conclusions and Future Work

We have described an approach for using trust assumptions while reasoning about security requirements. The approach makes a strong distinction between system requirements and machine specifications, permitting the requirements engineer to choose how to conform to the requirements. The trust assumptions embedded in the domain inform the requirements engineer, better enabling him or her to choose between alternate ways of satisfying the functional requirements while ensuring that vulnerabilities are removed or not created.

Work on trust assumptions is part of a larger context wherein security requirements are determined using the crosscutting properties of threat descriptions [5]. The trust assumptions will play a critical role in analyzing cost and risk. The quantification of the level of trust, not yet used, will be important in this context.

Acknowledgements. The financial support of the Leverhulme Trust is gratefully acknowledged. Thanks also go to Michael Jackson for his many insights about problem frames and requirements, and to the anonymous reviewers for their helpful comments.

References

1. Crook, R., Ince, D., Lin, L., Nuseibeh, B.: "Security Requirements Engineering: When Anti-Requirements Hit the Fan," In Proceedings of the IEEE Joint International Conference on Requirements Engineering (RE'02). Essen Germany (2002) 203-205.
2. Gans, G., et al.: "Requirements Modeling for Organization Networks: A (Dis)Trust-Based Approach," In 5th IEEE International Symposium on Requirements Engineering (RE'01). Toronto, Canada: IEEE Computer Society Press (27-31 Aug 2001) 154-165.
3. Giorgini, P., Massacci, F., Mylopoulos, J.: "Requirement Engineering Meets Security: A Case Study on Modelling Secure Electronic Transactions by VISA and Mastercard," In Proceedings of the 22nd International Conference on Conceptual Modeling. Chicago IL USA: Springer-Verlag Heidelberg (13-16 Oct 2003) 263-276.
4. Grandison, T., Sloman, M.: "Trust Management Tools for Internet Applications," In The First International Conference on Trust Management. Heraklion, Crete, Greece: Springer Verlag (28-30 May 2003).

5. Haley, C. B., Laney, R. C., Nuseibeh, B.: "Deriving Security Requirements from Cross-cutting Threat Descriptions," In Proceedings of the Fourth International Conference on Aspect-Oriented Software Development (AOSD'04). Lancaster UK: ACM Press (22-26 Mar 2004).

6. He, Q., Antón, A. I.: "A Framework for Modeling Privacy Requirements in Role Engineering" at Ninth International Workshop on Requirements Engineering: Foundation for Software Quality, The 15th Conference on Advanced Information Systems Engineering (CAiSE'03), Klagenfurt/Velden, Austria (16 Jun 2003).

7. ISO/IEC: *Information Technology - Security Techniques - Evaluation Criteria for IT Security - Part 1: Introduction and General Model*. ISO/IEC: Geneva Switzerland, 15408-1 (1 Dec 1999).

8. Jackson, M.: *Problem Frames*. Addison Wesley, 2001.

9. van Lamsweerde, A., Brohez, S., De Landtsheer, R., Janssens, D.: "From System Goals to Intruder Anti-Goals: Attack Generation and Resolution for Security Requirements Engineering" at Requirements for High Assurance Systems Workshop (RHAS'03), Eleventh International Requirements Engineering Conference (RE'03), Monterey, CA USA (8 Sep 2003).

10. Lin, L., Nuseibeh, B., Ince, D., Jackson, M., Moffett, J.: "Introducing Abuse Frames for Analyzing Security Requirements," In Proceedings of the 11th IEEE International Requirements Engineering Conference (RE'03). Monterey CA USA (8-12 Sep 2003) 371-372.

11. Moffett, J. D., Nuseibeh, B.: *A Framework for Security Requirements Engineering*, Department of Computer Science. University of York, UK, YCS368 (August 2003).

12. Pfleeger, C. P., Pfleeger, S. L.: *Security in Computing*. Prentice Hall, 2002.

13. Viega, J., McGraw, G.: *Building Secure Software: How to Avoid Security Problems the Right Way*. Addison Wesley, 2002.

14. Yu, E.: "Towards Modelling and Reasoning Support for Early-Phase Requirements Engineering," In Proceedings of the Third IEEE International Symposium on Requirements Engineering (RE'97). Annapolis MD USA (6-10 Jan 1997) 226-235.

15. Yu, E., Cysneiros, L. M.: "Designing for Privacy and Other Competing Requirements," In Second Symposium on Requirements Engineering for Information Security (SREIS'02). Raleigh, NC USA (15-16 Oct 2002).

16. Yu, E., Liu, L.: "Modelling Trust for System Design Using the i* Strategic Actors Framework," In *Trust in Cyber-societies, Integrating the Human and Artificial Perspectives*, R. Falcone, M. P. Singh, Y.-H. Tan, eds. Springer-Verlag Heidelberg (2001) 175-194.

Towards Trust Relationship Planning for Virtual Organizations

Philip Robinson, Jochen Haller, and Roger Kilian-Kehr

SAP Corporate Research, Vincenz-Prießnitz-Str.1, 76131 Karlsruhe, Germany
{Philip.Robinson, Jochen.Haller, Roger.Kilian-Kehr}@sap.com

Abstract. Virtual Organizations (VO) continue to inspire marketing specialists, technologists and researchers. However, with automation of security and trust necessary, this adds to the complexity of the dynamically networked relationships. This paper identifies Trust Relationship Planning as an advanced feature missing from Trust Management in the context of VO's. We define and motivate this claim, by aligning Trust Management with other relationship management systems, and derive core concepts for the planning component.

1 Introduction

Virtual Organizations (VO's) are proposed as the future of collaborative business systems. VO proponents suggest that there will be key advantages for production and profitability realized, when short-term, specially contracted and objective-oriented cross-domain relationships are formed, without extensive geographic dislocation of physical resources and people [5]. In terms of a single definition for a VO, we agree with Wolters and Hoogeweegen that authors vary in their definitions but there are some recurring properties across publications [9]. They identify these as:

Temporary alignments of a network of independent organizations, dynamic switching between network partners, end-customer requirements as starting point, bringing together the core competencies of the partners and intensive use of ICT (Information and Communication Technologies).

The motivation for writing this paper grew as we were deliberating over the new issues for trust management in these VO environments. We started by considering each of the recurring properties above and derived the following:

- There is the preconceived understanding that the relationships are temporal. Partners are therefore reluctant to sustain a long and costly trust development process that still involves legal and network administration expertise.
- Partners maintain their independent, more long-term portfolios and interests, and may prioritize them above those of the VO.
- External parties, such as customers, create the demand for relationship formation; there is therefore the question of per-partner risk incurred when committing to requirements that may not be core to their business but of a collaborative entity.

C.D. Jensen et al. (Eds.): iTrust 2004, LNCS 2995, pp. 355–361, 2004.

- The competencies and intellectual capital of partners must be disclosed for meeting short-term objectives, yet this knowledge is persisted within organizations that may be competitors within other or future contexts.
- VO's require heavy <u>automation</u>. Supporting ICTs, such as Grids and Web Services, still have unresolved security and trust issues including accepted standards [7].

When one reflects on these trust issues above, the emphasis is not on technology for credential, policy and permissions management, rather, the new issues for VO trust relationship management appear to be strategic. While existing trust management systems are at this time concerned with "live" operational issues (such as codifying credentials, policies and permissions), we suggest that a trust management solution adequate for the needs of a VO must support strategic forecasting, process optimization, service and resource selection, monitoring and decision support – the essence of planning.

Section 2 goes on to further develop this argument, with reference to established "relationship management" systems, namely, SRM (supplier relationship management) and CRM (customer relationship management), followed by a brief study of related work. Section 3 then presents our derivation of a trust relationship lifecycle, which we consider and position as the core concept towards trust relationship planning. We then conclude by summarizing our contributions and identifying further work in this area.

2 The Motivation for Planning in Trust Management

Firstly, we want to create an understanding that Trust Management can be considered alongside what are known as relationship management systems. Blaze, Feigenbaum and Lacy define the "trust management problem" as the collective study of *security policies, security credentials and **trust relationships***, in their 1996 paper [1]. Patton and Jøsang, even though in the specific context of e-Commerce, defines Trust Management as *"the activity of collecting, codifying, analyzing and evaluating evidence relating to competence, honesty, security or dependability with the purpose of making assessments and decisions regarding e-commerce **transactions**"* [4]. The term "transaction" encompasses a deal or communication, and thus refers to a particular relationship. We must note here that although the concern of managing a relationship has been established as an essential part of the trust management problem, most trust management research tends to treat trust as an atomic unit and incidentally abstract relationships from the goals of trust management. We found it more enlightening to refer to *"dynamic [trust] relationships"* as opposed to *"dynamic trust"*, and thus obtained a better understanding of the sincere nature of the issues for VO trust management.

Secondly, having labeled Trust Management as a Relationship Management System, we proceeded to look at two other well-known solutions that also assume this classification. SRM (Supplier Relationship Management) and CRM (Customer Relationship Management) are concerned with forging mutually beneficial, efficient and profitable relationships between a business, its suppliers and customers respectively. When reading marketing statements or technical white papers on these products, support for activities associated with planning resources, production cycles, marketing, investment, and other strategic decisions are always the key system features [6]. We can also correlate these features to the perceived strategic needs for trust in VO's:

- **Forecast and Analysis**: determination of trustworthiness of target VO communities
- **Administrative and Resource Efficiency**: Eliminate redundant policies, permissions and credentials in the VO
- **Monitoring and Measuring**: Establish sound measurements for trust before VO is operational
- **Process Efficiency**: Optimally maintain trust throughout the VO lifetime
- **Relationship Advancement**: Nurture trust beyond "active" VO relationships
- **Decision Support**: Make more informed relationship agreements

A VO is a system of multiple relationships, which go through the states of **Identification** (identifying potential opportunities and objectives), **Formation** (identifying and selecting partners, as well as committing resources), **Operation** (the functional activities towards meeting the objectives), and **Termination** (the dissolution of the VO and dispersal of assets), as defined by Strader in [8]. Existing work in operational risk management [10] and trust analysis [3, 11] were the notional starting points for associating the above features list with the lifecycle of the VO. However, we found that current methods are relevant within discrete phases of a system's existence, when the system is pending towards operational, or when the system is operational. Consider the definition of Operational Risk Management (ORM) in [10]: a decision-making tool to systematically help identify operational issues and benefits and determine the best course of action for any given situation. What we seek in trust relationship planning is a means of also identifying transitional issues and those beyond (before and after) operation, which may influence or result from the trustworthiness of relationships during operation of the VO. Additionally, in [11], Abdul-Rahman and Hailes state that the general models of trust are for a specific domain and were not designed to be automated. They proceeded to present their model, which very closely represents the sociological and dynamic properties of trust in Virtual Communities. We propose that a trust relationship planning model and system can offer a baseline for automated trust management, and hence equip existing trust models with a facility for utilization and integration in VO trust management. Our vision is an application independent process model based on capturing states and lifecycle of dynamic VO relationships. Trust models can be flexibly selected for use in discrete states of the VO relationships, based on the context, available knowledge and resources.

3 The Trust Relationship Lifecycle

According to Grandison and Sloman, the essential components of a "trust relationship" are: *the trustor, the trustee, a specific context with associated level of trust, and the conditions under which **the relationship becomes active*** [3]. We therefore gave thought to the states prior and subsequent to the active state, and the factors denoting that a relationship between a trustor and a trustee is "active" or "inactive".

Strader's model [8], already mentioned in the preceding section, provides discrete states of the complex VO relationships but does not contribute to defining the implications of trust within or between these states. Nevertheless, the SECURE project proposes that trust itself may be abstracted into states, and defines the phases of **Formation** (establishing initial trustworthiness), **Evolution** (iterating the process of trust formation) and **Exploitation** (determination of behaviour on the basis of trust) [2]. When considering the semantics of these two state models, they appear to be complementary and transitionally related. That is, we can either view the trust state as the conditions under which a relationship is advanced, or, vice-versa, the relationship state as the context within which trust is advanced. This is represented in figure 1: •

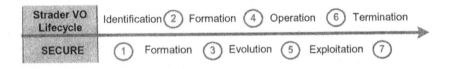

Fig. 1. Combination of VO and Trust Lifecycles

From figure 1 we derived new designations for the complementary phases labeled 1 to 7, and propose a single lifecycle for trust relationships (figure 2). Upon further consideration, we theorized that trust relationships are advanced based on the proximity and awareness of related entities (trustee and trustor), as well as their willingness to interchange knowledge or other productive resources. This was influenced by a notional correspondence with chemical reactions: if we consider each entity in a relationship as an atom (such as is the case in molecules), its properties (or what we refer to as "Awareness Horizon") would hold a likeness to the electron shell of the atom. Atoms may under some conditions *exist* in an atomic or isotopic form, until the proximity to (or *awareness* of) atoms of another element influences the probability of a reaction. Likewise, the proximity or awareness of entities influences the probability that they form relationships, and is a first state of information exchange, be it somewhat subliminal. Reactivity of atomic elements is also dependent on their relative electron richness or dearth. In comparison, we can also consider relationships between entities to be preceded by motive and *expression of intent*, based on their respective properties. Reaction between atoms results in bonds. These bonds can either be the sharing (covalent bonds) or unidirectional giving of electrons (ionic bonds) from one atom to the next. We see this as analogous to two entities *committing* to a relationship and at that moment determining the nature of the bond.

Some chemical reactions change colour, release gases or become explosive, which distinguishes the nature of the bond and the molecular product(s). Relationships also go through a phase of *activity*, which is their mark of productivity. However, at a point of neutrality, when there are no more electrons to be interchanged, the reaction ceases to show signs of productivity and is thus rendered *inactive*. Such is the case with relationships, which can also return to "active" given the appropriate conditions. Nevertheless, if the conditions imposed on chemical bonds exceed some threshold, the bonds may be broken. The effort to break a bond depends on the effort put into forming the bond. Relationships may also go into an *unrecoverable* state, if the conditions for dissolving the relationship are unexpectedly or purposefully incurred. Figure 2 diagrammatically summarizes these analogies from the perspective of entities, their properties or "Awareness Horizons" and the knowledge used to be cooperative and productive.

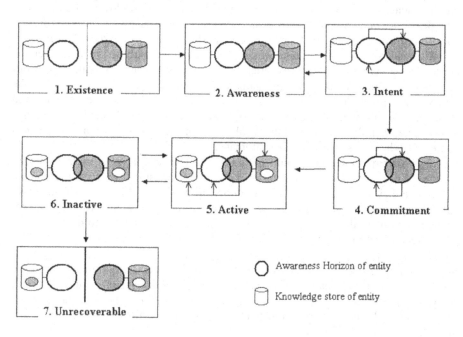

Fig. 2. Derived Trust Relationship Lifecycle

In order to make the contribution of the trust relationship lifecycle a bit clearer, we use the example of a research project. Consider the entities A (a medical research team) and B (cryptography research group) going through the phases of forming a VO to tackle a project on an online medical records management system. A is the "planner" of the VO and therefore is the initial controller of the objectives and opportunity.

(1) Existence: A and B exist in two very disparate domains of expertise and are hence unaware of each other. A has a set of objectives but is uncertain of how to go about locating trustworthy partners. Through recommendation at this state, A is informed of the communities of trustworthy entities commensurate with their objectives.

(2) Awareness: A may have performed a search, within a given community, or announce a tender. The information disclosed by A at this stage, could be critical.

(3) Intent: A decides that medical data needs to be kept in secure, distributed data stores and contacts B. However, A makes no commitment of its behaviour to B nor provides immediate access to its Domain Knowledge.

(4) Commitment: At this phase, the entities commit to an expected behaviour, use of capability and representative attributes. Decisions are made regarding access controls and disclosure of intellectual property and other domain knowledge. E.g. A may tell B that they can have access to patient data, once the names remain anonymous.

(5) Active: This state is the exploitation of the commitment gained in the previous state. Entities should be aware of their access controls allowed and those that they permit as well. A and B learn from each other and exchange knowledge of their domain influenced by the combined desire to meet the objectives of the relationship.

(6) Inactive: This is a state where the binding properties still hold, yet the exchange of domain knowledge goes into a lapsed phase, although previous knowledge is retained. B may have gathered the requirements from A and just be focused on applying its own domain knowledge for a period of time, or A may need some time to adjust its access controls. If these access controls could be planned before hand, then the inactivity status could be minimized. This is even more critical in the VO, where these activities are automated.

(7) Unrecoverable: This could be due to the termination of a contract, lack of funding or death of an entity. However, the entities may still leave with the domain knowledge they gained, and the trust relationship may be at the mercy of goodwill, unless some long-term measures are in place. These measures should also be planned, or the risk of dependency on goodwill. For example, A may bind B to destroying all patient records when the project is terminated.

In the future, this sort of searching, bartering and relationship formation may be conducted between automated agents, acting on behalf of the originator of the VO and competing prospective members. The originator or planner must be strategic in terms of information disclosed, permissions and transient relationship selectivity throughout these phases.

4 Conclusion

We have reemphasized in this paper that the VO age will demand advanced features for Trust Management. However, we have motivated that these advanced features are comparable to those in other Relationship Management systems, which are based on supporting strategic resource management. We then presented our first steps towards trust relationship planning, which is defining a possible lifecycle for trust relationships. In addition, we found that many of the issues identified during our relationship-oriented investigation of trust, resembled the issues for risk management in VO's. We therefore suspect that this approach to understanding trust may actually contribute to the discussions on the relationship between trust management and risk management. While our work has been a semi-formal approach up to the time the paper was written, we plan to carry on with a formalization of the unified state model, as we have already identified some convincing axioms and existing analogies from which we can draw. The structural components of such a system are also in the process of being thought through.

Acknowledgements. Members of TrustCoM consortium for already allowing us access to their domain knowledge, as we advance towards an active relationship

References

1. Blaze M., Feigenbaum J. & Lacy J. (1996) 'Decentralized Trust Management', Proc. 17th IEEE Symp. on Security and Privacy, pp 164-173, IEEE Computer Society, 1996
2. Cahill,V., Gray, E., Seigneur, J-M., Jensen, C.D., Chen, Y., Shand, B., Dimmock, N., Twigg, A., Bacon, J., English, C., Wagealla, W., Terzis, S., Nixon, P., Serugendo, G.M., Bryce, C., Carbone, M., Krukow, K., Nielsen, M. Using Trust for Secure Collaboration in Uncertain Environments. IEEE Pervasive Computing 2(3), July-September, 2003.
3. Grandison, T. and M. Sloman, Proceedings of 2nd IFIP Conference on e-Commerce, e-Business, e-Government, I3e2002, Lisbon, portugal. Oct 2002.
4. M.A.Patton and A.Jøsang. Technologies for Trust in E-Commerce. In the proceedings of the IFIP working conference on E-Commerce, Salzburg, Austria, June 2001
5. Mowshowitz, A. (1994), Virtual Organization: A Vision of Management in the Information Age, The Information Society, 10, pp. 267 – 288.
6. mySAP™ Supplier Relationship Management Press Fact Sheet, June 2003 (http://www.sap.com/company/press/factsheets/solution/srm.asp, December 2003)
7. Security in a Web Services World: A Proposed Architecture and Roadmap - A joint security whitepaper from IBM Corporation and Microsoft Corporation. April 7, 2002, Version 1.0 (http://www-106.ibm.com/developerworks/webservices/library/ws-secmap/? dwzone =webservices - accessed Dec 2003)
8. Strader, T.J., Lin, F. and Shaw, M.J. (1998), Information structure for electronic virtual organization management, Decision Support Systems, 23, pp. 75-94
9. Wolters, M.J.J., M.R. Hoogeweegen, Management Support for Globally Operating Virtual Organizations: The Case of KLM Distribution, Proceedings of the 32nd Hawaii International Conference on System Sciences (HICSS-32), January 5-8, 1999, Maui, Hawaii
10. FAA System Safety Handbook, Chapter 15: Operational Risk Management. December 30, 2000: http://www.asy.faa.gov/Risk/SSHandbook/Chap15_1200.PDF
11. Alfarez Abdul-Rahman, Stephen Hailes, "Supporting Trust in Virtual Communities", Proceedings of the 33rd HICCS, 2000

Trust, Security, and Contract Management Challenges for Grid-Based Application Service Provision

M. Gaeta[1], G. Laria[1], P. Ritrovato[1], N. Romano[1], B. Serhan[2], S. Wesner[2], T. Dimitrakos[3], and D. Mac Randal[3]

[1] CRMPA, Università di Salerno, Italy,
{ritrovato, gaeta, romano, laria}@crmpa.salerno.it
[2] High Performance Computing Centre, University of Stuttgart, Stuttgart, Germany
{wesner, serhan}@hlrs.de
[3] Central Laboratory of the Research Councils, Rutherford Appleton Lab., UK
{t.dimitrakos, d.f.mac.randal}@rl.ac.uk

Abstract. The GRASP project aims to provide an OGSA compliant infrastructure to allow Application Service Providers to exploit Grid concepts and infrastructure. Orchestration of grid service instances running "somewhere on the Grid" to deliver a service raises a number of trust, security and contract management challenges, especially in a business context. This paper describes the issues relating to SLA negotiation and management and to the trust and security of dynamically created, distributed virtual organizations, based on the experiences of developing the GRASP architecture and implementing an initial prototype infrastructure.

1 Introduction

During the last years, there was a growing interest in the service oriented architectures (SOA) that aim to become the enabling architecture to provide resource in a dynamic and distributed manner (Web Services are a typical approach to SOA). On the basis of this trend, the Grid Service concept was introduced (see Open Grid Service Architecture OGSA [2, 3]) that is the building block for creating service oriented grid architecture.

These Grid Services offer a well defined interface to different kinds of potentially stateful and transient resources, whether hardware, system resources or applications, so that they can be easily located, instantiated on demand (where applicable) and accessed dynamically.

An infrastructure that deals with dynamic location and usage of transient services naturally attracts attention from companies in the domain of Application Service Provision (ASP). The core business of such companies is the provision of services that deliver business processes in whole or in part. These services can then be contracted by companies who are interested in outsourcing parts of their business processes. The GRASP project will provide an OGSA compliant infrastructure, targeting the specific needs of ASPs, so that they can exploit Grid concepts and infrastructure in an economic way.

C.D. Jensen et al. (Eds.): iTrust 2004, LNCS 2995, pp. 362–368, 2004.

In particular, this infrastructure will allow the adoption of innovative business models where an ASP can leverage on transient grid services provided on demand by Grid Service Provider (GSP) to build more complex application to be provided to their own clients. In this scenario the role of GSP arises, as well. This collaborative business environment will allow the delivery of more suitable service to the final users with a general cost reduction for development and delivery.

Since the concept of (Grid) Service Provision is fundamental in SOA approaches to Grid Computing, many of the GRASP project results have a wider applicability than in the ASP domain.

2 A Simplified GRASP Scenario

We briefly explain a simplified GRASP scenario, introducing the basic concepts of Service Location, Instantiation, Hosting Environment and its relationship to the overall Virtual Organization (VO).

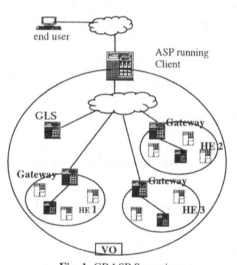

Fig. 1. GRASP Scenario

An end user will contact an ASP machine which is offering a client application. The end user starts the application and its results are obtained by orchestrating third party's (GSPs) grid services, instantiated at runtime somewhere in the VO. In fact, the ASP participates in a VO and thus can use services deployed anywhere within the VO in order to integrate them with their own value added service to deliver the overall application service. The VO is divided into Hosting Environments (HE), limited administrative domains which encompass a set of machines (Hosts) that can host grid services (potentially, the owner of the machine and the owner of the running grid services can be different). The ASP can locate services within the VO through a specific service: the GRASP Locator Service (GLS).

A client (in our case the ASP) interested in the usage of a specific Grid Service contacts a *GLS* and retrieves a list of GSP that can provide the desired Grid Service in accordance with the specified Quality of Services (QoS). Then the client enters a *negotiation* with the short-listed GSPs in order to reach and contract a specific *Service Level Agreement (SLA)* for the requested service. The actual content of the SLA instance is subject to the expected availability of resources in the selected *Hosting Environments* (HE), potentially owned by third parties, and on which the GSP intends to have an instance of the service created.

Finally, the selected Grid Service instance(s) must be created and/or started by an *Instantiator* and run in some HE(s). In this phase, on the basis of the current status, the *Instantiator* will check if the HE can actually provide the prefixed SLA for the instance that it is going to instantiate.

As a number of different service instances of potentially different GSPs serving potentially different clients may compete for the same resources in a HE, their execution must be

1. supported by a distributed performance monitoring and accounting scheme that collects and correlates resource usage information across HE
2. protected by dynamic service security perimeters that encircle Grid Service instances contributing to the same application instance across potentially different HE

3   General Trust and Contract Management Challenges

The following highlights (from the negotiation, monitoring, security and trust viewpoint) some issues, arising in the depicted scenario characterized by a dinamic and evolving environment:

- We need machine-readable semantics for contract description, that allow the definition of final contract instances (stored in specific contract repository)
- We have to guarantee the meeting of agreed contract both from the client (assurance of expected QoS) and GSP (grid services won't consume unaccounted resource on the HE and won't perform malicious or incompetent actions) viewpoint
- the ASP needs to be assured that optimal utilization of resources has been achieved across all contributing GSP and HE;
- Due to the separation of concerns between ASP, GSP, HE and user there is a need for policy languagues that allow enforcement across different administrative domain and are sufficiently powerfull to describe the necessary term and conditions. Conflicting policies will have to be consolidated and resolved in real time;
- mutual trust needs to be established between the service requestor, the GSP and the HE for a grid service instance to be successfully instantiated, invoked and executed;
- performance monitoring results from executions of component services in different HE may have to be reported and correlated; GSP and client must take into account their confidence in the monitor capability of the corresponding HE.

The following sections give an overview of how some of these issues are being addressed in the GRASP infrastructure (for details on GRASP architecture see [1]).

3.1   The GRASP Contract Management Subsystem

Although GRASP is researching generally applicable contract management techniques in an OGSA compliant Grid environment, our main focus is on Service Level Agreements: notably a SLA contract between a client and a service provider which may comprise different services running on different hosts at different times. The autonomic management and monitoring of such contracts execution is crucial for business oriented Grid environments. In addition, SLAs can be used at the back-end implementation of a GRASP environment to determine the constraints under which the GRASP environment operates. GRASP distinguishes two main phases of Contract Management:

Contract negotiation: The first step of contract negotiation is the discovery, comparison and establishment of suitable service offers as well as the "logical" and "physical" location of the corresponding service providers. GRASP GSLuses an appropriate SLA language that allows comparison of the client request against the SLA description and returns to the client a list of potential service providers that can potentially meet the requested QoS. As the proposed QoS might not be feasible at the moment of request, the client can negotiate directly, in two different ways, with the service provider about the currently available QoS in order to reach a specific SLA for a service instance:

- One phase negotiation: the client prioritises the received list, then works down the list until a service provider confirms acceptance of the requested QoS.
- Multi-phase negotiation: If a service provider is not able to deliver the requested QoS, an alternative QoS may be proposed for further negotiation.

There are some differences between the above approaches that impact the architecture of the Service Level Agreement management. In particular, a second phase requires the client to take into account feedback from the GSPs and converse with some of them. Further, GSPs and HEs need to implement a resource reservation capability, because GSPs need to ensure that there are resources available somewhere to execute a service instance. Even non-existing or idle instances of services under negotiation need to be considered when creating a QoS offer or assessing resource availability.

Contract monitoring: GRASP address the problem of monitoring SLA contract execution of dynamic entity as the Grid Services via dedicated *agreement services* i.e. each grid service is accompanied by an agreement service that monitors compliance with the SLA instance for this service. This approach is compatible with the recent proposal for the OGSI-Agreement specification [4].

Another issue arises from the divergence in the focus and objectives of metrics associated with SLA. Business logic metrics explicitly identified in an SLA are likely to be result/goal oriented rather than resource oriented. Monitoring of grid service instance execution however is by definition resource oriented. To overcome this, services translating metrics identified in the SLA to metrics that can be monitored during service execution must be provided. These *monitored metrics* fall into two types. Firstly conventional resource–based metrics such as elapsed time, amount of storage, etc. These can be obtained from the host system. Secondly, service-based metrics (such as accuracy of results, number of iterations, etc.) that can only come from the service itself. Hence, GRASP exposes monitoring related data as Service Data Elements and provides a Host monitoring service exposing system data.

Figure 3 provides a simplified overview of a GRASP hosting environment emphasising those components of interest for contract negotiation and monitoring. It also reflects our opinion that QoS monitoring and prediction must be done on the Gateway as well as on the Host systems.

The first GRASP infrastructure release is restricted to a one phase negotiation. Fig. 3 depicts a simplified GRASP Hosting Environment (HE) showing a Negotiation Handler that receives incoming requests. This uses a SLA Parser to analyzes the requests and asks the Agreement and HE Monitor if the request can be met. The latter, aware of all running Agreements Services on the different hosts, compiles a priority list of potential Hosts in this HE for an instance of the requested service and starts asking the Negotiator of each listed Host in priority order to instantiate the Grid Service, until the first one confirms. When the Negotiator at a Host receives a request its response is based on information provided by the Host Monitor and a comparison of the request against host-specific SLA rules stored in the SLA Host Template Pool.

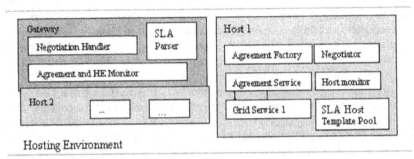

Fig. 3. Simplified GRASP hosting environment

3.2 The GRASP Secure Collaboration Management System

In GRASP a single application may be enacted by grid services executing on different hosts controlled by different institutions, each defining its own security policy.

To address trust establishment and secure collaboration, we use a specifically adapted implementation of the "virtual firewall" architecture provided by the dynamic service security perimeter model described in [5], based on a group oriented mechanism.

To enable this mechanism, we provide a GroupManagerService (GMS) responsible for managing group membership by defining authorization privileges, delivering and updating a group certificate to members. In every HE there is a GMS managing the group associated with that HE (all service instances within a HE belong to the same security group). Thus, the service instances set running in the same HE are included in a *local group* upon creation and have specific privileges related to that HE.

A service instance belonging to a HE (and so to a local group) may need P2P communication with another instance belonging to another HE (e.g to participate in an orchestrated service). We allow this P2P communication by creating another *virtual group,* which spans different local groups and it is administrated by a GMS running in any of the HEs involved. The same GMS can oversee a local group and

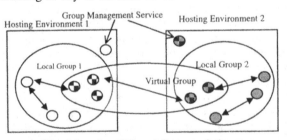

Fig. 4. Local and Virtual Groups relations

many virtual groups, performing different roles in each context. In particular, the notion of local group could be treated as a special case of virtual group.

In general, group creation/ expansion can be initiated by any group member or by any GMS, using an "invitation protocol". When a service receives an invitation message, it starts a registration phase with the GMS. Once admitted, a service interacts directly with other group members without the manager's participation.

GRASP *secure collaboration management* components are Grid services extending customized GRASP security PortTypes: GroupManagementPortType and GroupMembershipPortType. The former (extended by GMS) supports dynamic group composition (creation, expansion, shrinkage and dissolution) and provides group members authentication. The latter (extended by every service which needs to be secure) allows initiation of the group registration phase.

Upon creation each service instance becomes a member of the HE local group. The ServiceInstantiator receives the service reference from the Factory and sends it to the HE's GMS to start the local group registration phase. The GMS sends an invitation message to the service instance which returns all the necessary information for participation in the group. The GMS checks the received service data and returns the group certificate if security policies are satisfied. Now, the service instance can establish P2P communication inside the HE regulated by the GMS policies, using local group certificate as authentication token.

For a service instance to communicate with a member of another local group, it has to participate in the same virtual group as it. For a service instance join the virtual group it needs to be "invited" by another member of that virtual group or the GSM of that virtual group. A service instance can also invite itself by asking its own local manager to send such a request to the GMS of that virtual group. To be able to generate an invitation message, the service has to extend the GroupMembershipPortType which defines the startGroupRegistration method. This method contacts the specified Local Group manager[1] and obtains the group certificate for the invited group member.

One remaining issue is the enforcement of access restrictions and contractual obligations at the services themselves. In our reference model (see [5]), this is performed through dedicated enforcement agents at each member of a (virtual) group, i.e. each grid service instance contributing to the execution of an application on a HE. The enforcement agent (they can be a part of the grid service instance) is responsible for enforcing the security policies set by the Group Manager for both the Local Group and the Virtual Group.

At its simplest, the enforcement agent ensures that messages arriving for or originating from a service instance are encrypted with a valid key and signed with a valid certificate (i.e. are valid virtual group messages) and are valid service communications (i.e. the content is acceptable to the service instance and the HE's Group Manager). Enforcement of contracts and more sophisticated policies requires that the enforcement agents are able to execute commands that amount to the enactemnt of (a relevant part of) a contract clause or a security policy. [7, 8].

---

[1] It is the Group Manager Service of the HE. Each HE has a default Local Group Manager.

4 Conclusions

In this paper we have discussed several of the issues that have been tackled within the GRASP project while developing the GRASP architecture and implementing an initial prototype infrastructure.

Notwithstanding the considerable effort by the GRASP project in providing realistic solutions to the demanding problems that we predict will concern the next generation of Application Service Providers that chose to take advantage of the Grid in offering their services, many of the challenges identified in section 3 of this paper have only been partly addressed. Sometimes this was because of limitations of the existing technology (e.g. the lack of sufficiently rich and established service conversation protocols for agreeing QoS or access rights) or because of limitation on how well a community understands a problem (e.g. the lack of an established method for correlating business logic objectives to service execution and resource consumption, lack of establish models for separation of concerns, rights and liability and for delegation in multi institutional Virtual Organizations).

References

1. Dimitrakos T., Mac Randal D., Yuan F., Gaeta M., Laria G., Ritrovato P., Serhan B., Wesner S., Konrad W., An emerging architecture enabling Grid based Application Service Provision, 7th IEEE EDOC Conf. 2003.
2. I. Foster, C. Kesselman, J. Nick, S. Tuecke, The Physiology of the Grid: An Open Grid Services Architecture for Distributed Systems Integration. Open Grid Service Infrastructure WG, Global Grid Forum, June 22, 2002
3. *Grid Service Specification V1.0*. Open Grid Service Infrastructure WG, Global Grid Forum, Draft 29, 5/4/2003.
4. K. Czajkowski, A. Dan, J. Rofrano, S. Tuecke, M. Xu. Agreement-based Grid Service Management (OGSI-Agreement). Open Grid Service Infrastructure WG, Global Grid Forum, Draft, 12/06/2003.
5. Djordjevic I., Dimitrakos T., Phillips C.: *An Architecture for Dynamic Security Perimeters of Virtual Collaborative Networks*. Proc of 9th IEEE/IFIP Network Operations and Management Symposium (NOMS 2004), 19-23 April 2004, Seoul, Korea
6. T. Dimitrakos, D. Mac Randal, S. Wesner, B. Serhan, P. Ritrovato, G. Laria. Overview of an architecture enabling Grid based Application Service Provision. 2nd European Across Grids Conference, Nicosia, Cyprus, Jan. 2004
7. Damianou N., Dulay N., Lupu E., Sloman M.: *The Ponder Policy Specification Language*. Proc. Policy 2001: Workshop on Policies for Distributed Systems and Networks, Bristol, UK, 29-31 Jan. 2001, Springer-Verlag LNCS 1995, pp. 18-39
8. Bradshaw, J., et al. Representation and reasoning about DAML-based policy and domain services in KAoS. In Proceedings of The 2nd International Joint Conference on Autonomous Agents and Multi Agent Systems (AAMAS2003).
9. Johnson, M., Chang, P., et al. KAoS semantic policy and domain services: An application of DAML to Web services-based grid architectures. Proc. of the AAMAS 03 Workshop on Web Services and Agent-Based Engineering. Melbourne, Australia

Deploying Trust Policies on the Semantic Web
(Position Paper)

Brian Matthews and Theo Dimitrakos

CCLRC Rutherford Appleton Laboratory
Didcot, Oxon, OX11 0QX, UK
{b.m.matthews, t.dimitrakos}@rl.ac.uk

Abstract. Automated services over open distributed systems have been advocated as the future for conducting business. However, in order for such services to be successfully deployed, confidence in the system and its participants needs to established. The use of trust policies and trust management has been proposed to raise the level of trust whilst still maintaining a practical level of automation. To define, deploy and enforce trust policies a level of common vocabulary and understanding between participants needs to be established. The Semantic Web initiative of the W3C has been developing common languages and tools to allow the exchange and processing of common vocabularies, in the form of a graph-based description format, and an ontology language. In this paper we discuss the steps required to establish a policy-based service architecture, discuss the role of the Semantic Web initiative in enabling the practical deployment of this architecture, and highlight the work required to enable this.

1 Introduction

Automated services delivered over open distributed systems are seen as the next major development in science, commerce and government. However, this service vision will only come about if enterprises and individuals are confident that it will deliver services 'as advertised', not only in terms of functionality but also in the behaviour of participating agents. For example, agents can reasonably be expected to prevent unauthorised access to information and consequent malicious action, to respect confidentiality and privacy of all parties, and to supply accurate and timely results. These requirements are particularly challenging when the services depend on multiple contributing providers, who may not be known to the consumer of the overall service. Participants may gain by sharing resources, while being concerned about protecting their assets and reputation. Confidence that a party will behave well comes from a combination of **trust** between parties, and **control measures** that constrain behaviour.

In this new world, collaborations are fluid, linked by networks of trust and contracts, mediated via brokering and monitoring agents. Contracts formalise agreements among partners, stating the rights and obligations of the parties as well as sanctions to be applied if obligations are not fulfilled or rights exceeded. Contracts may then form the basis of behavioural norms and control policies applied under it.

C.D. Jensen et al. (Eds.): iTrust 2004, LNCS 2995, pp. 369–375, 2004.

Dependence on trust (that a partner will abide by agreements and policies) in such collaborations increases the efficiency of collaborations, but makes the collaborators more vulnerable. In contrast, enforcement of policies and contracts limits the risk of malicious or unintentional damage, at the price of increased overheads. The level of trust changes with time and with the importance of the interaction, and prescriptive contracts and policies cannot predict all possible behaviours in dynamic open systems. Consequently, trust and contract management frameworks need to be complemented by adaptive deployment mechanisms that resolve conflicts and support renegotiation and amendment in real time.

Existing tools and techniques for security management rely heavily on human intervention from system administrators and systems security officers using separate management applications in order to effect changes to the security configurations in response to security relevant events. In establishing dynamic collaborations on-demand, the scale, impact and frequency of changes increases dramatically and the variety of security mechanisms employed by the partners further impedes their deployment. Consequently, security management must become autonomic and adaptation must occur automatically in real-time, rather than through human intervention. Furthermore, autonomic security management will have to be complemented by extensible and machine processable standards for negotiating, validating and amending collaboration agreements, encoded by means of electronic contracts, which can be autonomically enacted by the platform.

Such extensible and machine processable standards require the development of common vocabularies and negotiation protocols. The Semantic Web initiative of the World Wide Web Consortium (W3C) is an effort to provide common machine-readable data onto the web, by allowing common vocabularies and conventions to be defined to describe web accessible resources. The aim of the Semantic Web is to be: *"... an extension of the current web in which information is given well-defined meaning, better enabling computers and people to work in cooperation."*[1]. The major components of the Semantic Web are the Resource Description Framework [13] for assigning properties and values to web resources, and for defining simple vocabularies, and the Web Ontology Language OWL [16], for defining more expressive vocabularies with additional constraints. Many tools and applications have now been produced on top of these basic Semantic Web tools.

In this paper we propose that the Semantic Web of the W3C provides an underlying framework to allow the deployment of a service architecture, as first suggested in [5]. We provide a survey of existing work which has been carried out to achieve this, and suggest how this and further work may be drawn together to support a complete Semantic Web enabled policy-based service architecture.

2 A Service Architecture

A service based architecture which is augmented with trust policies and trust management would have the following stages.

1. **Semantic Web Services:** in addition to publishing their interfaces, Web Services would need to publish statements describing their intended or normative behaviour.

These statements should be given common, machine processable, extensible semantics that support judgment of :
- whether a service can perform a given task;
- the relative ranking of a set of services with respect to basic QoS criteria.

2. **Trust policy publication:** service providers will publish policies for their use, detailing the obligations, privileges and expected levels of service which a user
should accept before using the service.
3. **Service discovery:** users of services will seek services which satisfy their requirements, via automated search and negotiation mechanisms, to find the "best available" service. The criteria of "best" should include not only the functional requirements of the service delivering the service to the required quality, but also
include both whether the published policy is acceptable to the user, and the reputation of the service provider, using any previous experience of using the provider,
and any recommendations or guarantees provided by third parties.
4. **Service negotiation:** once a service has been selected, there needs to be a negotiation between service and user. As part of this process, the policies of both parties have to be interrogated and a contract of use established. As part of this process, a conversation needs to take place between the parties, establishing a mutually
intelligible vocabulary of terms for data and process descriptions. This negotiation
may involve third parties (brokers, guarantors, service framework providers etc)
which may facilitate the relationship and foster trust between the parties.
5. **Experience monitoring:** during the execution of the service, which may be over a
long period, its progress is monitored. The experience of the quality of the service
may modify the relationship between the parties. For example, if the experience so
far is good, then the parties may relax restrictions for the remainder of the service.
6. **Policy Enforcement:** policy statements need to be interpreted into lower-level
rules which are then enforced at each network end-point.
7. **Service review:** after the end of the service the parties will review the progress of
the service, and modify appropriately the trust evaluation of the other party, and
modify the policies it will apply in future collaborations.

Thus at all stages of the process, a vocabulary describing the service needs to be established and exchanged between the parties.

3 Using the Semantic Web

We consider how the Semantic Web can support the deployment of the policy-
augmented service architecture described above.

3.1 Policy Publication and Enforcement

Web Services standards for SOAP-based message security and XML-based languages
for access control (e.g. XACML [19]) are emerging. The use of XML as a basis for
expression specification has the advantage of extensibility. Its semantics however are
mostly implicit as meaning depends on a shared understanding derived from human
consensus, and allow incompatible representation variations. Semantic Web-based

policy representations could be mapped to lower level XML representations if required by an implementation.

Some initial efforts in the use of Semantic Web representations for basic security applications (authentication, access control, data integrity, encryption) have begun to bear fruit. For example, Denker et al. [4] have integrated a set of ontologies (credentials, security mechanisms) and security extensions for Web Service profiles with the CMU Semantic Matchmaker. Kagal et al. [9] are also developing Rei, a Semantic Web based policy language. Furthermore, KAoS services and tools allow for the specification, management, conflict resolution, and enforcement of policies within the specific contexts established by complex organizational structures represented as domains [2; 8; 17; 18]. A comparison of KAoS, Rei, and more traditional policy approaches such as Ponder can be found in [15].

The KAoS policy ontology distinguishes between authorizations and (state or event triggered, conditional) obligations. Other policy constructs, including delegation and role-based authorisations, are built out of the basic primitives of domains and the basic policy types. "Action" is defined as the ontological class used to classify instances of intended or performed actions. Applicability of action instances relates to a policy (instance) through the association of the corresponding classes. The use of OWL enables reasoning about the controlled environment, policy relations and disclosure, policy conflict detection, and harmonization, as well as about domain structure and concepts exploiting the description logic subsumption and instance classification algorithms. Taking advantage of OWL, platform/application-specific ontologies are easily loaded on top of the core policy classes.

KAoS provides a powerful tool-set that appears to be capable to address publication and deployment of complex policies for Semantic Web Services. However the incorporation of trust metrics and a distributed enforcement and performance assessment schemes remain the main challenges, in addition to the production of a critical mass of domain/application-specific ontologies to allow its uptake and validation in large scale systems. With repect to the latter there is an ongoing effort to adapt KAoS for use in Grid Computing environments in conjunction to OGSA [8].

3.2   Service Discovery

In order for a new service to be used it needs to be discovered and a mapping needs to be established between the requirements of the client and the capabilities of the service. On the service side, discovery is facilitate in the presence of a set of semantic descriptions. WSDL descriptions can be used to support this, but they fall short in providing any unambiguous semantic content for the service interface description they provide; OWL has been used to provide descriptions of the functionality of web services, (e.g. DAML-S [3]), but not as yet to describe their quality of service.

On the client side, the client objectives must also be given semantics in order to enable achieving a "sufficiently good" similarity between objectives of requestor and the capabilities of the service, advertised by its provider. Generally, a match can be determined by heuristic algorithms, aided by domain-specific ontologies that define the terms used for service description as well as the objectives of the requestor. Again, there is a need to extend this work to non-functional requirements. P3P [10, 12] adds policies and requirement of the client with respect to Privacy; this would need to be extended to express the wider quality-of-service expectations of the client.

3.3 Service Negotiation

Once services have been discovered, there is a need to establish a relationship between the parties, (possibly mediated via third parties) and to negotiate the terms and conditions for the use of the service.

As part of this process, there is a step of trust evaluation, either from previous experience of one another, as recorded in a "trustbase" of trust valuations, or an evaluation of the trust value from recommendations from third parties, or a calculation of trust across the network via intermediate trust valuations. Preliminary work in calculating trust values across trust networks in the semantic web have been studied by Goldbeck, Hendler and Parsia [6; 7], and Richardson, Agrawal, and Domingos [14] which use a relatively straightforward model of trust which does not take into account context or uncertainty. They also consider reputation management, although this could be handled via an existing W3C recommendation, the Platform for Internet Content Selection (PICS [11]). This standard, designed originally for content filtering of web pages, can be used to express a general rating scheme, including for standards of reliability of web entities.

Once a trust valuation of the parties involved has been established an agreement needs to negotiated between the parties. This requires the interchange of vocabulary, and again the Ontology support provided via OWL in the Semantic Web is able to provide this mechanism; indeed as already noted, DAML-S has already started this for service descriptions, and KAoS for policies. We need to embed the trust valuations into the process, to use the expression of user requirements and preferences.

3.4 Experience Monitoring and Policy Enforcement

Once an agreement has been established, then the client can start using the service. This usage may be long-lived, and the experience of the parties during the interaction may modify their behaviour for its remainder. For example, good experience may result in the loosening of restrictions and a higher-level of trust, changing the valuations in internal "trustbases", and reducing the policy enforcement overhead.

End-point enforcement of a web service in particular requires an agent:

- to interpret the data elements and procedure calls of messages, compare them with the rules in a policy statement and block unauthorized requests;
- to interpret outgoing messages in order to ensure that the service does not initiate communication with malicious agents or send unauthorized requests;
- to initiate an action or a specific request to another service in order to meet an obligation associated with the enforcement of a policy statement.

These processes are likely to take place largely internally to the services taking part, but nevertheless a common vocabulary for interpreting the action of the other and third parties is needed.

3.5 Service Review

After the interaction has been completed, there should be a stage of review when trust valuations are reassessed, policies modified in the light of experience, and any recommendations to third parties propagated, within the common vocabularies provided within the Semantic Web.

4 Conclusion

Clearly, trust management, contract management and autonomic security mechanisms are important aspects in the practical deployment of the service architecture across different organisations, especially involving governmental and commercial organisations. Failure to provide adequate technical, legal and economic mechanisms to allow participants to act with confidence, will slow the acceptance the service architecture as an enabler of collaborations, and may prevent its uptake altogether, users instead using closed proprietary solutions which lack the benefits of an open system.

Semantic Web Services (e.g. http://www.swsi.org/) complement the rapidly advancing Web Services technology by defining and implementing new capabilities which more fully harness the power of Web Services through explicit representations of the semantics underlying Web resources. They provide an infrastructure capable of fully exploiting these semantics. Semantic Web Languages such as OWL extend RDF to allow users to specify ontologies composed of taxonomies of classes and inference rules. This is expected to allow software agents to understand and autonomously manipulate other agents or services, therefore enabling discovery, meaningful communication and collaboration among software agents and services, relying on control mechanisms that implement policy statements capturing human imposed constraints.

Thus the Semantic Web offers the infrastructure to share the vocabulary and semantic of policies and trust valuations. This has the advantage of using an established body of languages and tools designed to function over open distributed systems to leverage this sharing in an effective and economic manner. There has been some preliminary work in providing piece of this architecture carried out in different places. However, there has been no coherent scheme to bring these together in one policy-based service architecture, as outlined in this paper. In future work, we propose to provide a unified view to instantiate this architecture and consider how to deploy it in practice.

Acknowledgements. This work was supported by the European Commission funded project *Semantic-Web Advanced Development in Europe (SWAD-Europe).*

References

[1]   Berners-Lee, T., Hendler, J., and Lassila, 0.: The Semantic Web. Scientific American, May 2001

[2]   Bradshaw, J., Uszok, A., Jeffers, R., Suri, N., Hayes, P., Burstein, M., Acquisti, A., Benyo, B., Breedy, M., Carvalho, M., Diller, D., Johnson, M., Kulkarni, S., Lott, J., Sierhuis, M. and Van Hoof, R. Representation and reasoning about DAML-based policy and domain services in KAoS. In Proc. of The 2nd Int. Joint Conf. on Autonomous Agents and Multi Agent Systems (AAMAS2003).

[3]   DAML Services homepage http://www.daml.org/services/

[4]   Denker, G., Kagal, L., Finin, T., Paolucci, M. and Sycara, K. Security for DAML Web Services: Annotation and Matchmaking. In D. Fensel, K. Sycara, & J.Mylopoulos (Ed.), The Semantic Web—ISWC 2003. Proceedings of the 2nd International Semantic Web Conference, Sanibel Island, Florida, USA, October 2003, LNCS 2870.

[5]   Dimitrakos, T., Matthews, B. and Bicarregui, J. Towards supporting security and trust management policies on the Web. ERCIM Workshop 'The Role of Trust in e-Business' in conjunction with IFIP I3E conference on October 3, 2001.

[6]   Golbeck J., Parsia B., and Hendler J.: Trust networks on the semantic web. In Proceedings of Cooperative Intelligent Agents 2003, Helsinki, Finland, August 2003.

[7]   Golbeck, J. and Hendler, J. Inferring Reputation on the Semantic Web. http://www.mindswap.org/papers/GolbeckWWW04.pdf, submitted to WWW'04.

[8]   Johnson, M., Chang, P., Jeffers, R., Bradshaw, J. M., Soo, V.-W., Breedy, M. R., Bunch, L., Kulkarni, S., Lott, J., Suri, N., & Uszok, A. KAoS semantic policy and domain services: An application of DAML to Web services-based grid architectures. Proceedings of the AAMAS 03 Workshop on Web Services and Agent-Based Engineering. Melbourne, Australia, 2003.

[9]   Kagal, K., Finin, T. and Anupam, J. A Logical Policy Language for a Pervasive Computing Environment., 4th IEEE Int. Workshop on Policies for Distributed Systems and Networks, Lake Como, 4-6 June, 2003.

[10]   McBride, B., Wenning, R. and Cranor, L.: An RDF Schema for P3P. W3C Note 25 January 2002 http://www.w3.org/TR/p3p-rdfschema

[11]   Platform for Internet Content Selection (PICS) http://www.w3.org/PICS

[12]   Platform for Privacy Preferences (P3P) Project http://www.w3.org/P3P/

[13]   Resource Description Framework homepage http://www.w3.org/RDF/

[14]   Richardson, M., Agrawal, R. and Domingos, P. Trust Management and the Semantic Web In D. Fensel, K. Sycara, & J.Mylopoulos (Eds.), The Semantic Web—ISWC 2003. Proc. of the 2nd Int. Semantic Web Conf., Sanibel Island, Florida, USA, October 2003, LNCS 2870.

[15]   Tonti, G., Bradshaw, J. M., Jeffers, R., Montanari, R., Suri, N., & Uszok, A. (2003). Semantic Web languages for policy representation and reasoning: A comparison of KAoS, Rei, and Ponder. In D. Fensel, K. Sycara, & J.Mylopoulos (Eds.), The Semantic Web— ISWC 2003. Proc. of the 2nd Int. Semantic Web Conf., Sanibel Island, Florida, USA, October 2003, LNCS 2870.

[16]   Web-Ontology (WebOnt) Working Group homepage http://www.w3.org/2001/sw/WebOnt/

[17]   Uszok, A., Bradshaw, J., Jeffers, R., Suri, N., Hayes, P., Breedy, M., Bunch, L., Johnson, M., Kulkarni, S. and Lott, J. (2003). KAoS Policy and Domain Services: Toward a Description-Logic Approach to Policy Representation, Deconfliction and Enforcement. In Proc. of the IEEE Workshop on Policy 2003.

[18]   Uszok, A., Bradshaw, J., Jeffers, R., Johnson, M., Tate, A., Dalton, J. and Aitken, S. Policy and Contract Management for Semantic Web Services. to appear AAAI Spring Symposium, Stanford University, California, USA, March 2004.

[19]   XACML: Extensible Access Control Markup Language http://www.oasis-open.org/committees/tc_home.php?wg_abbrev=xacml

Author Index

Lecture Notes in Computer Science

For information about Vols. 1–2874

please contact your bookseller or Springer-Verlag